Animals and Animality in the Babylonian Talmud

Animals and Animality in the Babylonian Talmud selects key themes in animal studies – animal intelligence, morality, sexuality, suffering, danger, personhood – and explores their development in the Babylonian Talmud. Beth Berkowitz demonstrates that distinctive features of the Talmud – the new literary genre, the convergence of Jewish, Christian, and Zoroastrian cultures, the Talmud's remove from Temple-centered biblical Israel – led to unprecedented possibilities within Jewish culture for conceptualizing animals and animality. She shows that the Babylonian Talmud is ripe for reading with a critical animal studies perspective. When we do, we find waiting for us a multilayered, surprisingly self-aware discourse about animals as well as about the anthropocentrism that infuses human relationships with them. For readers of religion, Judaism, and animal studies, this book offers new perspectives on animals from the vantage point of the ancient rabbis.

Beth A. Berkowitz is the author of *Execution and Invention: Death Penalty Discourse in Early Rabbinic and Christian Cultures* (2006, winner of the Salo Baron Prize for First Book in Jewish Studies) and *Defining Jewish Difference: From Antiquity to the Present* (Cambridge University Press, 2012). She is a coeditor of *Religious Studies and Rabbinics: A Conversation* (2017).

Animals and Animality in the Babylonian Talmud

BETH A. BERKOWITZ

Barnard College

CAMBRIDGE
UNIVERSITY PRESS

CAMBRIDGE
UNIVERSITY PRESS

University Printing House, Cambridge CB2 8BS, United Kingdom

One Liberty Plaza, 20th Floor, New York, NY 10006, USA

477 Williamstown Road, Port Melbourne, VIC 3207, Australia

314–321, 3rd Floor, Plot 3, Splendor Forum, Jasola District Centre, New Delhi – 110025, India

79 Anson Road, #06–04/06, Singapore 079906

Cambridge University Press is part of the University of Cambridge.

It furthers the University's mission by disseminating knowledge in the pursuit of education, learning, and research at the highest international levels of excellence.

www.cambridge.org
Information on this title: www.cambridge.org/9781108423663
DOI: 10.1017/9781108529129

First published 2018

Printed in the United Kingdom by Clays, St Ives plc

A catalogue record for this publication is available from the British Library.

ISBN 978-1-108-42366-3 Hardback

Contents

Acknowledgments   *page* vii

1   Introduction: Balaam's Ass, the Babylonian Talmud,
    and Critical Animal Studies   1

    ORIENTATION TO THE BABYLONIAN TALMUD   31

2   Animal Intelligence: Bava Qamma 34b–35a   37
3   Animal Morality: Sanhedrin 55a–b   63
4   Animal Suffering: Bava Metzia 32a–33a   89
5   Animal Danger: Bava Qamma 80a–b   120
6   Animals as Livestock: Sukkah 22b–23b   153
7   Conclusion: Jewish Animals   180

Works Cited   193
Index   221

Acknowledgments

I have presented ideas from this book in a variety of venues. I would like to thank the many people who gave me feedback in those venues: the American Academy of Anthropology Annual Meeting in 2015; the American Academy of Religion Meeting in 2013; the Association of Jewish Studies Conferences in 2011 and 2014; Bard College's conference "Make It New Again" in 2017; Barnard College's Rennert Forum in 2013; Brandeis University's Jewish Studies Colloquium in 2016; Columbia University's workshop "Religion Unwound" in 2013; Northwestern University's conference "At the Crossroads" in 2015; the University of Chicago's Animal Studies Workshop, cosponsored with Jewish Studies, in 2015; the Workshop on Animals, Law, and Religion at Harvard University Law School in 2016; the multiyear Workshop in Islamic and Jewish Legal Reasoning at the University of Toronto; and Yale University's Ancient Judaism Workshop in 2013. My gratitude goes to those who invited me to participate in these forums: Febe Armanios, Mira Balberg, Anver Emon, Boğaç Ergene, ChaeRan Freeze, Bill Hutchison, Katharine Mershon, James Redfield, Annie Schiff, Shai Secunda, Kristen Stilt, and Barry Wimpfheimer.

I would like to thank my colleagues in the Religion Department at Barnard College, which I joined just as this project was getting under way. I am deeply grateful for the camaraderie that we share. I would also like to thank my colleagues in the Columbia University Religion department and at Columbia University's Institute for Israel and Jewish Studies, both of which are welcoming homes for me within the larger university. I am grateful to Michelle Chesner, the librarian for Jewish Studies at Columbia University, who is ever ready to offer assistance. I would like to thank the students in courses I taught at the Jewish Theological Seminary and at Barnard College who read sources and scholarship on animals with me and whose observations have left their mark on this book. Their final projects – on "magizoology" in Harry Potter, the depiction of pets in Frida Kahlo's painting, and the mummification of animals in ancient Egypt, to name a few – were inspirational.

I would like to thank Barnard College for the Senior Faculty Research Leave that gave me time off from teaching to work on this project.

An earlier version of Chapter 2 was published as "Animal." In *Late Ancient Knowing: Explorations in Intellectual History*. Edited by Catherine Chin and Moulie Vidas. Berkeley: University of California Press, 2015, pp. 36–57.

An earlier version of Chapter 4 was published as "The Slipperiness of Animal Suffering: Revisiting the Talmud's Classic Treatment." In *Jewish Veganism and Vegetarianism*. Edited by Jacob Labendz and Shmuly Yanklowitz. State University of New York Press, forthcoming.

An earlier version of Chapter 6 was published as "Revisiting the Anomalous: Animals at the Intersection of Persons and Property in Bavli Sukkah 22b–23b." In *The Faces of Torah: Studies in the Texts and Contexts of Ancient Judaism in Honor of Steven Fraade*. Edited by Christine E. Hayes, Tzvi Novick, and Michal Bar-Asher Siegal. Göttingen, Germany: Vandenhoeck and Ruprecht, Supplements to the *Journal of Ancient Judaism*, Vol. 22, 2017, pp. 239–256.

Sections of the book appeared in earlier form in "The Cowering Calf and the Thirsty Dog: Narrating and Legislating Kindness to Animals in Jewish and Islamic Texts." Coauthored with Marion Katz. In *Islamic and Jewish Legal Reasoning*. Edited by Anver M. Emon. London: Oneworld Press, 2016, pp. 61–112.

I would like to thank the editors of these essays – CM Chin, Anver Emon, Marion Katz, Jacob Labendz, Michal Bar-Asher Siegel, Moulie Vidas, and Shmuly Yanklowitz – for their attentive reading and superb editing. I would like to thank Elizabeth Shanks Alexander for what has been an extraordinary academic partnership these past years. Thanks go also to Ben Baader, Chaya Halberstam, and Lisa Silverman for our fruitful conversations about Jewish difference. I thank Seth Schwartz for his unfailing friendship, Moshe Simon-Shoshan for reading Chapter 1, and the anonymous readers of Cambridge University Press for their many insightful comments and suggestions.

I would like to thank those at Cambridge University Press who have ushered this book from manuscript to the printed page: Lew Bateman,

Beatrice Rehl, Edgar Mendez, Katherine Tengco-Barbaro, Vincent Rajan, and Dee Josephson.

My family knows firsthand my love for animals and shares that love with me. We will always cherish the memory of Dulcie, our first dog. We are now blessed with a big, lumbering Newfoundland puppy, Burt, who is a source of constant delight and amusement. I would like to thank my family – Josh, Orly, Tamar, and Burt – for the pleasure and love they give me. I want to thank the rest of my family – my parents, sister, sister-in-law, brothers-in-law, nieces, and nephew – for their love and for their tolerance of our family's fondness for big dogs.

I

Introduction

Balaam's Ass, the Babylonian Talmud, and Critical Animal Studies

REMBRANDT'S ASS

In Rembrandt's "The Prophet Balaam and the Ass," Balaam is at the center of the painting, his turbaned white hair streaming, his red cloak billowing around him.[1] With one hand Balaam pulls his donkey with a rope. In his other hand he holds a club that he is about to bring down on the recalcitrant donkey. An angel stands above Balaam in a pose that mirrors Balaam's. The angel is about to strike Balaam with a sword, but Balaam does not see him. Balaam looks at the donkey, the angel looks at Balaam, each in consternation. The two figures are a physics lesson in potential energy. Rembrandt has captured them at a moment of great dramatic tension.

In between the two human figures is the donkey. She has been brought to her knees, her saddlebag almost level with the ground, her head turned back toward Balaam as she, with terrified eyes and mouth agape, awaits the strike.[2] Is she looking at the angel or at Balaam? Whom does she fear more? In the painting of Balaam by Rembrandt's teacher Pieter Lastman

---

[1] Rembrandt Harmenszoon van Rijn, 1626, in the Musée Cognacq-Jay in Paris. The image can be viewed at www.museecognacqjay.paris.fr/en/la-collection/ass-prophet-balaam.
[2] The Numbers narrative describes the donkey as "crouched down under Balaam" (Numbers 22:27), which, according to Baruch Levine, suggests that the donkey either had prostrated herself before the angel or was waiting for the angel's command. The crouching is not a consequence of Balaam's blows, says Levine, though that is how Rembrandt seems to be rendering it. See Baruch A. Levine, *Numbers 21–36: A New Translation with Introduction and Commentary*, vol. 4A, The Anchor Bible (New York: Doubleday, 2000), 156–7.

I

the angel stands to the side of the donkey rather than above her, so it is clear that the object of the donkey's gaze is Balaam.[3] The ambiguity in Rembrandt's version is only one of the ways in which the painting surpasses his teacher's.

In the lower right foreground of Remrandt's portrait are dark furrowed leaves that suggest the vineyard described in the biblical narrative (Numbers 22:24), while in the far shadows stand the two servants who accompany Balaam (Numbers 22:22), and lit up and on higher ground wait the Moabite dignitaries who have invited Balaam at the Moabite king Balak's behest (Numbers 22:21). But it is the donkey who is meant to occupy the viewer's interest. The angel's illuminated white robe forms the background to the donkey's head and draws the eye to it. The white both of the donkey's teeth and of the documents protruding from her saddlebag match the white of the angel's robe behind them. The donkey's agitated expression contrasts with the impassive, partially obscured face of the Moabites' horse shown in the background. Our compassion is stirred for the donkey so unjustly treated.[4]

Balaam's readers are divided between those who admire him as a rare gentile prophet and those who revile him for his mission to curse Israel and his obstinacy in this scene. Rembrandt's portrait clearly falls into the second camp.[5] For Rembrandt and his seventeenth-century Dutch audiences, Balaam would have represented the faithless persecutors of Christ, in line with conventional Christian understandings of the story, and perhaps also the contemporaneous Counter-Remonstrants in their persecution of the Remonstrants.[6] The donkey is the figure with whom

[3] Pieter Lastman, 1622, in the Israel Museum in Jerusalem. For comparison of Lastman's Balaam to Rembrandt's, see Shimon Levy, "Angel, She-Ass, Prophet: The Play and Its Set Design," in *Jews and Theater in an Intercultural Context*, ed. Edna Nahshon (Leiden: Brill, 2012), 14–17.

[4] See discussion of this painting in Eric Jan Sluijter, *Rembrandt and the Female Nude* (Amsterdam: Amsterdam University Press, 2006), 106–7.

[5] See Ed Noort, "Balaam the Villain: The History of Reception of the Balaam Narrative in the Pentateuch and the Former Prophets," in *The Prestige of the Pagan Prophet Balaam in Judaism, Early Christianity and Islam*, ed. Geurt Hendrik van Kooten and J. van Ruiten, Themes in Biblical Narrative Conference (Leiden: Brill, 2008), 8–9. The interpretive division begins already in the Hebrew Bible itself, as Noort discusses; see also the excursus in Jacob Milgrom, *Numbers = [Ba-Midbar]: The Traditional Hebrew Text with the New JPS Translation*, JPS Torah Commentary (Philadelphia: Jewish Publication Society, 1990), 469–71.

[6] This interpretation of the painting is suggested by Shelley Perlove and Larry Silver, *Rembrandt's Faith: Church and Temple in the Dutch Golden Age* (University Park: Penn State Press, 2009), 28–32. The conflict between Remonstrants and Counter-Remonstrants was generated by a difference in views between two professors at Leiden University

one is meant to identify. She is the Christian in opposition to the Jew, the Remonstrant imprisoned and exiled by the Counter-Remonstrants.

BALAAM'S RIDE

I begin this book with Balaam's donkey as Rembrandt portrays her because she captures the complexity of anthropocentrism in canonical religious texts, the subject of this book. The texts are anthropocentric, yet animal perspectives percolate up. In this introductory chapter I will stay with Balaam's donkey a little longer in order to illustrate the major currents within contemporary critical animal studies, the field on which this book draws. I will then make my way to the Babylonian Talmud, the late ancient literary work prized by Jewish law and culture, which is the primary text for this book.[7] I will lay out the book's purpose, which is to explore the anthropocentrism that structures talmudic discourse and to tease out the animal subjectivities that have gone unseen there. The book's broader goal is to offer some new perspectives on animals and animality from the vantage point of the rabbis.

In the Balaam tale, the donkey is the literal vehicle on whom Balaam rides toward Balak and the metaphorical vehicle through which God teaches Balaam obedience.[8] She will also be *my* vehicle for introducing the central concerns of critical animal studies. As the story begins, Balaam is traveling to King Balak, who is pressuring him to curse the people of Israel (Numbers 22:21). God is angry with Balaam for his compliance with Balak's request (Numbers 22:22).[9] The action

and had torn apart the Dutch Reformed Church at the time that Rembrandt made this painting. While not himself a Remonstrant, Rembrandt had many ties to the group; see ibid., 25. For early Christian understandings of Balaam (key texts are Revelation 2:14, 2 Peter 2:15–16, and Jude 11), see Geurt Hendrik van Kooten and J. van Ruiten, eds., *The Prestige of the Pagan Prophet Balaam in Judaism, Early Christianity and Islam*, Themes in Biblical Narrative Conference (Leiden: Brill, 2008), 233–302.

Rembrandt had many relationships with Jews, painted them in a surprisingly dispassionate mode given European painting's tradition of grotesque depiction of Jews, and sold this particular painting to a Jew named Alfonso Lopez, so one might plausibly interpret this painting also in more Judaism-friendly terms; see Steven M. Nadler, *Rembrandt's Jews* (Chicago: University of Chicago Press, 2003), 82.

7 On what makes animal studies "critical," see Dawne McCance, *Critical Animal Studies: An Introduction* (Albany: State University of New York Press, 2013), 4–5.

8 The donkey's role is described this way in Kenneth C. Way, *Donkeys in the Biblical World: Ceremony and Symbol* (Winona Lake, IN: Eisenbrauns, 2011), 187.

9 God is angry even though just two verses prior God tells Balaam in a dream to go to Balak. That is one feature among many suggesting to source critics that the story with

proceeds by patterns of three. The donkey tries three times to avoid the angel (Numbers 22:23, 25, 27). Each time Balaam does not see the angel and is angry at the donkey for her seemingly unwarranted stop. Over the course of the repetitions, the drama intensifies.[10] The angel keeps advancing, the donkey finds herself with less and less room to move, trapped between the angel and Balaam, and Balaam grows increasingly aggressive. The drama culminates in a tête à tête between Balaam and the donkey, whose mouth God miraculously opens. God finally permits Balaam to see the angel, Balaam realizes his error and offers to turn back, but the angel urges him on to his prophetic task now that he has been prepared to speak only God's word. The story is filled with irony[11]: a seer who cannot see, a man more stubborn than his mule, an ass who is anything but asinine.[12] At the very moment that the angel's sword is under his nose, Balaam says in exasperation that, if he had a sword, he would slay the donkey with it – an irony made visual in Rembrandt's painting. By the end of the story, the irony is resolved. The seer has learned to see; Balaam has gone from stubborn to subservient. The ass presumably goes back to being asinine, since we never hear from her again.

---

the donkey is an interpolation in the larger Balaam narrative. See Clinton J. Moyer, "Who Is the Prophet, and Who the Ass? Role-Reversing Interludes and the Unity of the Balaam Narrative (Numbers 22–24)," *Journal for the Study of the Old Testament* 37, no. 2 (2012): 169–74. Moyer himself argues for the donkey episode being an integrated part of the narrative. Building on Moyer's approach but arguing with his conclusions is Amos Frisch, "The Story of Balaam's She-Ass (Numbers 22: 21–35): A New Literary Insight," *Hebrew Studies* 56, no. 1 (2015): 103–13.

[10] On the patterns of three and their intensification, see Way, *Donkeys in the Biblical World*, 183–4.

[11] On the ironies in the story, see Milgrom, *Numbers*, 469. To them can be added the gendering of the characters – the femaleness of the ass versus the maleness of the prophet – which Kirova sees as contributing to the carnivalesque dimensions of the story; see Milena Kirova, "Eyes Wide Open: A Case of Symbolic Reversal in the Biblical Narrative," *Scandinavian Journal of the Old Testament* 24, no. 1 (2010): 85–98. Kirova points to the role of the ass's female gender in the lesson of subordination that she teaches, and compares the miracle of God's opening the donkey's mouth to the miracle of God's opening wombs (the first observation is seriatim through the article; the latter point is on p. 94).

[12] I borrow that last locution about the ass from Heather A. McKay, "Through the Eyes of Horses: Representation of the Horse Family in the Hebrew Bible," in *Sense and Sensitivity: Essays on Reading the Bible in Memory of Robert Carroll*, ed. Alastair G. Hunter and Philip R. Davies (London: Sheffield Academic Press, 2002), 138. On the stereotype of the donkey as stubborn, see the cultural history in Jill Bough, *Donkey* (Chicago: University of Chicago Press, 2011).

TALKING ANIMALS

Animals such as Balaam's donkey who speak in human language have a long history in western culture. From the "contest literatures" of the ancient Sumerians and Babylonians in which two animals spar over who is better, to the talking dogs of Lucian's *Dialogues of the Dead* in ancient Rome, right up to Tony the Tiger selling Frosted Flakes, speaking animals would seem to be the ultimate in what primatologist Frans de Waal calls anthropocentric anthropomorphism.[13] Anthropomorphism – the attribution of human characteristics to the nonhuman – is not all bad, says de Waal. The continuity between human beings and other species, however minimal it may be in some cases, means that human beings can use their own experience to understand other species. Yet one must also take into account the many differences between a human being and a chimpanzee, or dog, or bat.[14] De Waal suggests that an anthropomorphism that considers both continuity and difference be called "animal-centric." An example would be recognizing that a dog's "smile" may be expressing fear or submission. Anthropocentric anthropomorphism, by contrast, would presume that the dog is happy. Anthropocentric anthropomorphism imposes human systems of meaning on other species and effaces the systems that other species make for themselves. It is the difference, de Waal observes, between giving someone a gift that *they* would want and giving someone a gift that *you* would want. Animals such as Balaam's donkey who speak in human language are giving us a gift that we would want.[15]

Their anthropocentrism notwithstanding, animals who speak in human language do reflect a genuine desire to see the world from an animal's perspective, Karla Armbruster argues.[16] Balaam's donkey, in my

[13] On the "contest literatures," see Cameron B. R. Howard, "Animal Speech as Revelation in Genesis 3 and Numbers 22," in *Exploring Ecological Hermeneutics*, ed. Norman C. Habel and Peter L. Trudinger (Atlanta, GA: Society of Biblical Literature, 2008), 23. On anthropocentric vs. animalcentric anthropomorphism, see Frans B. M. de Waal, *The Ape and the Sushi Master: Cultural Reflections of a Primatologist* (New York: Basic Books, 2001), 74–8.

[14] Echoing, "What Is It Like to Be a Bat?," in *Mortal Questions*, ed. Thomas Nagel (New York: Canto, 1979), 165–80.

[15] See Karla Armbruster, "What Do We Want from Talking Animals? Reflections on Literary Representations of Animal Voices and Minds," in *Speaking for Animals: Animal Autobiographical Writing*, ed. Margo DeMello (New York: Routledge, 2013), 17–33. Armbruster cites Erica Fudge, who says that speaking animals in literature say what we want to hear, e.g., Lassie tells us she wants to come home (p. 21). Armbruster also calls speaking animals a form of "speaking for others," a practice conceptualized and critiqued by feminism (pp. 22–3).

[16] See ibid.

reading of her, is such a case. In her dialogue with Balaam, the donkey reproaches him not only for his physical blows but also for his betrayal of their trust[17]:

> Then the Lord opened the ass's mouth, and she said to Balaam, "What have I done to you that you have beaten me these three times?"
> Balaam said to the ass, "You have made a mockery of me! If I had a sword with me, I'd kill you!"
> The ass said to Balaam, "Look, I am the ass that you have been riding all along until this day! Have I been in the habit of doing thus to you?"
> And he answered, "No."
> Then the Lord uncovered Balaam's eyes, and he saw the angel of the Lord ...[18]

The donkey's opening line challenges Balaam's repeated beatings. All the donkey has done is stop walking. The punishment, if merited at all, is out of proportion to the crime. Balaam retorts that the harm done by the donkey is to Balaam's dignity ("You have made a mockery of me!") and that, in fact, the donkey deserves a worse punishment than Balaam has so far inflicted ("If I had a sword with me, I'd kill you!").[19] The donkey in response reminds Balaam of her loyalty to him ("Look, I am the ass that you have been riding all along until this day! Have I been in the habit of doing thus to you?"). The response seems to put Balaam in his place. His one-word answer "No" is the turning point in the tale. At that moment God opens Balaam's eyes so that he can see the angel. The dialogue between Balaam and the donkey begins with God's opening the donkey's mouth and closes with God's opening Balaam's eyes.

The impact of the donkey's speech on Balaam is due to her (and, obviously, the storyteller's) prodigious rhetorical talents. Most of us in the

---

[17] To see how the rabbis cleverly fill out the dialogue, see Babylonian Talmud Sanhedrin 105b and discussion in Ronit Nikolsky, "Interpret Him as Much as You Want: Balaam in the Babylonian Talmud," in *The Prestige of the Pagan Prophet Balaam in Judaism, Early Christianity and Islam*, ed. Geurt Hendrik van Kooten and J. van Ruiten, Themes in Biblical Narrative Conference (Leiden: Brill, 2008), 213–30. One of the more intriguing rabbinic interventions is the claim that Balaam has sex with his donkey every night, the product of a wordplay on the name Balaam ben Be'or that reads it as *ba'al be'ir* ("he has sexual intercourse with cattle").

[18] Numbers 22:28–31.

[19] The Hebrew for "You have made a mockery of me" is הִתְעַלַּלְתְּ בִּי (*hitalalt bi*). The verb's usage elsewhere suggests not light mockery but traumatic humiliation. It is used to describe God's mockery of the Egyptians (Exodus 10:2, 1 Samuel 6:6), the rape of the concubine (Judges 19:25), Saul's fear of what the Philistines might do to him (1 Samuel 31:4), and Zedekiah's fear of what the Judeans might do to him (Jeremiah 38:19). See Milgrom, *Numbers*, 320, n. 71.

donkey's place would have responded to Balaam with some version of "Can't you see that there's an angel standing in my way?" (Most of us in Balaam's place, for that matter, would have reacted to the donkey with some version of "I must be crazy if my donkey is talking to me," but Balaam takes it in stride.) The donkey never mentions the elephant in the room (i.e., the angel in the vineyard) and instead calls attention to their own relationship.[20] This choice on the donkey's part – and it is a choice, since while God opens the donkey's mouth, God is not said to be putting words into it – is critical to the donkey's lesson to Balaam.[21] Just as the donkey is subservient to his master, so too should Balaam be subservient to his master – God.

While the moral of the story is human obedience to God, the story does not skirt the subjectivity of the donkey. What does it feel like to be a donkey, the story implicitly wonders, saddled and weighed down with cargo, beaten for not going fast enough? When the donkey teaches God's lesson to Balaam, she is also teaching him, and the story's readers, about her experience as a donkey. She may be speaking God's words, but she is also speaking her own. A person can never really understand what it feels like to be a donkey, and the story evinces interest neither in how donkeys normally express themselves nor in liberating them from human servitude. When the story describes the donkey's mouth being opened, it presumes that prior to that moment the donkey's mouth was "closed," even though braying constitutes speech, albeit not a speech in which human beings are fluent.[22] Moreover, the story holds up the subordination of animals to people as a model for the subordination of people to God.

---

[20] The donkey speaks of her past subservience to Balaam using unusual language (הַהַסְכֵּן הַסְכַּנְתִּי לַעֲשׂוֹת לְךָ כֹּה, *ha-hasken hiskanti la'asot lekha koh*). Milgrom understands the phrase ("Have I been in the habit of doing thus to you?") in the tradition of Targum Onkelos and Rashi; see Milgrom, *Numbers*, 320, n. 74. Highlighting the power dynamics between the donkey and Balaam, Levine renders it as "Have I ever before sought to gain an advantage by behaving towards you in such a manner?" Levine describes his translation as "merely an educated guess"; Levine, *Numbers 21–36*, 4A:142. The Rabbis point to the same root's use in 1 Kings 1:2 to describe Avishag's "warming" of David by lying with him at night, and they understand the phrase here to be a reference to the donkey's sexual relationship with Balaam (Sanhedrin 105b; see note 17). The high-flown language of the donkey may be meant to contrast ironically with the one-word simple answer to which Balaam is reduced.

[21] God is described several times later in the narrative (Numbers 23:5, 12, 16) as putting words into Balaam's mouth, but God is not described as doing so here.

[22] Levine misses this when he says that "speech comes naturally to humans, but not, of course, to animals, who are given this exceptional faculty in fables"; Levine, *Numbers 21–36*, 4A:157.

The only challenge that the donkey poses to Balaam is why he does not act more responsibly as a master. Nevertheless, the story's choice to have the donkey speak from her own position as a donkey, even if not in her own language, suggests that at the heart of the story is curiosity about the animal's experience, even if that experience serves human purposes and is wrapped up in human perspectives. It is no surprise that Rembrandt chose to portray the donkey with mouth open, at the moment that she speaks, since this is the moment in the story filled with greatest pathos. In Rembrandt's portrait and in the biblical story itself, the donkey is a vehicle, but she is also more.

CRITICAL ANIMAL STUDIES

Mainstream Jewish understandings of Balaam's ass have resisted seeing her as anything more than a vehicle.[23] Maimonides chalked the whole incident up to a dream.[24] These traditions of reading have solidified and in many cases amplified the anthropocentrism of the ancient texts such that the anthropocentrism seems inevitable and invisible rather than historically conditioned and actively ideological. The posthumanist perspective offered by critical animal studies brings that anthropocentrism to light, making it possible to encounter Balaam's donkey, and the talmudic animals who will be introduced in the chapters that follow, as characters in their own right even as they are trapped in human perspectives and products of them.[25]

The story of animal studies has philosophy as its main character.[26] Matthew Calarco describes a shift within animal studies from its early

[23] Howard, "Animal Speech as Revelation in Genesis 3 and Numbers 22" tries to offset the anthropocentrism with theology: "For the animals to appear only as servants of *human* needs would be an unmitigated anthropocentrism. For them to be presented as agents of *divinity* is another matter" (p. 28). The animal is still a vehicle in the theological model, however.

[24] *Guide of the Perplexed* II:42. See discussion of Maimonides's view of animals in Hannah Kasher, "Animals as Moral Patients in Maimonides' Teachings," *American Catholic Philosophical Quarterly* 76, no. 1 (2002): 165–80.

[25] "Posthumanities" and "posthumanism" are interested in the implications of artificial intelligence as much as in animals. See Cary Wolfe, *What Is Posthumanism?* (Minneapolis: University of Minnesota Press, 2010); Stefan Herbrechter, *Posthumanism: A Critical Analysis* (New York: Bloomsbury Academic, 2013); Pramod K. Nayar, *Posthumanism* (Cambridge, UK: Polity, 2014). Bringing together the interests in artificial intelligences and animals is "From Cyborgs to Companion Species," in Donna Jeanne Haraway, *The Haraway Reader* (New York: Routledge, 2004), 295–320.

[26] Article-length accounts of animal studies include one oriented toward Continental philosophy – Cary Wolfe, "Human, All Too Human: 'Animal Studies' and the Humanities,"

years, when Peter Singer's *Animal Liberation* popularized the term
"speciesism" and advocated for equal consideration for animals, to
a second wave, when Derrida's "The Animal That Therefore I Am"
reflected on the violence in the homogenizing term "animal" and developed an animal ethics based on alterity.[27] Calarco calls early thinkers
like Singer the "identity theorists." They attacked the prejudice against
other species at the core of classical philosophy and advocated for the

Proceedings of the MLA 124, no. 2 (2009): 564–75 – and another oriented toward
history – Erica Fudge, "A Left-Handed Blow: Writing the History of Animals," in
Representing Animals, ed. Nigel Rothfels (Bloomington, IN: Indiana University Press,
2002), 3–18. Monographs include Kari Weil, *Thinking Animals: Why Animal Studies
Now?* (New York: Columbia University Press, 2012); McCance, *Critical Animal Studies*;
Anthony J. Nocella et al., eds., *Defining Critical Animal Studies: An Intersectional Social
Justice Approach for Liberation* (New York: Peter Lang, 2013); Paul Waldau, *Animal
Studies: An Introduction* (New York: Oxford University Press, 2013); John Sorenson,
Critical Animal Studies: Thinking the Unthinkable (Toronto: Canadian Scholars' Press,
2014); Nik Taylor and Richard Twine, eds., *The Rise of Critical Animal Studies: From
the Margins to the Centre* (Abingdon, UK: Routledge, 2014); Derek Ryan, *Animal
Theory: A Critical Introduction* (Edinburgh: Edinburgh University Press, 2015).
   Recent readers in animal studies include Matthew Calarco and Peter Atterton, eds.,
Animal Philosophy: Essential Readings in Continental Thought (New York: Continuum,
2004); Josephine Donovan and Carol J. Adams, eds., *The Feminist Care Tradition in
Animal Ethics: A Reader* (New York: Columbia University Press, 2007); Linda Kalof
and Amy Fitzgerald, eds., *The Animals Reader: The Essential Classic and Contemporary
Writings* (New York: Berg, 2007); Susan Jean Armstrong and Richard G. Botzler, eds.,
The Animal Ethics Reader (New York: Routledge, 2008); Jodey Castricano, ed., *Animal
Subjects: An Ethical Reader in a Posthuman World* (Waterloo, ON: Wilfrid Laurier
University Press, 2008); Aaron S. Gross and Anne Vallely, eds., *Animals and the Human
Imagination: A Companion to Animal Studies* (New York: Columbia University Press,
2012); Louisa Mackenzie and Stephanie Posthumus, eds., *French Thinking about
Animals, The Animal Turn* (East Lansing: Michigan State University Press, 2015).
   For a brief but useful discussion of the significance of literary studies (like this one)
to critical animal studies, see Colleen Glenney Boggs, *Animalia Americana: Animal
Representations and Biopolitical Subjectivity* (New York: Columbia University Press,
2013), 19–21. She describes literature as "the site where the relationship with animals
is worked out ..." where "we confront the irreducible alterity of animals that is the
basis for a relationship beyond anthropomorphism" (p. 20). For more on animal studies and literary studies, see Carrie Rohman, *Stalking the Subject: Modernism and the
Animal* (New York: Columbia University Press, 2012); Scott M. DeVries, *Creature
Discomfort: Fauna-Criticism, Ethics and the Representation of Animals in Spanish
American Fiction and Poetry* (Leiden: Brill, 2016). The classic work treating literature's
contribution to thinking about animals is J. M. Coetzee, *The Lives of Animals*, Princeton
Classics (Princeton, NJ: Princeton University Press, 2016).
[27] Matthew Calarco, *Thinking Through Animals: Identity, Difference, Indistinction* (Palo
Alto, CA: Stanford University Press, 2015). This section is an encapsulation of his
arguments.

inclusion of other species within the circle of moral accountability.[28] These theorists changed the terms of philosophical reflection by uprooting human exceptionalism and by stressing instead the features that human beings share with other animals. Singer's arguments against speciesism are, however, themselves rife with speciesism. His assumption in *Animal Liberation* is that while animals may suffer as human beings do, they are inferior creatures in most other ways. Even when corrected for speciesism, critics argue that such an approach remains logocentric, grounding its arguments in appeals to human rationality, attributing the problem of speciesism to an individual's irrational biases, and predicating the moral status of other species on their approximation to human beings. The more similar an animal is to a human, the more likely it is that identity theorists will attribute moral significance to them.

For "difference theorists," associated with the continental tradition and the postmodern rather than the analytic and the modern, the basis of ethics is not empathy with a fellow creature, but encounter with the Other. The animal demands an ethical response not because they are in some way or another the same as human beings (e.g., the capacity to suffer, to have intention, to communicate, and so forth), but because they are irreducibly different. Difference theorists see the roots of species hierarchy not, as the analytic philosophers tend to, in an individual's irrational bias on behalf of his or her own species, but in elaborate and frequently invisible infrastructures of power that maintain the privilege of the human.[29] Difference theorists critique the apparatus that melds all life forms other than the human into the single essence known as "the animal," and they see the human/animal binary as similar and related to other reductive binaries: white/black, male/female, straight/gay, able-bodied/disabled, culture/nature, and so forth.

---

[28] On the classical philosophical background, see Richard Sorabji, *Animal Minds and Human Morals: The Origins of the Western Debate* (Ithaca, NY: Cornell University Press, 1993). On the view of animals as *automata* promulgated by Descartes, the "villain" of the animal rights narrative if there were one, see Tom Regan, *The Case for Animal Rights* (Berkeley: University of California Press, 2004), 1–33. On Descartes's reliance on Aristotle, see Catherine Osborne, *Dumb Beasts and Dead Philosophers* (New York: Oxford University Press, 2007), 63–97.

[29] On the distinction between "speciesism" and "anthropocentrism," see Calarco, *Thinking Through Animals*, 25–6. For further on anthropocentrism, see Rob Boddice, ed., *Anthropocentrism: Human, Animals, Environments* (Boston: Brill, 2011).

While resolving some of the dilemmas left by the sameness theorists, the difference theorists create new ones. Where do ethics stop? If ethics extend to the ape, the toad, and the amoeba, do they extend also to the fern and flower, the rock, the grain of sand? Ethical principles require reworking if they are to incorporate so many new ethical subjects. Difference theorists also leave dormant the power of identification to shape ethics, and they leave little room for individual agency, which seems to dissolve into false consciousness within the systems of power to which these theorists point. The newest turn in critical animal studies – Calarco calls it "indistinction" – aims to recover sameness but along new lines, so that instead of seeing the ways that animals are like us, we notice how we are like them.[30] We might consider, with Gilles Deleuze, that we too are slabs of meat, and that the packaged meat in the butcher section of the supermarket looks remarkably like our own body parts. We might think, with Jason Hribal, of an animal's escape from a slaughterhouse, zoo, circus, or water park not as the exercise of instinct but as a desperate break for freedom.[31] "Indistinction" is interested in the commodification of animals within global capitalism and in the intersectionality of oppressions.[32] In this set of approaches can be located the new materialism, a branch of feminist theory that returns to the material as the ground of being.[33] It tries to

[30] Scholars Calarco discusses under this rubric are Gilles Deleuze, Giorgio Agamben, Donna Haraway, Rosi Braidotti, Val Plumwood, Elizabeth Grosz, Jason Hribal, and Brian Massumi.

[31] See Gilles Deleuze, *Francis Bacon: The Logic of Sensation* (Minneapolis: University of Minnesota Press, 2003); Jason Hribal, *Fear of the Animal Planet the Hidden History of Animal Resistance* (Oakland, CA: AK Press, 2010). A similar approach to Hribal's is found in Sarah E. McFarland and Ryan Hediger, eds., *Animals and Agency: An Interdisciplinary Exploration* (Leiden: Brill, 2009).

[32] Works that emphasize the overlap between critical animal studies and other critical studies like those of the environment, race, class, ethnicity, and sexuality include Mel Y. Chen, *Animacies: Biopolitics, Racial Mattering, and Queer Affect* (Durham, NC: Duke University Press, 2012); Nocella et al., *Defining Critical Animal Studies*; Kathryn Gillespie and Rosemary-Claire Collard, eds., *Critical Animal Geographies: Politics, Intersections and Hierarchies in a Multispecies World* (New York: Routledge, 2015); Claire Jean Kim, *Dangerous Crossings: Race, Species, and Nature in a Multicultural Age* (New York: Cambridge University Press, 2015); Anthony J. Nocella, Amber E. George, and J. L. Schatz, eds., *The Intersectionality of Critical Animal, Disability, and Environmental Studies: Toward Eco-Ability, Justice, and Liberation* (Lanham, MD: Lexington Books, 2017).

[33] See the collections: Stacy Alaimo and Susan Hekman, eds., *Material Feminisms* (Bloomington, IN: Indiana University Press, 2008); Diana Coole and Samantha Frost, eds., *New Materialisms: Ontology, Agency, and Politics* (Durham, NC: Duke University Press, 2010).

correct the radical constructionism of some modern feminist theory by highlighting human animality, mortality, physicality, and relationality.

Scientific research plays a critical role in animal studies. It shows in other species previously unimagined capacities to feel, think, speak, sing, learn, teach, plan, recognize, remember, share, trick, play, flirt, grieve, judge, and self-reflect.[34] De Waal tells the story of Binti Jua, a gorilla who saved a three-year-old boy who had fallen into the primate exhibit at the Chicago Brookfield Zoo.[35] As de Waal recounts it, the gorilla was seen to scoop up the boy, give him a gentle pat on the back, and send him on his way. The gorilla's kindness earned her a spot on *Time*'s list of "best people" of 1996. De Waal marvels at how some scientists dismissed the gorilla's act as the product of a "confused maternal instinct" or a desire for a reward from her zookeeper. They were willing to entertain any explanation other than one that saw moral significance in the gorilla's behavior.[36] De Waal's work with bonobos and chimpanzees shows consistently, however, that other primates exhibit many behaviors people normally consider to be moral, such as peacemaking and reconciliation. Some scientists have attributed religion to other species. Observing a chimpanzee community performing what she calls a "waterfall dance," Jane Goodall suggests that it be interpreted as a form of religious expression.[37] Goodall's and de Waal's work is

---

[34] Some well-known works on animal capacities include Marc Bekoff, *The Emotional Lives of Animals: A Leading Scientist Explores Animal Joy, Sorrow, and Empathy – and Why They Matter* (Novato, CA: New World Library, 2008); Jeffrey Moussaieff Masson, *When Elephants Weep: The Emotional Lives of Animals* (New York: Random House, 2009); Alexandra Horowitz, *Inside of a Dog: What Dogs See, Smell, and Know* (New York: Scribner, 2010); Barbara J. King, *How Animals Grieve* (Chicago: University of Chicago Press, 2013); Helen Macdonald, *H Is for Hawk* (New York: Grove/Atlantic, 2015); Sy Montgomery, *The Soul of an Octopus* (New York: Simon & Schuster, 2015); Jennifer Ackerman, *The Genius of Birds* (New York: Penguin, 2016); Abigail Tucker, *The Lion in the Living Room: How House Cats Tamed Us and Took Over the World* (New York: Simon & Schuster, 2016).

[35] de Waal, *The Ape and the Sushi Master*, 78–81.

[36] Resistance to attributing moral significance to an animal's act, and ridiculing of people who do, can be found in the recent incident in which a golden retriever saved a fawn who was drowning; note the *New York Times* headline: Sarah Maslin Nir, "Dog Praised as Hero for Saving Deer (Whether He Meant To or Not)," *The New York Times*, July 18, 2017, sec. N.Y. / Region, www.nytimes.com/2017/07/18/nyregion/dog-rescues-a-drowning-deer-and-becomes-a-social-media-hero.html.

[37] See Barbara J. King, "Anti-Stress Serenity Injection: The Chimpanzee Waterfall Video," *NPR.org*, accessed January 14, 2016, www.npr.org/sections/13.7/2012/03/28/149531687/anti-stress-serenity-injection-the-chimpanzee-waterfall-video. On animal

with species with whom human beings can relatively easily relate, i.e., other primates, but more and more is being observed and appreciated also about the capacities of species distant from human beings, such as in Helen MacDonald's popular and acclaimed *H Is for Hawk* and Sy Montgomery's *Soul of an Octopus*.[38]

ANIMALITY

I use the notion of animality in this book with two aims in mind: 1) to point to this expanding way of seeing other species in relation to our own, and 2) to cultivate greater sensitivity to anthropocentrism or what Giorgio Agamben called the "anthropological machine."[39] With that first aim in mind, "animality" is intended to echo "personality" as an index of difference at the level of the individual. The notion of personality presumes that every person possesses their own peculiar combination of traits that makes them who they are and that distinguishes them from everyone else.[40] The notion of "animality" attributes individual significance to nonhuman persons as well, without getting tangled up in the linguistic paradox of attributing a "personality" to an animal.[41] "Animality" used in this sense represents an effort to claim distinctiveness, agency, and subjectivity for individuals who belong to a species category other than the human.

The second aim of "animality" is to make anthropocentrism more visible. "Animality" in this sense points to the constructedness of species difference and to the violence done to other species and to some human

religion, see Donovan O. Schaefer, "Do Animals Have Religion? Interdisciplinary Perspectives on Religion and Embodiment," *Anthrozoös* 25, no. 1 (August 1, 2012): 173–89; Donovan O. Schaefer, *Religious Affects: Animality, Evolution, and Power* (Durham, NC: Duke University Press, 2015). On the animal in modern theories of religion, see Aaron S. Gross, *The Question of the Animal and Religion: Theoretical Stakes, Practical Implications* (New York: Columbia University Press, 2015).

[38] See footnote 34 for references.

[39] Giorgio Agamben, *The Open: Man and Animal* (Palo Alto, CA: Stanford University Press, 2004), 33–8.

[40] Personality psychology's central question is how human beings differ from each other; see Albert Ellis, Mike Abrams, and Lidia Abrams, *Personality Theories: Critical Perspectives* (Los Angeles: Sage, 2009), 1.

[41] Though animal scientists do use the term "personality" this way; see Claudio Carere and Dario Maestripieri, eds., *Animal Personalities: Behavior, Physiology, and Evolution* (Chicago: University of Chicago Press, 2013). In Chapter 6, I discuss the application of the notion of "personhood" to animals.

beings by that construction.[42] The use of the adjective "animalistic" to criticize certain human behaviors as overly aggressive or hyper-sexual demonstrates the manipulability of the notion of the animal and the flexibility of the binary of human/animal. In the discourse of animality, a person can easily end up on the animal side, and an animal on the human side. To capture this elasticity, Colleen Glenney Boggs describes a grid of four figures: the animalized animal, the humanized human, the humanized animal, and the animalized human.[43] The animalized animal possesses no subjectivity whatsoever; the humanized human, at the other end of the spectrum, has the monopoly on subjectivity; the humanized animal can participate in subjectivity by being considered non-"animalistic" despite her formal features as an "animal"; and, finally, the animalized human loses the claim to subjectivity and is thought of as an animal despite sharing the formal features of a human being. Animality and humanity within this grid erect boundaries, organize relationships, and justify behaviors, such as the abuse by American soldiers of Iraqi prisoners at Abu Ghraib prison, one of the subjects that Boggs considers. This notion of "animality" is linked to what de Waal calls anthropodenial, the rejection of human continuity with other species, and to a human exceptionalism that privileges not only human beings over other species but also some human beings over other ones. "Animality" used in this second sense is set to a much darker shade than "animality" used in the first sense, here representing the side of animal studies that has little to do with liking animals or even reckoning with real animals at all and that instead calls attention to the ideological deployment of species difference.[44]

[42] Weitzenfeld and Joy describe four categories of violence; see Adam Weitzenfeld and Melanie Joy, "An Overview of Anthropocentrism, Humanism and Speciesism in Critical Animal Theory," in *Defining Critical Animal Studies: An Intersectional Social Justice Approach for Liberation*, ed. Anthony J. Nocella, John Sorenson, Atsuko Matsuoka, and Kim Socha (New York: Peter Lang, 2013), 3–27.

[43] See Boggs, *Animalia Americana*, 71. She is drawing on Cary Wolfe and Jonathan Elmer, "Subject to Sacrifice: Ideology, Psychoanalysis, and the Discourse of Species in Jonathan Demme's Silence of the Lambs," *Boundary* 2 (1995): 141–70.

[44] See a dual approach to animality also in Michael Lundblad, "From Animal to Animality Studies," *Proceedings of the MLA* 124, no. 2 (2009): 496–502: "I want to argue for 'animality studies' as a way to describe work that expresses no explicit interest in advocacy for various nonhuman animals, even though it shares an interest in how we think about 'real' animals. I use 'animality' to refer *both* to real animals and concern with their welfare and the recognition of their subjectivity, *and* to the dynamics and politics of species representation and especially to its intersectionality with race, gender, sexuality, etc." (497)

ANIMALITY IN THE TALMUD

This book brings the multiple meanings evoked by "animality" and the multiple sides of animal studies to the animals that appear in the Babylonian Talmud. The book selects five extended passages within the Babylonian Talmud and marries each one with a contemporary animal studies perspective. Each passage has been chosen for its sustained engagement with a significant dimension of animality as I have described it. One talmudic passage is concerned with the capacities of animal cognition; another with animal moral accountability; a third with animal suffering; the fourth with the idea of the "dangerous" animal; the final passage is concerned with the status of animals as property and as things. These passages are not, for the most part, well-known, the ones pored over in yeshivas or discussed in academic works (with the exception of the passage on animal suffering, which is foundational to Jewish animal ethics and law). These are passages that seemed to me to offer new paths for thinking about animality in the Talmud and in Jewish culture more generally. By choosing these passages I hope to expand the canon and also to inspire readers of the Talmud to revisit their favorite passages from a critical animal studies perspective.

The Babylonian Talmud's new perspectives on other species are the product of a perfect storm of forces: the new literary genre of the Babylonian Talmud, the Talmud's cultural eclecticism, and its remove from the Jerusalem Temple. I will discuss each in turn. While having much in common with the Palestinian Talmud, the Babylonian Talmud displays a degree of abstraction and reflexivity that is unique within rabbinic literature.[45] The editorial layers of the Babylonian Talmud, the so-called Stam (for further discussion of the Stam, see the orientation to the Talmud that follows this chapter), exhibit an unprecedented interest in defining and refining categories. The talmudic editors engage in a meta-critique of law, tradition, culture, identity, and of thought itself, as Talmud scholarship in the past twenty-five years has explored.[46] This scholarship shows the

---

[45] See Leib Moscovitz, *Talmudic Reasoning: From Casuistics to Conceptualization* (Tübingen: Mohr Siebeck, 2002).

[46] See, for example, David Charles Kraemer, *The Mind of the Talmud: An Intellectual History of the Bavli* (New York: Oxford University Press, 1990); Jeffrey L. Rubenstein, *Talmudic Stories: Narrative Art, Composition, and Culture* (Baltimore: Johns Hopkins University Press, 1999); Jeffrey L. Rubenstein, *The Culture of the Babylonian Talmud* (Baltimore: Johns Hopkins University Press, 2005); Daniel Boyarin, *Socrates and the Fat Rabbis* (Chicago: University of Chicago Press, 2009); Barry S. Wimpfheimer, *Narrating the Law: A Poetics of Talmudic Legal Stories* (Philadelphia: University of Pennsylvania

Babylonian Talmud editors to be manufacturers of a new discourse that probes, expands, alters, and frequently undermines inherited traditions. Emerging scholarship is revealing the grand scope of the Stam's literary artistry, legal innovation, and self-awareness.[47] My arguments build on this work by exploring the metacritical dimensions of the Babylonian Talmud's discourse of animals and animality. The Talmud's new perspectives on other species are part of this new literary project.

Second, the Babylonian Talmud sits at a cultural crossroads. One of various tolerated minorities within the Sasanian empire, Babylonian Jews lived in a diverse, culturally rich world.[48] Scholars today are reading the Babylonian Talmud alongside ambient Zoroastrian and Syriac Christian literatures to see how those literatures might illuminate it.[49] They are also assessing the ongoing influx of Hellenistic culture not only into Palestinian rabbinic circles – that "influence" has long been studied (and the notion of "influence" problematized) – but also into Babylonian

Press, 2011); Moulie Vidas, *Tradition and the Formation of the Talmud* (Princeton, NJ: Princeton University Press, 2014).

[47] Examples include Shana Strauch Schick, "Intention in the Babylonian Talmud: An Intellectual History" (PhD diss., Yeshiva University, 2011); Zvi Septimus, "The Poetic Superstructure of the Babylonian Talmud and the Reader It Fashions" (PhD diss., University of California, Berkeley, 2011); Lynn Kaye, "Law and Temporality in Bavli Mo'ed" (PhD diss., New York University, 2012); Sarit Kattan Gribetz, "Conceptions of Time and Rhythms of Daily Life in Rabbinic Literature, 200–600 CE" (PhD diss., Princeton University, 2013); Ayelet Libson, "Radical Subjectivity: Law and Self-Knowledge in the Babylonian Talmud" (PhD diss., New York University, 2014); Elana Stein, "Rabbinic Legal Loopholes: Formalism, Equity and Subjectivity" (PhD diss., Columbia University, 2014).

[48] On the experience of minorities within the Sasanian Empire, see Richard E. Payne, *A State of Mixture: Christians, Zoroastrians, and Iranian Political Culture in Late Antiquity* (Berkeley: University of California Press, 2015).

[49] On the Talmud's engagement with ambient Zoroastrian culture, see work by Yaakov Elman, Shaul Shaked, Geoffrey Herman, Shai Secunda, Yishai Kiel, Jason Mokhtarian, and Sara Ronis. New collections of such work include: Carol Bakhos and M. Rahim Shayegan, eds., *The Talmud in Its Iranian Context* (Tübingen: Mohr Siebeck, 2010); Geoffrey Herman, ed., *Jews, Christians, and Zoroastrians : Religious Dynamics in a Sasanian Context* (Piscataway, NJ: Gorgias Press, 2014); Shai Secunda and Uri Gabbay, eds., *Encounters by the Rivers of Babylon: Scholarly Conversations between Jews, Iranians, and Babylonians in Antiquity* (Tübingen: Mohr Siebeck, 2014). See also the exchange among Robert Brody, Shai Secunda, Richard Kalmin, and Simcha Gross in *Jewish Quarterly Review* 106/2 (2016): 209–55. On reading Syriac Christian literature in conjunction with Talmud, see Adam H. Becker, "The Comparative Study of 'scholasticism' in Late Antique Mesopotamia: Rabbis and East Syrians," *AJS Review* 34, no. 01 (2010): 91–113; Michal Bar-Asher Siegal, *Early Christian Monastic Literature and the Babylonian Talmud* (New York: Cambridge University Press, 2013).

ones.[50] This influx from the west would have included prior Jewish writings, such as the Septuagint, Philo and Josephus, and the Apocrypha and Pseudepigrapha, and it included the rabbinic traditions of Palestine found in the Tosefta, the Palestinian Talmud, and midrash collections.[51] What happened when all the various cultural traditions encountered by the Babylonian Rabbis – eastern, western, Zoroastrian, Christian, Second Temple period Jewish, Palestinian rabbinic – commingled with each other in their views of animals? Zoroastrianism's dualistic division of animals into beneficent or accursed would have met late antique philosophy's debates about animal minds.[52] Those traditions in turn would have mixed with the Hebrew Bible's menagerie, the Mishnah's laws of animal torts and sacrifices, and so on.[53] One can only imagine the cultural combustion. In producing their discourse on animals, the redactors of the Babylonian Talmud had an embarrassment of riches with which to work, and we should not be too surprised to see new lines of thinking there.

Third, the Babylonian Talmud is at a remove both chronologically and geographically from the Jerusalem Temple. The "substitution strategies"

---

[50] On Hellenism in the Babylonian Talmud, see Richard Lee Kalmin, *Jewish Babylonia between Persia and Roman Palestine* (New York: Oxford University Press, 2006); Richard Lee Kalmin, *Migrating Tales: The Talmud's Narratives and Their Historical Context* (Berkeley: University of California Press, 2014); Daniel Boyarin, "Hellenism in Jewish Babylonia," in *The Cambridge Companion to the Talmud and Rabbinic Literature*, eds. Charlotte Elisheva Fonrobert and Martin S. Jaffee, Cambridge Companions to Religion (New York: Cambridge University Press, 2007), 336–63.

On the problem of "influence," see Michael L. Satlow, "Beyond Influence: Toward a New Historiographic Paradigm," in *Jewish Literatures and Cultures: Context and Intertext*, ed. Anita Norich and Yaron Eliav (Providence, RI: Brown Judaic Studies, 2008), 37–54.

[51] On prerabbinic Jewish writings in the Talmud, see Jenny R. Labendz, "The Book of Ben Sira in Rabbinic Literature," *AJS Review* 30, no. 02 (2006): 347–92; Richard Kalmin, "Josephus and Rabbinic Literature," in *A Companion to Josephus*, ed. Zuleika Rodgers and Honora Howell Chapman (Malden, MA: Wiley Blackwell, 2016), 293–304. Theoretical models for rabbinic parallels can be found in Shaye J. D. Cohen, ed., *The Synoptic Problem in Rabbinic Literature* (Providence, RI: Brown Judaic Studies, 2000).

[52] On the classical Greek and Latin materials, see later in this chapter, and Chapter 2. On animals in Zoroastrianism, see Maria Macuch, "On the Treatment of Animals in Zoroastrian Law," *Iranica Selecta: Studies in Honour of Professor Wojciech Skalmowski on the Occasion of His Seventieth Birthday* Silk Road Studies VIII (2003): 167–90; Mahnaz Moazami, "Evil Animals in the Zoroastrian Religion," *History of Religions* 44, no. 4 (2005): 300–17; Richard Foltz, "Zoroastrian Attitudes toward Animals," *Society & Animals* 18, no. 4 (2010): 367–78; Mahnaz Moazami, "A Purging Presence: The Dog in Zoroastrian Tradition," *Anthropology of the Middle East* 11, no. 1 (Spring 2016): 20–9.

[53] A collection on the Hebrew Bible from a critical animal studies perspective is Jennifer L. Koosed, ed., *The Bible and Posthumanism* (Atlanta, GA: Society of Biblical Literature, 2014). On animals in the Mishnah, see references later in this chapter, and passim in this book.

devised by the Rabbis to fill the void left by the Temple's destruction are well-noted: repentance, good deeds, and prayer replaced purity practices and sacrificial offerings; the table replaced the altar; the seder replaced the Passover sacrifice.[54] More recently, scholars are considering the incompleteness of those strategies, with the temple and sacrifice retaining great symbolic power, and priests and purity retaining real social power.[55] Discourse about the Temple afforded the rabbis opportunity to argue for their authority, to order categories of privilege, to structure bodily experience, and to borrow from the Bible's prestige. The Babylonian Talmud

---

[54] See Baruch M. Bokser, "Rabbinic Responses to Catastrophe: From Continuity to Discontinuity," *Proceedings of the American Academy for Jewish Research* 50 (1983): 37–61; Baruch M. Bokser, *The Origins of the Seder: The Passover Rite and Early Rabbinic Judaism* (Berkeley: University of California Press, 1984); Steven Fine, "Did the Synagogue Replace the Temple?," *Bible Review* 12 (1996): 18–27; Dalia Marx, "The Missing Temple: The Status of the Temple in Jewish Culture Following Its Destruction," *European Judaism* 46, no. 2 (September 1, 2013): 61–78.

[55] On the symbolic power of the Temple and its cult post-70 C.E.: Michael D. Swartz, "Ritual about Myth about Ritual: Towards an Understanding of the Avodah in the Rabbinic Period," *The Journal of Jewish Thought and Philosophy* 6, no. 1 (1997): 135–55; Simon Goldhill, *The Temple of Jerusalem* (Cambridge, MA: Harvard University Press, 2005), 81ff.; Adiel Schremer, "Stammaitic Historiography," in *Creation and Composition: The Contribution of the Bavli Redactors (Stammaim) to the Aggada*, ed. Jeffrey L. Rubenstein (Tübingen: Mohr Siebeck, 2005), 219–36; Jonathan Klawans, *Purity, Sacrifice, and the Temple: Symbolism and Supersessionism in the Study of Ancient Judaism* (New York: Oxford University Press, 2006), 175–212; Steven D. Fraade, "The Temple as a Marker of Jewish Identity before and after 70 CE: The Role of the Holy Vessels in Rabbinic Memory and Imagination," in *Jewish Identities in Antiquity: Studies in Memory of Menahem Stern*, ed. Lee I. Levine and Daniel R. Schwartz (Tübingen: Mohr Siebeck, 2009), 237–65; Tamar Jacobowitz, "Leviticus Rabbah and the Spiritualization of the Laws of Impurity" (PhD, University of Pennsylvania, 2010); Naftali S. Cohn, *The Memory of the Temple and the Making of the Rabbis* (Philadelphia: University of Pennsylvania Press, 2013); Mira Balberg, *Blood for Thought: The Reinvention of Sacrifice in Early Rabbinic Literature* (Berkeley: University of California Press, 2017).

On priests and purity practices post-70 CE: Oded Irshai, "The Role of the Priesthood in the Jewish Community in Late Antiquity: A Christian Model?," in *Jüdische Gemeinden und ihr christlicher Kontext in kulturräumlich vergleichender Betrachtung: von der Spätantike bis zum 18. Jahrhundert*, ed. Christoph Cluse, Alfred Haverkamp, and Israel J. Yuval (Hannover: Hahnsche Buchhandlung, 2003), 75–85; Philip S. Alexander, "What Happened to the Priesthood after 70?," in *A Wandering Galilean: Essays in Honour of Seán Freyne*, ed. Zuleika Rodgers, Anne Fitzpatrick McKinley, and Margaret Daly-Denton (Boston: Brill, 2009), 5–34; David Amit and Yonatan Adler, "The Observance of Ritual Purity after 70 C.E.: A Reevaluation of the Evidence in Light of Recent Archaeological Discoveries," in *Follow the Wise: Studies in Jewish History and Culture in Honor of Lee I. Levine*, ed. Zeev Weiss (Winona Lake, IN: Eisenbrauns, 2010), 121–43; Mira Balberg, *Purity, Body, and Self in Early Rabbinic Literature* (Berkeley: University of California Press, 2014); Stuart S. Miller, *At the Intersection of Texts and Material Finds: Stepped Pools, Stone Vessels, and Ritual Purity Among the Jews of Roman Galilee* (Göttingen: Vandenhoeck & Ruprecht, 2015).

creatively reimagined the Temple – its spaces, rituals, functionaries, smells and sights, the theology that it represented, the catastrophe that befell it – and put it to new uses. What did this mean for the animals that had been at the heart of Temple ritual? The Babylonian Talmud would have faced pressing questions about the role of animals in Jewish life as it moved further and further away from the reality of animal blood and guts that constituted daily routine at the Temple. Finding new perspectives on animals was a desideratum for the composers of the Babylonian Talmud in their recreation of rabbinic religion for a new time and place.

These forces – a new literary discourse, a rich convergence of cultures, a greater remove from ancient Temple-centered Judaism – conspired to produce unprecedented possibilities within the Babylonian Talmud for conceptualizing animals and animality. The argument of this book is, in sum, that the Babylonian Talmud created a discourse about animals that imagines them as agents and subjects in new ways, as "persons" with the capacity to exercise intention and plan for the future, to experience pleasure and be held accountable for sin, to undergo suffering even if that suffering might most often be seen as a sacrifice necessary to satisfy human wishes, and to break free of the property category into which they are usually placed. Built into this new discourse of animal personhood is an engagement with and sometimes critique of the anthropocentrism that suppresses it, an anthropocentrism that results in ideas such as "dangerous" animals and "livestock," which hyper-animalizes the animal by representing "it" (using the grammar of objectification purposely here) as either a threat or a testament to human control. The following chapters propose that the Talmud is ripe for reading with a critical animal studies perspective, and that when we do we find waiting there a multilayered, surprisingly self-aware discourse about animals and the anthropocentrism that infuses human relationships with them. In making this case I connect to recent work on rabbinic anthropologies. I turn to those in the conclusion to consider how this book might contribute to contemporary conversations about selves and others in Jewish culture.

MICROREADING

The method that this book adopts is "microreading." It is modeled on microhistory, which developed in Italy in the 1970s as a response to master-narrative historiography.[56] Microhistory's aim was to reduce the

[56] See Sigurður G. Magnússon and István M. Szíjártó, *What Is Microhistory? Theory and Practice* (New York: Routledge, 2013); Hans Renders and Binne de Haan, eds.,

scale of observation and to pay attention to individuals, practices, and events that would normally have been considered historically unimportant. Rather than identify the major figures and events that changed the world, as master-narratives did, microhistories situated people within their worlds and tried to make sense of them there.

Reading Talmud might seem far removed from Italian history or any historiography whatsoever because the Talmud is notoriously resistant to historical reconstructions based on it.[57] Yet microhistory is surprisingly similar in spirit to the method by which the talmudic rabbis themselves approached their literary heritage, scrutinizing each sentence, phrase, word, and letter of biblical and prior rabbinic traditions. In that same spirit, I read talmudic texts here at the microlevel. At that level one is able to find animals such as Rav Pappa's clever ox (Chapter 2) and moments such as Rava proposing that an animal can enjoy sex (Chapter 3). Microreading allows the focus to shift away from the rabbis themselves and their study houses and study habits toward the animals who inhabit their farms, fields, and domiciles. By resizing the scope, microreading has the potential to modify the macro picture of rabbinic Judaism. That being said, its goal is not necessarily to do so, since it takes the small events and marginal figures to have their own significance, not only insofar as they fit into a master narrative.

Microreading also has in mind the notion of micro-aggression, another idea that goes back to the 1970s that has recently grown popular. "Micro-aggression" came from the mental health fields to extend the category of racism to more casual forms of discrimination and marginalization. A micro-aggression might involve the implicit underestimation of a person's ability (e.g., complimenting an African American for being "articulate"), neglecting to recognize their contributions and achievements (e.g., the repeated omission of African Americans from academy-award nominations), or retaining emblems of traumatic histories of violence and oppression (e.g., the Confederate flag, buildings named after slave owners). The term was soon applied to aggressions based also on gender, sexual orientation, religion, ethnicity, physical and

---

Theoretical Discussions of Biography: Approaches from History, Microhistory and Life Writing (Leiden: Brill, 2014), 105–65.

[57] On the problems of reconstructing history from rabbinic sources, see Seth Schwartz, "The Political Geography of Rabbinic Texts," in *The Cambridge Companion to the Talmud and Rabbinic Literature*, ed. Charlotte E. Fonrobert and Martin S. Jaffee, Cambridge Companions to Religion (New York: Cambridge University Press, 2007), 75–96.

mental health and ability, economic circumstance, educational level, immigration status, and so forth.[58] Micro-aggressions are frequently unconscious on the part of the aggressor, who consequently tends to disavow the harm they cause. Micro-aggressions presume certain identities and practices to be normative while subtly pathologizing other ones, often grouping pathologies across category lines so that a single individual will be marginalized along multiple lines at once. Anger, depression, shame, anxiety, and a feeling of isolation are common consequences of micro-aggressions, whose accumulated effect can be devastating, especially because of their invisibility to all but the individuals who experience them.

A microreading strategy with micro-aggression in mind is able to detect in the Talmud the thoroughgoing and normative anthropocentrism that a cruder reading strategy might skim over. The microreadings in this book seek to uncover the subtle, casual ways that the Talmud objectifies, underestimates, and neglects to consider other species, along with the Talmud's obliviousness to the devastating toll of such marginalization. Micro-aggression is often not all that "micro," and that is the case with talmudic animals too, such as in the talmudic passage that imagines tying up an elephant (Chapter 6) or that encourages the wanton killing of cats (Chapter 5). These texts can be read as micro-aggressions – or full-on aggression – not only on the part of the rabbis toward the animals they describe, however, but also on the part of those animals, whose will, desire, and experience in the world seem to speak back to the rabbis within their discussions.

THE ANIMAL IN JEWISH, RELIGIOUS, AND ANCIENT STUDIES

The animal has until only recently gone below the radar of subjects considered of serious scholarly interest in Jewish studies. In the past several years critical animal studies have crept into Jewish studies, not surprisingly clustered in the area of philosophy given the primacy of philosophy in critical animal studies.[59] The most sustained dialogue between

---

[58] See Derald Wing Sue, *Microaggressions in Everyday Life: Race, Gender, and Sexual Orientation* (Hoboken, NJ: John Wiley & Sons, 2010).

[59] On the animal in modern Jewish thought: Diane Perpich, *The Ethics of Emmanuel Levinas* (Palo Alto, CA: Stanford University Press, 2008), 150–76; Matthew Calarco, *Zoographies: The Question of the Animal from Heidegger to Derrida* (New York: Columbia University Press, 2008), 55–77; Andrew Benjamin, *Of Jews and Animals* (Edinburgh: Edinburgh University Press, 2010); Peter Atterton, "Levinas and Our Moral Responsibility toward Other Animals," *Inquiry* 54, no. 6 (2011): 633–49. What

critical animal studies and Jewish studies comes from the field of religious studies, however: Aaron Gross's *Question of the Animal and Religion,* which is framed by the scandal of human and animal rights abuses at the Agriprocessors kosher meat plant in Iowa.[60] The most well-known Jewish engagement with contemporary thinking on animals is Jonathan

constitutes "Jewish thought" is beyond the scope of this discussion, which means that the inclusion and omission of references here is easy to quibble with.

In medieval Jewish thought: Kalman P. Bland, "Construction of Animals in Medieval Jewish Philosophy," in *New Directions in Jewish Philosophy,* ed. Aaron W. Hughes and Elliot R. Wolfson (Bloomington, IN: Indiana University Press, 2010), 175–204; David I. Shyovitz, "Christians and Jews in the Twelfth-Century Werewolf Renaissance," *Journal of the History of Ideas* 75, no. 4 (2014): 521–43; David I. Shyovitz, "'How Can the Guilty Eat the Innocent?' Carnivorousness and Animal Eschatology in Medieval Jewish Thought," in manuscript.

See also Roberta Kalechofsky, "Hierarchy, Kinship, and Responsibility: The Jewish Relationship to The Animal World," in *A Communion of Subjects: Animals in Religion, Science, and Ethics,* ed. Paul Waldau and Kimberley Patton (New York: Columbia University Press, 2006), 91–9; Phillip Ackerman-Lieberman and Rakefet Zalashik, eds., *A Jew's Best Friend? The Image of the Dog Throughout Jewish History* (Portland, OR: Sussex Academic Press, 2013). See also the work of Marc Epstein on medieval Jewish art, which gives substantial attention to its animal depictions: Marc Michael Epstein, "The Elephant and the Law: The Medieval Jewish Minority Adapts a Christian Motif," *The Art Bulletin* 76, no. 3 (September 1, 1994): 465–78; Marc Michael Epstein, *Dreams of Subversion in Medieval Jewish Art and Literature* (University Park: Pennsylvania State University Press, 1997); Marc Michael Epstein, *The Medieval Haggadah: Art, Narrative, and Religious Imagination* (New Haven, CT: Yale University Press, 2011).

A work of Talmud scholarship that draws on critical animal studies is Mira Beth Wasserman, *Jews, Gentiles, and Other Animals: The Talmud After the Humanities* (Philadelphia: University of Pennsylvania Press, 2017).

The one comprehensive academic work on animals in rabbinic literature is Jacob Neusner, *Praxis and Parable: The Divergent Discourses of Rabbinic Judaism: How Halakhic and Aggadic Documents Treat the Bestiary Common to Them Both* (Lanham, MD: University Press of America, 2006). That work's primary interest is differentiating the legal (halakhic) materials from the narrative and homiletical (aggadic) ones, and animals serve as the sample case for that binary. An interesting treatment from nearly a century ago of animals in rabbinic literature is that of Victor Aptowitzer, "The Rewarding and Punishing of Animals and Inanimate Objects: On the Aggadic View of the World," *Hebrew Union College Annual* 3 (1926): 117–55.

General treatments of animals in Judaism not from a critical animal studies perspective (some predating it) include: Arieh Shoshan, *Ba'ale hayim be-sifrut Yisrael: ben Yehudi li-vehemto* (Rehovot, Israel: Shoshanim, 1971); Elijah Judah Schochet, *Animal Life in Jewish Tradition: Attitudes and Relationships* (Brooklyn, NY: Ktav, 1984); Shlomo Pesach Toperoff, *The Animal Kingdom in Jewish Thought* (Northvale, NJ: Jason Aronson, 1995); Ronald H. Isaacs, *Animals in Jewish Thought and Tradition* (Northvale, NJ: Jason Aronson, 2000); Natan Slifkin, *Man and Beast: Our Relationships with Animals in Jewish Law and Thought* (Brooklyn, NY: Zoo Torah; Yashar Books, 2006).

60   Gross, *The Question of the Animal and Religion.* The owner, Sholom Rubashkin, went to prison only on the basis of the financial malfeasance.

Safran Foer's *Eating Animals*, a memoir, meditation, and manifesto on the massive scope of daily violence against animals.[61]

The animal has for some time been a "person" of interest in religious studies. Peter Singer's denunciation of the Bible, Augustine, and Aquinas for their dominionist ideology has sparked prolific response from Bible scholars and Christian theologians.[62] Studies of animals in Islam, indigenous American religions, and eastern religions have all appeared.[63] Some works span many religions.[64] Theoretically inflected scholarship

---

[61] Jonathan Safran Foer, *Eating Animals* (New York: Little, Brown and Company, 2009).

[62] Works of Bible scholarship from a Christian perspective and Christian or Christian-oriented theology include Andrew Linzey, *Animal Gospel* (Louisville, KY: Westminster John Knox Press, 2000); Laura Hobgood-Oster, *Holy Dogs and Asses: Animals in the Christian Tradition* (Urbana: University of Illinois Press, 2008); Celia Deane-Drummond and David L. Clough, eds., *Creaturely Theology: On God, Humans and Other Animals* (London: SCM Press, 2009); David L. Clough, *On Animals: Volume I: Systematic Theology* (London: A&C Black, 2012); Nicola Hoggard Creegan, *Animal Suffering and the Problem of Evil* (New York: Oxford University Press, 2013). Collections of Christian animal theology include Charles Pinches and Jay B. McDaniel, eds., *Good News for Animals? Christian Approaches to Animal Well-Being* (Maryknoll, NY: Orbis Books, 1993); Andrew Linzey and Dorothy Yamamoto, eds., *Animals on the Agenda: Questions about Animals for Theology and Ethics* (Urbana: University of Illinois Press, 1998).

[63] On animals in Islam, see Richard Foltz, "This She-Camel of God Is a Sign to You": Dimensions of Animals in Islamic Tradition and Muslim Culture," in *A Communion of Subjects: Animals in Religion, Science, and Ethics*, ed. Paul Waldau and Kimberley Patton (New York: Columbia University Press, 2006), 146–59; Sarra Tlili, *Animals in the Qur'an* (New York: Cambridge University Press, 2012); Richard Foltz, *Animals in Islamic Traditions and Muslim Cultures* (London: Oneworld, 2014); Alan Mikhail, *The Animal in Ottoman Egypt* (New York: Oxford University Press, 2013); Al-Hafiz Basheer Ahmad Masri, *Animal Welfare in Islam* (Markfield, UK: The Islamic Foundation, 2016); Alan Mikhail, "Dogs in Ancient Islamic Culture," *OUPblog*, July 13, 2017, https://blog .oup.com/2017/07/dogs-ancient-islamic-culture/.
    On indigenous traditions, see Howard L. Harrod, *The Animals Came Dancing: Native American Sacred Ecology and Animal Kinship* (Tucson: University of Arizona Press, 2000); Emil Her Many Horses and George P. Horse Capture, eds., *A Song for the Horse Nation: Horses in Native American Cultures* (Golden, CO: Fulcrum, 2006); Shepard Krech, *Spirits of the Air: Birds & American Indians in the South* (Athens: University of Georgia Press, 2009); Michael M. Pomedli, *Living with Animals: Ojibwe Spirit Powers* (Toronto: University of Toronto Press, 2014). On animals in eastern traditions, see Paul Waldau, *The Specter of Speciesism: Buddhist and Christian Views of Animals* (New York: Oxford University Press, 2002); Arvind Kumar Singh, *Animals in Early Buddhism* (Delhi: Eastern Book Linkers, 2006); David Jones, *Buddha Nature and Animality* (Fremont, CA: Jain, 2007); Pu Chengzhong, *Ethical Treatment of Animals in Early Chinese Buddhism: Beliefs and Practices* (Newcastle upon Tyne: Cambridge Scholars Publishing, 2014); Neil Dalal and Chloe Taylor, eds., *Asian Perspectives on Animal Ethics: Rethinking the Nonhuman* (New York: Routledge, 2014).

[64] For discussions or anthologies that span religions, see Paul Waldau and Kimberley Patton, eds., *A Communion of Subjects: Animals in Religion, Science, and Ethics* (New York: Columbia University Press, 2006); Katherine Wills Perlo, *Kinship and*

in religious studies that addresses animals includes Wendy Doniger on Hindu animal myths, Donovan Schaefer on animal religion, Jonathan Crane's collection on animal agency, and Stephen Moore's on theology.[65]

Closer in place and time to the Talmud are works on the animal in Greek and Roman philosophy, Second Temple period Jewish literature, and early Christian writings.[66] Ingvild Gilhus's study of the animal in ancient Judaism, early Christianity, and late Roman imperial life combines all these

Killing: The Animal in World Religions (New York: Columbia University Press, 2009); Lisa Kemmerer, *Animals and World Religions* (New York: Oxford University Press, 2012); Celia Deane-Drummond, David L. Clough, and Rebecca Artinian-Kaiser, eds., *Animals as Religious Subjects: Transdisciplinary Perspectives* (London: Bloomsbury T&T Clark, 2013); Stephen D. Moore, ed., *Divinanimality: Animal Theory, Creaturely Theology* (New York: Fordham University Press, 2014); Barbara Allen, *Animals in Religion: Devotion, Symbol and Ritual* (London: Reaktion Books, 2016).

[65] Stella Snead, Wendy Doniger, and George Michell, *Animals in Four Worlds: Sculptures from India* (Chicago: University of Chicago Press, 1989); Wendy Doniger, *Implied Spider: Politics and Theology in Myth* (New York: Columbia University Press, 2010); Moore, *Divinanimality*; Jonathan K. Crane, ed., *Beastly Morality: Animals as Ethical Agents* (New York: Columbia University Press, 2015); Schaefer, *Religious Affects*.

[66] Sorabji, *Animal Minds*; Roger Kenneth French, *Ancient Natural History: Histories of Nature* (New York: Routledge, 1994); Stephen Thomas Newmyer, *Animals, Rights, and Reason in Plutarch and Modern Ethics* (New York: Routledge, 2006); Osborne, *Dumb Beasts and Dead Philosophers*; Stephen Thomas Newmyer, *Animals in Greek and Roman Thought: A Sourcebook* (New York: Routledge, 2011); Alastair Harden, *Animals in the Classical World: Ethical Perspectives from Greek and Roman Texts* (New York: Palgrave Macmillan, 2013).

See also the reference works: Gordon Lindsay Campbell, ed., *The Oxford Handbook of Animals in Classical Thought and Life* (New York: Oxford University Press, 2014); Kenneth F. Kitchell, Jr., *Animals in the Ancient World from A to Z* (New York: Routledge, 2014). For bibliography on animals in antiquity (stopping with 2006), see "Animals in Graeco-Roman Antiquity and Beyond," at www.telemachos.hu-berlin.de/esterni/ Tierbibliographie_Foegen.pdf. See also the well-organized but now dated bibliography at the end of Sorabji, *Animal Minds*, 220–32.

Still classic are George Jennison, *Animals for Show and Pleasure in Ancient Rome* (Manchester, UK: Manchester University Press, 1937) and J. M. C. Toynbee, *Animals in Roman Life and Art* (Barnsley, UK: Pen & Sword Books, 2012). Recent work on animals in the Roman games includes Peter Nicholson, *Pure History Specials. Beasts of the Roman Games* (London: Digital Rights Group, 2009); Donald G. Kyle, *Spectacles of Death in Ancient Rome* (New York: Routledge, 2012); Roger Dunkle, *Gladiators: Violence and Spectacle in Ancient Rome* (New York: Routledge, 2013); Jerry P. Toner, *The Day Commodus Killed a Rhino: Understanding the Roman Games* (Baltimore: Johns Hopkins University Press, 2014).

More specialized studies include Cristina Mazzoni, *She-Wolf: The Story of a Roman Icon* (New York: Cambridge University Press, 2010); Steven D. Smith, *Man and Animal in Severan Rome: The Literary Imagination of Claudius Aelianus* (New York: Cambridge University Press, 2014); Porphyry, *Porphyry: On Abstinence from Killing Animals*, trans. Gillian E. Clark (London: A&C Black, 2014).

strands.[67] There is a massive body of work on ancient animal sacrifice, and substantial ancient "zooarcheology," the study of animal remains from antiquity.[68] Some of these books, like Gilhus's, actively inform the work in the following chapters, while others form the scholarly context for it. Together with this book all of them show that the animal is gaining ground in Jewish studies, religious studies, and the study of the ancient world.

The following chapters draw upon animal studies from other areas too, such as philosophy, law, and literature, but before turning to a brief description of the chapters and then to the chapters themselves, I would like to mention another influence upon this book, and that is my personal investment in "the animal." I became a vegetarian at age twelve, after my sister became vegetarian; my parents soon followed. For me it began with the tiny hairs on the skin of the chicken that my sleepaway camp served at Sabbath evening dinner, causing in me a feeling of such

On ancient Jewish and Christian writings: Robert McQueen Grant, *Early Christians and Animals* (New York: Routledge, 1999); Katell Berthelot, "Philo and Kindness towards Animals (De Virtutibus 125–47)," *The Studia Philonica Annual*, no. 14 (2002): 48–65; Janet E. Spittler, *Animals in the Apocryphal Acts of the Apostles: The Wild Kingdom of Early Christian Literature* (Tübingen: Mohr Siebeck, 2008).

[67] Ingvild Sælid Gilhus, *Animals, Gods and Humans: Changing Attitudes to Animals in Greek, Roman and Early Christian Ideas* (New York: Routledge, 2006).

[68] Works on animal sacrifice include: Klawans, *Purity, Sacrifice, and the Temple*; M.-Z. Petropoulou, ed., *Animal Sacrifice in Ancient Greek Religion, Judaism, and Christianity, 100 BC–AD 200* (New York: Oxford University Press, 2008); Jennifer Wright Knust and Zsuzsanna Várhelyi, eds., *Ancient Mediterranean Sacrifice* (New York: Oxford University Press, 2011); F. S. Naiden and Christopher A. Faraone, eds., *Greek and Roman Animal Sacrifice: Ancient Victims, Modern Observers* (New York: Cambridge University Press, 2012); Anne M. Porter and Glenn M. Schwartz, eds., *Sacred Killing: The Archaeology of Sacrifice in the Ancient Near East* (Winona Lake, IN: Eisenbrauns, 2012); Daniel C. Ullucci, *The Christian Rejection of Animal Sacrifice* (New York: Oxford University Press, 2012); Nicole J. Ruane, *Sacrifice and Gender in Biblical Law* (New York: Cambridge University Press, 2013); Yvonne Sherwood, "Cutting up 'Life': Sacrifice as a Device for Clarifying – and Tormenting – Fundamental Distinctions Between Human, Animal and Divine," in *The Bible and Posthumanism*, ed. Jennifer L. Koosed (Atlanta, GA: Society of Biblical Literature, 2014), 247–97.

See the zooarcheological studies of Maaike Groot, *Animals in Ritual and Economy in a Roman Frontier Community: Excavations in Tiel-Passewaaij* (Amsterdam: Amsterdam University Press, 2008); Maaike Groot, *Livestock for Sale: Animal Husbandry in a Roman Frontier Zone* (Amsterdam: Amsterdam University Press, 2016).

There is extensive discussion of dog burials found in Ashkelon: Lawrence E. Stager, "Why Were Hundreds of Dogs Buried at Ashkelon?," *Biblical Archaeology Review* 17, no. 3 (1991): 26–42; Paula Wapnish and Brian Hesse, "Pampered Pooches or Plain Pariahs? The Ashkelon Dog Burials," *The Biblical Archaeologist* 56, no. 2 (1993): 55–80; Baruch Halpern, "The Canine Conundrum of Ashkelon: A Classical Connection," in *The Archaeology of Jordan and Beyond: Essays in Honor of James A. Sauer*, ed. Michael D. Coogan, Lawrence E. Stager, and Joseph A. Greene (Winona Lake, IN: Eisenbrauns, 2000), 133–44; Meir Edrey, "The Dog Burials at Achaemenid Ashkelon Revisited," *Tel Aviv* 35, no. 2 (2008): 267–82.

revulsion that I could not take another bite and have not since. In the intervening years I have augmented my story with nobler justifications for my vegetarianism – factory farming, environmental sustainability – but were those other explanations to vanish, I would still be left with that feeling described by philosopher Cora Diamond that animals are "fellow creatures" and not food.[69] Those tiny hairs would still bother me. That sense of animals as fellow-creatures was made more real for me when my then-boyfriend-now-husband and I got a dog right after I turned in my dissertation. That dog, Dulcie, has since died, and we recently welcomed a new dog into our home, and it is they whom I have in mind when I speak of dogs as having "animalities" along the lines of people's personalities. They are individuals as much as I am. I do not pretend to be an animal saint. Dulcie and our puppy Burt were pure-breds bought from breeders, I am a vegetarian and not a vegan, and now and then I get tired of the vegan shoe options and buy a pair of leather shoes. I agreed when my neighbors asked us to have the exterminator set rat traps in our backyard, and I will kill a mosquito if it looks like it is about to sting me. My relationship with other species is, in sum, as complex as anyone else's. I only mean to say that for this study of animals, I have "skin in the game" and it is not a neutral subject of research. With the mass-scale slaughter of animals and the accelerating shrinkage of animal habitats – with animal experimentation going on in the rooms upstairs from my college office – neutrality hardly seems possible or desirable.

THE CHAPTERS

This chapter's aim was to introduce the contours and contributions of critical animal studies, to argue for their relevance to the Babylonian Talmud, and to describe the current state of scholarship at the point where animal studies, Jewish studies, religious studies, and the study of antiquity converge. Following this introductory chapter is a brief orientation to the Talmud for those readers unfamiliar with that ancient Jewish literary corpus.

Chapter 2, "Animal Intelligence," takes up a passage in Bava Qamma 34b–35a that probes the scope of animal cognition. The passage begins with a mishnah that compares the liability of a person for his own actions

---

[69] Cora Diamond, "Eating Meat and Eating People," *Philosophy* 53, no. 206 (October 1978): 465–79.

to the liability of a person for his ox's actions. One case that the Mishnah mentions is setting fire to a stack of grain on the Sabbath. The talmudic commentary considers whether that case represents a purely destructive act – this does not constitute a violation of the Sabbath, according to the Mishnah – or whether the act may have some productive purpose, such as generating ashes to be used for medicinal purposes, in which case the act would constitute a Sabbath violation. The commentary goes on to claim, then to challenge, and finally to prove that an animal is capable of the step-by-step, intention-driven plan that setting a fire to produce ashes would require. In making these generous claims about animal cognition, the talmudic authors speak of a "clever ox" (*shor piqe'ah*), and they tell a story of a particular ox who was known to assuage the pain of his toothaches by lifting the lid of a beer vat and helping himself to a swig. The talmudic editors pose rhetorical questions that project onto the reader resistance to the notion of a clever animal with human-like needs and human-like abilities to fulfill them. The redactors also set clear limits on animal cognition when they deny to animals the capacity to intend to cause shame. This chapter contextualizes the talmudic passage within ancient and modern debates about animal intelligence.

Chapter 3, "Animal Morality," looks at the laws of bestiality in Sanhedrin 55a–b. Leviticus 20:15–16 dictates the death penalty for an animal and person who have sex with each other. The Mishnah calls for a full-scale criminal trial for the suspected couple – the person *and* the animal – and judicial execution for the couple if they are found guilty. The Mishnah's procedure would seem to imply that the animal has moral culpability akin to that of his or her human sexual partner. Yet the Mishnah elsewhere explicitly denies that an animal has the capacity to sin, claiming instead that the animal's punishment is "collateral damage" for the human partner's sin. The Talmud is left, then, with an ambiguity: Is the animal morally culpable or not? The Mishnah's procedure suggests yes, but its explicit statement suggests no. To address the ambiguity, the talmudic commentary poses a borderline case. What if the person in question is not Jewish? Does the animal still deserve to be executed? Chapter 3 argues that the question is itself ambiguous. The chapter discusses not only how various rabbis ruled on the question of the animal's culpability in this case but also how they understood the question to begin with. The chapter argues that the talmudic editors then reframed the earlier rabbinic rulings to produce an account of sin, pleasure, moral accountability, and God's judgment and mercy. This chapter considers the talmudic discussion in light of medieval and early modern animal trials in Europe and the scholarship that has struggled to make sense of the phenomenon.

Chapter 4, "Animal Suffering," revisits the classic discussion of animal suffering from Bava Metzia 22a–23a. In this chapter, I consider the complexity of human responses to animal suffering, drawing on Peter Singer's treatment of animal suffering from the perspective of his feminist critics. The basis for the talmudic discussion is a section of Bible and Mishnah describing a burdened donkey stopped on the side of the road. The biblical and Mishnaic passages seem almost completely uninterested in the suffering of the animal; their concern is the interpersonal dynamics between the animal owner and the passersby. That lack of interest does not stop the Babylonian rabbi Rava from issuing a grand statement, based on those very passages, that animal suffering is a concern of scriptural origin. The talmudic commentary goes on to show, over and over again, that the early rabbinic texts simply do not support Rava's claim. The early rabbinic traditions instead feature a series of cases in which animal suffering slides to the bottom of the list of priorities, even when at first glance the suffering of the animal appears to be the most pressing concern. The talmudic passage in my reading of it shows, contrary to conventional apologetics, that animal suffering is not a concern present in inherited canonical sources, and that the Talmud's aim is for its readers to recognize this. The Talmud invites readers to see that their own sensitivity to animal suffering is spotty, and that Rava's claim about it, though bold, is not all that convincing.

Chapter 5, "Animal Danger," takes up several legal motifs in the Mishnah – the goring ox, a list of "dangerous" animals, and restrictions on household animals – to show that a new discourse of animal nature is being produced there. Drawing on moral panic and risk theory, I read a narrative on Bava Qamma 80a–b in which three rabbis attend a celebration for a baby. They become so preoccupied with the question of which rabbi should enter the room first that no one notices when a cat attacks the baby. After the cat bites off the baby's hand, one of the rabbis issues a set of harsh legislations about cats. The danger to the baby seems to have come less from the cat, however, than from the rabbis who drew attention away from the baby and left him vulnerable. This chapter argues that the cat attack story intends to raise provocative questions about discourses of animal danger.

Chapter 6, "Animals as Livestock," reads a talmudic passage on Sukkah 22b-23a in light of contemporary conversations about animal personhood. Early rabbinic teachings describe the use of a live animal to constitute the floor or wall of a sukkah (fall festival booth) and to serve other purposes normally fulfilled by inanimate objects. When two later rabbis disagree over why an animal-walled sukkah should be prohibited, the talmudic commentary launches into an investigation of what makes an animal a bad "thing." Is it the animal's will? Their mortality? The animal's body? In an epilogue, the Talmud imagines immobilizing an animal such that he could never escape, and so that his dying body would not jeopardize the stability of the sukkah. It is a grim ending to the Talmud's reflections on animal objectification.

Chapter 7, the Conclusion, considers the contribution of this book to understanding the selves and Others that populate rabbinic literature. What impact might the animalities featured in this book have on contemporary views of the Talmud's anthropologies? The conclusion reviews recent scholarship on the rabbinic self and Other along with Jewish pet-related practices to reflect on the challenges that animals pose to Jewish self/Other binaries.

The chapters together show that talmudic texts are deeply engaged in the problems and possibilities of animality. Colleen Glenney Boggs writes that "animals are animals in American literature and ... we have not adequately accounted for them as such."[70] This book makes a comparable claim for the Babylonian Talmud. Boggs continues: "accounting for them as such will change how we read that literature."[71] So too will accounting for animals change how we read Talmud and, beyond that, the classic texts of western religion. For Boggs, accounting for animals means deconstructing the biopolitics of modernity; here it means returning to late antiquity and to the roots of contemporary religion, to find that it is a time neither of irredeemable speciesism nor of romanticized harmony between man and nature. Ancient texts like the Talmud allow us to take biopolitics back to its formative years, to reveal how animals came to occupy the margins of personhood and how their only partially suppressed subjectivities formed the backdrop for the emergence of the human self.

[70] Boggs, *Animalia Americana*, 29.
[71] Ibid.

ORIENTATION TO THE BABYLONIAN TALMUD

My ten-year-old daughter, who sat next to me in the movie theater as we watched "The Big Short," kept whispering to me in frustration, "I don't understand!"[1] She was referring to the collateralized debt obligations that contributed to the collapse of the global economy in 2008. I kept trying to explain to her – that's the point, *nobody* understood. Something similar can be said about the Babylonian Talmud. Even for those who spend a lifetime studying the Talmud, its discourse is difficult, and its logic can come across as convoluted. Academic scholars are still debating just what the Talmud *is*. Readers might keep that in mind as I give a brief orientation to the Talmud to those who are unfamiliar with the joys and challenges that this ancient literary corpus presents.[2]

---

[1] Adam McKay, *The Big Short*, 2015.
[2] See the following reference works on the Talmud: Shemuel Safrai, ed., *The Literature of the Sages, First Part: Oral Tora, Halakha, Mishna, Tosefta, Talmud, External Tractates*, vol. 3, Compendia Rerum Iudaicarum ad Novum Testamentum (Philadelphia: Fortress Press, 1987); Hermann L. Strack and Gunter Stemberger, *Introduction to the Talmud and Midrash*, trans. Markus Bockmuehl, Reprint edition (Minneapolis: Fortress Press, 1992); Steven T. Katz, ed., *The Cambridge History of Judaism: The Late Roman-Rabbinic Period*, vol. 4 (New York: Cambridge University Press, 2006); Charlotte Elisheva Fonrobert and Martin S. Jaffee, eds., *The Cambridge Companion to the Talmud and Rabbinic Literature*, Cambridge Companions to Religion (New York: Cambridge University Press, 2007); David Weiss Halivni, *The Formation of the Babylonian Talmud*, trans. Jeffrey L. Rubenstein (New York: Oxford University Press, 2013); Joshua Kulp and Jason Rogoff, *Reconstructing the Talmud: An Introduction to the Academic Study of Rabbinic Literature* (New York: Hadar Press, 2017). See also the helpful brief introduction to the Talmud found in Julia Watts Belser, *Power, Ethics, and Ecology in Jewish Late Antiquity: Rabbinic Responses to Drought and Disaster* (New York: Cambridge University Press, 2015), 24–33.

The Rabbis first emerged as an identifiable group sometime in the first two centuries of the millennium in Roman Palestine, possibly as an extension of the first-century Pharisees mentioned in the New Testament though the precise relationship and extent of continuity is murky.[3] The rabbis fashioned themselves as a religious elite, heir to the scriptures and oral traditions of ancient Israel, and arbiters of proper Jewish practice. The earliest generations of Rabbis were known as Tannaim, "repeaters," since teaching was done almost exclusively orally, through repetition. The literary work composed by the Tannaim that achieved the most prominence is "The Mishnah."[4] Later tradition attributed the editing of the Mishnah to Rabbi Judah the Patriarch, often known simply as "Rabbi." The final editing of the Mishnah was thought to have taken place around the year 200 CE, which consequently came to be considered a turning point in the history of the rabbinic movement.

The Mishnah is organized into six legal rubrics called "orders" (singular: *seder*; plural: *sedarim*). These orders are 1. agricultural law (*Zera'im*; literally, "Seeds"); 2. festival law (*Mo'ed*; literally, "Appointment"); 3. family law (*Nashim*, literally, "Women"); 4. torts and procedural law (*Neziqin*, literally "Damages"); 5. laws of sacrificial offerings (*Qodashim*, literally "Holy Things"); 6. purity law (*Teharot*, literally "Purities"). The topics reflect the world as it had been before the rabbis came along, or as the rabbis wished it to be, rather than as it was, since the rabbis of second and third-century Roman Palestine had neither a temple in Jerusalem in which to celebrate festivals and offer sacrifices nor the political clout to control marriage and divorce, adjudicate most disputes, or punish criminals. Each order is divided into numerous tractates (singular: *masekhet*;

Helpful websites include: "Rabbinics Resources Online," accessed March 9, 2016, www.rabbinics.org/; "The Talmud Blog," *The Talmud Blog*, accessed March 9, 2016, https://thetalmudblog.wordpress.com/; "Printing the Talmud Web Site," accessed March 9, 2016, http://jewishhistory.com/PRINTINGTHETALMUD/home.html; "TheGemara .com – A Historical and Contextual Approach," *TheGemara.com*, accessed July 11, 2017, http://thegemara.com/.

[3] The classic treatment of the question is Shaye J. D. Cohen, *The Significance of Yavneh and Other Essays in Jewish Hellenism* (Tübingen: Mohr Siebeck, 2010), 44–70. See the revisiting of Cohen's argument in Hayim Lapin, *Rabbis as Romans: The Rabbinic Movement in Palestine, 100–400 CE* (New York: Oxford University Press, 2012), 45–9. On how later talmudic narratives about rabbinic origins have skewed the historical picture, see Schremer, "Stammaitic Historiography."

[4] Other works attributed to the Tannaim, aside from the Tosefta discussed below, are collections of midrash halakhah (which loosely translates as "legal exegesis"), organized according to the books of the Pentateuch (excluding Genesis, since Genesis has little legal material to interpret).

plural: *masekhtot*), and each tractate into chapters (singular: *pereq*; plural: *peraqim*). An individual teaching is called *a* mishnah, not to be confused with *the* Mishnah, which refers to the corpus in its entirety. Other teachings of a mishnah-like character that were not included within the Mishnah proper were collected in a parallel work called the Tosefta, whose individual teachings are known as *baraitot*, the root of which means "outside" and refers to their exclusion from the Mishnah.

After the editing of the Mishnah, rabbis ceased to be known as Tannaim and began to be called Amoraim ("sayers" or "explainers"). The shift in title reflects a perception that a new era had begun, one dedicated less to the production of new rabbinic teachings than to the interpretation and harmonization of old ones such as those found in the Mishnah and Tosefta. At this point the rabbinic movement breaks into two, with one geographical center remaining in Palestine, and one developing in Sassanid-held Babylonia (current-day Iraq). Amoraim traveled back and forth between the two centers, which entered into a vigorous competition with each other. Aramaic crept into the language of rabbinic teachings, which became more variegated not only in language but also in genre, with narratives and homilies becoming popular rabbinic forms alongside legal exegesis and legislation. The fourth century CE seems to have been a watershed era for the Amoraim: Christianity became the dominant religion in the West; the Palestinian Amoraim faded out; the two most well-known Babylonian Amoraim, Abaye and Rava, were purportedly active in this period; and a mass of literary materials passed from west to east.

Two towering literary corpora began to form in the amoraic period: the Talmuds (the Hebrew means "study" or "curriculum"), one in Palestine (known as "The Yerushalmi"), and one in Babylonia (known as "The Bavli"), both structured as commentaries on the Mishnah. The Talmuds ask about the meaning of words or syntax in the Mishnah; they juxtapose the Mishnah with other early rabbinic (i.e., tannaitic) teachings (i.e., baraitot); they hypothesize legal scenarios similar to those in the Mishnah; they speculate on the principles that underlie the Mishnah's cases. The Babylonian Talmud is the more well-developed of the two Talmuds due to its voluminous anonymous editorial materials, which give the Babylonian Talmud its distinctive stamp. Nearly every passage of the Babylonian Talmud – a bounded literary unit within the Talmud is called a *sugya* – is defined by its anonymous voice, which is responsible for the back-and-forth dialectic for which the Talmud is famous.

Contemporary scholars have come to call the authors of this editorial material "the Stammaim," which means literally "the anonymous ones."

Their identity and chronology are much debated. The consensus is that they lived after the Amoraim, though some scholars maintain, echoing the traditional view, that the editing was continuous throughout the period of the Amoraim and did not take place in a subsequent burst. Were the Stammaim a coherent group, or should the editing be understood more strictly as a literary function, perhaps taken on by some of the Ge'onim, the rabbinic leaders and institution builders who lived in the heart of the Abassid Islamic empire? My discussion of talmudic texts will take an agnostic approach to these questions, though my general assumption follows the consensus that the editorial materials are largely later than the teachings of the Amoraim and reflect a more institutionalized phase of rabbinic culture.

Scholars also debate the nature of the literary activity of the Stammaim. Did the Stammaim preserve texts as they found them, or did they alter them, and if so, to what extent and with what motivation? Did they sometimes fabricate texts to look old when they really weren't? I will take a moderate position on the question of editorial intervention, supposing that the Stammaim did not entirely make up or even drastically alter traditions but that they did have a radical impact on how those traditions are read.

Thanks to the Talmud's full-bodied literary style and to the influence of the Ge'onim, who transmitted and codified the Talmud, it came to occupy a distinguished place in Jewish literature and life. Just how canonical was the Talmud in the early medieval period, certainly for the Jewish populace, but even for Jewish jurists, is still being hashed out, but if the burgeoning of exegetical works is any indication, the Talmud was making great gains in its influence. The commentary that became most central to the study of the Talmud was that of Rashi, the acronym for Rabbi Solomon ben Isaac (1040–1105, born in Troyes, France), who offered short, straightforward glosses that helped to make basic sense of the text. The Tosafists were Rashi's intellectual descendants (some Tosafists were Rashi's genealogical descendants as well) and often expanded on Rashi's comments, but their chief aim was to harmonize conflicting traditions within the Talmud. The Tosafists were among the Rishonim, "first ones," the rabbinic scholars of medieval Europe and North Africa who composed foundational talmudic commentaries and codes. I draw upon these interpretive traditions at various points in the book.

No manuscript of the Babylonian Talmud exists from the period of its composition. The earliest extant Talmud manuscript may be a fragment of tractate Hullin that possibly dates to around 750 C.E. Only one medieval manuscript of the entire Talmud exists; it is known as the Munich manuscript after its library location. No modern critical edition of the entire Talmud exists either. The textual variants, which come from manuscripts, early printings, geniza fragments, and citations in medieval commentaries, are still being collated and analyzed in order to produce not a definitive text – scholars doubt an urtext exists – but a comprehensive synopsis as well as a plausible reconstruction of the major textual branches. Digital media play a vital role in these efforts. Because of the absence of a definitive critical text, I cite the Talmud in this book according to the standard printed edition that harks back to nineteenth-century Vilna. I have relied upon the Saul Lieberman Institute for Talmudic Research for its transcription of major Talmud manuscripts and early printings; I cite textual variants from that database when they bear significance for interpretation.[5] When I cite only the tractate followed by the folio number and side (e.g., Sanhedrin 55a), it refers to the Babylonian Talmud. When I cite the Palestinian Talmud, I specify it as such and cite the Leiden manuscript. I cite the Mishnah from the Kaufmann manuscript, widely considered to be the most important, and in footnotes I cite Mishnah variants from the Parma and Cambridge manuscripts, as well as the standard printed edition, when they are significant. For the Kaufmann manuscript, I have relied upon the digitized photographs in the "Online Treasury of Talmudic Manuscripts" sponsored by the Jewish National and University Library in Jerusalem.[6]

---

[5] "The Saul Lieberman Institute | Home Page," accessed March 9, 2016, http://eng.lieber maninstitute.org/. For geniza fragments, manuscripts, and early printings of the Talmud, see "Hachi Garsinan: The Friedberg Project for Talmud Bavli Variants," accessed July 17, 2017, https://bavli.genizah.org/Global/homepage?lan=eng&isPartial=False&isDoubleLo gin=False&TractateID=0&DafID=0. Resources for the text of the Talmud can also be found in "The Society for the Interpretation of Talmud," accessed July 17, 2017, www .talmudha-igud.org.il/content.asp?lang=en&pageid=1.

[6] "Online Treasury of Talmudic Manuscripts," accessed March 9, 2016, http://jnul.huji .ac.il/dl/talmud/intro_eng.htm.

2

Animal Intelligence

Bava Qamma 34b–35a

ANIMALS AT THE EDGE

According to one early rabbinic law, a person who makes an oath about something ridiculous should be flogged:

What is a vain oath?
... He swore regarding a matter that is impossible to him.
He said, "If I have not seen a camel flying in the air," or "If I have
not seen a snake like the beam of an olive press."[1]

איזו היא שבועת שוא

...נשבע על[2] דבר שאי[3] אפשר לו

אמ' אם לא ראיתי גמל פוריח באויר ואם לא ראיתי נחש כקורת בית הבד

Given that there are almost infinite ways to imagine the impossible, it is interesting to see what the Mishnah conjures up: a flying camel and a gargantuan snake. Later rabbinic commentators wondered: Why not a flying mouse? Isn't that just as ridiculous? And, conversely, they challenged: Is a gargantuan snake really so impossible?[4] The two Talmuds ponder these

---

[1] Mishnah Shevuot 3:8 (Kaufmann manuscript). See parallel Mishnah Nedarim 3:2. The famous Mishnah Hagigah 1:8 declares that the legal practice of annulling vows, like this camel, "flies in the air." According to Mishnah Avot 5:9 (and parallel Sifra Qedoshim Parshata 2:7), attacks by wild animals (*hayah ra'ah*) are God's punishment for vain oaths.

[2] The word *al* ("regarding") is written into the margins by the scribe.

[3] *Aleph-yud* (the "im-" in "impossible") is inserted above the line by the scribe.

[4] Palestinian Talmud Nedarim 3:2 (37d), Shevuot 3:8 (34d); Babylonian Talmud Nedarim 25a, Shevuot 29a–b. Shevuot 29a also asks: What if the oath-taker in fact saw a large bird but described it as a camel (in which case the subject of the oath would no longer be ridiculous)?

questions, but I start with this mishnah to suggest that animals serve frequently in rabbinic literature to define the limits of reality. Animals sit at the edge of personhood, like a variety of human characters – women, children, slaves, foreigners.

A problem of knowability is distinctive to animals, however, and goes back in Jewish discourse to the goring ox in Exodus. Can the owner of an animal know his animal's character and predict his animal's behavior? If so, then he becomes accountable for damage his animal causes. Colin Dayan, in her *The Law Is a White Dog*, puts it this way with respect to common law torts:

> Harm is ... determined by the "nature" or "propensities" of an animal, whether luxury or useful, tame or wild. Crucial also to this judgment is what can be known by a human about an animal, or what can never be known or understood or foreseen.[5]

Animals press the boundaries of what we know, and that is why, I would speculate, the preceding rabbinic legal passage uses animals to imagine the unimaginable.

This chapter deals with what the Babylonian Talmud "knows" about animals. My interest is in knowledge on a number of levels: knowledge possessed by animals, knowledge possessed about animals, and knowledge possessed about knowledge. To put all this together, my question is: What did the talmudic composers think they knew about what animals know, and how did they think they knew it? It is a question about animal intelligence and human intelligence and the variety of ways in which the relationship between them is configured within the Talmud.

ANIMAL MINDS

In modern times, that question has been addressed empirically by cognitive ethologists, the scientists who study animal minds.[6] The field of ethology, the study of animal behavior, took off when the Nobel Prize was granted in 1973 to ethologists Niko Tinbergen, Konrad Lorenz, and Karl von Frisch. Donald Griffin's landmark *Question of Animal Awareness* launched the subfield of cognitive ethology a few years later.[7]

---

[5] Colin Dayan, *The Law Is a White Dog: How Legal Rituals Make and Unmake Persons* (Princeton, NJ: Princeton University Press, 2011), 207.

[6] For an overview of the history, goals, and methods of cognitive ethology, see Chapter 5, written by the editors, in Marc Bekoff and Dale Jamieson, eds., *Readings in Animal Cognition* (Cambridge, MA: MIT Press, 1996).

[7] Donald Redfield Griffin, *The Question of Animal Awareness: Evolutionary Continuity of Mental Experience* (New York: Rockefeller University Press, 1981). For reflections on the

Now scientists speak of the "cognitive revolution" of the 1960s and 1970s.[8] The most visible advocates of cognitive ethology have been Marc Bekoff and Frans de Waal, though the inspiration for the field comes straight from Darwin, who took great interest in animal minds and stressed continuities between human beings and other animals in their cognitive capacities.[9] Ethologists are distinctive among biologists in their concern with the whole animal in its habitat, rather than in genetics and

field two decades later, see Donald Redfield Griffin, *Animal Minds: Beyond Cognition to Consciousness* (Chicago: University of Chicago Press, 2013).

[8] See Bernard J. Baars, *The Cognitive Revolution in Psychology* (New York: Guilford Press, 1986); William O'Donohue, Kyle E. Ferguson, and Amy E. Naugle, "The Structure of the Cognitive Revolution: An Examination from the Philosophy of Science," *The Behavior Analyst* 26, no. 1 (2003): 85–110.

[9] See, for example, Bekoff, *The Emotional Lives of Animals*; Marc Bekoff, *Wild Justice: The Moral Lives of Animals* (Chicago: University of Chicago Press, 2009); Frans B. M. de Waal, *Chimpanzee Politics: Power and Sex among Apes* (Baltimore: Johns Hopkins University Press, 1998); de Waal, *The Ape and the Sushi Master.*

A selection of other work on animal minds and cognition includes Marian Stamp Dawkins, *Through Our Eyes Only? The Search for Animal Consciousness* (New York: Oxford University Press, 1998); Marc Bekoff, Colin Allen, and Gordon M. Burghardt, eds., *The Cognitive Animal: Empirical and Theoretical Perspectives on Animal Cognition* (Cambridge, MA: MIT Press, 2002); Frans B. M. de Waal and Peter L. Tyack, eds., *Animal Social Complexity: Intelligence, Culture, and Individualized Societies* (Cambridge, MA: Harvard University Press, 2003); Matthew Nudds and Susan Hurley, eds., *Rational Animals?* (New York: Oxford University Press, 2006); Irene Maxine Pepperberg, *The Alex Studies: Cognitive and Communicative Abilities of Grey Parrots* (Cambridge, MA: Harvard University Press, 1999); Dorothy L. Cheney and Robert M. Seyfarth, *Baboon Metaphysics: The Evolution of a Social Mind* (Chicago: University of Chicago Press, 2007); Jonathan Balcombe, *Second Nature: The Inner Lives of Animals* (New York: Macmillan, 2010); Julie Ann Smith and Robert W. Mitchell, eds., *Experiencing Animal Minds: An Anthology of Animal-Human Encounters* (New York: Columbia University Press, 2012). For a collection from a philosophical perspective, see Robert W. Lurz, ed., *The Philosophy of Animal Minds* (New York: Cambridge University Press, 2009). Combining science and philosophy is Colin Allen and Marc Bekoff, *Species of Mind: The Philosophy and Biology of Cognitive Ethology* (Cambridge, MA: MIT Press, 1997). On the critical side of ethology is Clive D. L. Wynne, *Do Animals Think?* (Princeton, NJ: Princeton University Press, 2004).

There is much popular coverage of animal minds. A sampling includes Virginia Morell, "Animal Minds – National Geographic Magazine," accessed July 10, 2017, http://ngm.nationalgeographic.com/2008/03/animal-minds/virginia-morell-text; Jeffrey Klu ger, "What Are Animals Thinking? (A Lot, as It Turns Out)," *Time*, accessed July 10, 2017, http://time.com/3173937/what-are-animals-thinking-hint-more-that-you-suspect/; "Inside the Animal Mind – BBC Two," *BBC*, accessed July 10, 2017, www.bbc.co.uk/programmes/b03thwhf; "NOVA | Inside Animal Minds," accessed July 10, 2017, www.pbs.org/wgbh/nova/nature/inside-animal-minds.html.

This is Darwin: "there is no fundamental difference between man and the higher mammals in their mental faculty." Charles Darwin and Sir Francis Darwin, *Charles Darwin's Works: The Descent of Man and Selection in Relation to Sex* (New York: D. Appleton, 1896), 66.

in laboratory experiments, and in their bottom-up rather than top-down approach, in which they ask open-ended questions about the capabilities of various species and avoid using human capabilities as the yardstick.[10] Cognitive ethologists have been derided by other biologists for being fanciful "mentalists" who attribute too much intelligence to other species. Ethologists respond that their behaviorist biology colleagues are too quick to deny capacities to other species.[11] Cognitive ethologists break their work down into four areas of interest: navigation, decision-making and planning, communication, and social knowledge.[12] The second area, decision-making and planning, is the type of animal cognition this chapter will discuss, and it is at the core of studying animal cognition since it deals with the animal's ability to remember the past, make choices in the present, and plan for the future.

The intellectual elites of antiquity cast the question of animal cognition in terms of animal reason (*logos*). Do other species possess reason and, if they do, is their reason comparable to that of human beings? The stakes of this debate were high, since a creature without reason could have no share in human justice. For rabbinic authors, it was the prosaic framework of torts liability, not the discourse of reason, that afforded the opportunity to reflect on animal intelligence. Knowledge about animals, for the rabbinic legal texts, continually circles back to the question of who pays for what when. Reading those texts creatively, however, reveals a rabbinic theory of animal intelligence.

In this chapter, I will first give a brief survey of perspectives on animal intelligence in the larger landscape of late antiquity, and I will then examine a series of rabbinic texts about an ox who sets fire to a stack of grain on the Sabbath. This "clever ox," as Rashi describes him, is the vehicle (recalling Balaam's donkey in the previous chapter) through which I will explore the Talmud's approach to animal cognition. The texts I will treat demonstrate not a turn away from the animal, as is sometimes thought to have transpired in late antiquity, a rejection of things corporeal or carnal,

---

[10] On the bottom-up approach, see introduction in Frans B. M. de Waal and Pier Francesco Ferrari, eds., *The Primate Mind: Built to Connect with Other Minds* (Cambridge, MA: Harvard University Press, 2012).

[11] For criticism along those lines, see Edward A. Wasserman and Thomas R. Zentall, eds., *Comparative Cognition: Experimental Explorations of Animal Intelligence* (New York: Oxford University Press, 2006). On these debates, see de Waal, *The Ape and the Sushi Master*.

[12] See introduction by Randolf Menzel and Julia Fischer, eds., *Animal Thinking: Contemporary Issues in Comparative Cognition* (Cambridge, MA: MIT Press, 2011), 3.

but rather an outpouring of interest in animals, their capacity to know, and the human capacity to know them. Certain questions at the center of today's debates – Are animals goal-seeking agents, possessing mental states that motivate and guide their behaviors? On what basis can inferences about animal mental states be made? – were the same ones posed within the ancient texts.

CLASSICAL PHILOSOPHY ON ANIMAL REASON: "ELEPHANTS EMPLOY SURGERY"

Across the span of his writings, Aristotle denies to animals reason (*logos*), reasoning (*logismos*), thought (*dianoia*), intellect (*nous*), and belief (*doxa*).[13] By withholding from animals all these attributes, Aristotle produced a logical conundrum. If animals have no reason, intellect, or belief, how do they do all the things that we see them do? Aristotle's answer was perception (*aesthesis*), says Richard Sorabji. Aristotle restricted the category of reason to the development of beliefs and beliefs about beliefs, which he considered unique to human beings, and he expanded the category of perception, which he attributed to all living beings.[14]

Stoic writers resisted Aristotle's contraction of the category of reason and reincorporated into it a good deal of perception, memory, intention, and emotion. Yet, following Aristotle, they still denied reason to animals. The consequence was that Stoics attributed to animals – whom they called *aloga*, creatures without reason, rather than the more inclusive *zōa* (living beings) or the conventional *thēria* (beasts) – very little capacity beyond the most superficial apprehension of appearances.[15] The Stoics, along with Epicureans and Peripatetics, became responsible for a view of animals that took them to be radically limited in cognitive ability.

The Pythagorean, Cynic, and Platonist traditions of late antiquity challenged this philosophical turn, pointing to animal speech, skills, virtues, and vices as indicators of animal reason.[16] The late ancient writers presented animal reason as a question to debate, for and against, with their own ancient texts lining up on one side or the other. A case in point is the first-century CE Jewish philosopher Philo, in his essay, "On Animals," which he stages as a debate between his nephew Alexander

---

[13] See Sorabji, *Animal Minds*, 12.
[14] Ibid., 67–71.
[15] Ibid., 20–9, 40–4, 71–2. On use of the term *aloga*, see ibid., 46.
[16] Ibid., 78–89.

and an interlocutor, Lysimachus, joined by Philo himself, on the question of whether animals possess reason.[17] Lysimachus and Philo adopt the Stoic/Epicurean dismissal of animal reason after entertaining Alexander's Pythagorean/Cynic sympathies. Writing a generation after Philo and using many of the same sources, Plutarch structures his essay "Whether Land or Sea Animals are Cleverer" as a competition between land and sea animals. It is really a unified argument for the cleverness of all animals, with colorful evidence like the elephant who employs surgery to remove javelins from his beloved master (970:14), and the snake who eats fennel to restore his fading sight (974:20).[18] Another Plutarch essay, "Beasts Are Rational," rewrites the tenth book of the Odyssey from the perspective of the nameless men whom Circe turns into pigs.[19] In Plutarch's imagining, Circe gives the men the chance to be turned back into humans. Plutarch's joke is that the men prefer to stay pigs. A character named Gryllus ("the grunter") enumerates all the ways that it is better to be an animal than a person. The third-century Neoplatonic philosopher Porphyry, in his essay "On Abstinence from Killing Animals," disposes of Stoic arguments that animals lack reason and advocates instead the Pythagorean position that animals possess reason and deserve justice.[20] Porphyry goes so far as to claim Aristotle, along with Pythagoras, Empedocles, Democritus, and Plato, for the pro-animal reason side, even though Aristotle was more typically and persuasively marshaled for arguments against animal reason. The implications for moral philosophy and practical ethics were never far behind in these discussions.[21] Animal sacrifice loomed particularly large as an enduring Greek and later Roman practice at stake in the debates. If animals have reason, how can one justify killing them and offering them to the gods?[22] The widespread belief in the

---

[17] The text was preserved only in Armenian; see Philo, *Philonis Alexandrini de Animalibus: The Armenian Text*, trans. Abraham Terian (Chico, CA: Scholars Press, c1981), and discussion in Gilhus, *Animals, Gods and Humans*, 42–4.

[18] Plutarch, *Plutarch's Moralia*, trans. William C. Helmbold and Harold Cherniss, vol. 12, Loeb Classical Library (Cambridge, MA: Harvard University Press, 2001), 309–486. For discussion of Plutarch on animals, see French, *Ancient Natural History*, 178–84.

[19] Plutarch, *Plutarch's Moralia*, 12:487–533. For discussion of both these essays, see Gilhus, *Animals, Gods and Humans*, 44–52.

[20] See Porphyry, *On Abstinence from Killing Animals*, trans. Gillian E. Clark (Ithaca, NY: Cornell University Press, 2000).

[21] The ancient touchstone on the subject is the much-cited Stoic Chrysippus, who is reported to have declared that no relation of justice can exist between man and irrational animals because of their essential unlikeness (*Stoicorum Veterum Fragmenta* 3.367:89 and 3.371:90).

[22] See Gilhus, *Animals, Gods and Humans*, 114–60. On the ancient conversations about animal sacrifice, see Knust and Várhelyi, *Ancient Mediterranean Sacrifice*; Petropoulou, *Animal Sacrifice in Ancient Greek Religion, Judaism, and Christianity, 100 BC–AD 200*.

transmigration of souls between human beings and other species posed the reverse problem. If animals do not have reason, how are they able to be reincarnated as humans, who do?[23]

These positions repeat over and over in an intertextual trail typical of ancient writings: Porphyry borrows heavily from Plutarch, who draws on the same Neoplatonic sources as Philo, which can be traced through a variety of other ancient writers. The same themes crop up in other genres of Roman writing – in the Digest of Justinian, when it declares animals devoid of reason – as well as in some early Christian texts.[24] In *Against Celsus*, Origen draws on conventional Stoic arguments to deny Celsus's accusation that Christian theology is narrowly anthropocentric.[25] At stake in Origen's polemics about animals is the elected status of Christians, Ingvild Gilhus proposes, since in Origen's logic, Christians are to pagans as human beings are to animals.[26] The Christian vis à vis the pagan, like the human vis à vis the animal, is uniquely qualified to discern truth and to exercise the proper behavioral restraints.[27] Augustine echoes the Stoic line of thinking denying reason to animals when in the *City of God* he limits the prohibition on murder in the sixth commandment to human victims, and he polemicizes against Manichaean vegetarian practices and ideas.[28]

Alongside these philosophical and theological speculations arose a genre of natural history that also addressed animal intelligence.[29] Natural histories by Pliny, Aelian, and Oppian reproduce the full spectrum of

[23] See Gilhus, *Animals, Gods and Humans*, 78–92.

[24] Digest 9.1.3: *Nec enim potest animal iniuria fecisse, quod sensu caret.* "An animal is incapable of committing a legal wrong because it is devoid of reasoning." Alan Watson, trans., *The Digest of Justinian*, vol. 1 (Philadelphia: University of Pennsylvania Press, 2009), 278.

[25] The relevant section is Book 4: 74–99; Origen, *Contre Celse*, trans. Marcel Borret, 5 vols. (Paris: Éditions du Cerf, 1967). For translation into English, see Origen, *Contra Celsum*, trans. Henry Chadwick (New York: Cambridge University Press, 1980).

[26] Gilhus, *Animals, Gods and Humans*, 57–61.

[27] But see Patricia Cox Miller, *The Poetry of Thought in Late Antiquity: Essays in Imagination and Religion* (Burlington, VT: Ashgate, 2001), 35–59. She argues that while corporeal beasts are mute and morally neutral for Origen, Scripture's beasts are pregnant with meaning, an "amazing play of the soul," "vessels for the presence of God" (p. 42).

[28] Augustine, *City of God* 1.20; *On the Morals of the Manicahaeans* 2.17.54–59. See Sorabji, *Animal Minds*, 195–8. Gillian Clark, "The Fathers and the Animals: The Rule of Reason?," in *Animals on the Agenda*, ed. Andrew Linzey and Dorothy Yamamoto (Urbana: University of Illinois Press, 1998), 67–79; Gilhus, *Animals, Gods and Humans*, 267–8. For further discussion of relevant Christian writings, see Sorabji, *Animal Minds*, 198–205.

[29] See French, *Ancient Natural History*, pp. 149 and on, for the Roman period.

positions from Stoic to Platonist, sometimes presuming an ontological divide between reasoning humans and nonreasoning animals, at other times formulating what Gilhus calls "a web of correspondences between them that criss-cross the natural world."[30] The natural historians frequently attribute a menu of high-level cognitive capacities – wisdom, intelligence, cooperation, and justice – to horses, elephants, dogs, bees, and other species, and tell stories about intimate human/animal interactions, always to support some broader view of the natural world and its relationship to the divine realm, with some moral for the Roman man.[31] That animal lore was domesticated by Christian writers and linked to the Old and New Testaments, such as in the widely circulated *Physiologus*, in order to illustrate the wonders of God's creation and the many lessons animals held for the Christian man.[32] The scope of animal cognition is unresolved within and across these works, which take a variety of approaches to the kinds of thinking animals can do.

ANIMAL REASON IN THE MISHNAH

The same can be said of the Mishnah. The Mishnah sometimes grants to animals powers of discernment, sophistication of behavior, and a wide range of emotions, yet at other times the Mishnah conceptualizes animals as a form of animate property and presumes a stark ontological divide between human being and animal.[33] Passages that attribute to animals complex cognition include Mishnah Bava Qamma 4:2, which imagines an ox who habitually gores others of his own species but not animals of other species, an ox who gores people but not animals, an ox who gores only young animals but not mature ones, and an ox who gores only on Sabbaths but not on weekdays.[34] The presumption is that the ox is able to

---

[30] Gilhus, *Animals, Gods and Humans*, 71. On animals in Aelian, see Smith, *Man and Animal in Severan Rome*.

[31] On moralizing in the natural history genre, as well as the construction of Roman identity and ideology, see French, *Ancient Natural History*, focusing on Pliny, especially pp. 196, 207–18, 230, 248; on Aelian and Oppian, pp. 260–76.

[32] On the *Physiologus*, see French, *Ancient Natural History*, 276–86; Miller, *The Poetry of Thought in Late Antiquity*, 61–73. For an anthologizing of patristic texts on animals, see David Sutherland Wallace-Hadrill, *The Greek Patristic View of Nature* (New York: Barnes & Noble, 1968), 31–9.

[33] For a parallel "schizophrenia" regarding animals that Francione identifies in the contemporary United States, see the articulation in Gary L. Francione, *Animals Property & The Law* (Philadelphia: Temple University Press, 1995). For further discussion of Francione, see Chapter 6.

[34] And see parallel Tosefta Bava Qamma 4:5.

differentiate in all these ways – by species, age, size, or calendar – and to show preferences based on those distinctions.³⁵ Mishnah Bava Qamma 4:6 speaks of an ox who intends to kill another animal but accidentally kills a person, who intends to kill a gentile but accidentally kills a Jew, or who intends to kill an insufficiently developed infant but accidentally kills a fully developed one. The presumption throughout is that an ox is capable of differentiating by species, developmental stage, and possibly even religion.³⁶ The given in all these scenarios is that an ox is capable of purposeful, targeted behaviors.³⁷ According to Mishnah Bava Qamma 5:6, if a deaf, mentally unsound, or immature ox falls into a pit, the owner of the pit is declared liable, presumably because such an ox could not be expected to watch his step.³⁸ The categories that appear in this mishnah – deaf, mentally unsound, and immature – are typically applied to people and never to animals, befuddling the commentators on this passage, for whom the concept of a deaf or mentally unsound ox must have seemed strange.³⁹ *Disability* implies ability and is generally understood within the Mishnah to be a distinctively human category.⁴⁰

³⁵ The relevant legal principle is that if the ox commits harm according to these known preferences, the owner is considered negligent and is fully liable, but if the ox commits harm outside of these preferences, the owner cannot be expected to have anticipated the damage and would have less liability.

³⁶ See parallel Tosefta Bava Qamma 4:6.

³⁷ This is explicit in the Tosefta parallel: "'When he gores' – [the owner is liable for damages only] until he intends to gore." The rabbinic tort category called *qeren*, the word for an ox's horn, covers torts cases in which intention to harm is present, so that the goring ox becomes the paradigmatic case of intentional harm.

On the recognition of animal intention in contemporary American torts law, see Christopher D. Seps, "Animal Law Evolution: Treating Pets as Persons in Tort and Custody Disputes," *University of Illinois Law Review* 4 (2010): 1356.

³⁸ For discussion of this mishnah, see Daniel R. Schwartz, "Rabbinic Law between Biblical Logic and Biblical Text: The Pitfalls of Exodus 21:33–4," *Harvard Theological Review* 107, no. 3 (July 2014): 314–39.

³⁹ The wording and logic of the text are ambiguous. Bava Qamma 54a–b offers a variety of interpretive possibilities. See also parallel Tosefta Bava Qamma 6:13.

⁴⁰ Disability studies have many convergences with animal studies. See Lennard J. Davis, ed., *The Disability Studies Reader* (New York: Routledge, 2013).

For disabilities studies of the Hebrew Bible, see Hector Avalos, Sarah J. Melcher, and Jeremy Schipper, eds., *This Abled Body: Rethinking Disabilities in Biblical Studies* (Atlanta GA: Society of Biblical Literature, 2007); Saul M. Olyan, *Disability in the Hebrew Bible: Interpreting Mental and Physical Differences* (New York: Cambridge University Press, 2008); Rebecca Raphael, *Biblical Corpora: Representations of Disability in Hebrew Biblical Literature* (New York: Bloomsbury T&T Clark, 2009); Candida R. Moss and Jeremy Schipper, eds., *Disability Studies and Biblical Literature* (New York: Palgrave Macmillan, 2011).

For New Testament, see Chad Hartsock, *Sight and Blindness in Luke-Acts: The Use of Physical Features in Characterization* (Leiden: Brill, 2008); Louise J. Lawrence, *Sense and Stigma in the Gospels: Depictions of Sensory-Disabled Characters* (New York: Oxford University Press, 2013).

Animal intelligence is implicitly raised in other rabbinic legal areas as
well. Tosefta Hullin 1:1 hypothesizes an ape who is capable of slaughtering another animal for sacrifice and Mishnah Yadayim 1:5 an ape
who pours water for handwashing.[41] Mishnah Sanhedrin 1:4 requires
the administration of a full criminal trial for an animal suspected of a
capital crime (the two "animal" capital crimes are murder of a human
being and sexual intercourse with one – see Chapter 3 for further discussion).[42] Criminal trials for animals seems to imply moral culpability,
though a later mishnah rules out that possibility: "If the person sinned,
did the animal [too] sin?" (see Chapter 3 on this passage).[43] Other mishnahs present a parallelism between human beings and animals. Mishnah
Shabbat Chapters 5 and 6 deal successively with the question of what an
animal, woman, and man may go out wearing on the Sabbath in light of
the prohibition on bearing burdens.[44] Mishnah Bekhorot Chapters 5 and
6 compare the blemishes that disqualify an animal from sacrifice with
the blemishes that disqualify a priest from performing Temple worship.
Some early rabbinic traditions speak of human-animal hybrid creatures,
such as the *adne-hasadeh*, an ape-man, and the fish-man, associated with
the dolphin.[45] These teachings presume similarity, continuity, or hybridity

---

For late antiquity more generally, see Robert Garland, *The Eye of the
Beholder: Deformity and Disability in the Graeco-Roman World* (London: Bloomsbury
Academic, 2010). For disability in rabbinic literature, see Julia Watts Belser, "Reading
Talmudic Bodies: Disability, Narrative, and the Gaze in Rabbinic Judaism," in *Disability
in Judaism, Christianity, and Islam: Sacred Texts, Historical Traditions, and Social
Analysis*, ed. Darla Schumm and Michael Stoltzfus (New York: Palgrave Macmillan,
2011), 5–27.
   In "Whether Land or Sea Animals Are Cleverer," Plutarch argues that the customary
application of mental disability language to animals (e.g., a "mad" dog) presumes that
"normal" animals possess mental ability (963, pp. 344–7).
   On changing perceptions of animals with disabilities and the growing sophistication of devices used to assist disabled animals, see Neil Genzlinger, "The Lives of
Animals, Disabled and Otherwise," *The New York Times*, April 8, 2014, www.nytimes
.com/2014/04/09/arts/television/the-lives-of-animals-disabled-and-otherwise.html.
[41] On the ape in the Mishnah, see Yehuda Feliks, *Ha-hai ba-Mishnah* (Jerusalem: Institute
   for Mishna Research, 1982), 146–7.
[42] See the intriguing parallel Tosefta Sanhedrin 3:1, which expands the trials to other species and also systematically compares trial procedures for animals and humans. For further discussion of animal trials and these rabbinic passages in particular, see Chapter 3.
[43] Mishnah Sanhedrin 7:4.
[44] Jeremiah 17:21–2 speaks of a restriction on carrying burdens on the Sabbath. Later
   Jewish interpreters like the rabbis interpret Jeremiah broadly as denouncing virtually all
   kinds of carrying across spatial domains. See Alex Jassen, "Tracing the Threads of Jewish
   Law: The Sabbath Carrying Prohibition from Jeremiah to the Rabbis," *Annali Di Storia
   Dell'esegesi* 28, no. 1 (January 2011): 253–78.
[45] *Adne ha-sadeh*: Mishnah Kilayim 8:5, Sifra Shemini 6; *dolphin*: Tosefta Bekhorot 1:11.

between people and animals. Yet elsewhere the Mishnah groups animals with other types of property, such as Mishnah Sukkah 2:3, which permits building a sukkah on top of a camel the way one might on top of a ship or on top of a tree (see Chapter 6), or Mishnah Bava Metzia 2:9, which discusses lost donkeys and cows along with lost clothing and food (see Chapter 4).

The vocabulary that the early Rabbis use for animals points to the same variety of conceptualizations that the legal substance does. The Rabbis use the same generic word for animal, *behemah*, that the Bible does, which literally means mute or dumb, but they further subdivide the term, distinguishing between domesticated (*behemah*, used in a stricter sense) and undomesticated animals (*hayah*), and within domesticated animals between small species and large species (*behemah daqah* vs. *behemah gasah*) and between cattle and birds (*behemah* vs. *of*). At times, the early Rabbis refer to animals as "possessors of life" (*ba'ale hayim*) or "that which has in it the breath of life" (*davar she-yesh bo ru'ah hayim*).[46] They mention many common domesticated species such as dogs, cats, goats, sheep, pigs, chickens, and pigeons, and they develop a standardized list of "dangerous" species that includes the lion, wolf, bear, tiger, leopard, and snake (see Chapter 5 on this list).

The Mishnah at one point reflects on the Bible's habit of mentioning certain animal species and not other ones:

It is the same for the ox and for any domesticated animal regarding: falling into the pit; and for separating from Mount Sinai; and for double compensation; and for returning a lost object; for unloading; for muzzling; for mixed species; and for the Sabbath.[47]

And thus [it is also for] undomesticated animals and fowl [and] the like.

---

[46] Sources that use the term *davar she yesh-bo ru'ah hayim* are Mishnah Eruvin 1:7, Gittin 2:3, Bava Qamma 1:1, 7:1, Menahot 9:9, Ohalot 6:1; 15:9; Tosefta Gittin 2:4, Zavim 5:4. *Ba'ale hayim* is used largely in the Babylonian Talmud and forms part of the expression that became the major rabbinic resource for animal rights – "animal suffering," *tza'ar ba'ale hayim* – a concept that appears only in the Babylonian Talmud. On the classic talmudic passage discussing this concept, see Chapter 4. For further discussion of the rabbinic vocabulary for animals, see Chapter 5.

[47] The biblical cases are: Exodus 21:33–4 (the pit; ox and donkey are specified); Exodus 19:12–13 (separation at Sinai; this case uses the broader language of *behemah*); Exodus 22:3 (double-payment for theft; ox, donkey, and sheep are specified); Deuteronomy 22:1 (returning a lost animal; ox, sheep, and goat are specified); unloading (Exodus 23:5; donkey is specified); muzzling (Deuteronomy 25:4; ox is specified); mixed species (Leviticus 19:19 on cross-breeding; *behemah* is used; Deuteronomy 22:10 on cross-yoking; ox and donkey are specified); Sabbath (Exodus 20:10, which uses *behemah*; Deuteronomy 5:14; ox and donkey are specified, and *behemah* added).

If so, why was it said "ox or donkey"?

Rather since the biblical verse spoke in the present.[48]

אחד השור ואחד כל הבהמה לנפילת הבור ולהפרשת הר סיני לתשלומי כפל ולהשיב אבדה לפריקה
לחסימה לכלאיים ולשבת

וכן חייה ועוף כיוצא בהן

אם כן למה נאמר שור או חמור[49]

אלא שדיבר הכתוב בהווה

This mishnah anthologizes animal-related rulings from the Torah – resting on the Sabbath, returning a lost animal, and so forth – and affirms their application not only to the ox and donkey, the species typically mentioned, but to all domesticated animal species. The Torah mentions the ox or donkey not to exclude the other species, proposes the Mishnah, but to address "the present," that is, the most common scenario.[50] Evoking the creative and self-conscious intertextuality of the Roman philosophers and natural historians who adapted Plato's and Aristotle's views of animals, the Rabbis anchor their discourse on animals in the language and law of the Torah while establishing hermeneutical principles that give them relatively free rein in that discourse's development.[51]

MISHNAH BAVA QAMMA 3:10: SLAVERY, SABBATH OBSERVANCE, AND OTHER THINGS UNIQUELY HUMAN

In at least one case, the Mishnah posits a stark ontological break between human beings and animals, echoing Stoic traditions of thought.[52] Mishnah

---

[48] Mishnah Bava Qamma 5:7. See parallel in Mekhilta de-Rabbi Yishma'el Mishpatim 10 s.v. *ve-khi yigah shor.* H. Saul Horovitz and Israel Abraham Rabin, eds., *Mechilta d'Rabbi Ismael* (Jerusalem: Wahrmann Books, 1970), 280.

[49] Donkey (*hamor*) is written in smaller letters in the Kaufmann manuscript.

[50] The Mishnah applies the exclusio method to one case of biblical animal legislation, that of four- or five-fold compensation, which is contrasted with the inclusive hermeneutic employed for the double-compensation case; see Mishnah Bava Qamma 7:1.

[51] This is the only place in the Mishnah and Tosefta that the expression "the biblical verse spoke in the present" appears; it appears several times in midrash halakhah. A similar principle is furnished for interpreting the words of earlier sages; see Mishnah Shabbat 6:6, 6:9, Eruvin 1:9, Nedarim 5:5, Eduyot 1:12; Tosefta Gittin 3:12, Kelim (Bava Metzia) 7:6, Niddah 6:18.

[52] Scholarship in the past fifty years has shown rabbinic literature's multiple lines of familiarity with Greek and Roman culture. See, for example, Lapin, *Rabbis as Romans*, which argues that rabbinic literature is effectively approached as Roman provincial literature.

Bava Qamma 3:10 presents cases where the owner of an ox should not be held responsible for the damages caused by his ox:

There are [cases where a person] is liable for the act of his ox but exempt for his own act; [and there are cases where a person] is liable for his own act but exempt for the act of his ox:[53]

His ox who shamed [a person], he (the ox's owner) is exempt [from paying compensation for shame], but he who shamed, he is liable.

His ox who blinded the eye of his slave or knocked out his tooth, he is exempt, but he who blinded the eye of his slave or knocked out his tooth, he is liable.

His ox who injured his father or his mother, he is liable, but he who injured his father or his mother, he is exempt.

His ox who set fire to a stack of grain on the Sabbath, he is liable, but he who set fire to a stack of grain on the Sabbath, he is exempt because he is judged with his life.[54]

יש חייב על מעשה שורו ופטור על מעשה עצמו חייב על מעשה עצמו ופטור על מעשה שורו

שורו שבייש פטור והוא שבייש חייב

שורו שסימא את עין עבדו והפיל את שנו פטור והוא שסימא את עין עבדו והפיל את שינו חייב

שורו שחבל באביו ובאמו חייב והוא שחבל באביו ובאמו פטור

שורו שהדליק את הגדיש בשבת חייב והוא שהדליק את הגדיש בשבת פטור מפני שהוא נידון בנפשו

For the first two cases, shaming a person and blinding or knocking out the tooth of one's slave, the Mishnah dissociates the owner from his ox. If one's ox inflicts these damages, one is free from liability.[55] The second two cases, injury of parents and setting a fire on the Sabbath, presume no such dissociation, and the owner is held liable for the acts of his ox. Nevertheless, the degree of liability is marked as different depending on

It tends to be difficult to show, however, that particular rabbinic teachings are familiar with particular Greek or Roman ones.

[53] This line is in reverse order in the printed edition.

[54] The last line in the printed edition is somewhat different: "he is held liable with his life" (*mit'hayev be-nafsho* rather than *nidon be-nafsho*).

[55] Mishnah Bava Qamma 8:1 suggests that the exemption regarding shame has to do with the person's lack of intention to cause harm: "If he fell from the roof, and he injured and he shamed [a person below], he is liable for the injury but exempt for the shame (*boshet*), as it is said, 'and she puts out her hand and seizes him by his genitals (*mevushav*)' (Deut. 25:11) – he is not liable until he intends [it]."

Mishnah Bava Qamma 8:3–5's material on slaves suggests that the exemption regarding the slave is based on a rabbinic approach to Exodus 21:26–7 (which requires a master who blinds or knocks out the tooth of his slave to free him) that sees it as an exception rather than as a broad paradigm. Mishnah Bava Qamma 3:10 exempts the ox owner likely because the Mishnah considers the liberation of a slave to be an irregular and unusually severe penalty that should not be extended beyond the owner himself to the same damages when caused by his ox.

whether one's ox or one's own self is the agent of the injury. If the person himself commits either of these two acts, he is criminally liable; if his ox commits them, he has only civil liability. The principle underlying these two legislations appears to be that a person cannot receive capital punishment for an act his animal commits even if that act is normally a capital crime.[56] One is still, on some level, identified with one's animal, since one is held liable for the animal's act under civil law, but one is not identified to the extent that one can be executed for the animal's act. For the first two cases, by contrast, the owner does not seem to be identified with the animal at all; there is no liability of any sort.

This mishnah can be read as setting forth basic principles of difference between human beings and animals.[57] This mishnah anthologizes disparate cases, despite creating some ambiguity regarding liability structures – as well as repetition with other mishnahs, something that disturbed Talmud commentators – in order to reveal parallels among the cases and to draw out from them a paradigm of human difference.[58] Within these four legal areas – shame, slave ownership, honor of parents, and observance of the Sabbath – the human being is said to hold a greater degree of liability for himself than for his ox even though in most other cases the liability is understood to be roughly equivalent.[59] This mishnah seems to say that

[56] The last two cases may have a logic similar to that of the slave (see note 55): striking a parent and lighting a fire on the Sabbath are explicit prohibitions in the Torah whose uniquely severe penalties for these acts should not be extended to the case when one's animal commits them.

[57] This mishnah is difficult. It appears initially to claim that there are cases when one is more liable for an act if one's ox does it and cases when one is less liable if one's ox does it, but in fact one is more liable in all four cases if one does the act oneself. The second two cases do not in fact reverse the liability structure, as the Mishnah implies but, rather, up the ante from civil to criminal liability. "Exempt" shifts in meaning from the first case, where it refers to a full exemption from all penalties, to the last two cases, where it refers to an exemption from monetary penalties only, but asserts liability for criminal ones. In the second case, the word "exempt" has yet another referent, which is liberation of the slave. "Liable" may shift meanings too, since commentators understand the liability for the ox who lights the stack of grain to be a case of half rather than full liability.

[58] Mishnah Bava Qamma 8:2 repeats the same legislation about shame and expands the exemption to all other categories of personal injury compensation besides direct damages. See Tosafot on Bava Qamma 34b s.v. *shoro she-biyesh patur*.

[59] Tosefta Bava Qamma 3:4 adumbrates the cases when liability is the same for owner and animal:

There are [cases where a person] is liable for the damages [caused] by himself and for the damages by his ox or his donkey, and [there are cases where a person] is exempt for the damages by himself and for the damages by his ox.

In what manner is he liable for the damages by himself and for the damages by his ox and his donkey?

human beings are not like animals in their capacity to experience and inflict shame, to own members of the same species, and to sacralize and profane family and time. The implication of this mishnah is that it cannot be considered equivalent when an animal engages in these acts, even when that animal is one's own. Through its liability discourse, this mishnah articulates a conception of the uniquely human. That conception is rooted

He damaged on private property, he is liable; his ox and his donkey, they are liable.

He damaged intentionally, he is liable; his ox and his donkey, they are liable.

He set fire to the stack of grain of his friend on the Day of Atonement, he is liable; his ox and his donkey, they are liable.

In what manner is he exempt from paying for the damages by himself and for the damages by his ox and his donkey?

He damaged on public property while he is walking, he is exempt; his ox and his donkey, they are exempt.

He killed unintentionally, he is exempt; his ox and his donkey, they are exempt.

He injured the sanctified [animal], the convert, or the liberated slave, he is exempt; his ox and his donkey, they are exempt.

And he is exempt for the damages by his male slave and his female slave.

יש חייב על נזקי עצמו ועל נזקי שורו וחמורו ופטור על נזקי עצמו ועל נזקי שורו

כיצד חייב על נזקי עצמו ועל נזקי שורו וחמורו

הזיק ברשות היחיד חייב שורו וחמורו חייבים

הזיק במתכוין חייב שורו וחמורו חייבים

הדליק גדישו של חבירו ביום הכפורים חייב שורו וחמורו חייבין

כיצד פטור מלשלם על נזקי עצמו ועל נזקי שורו וחמורו

הזיק ברה"ר בדרך הלוכו פטור שורו וחמורו פטורין

המית בלא מתכוין פטור שורו וחמורו פטורין

חבל בהקדש בגר ועבד משוחרר פטור שורו וחמורו פטורין

ופטור על נזקי עבדו ואמתו

Both the Mishnah and Tosefta presume that for most tort cases, an animal's acts are considered equivalent to those of the owner himself. The mishnah upon which I am here focusing moves from that assumption of equivalency to pinpoint cases when this is not so.

In the area of personal injury compensation, the Mishnah requires the same basic compensation (the category called *nezeq*) whether it is oneself or one's ox who inflicted the injury, but the Mishnah levies extra payments (worker's compensation, pain and suffering, and so forth) when it is oneself, and adds liability for causing miscarriage; see Mishnah Bava Qamma 8:2 (and previous note). Contrast this approach to the one the Mishnah takes for injury caused by children, slaves, and wives, for which the father, master, or husband is exempt (Bava Qamma 8:4). A general analysis of "vicarious liability" in modern law can be found in Paula Giliker, *Vicarious Liability in Tort: A Comparative Perspective* (New York: Cambridge University Press, 2010). For discussion of liability in modern law for harm caused by animals, see Peter North, *Civil Liability for Animals* (New York: Oxford University Press, 2012).

in biblical themes like observance of the Sabbath and honor of parents but also in contemporaneous Roman ones like shame.[60] Many Mishnah passages presume a fairly high level of animal intelligence; this passage sets the animal's limits.

PALESTINIAN TALMUD BAVA QAMMA 3:10: THE NEEDY OX

This mishnah provides a forum for later rabbis to explore and extend the boundaries of animal intelligence. The Palestinian Talmud, which comprises commentary on the Mishnah from the generations of Rabbis (i.e., Amoraim) who lived two centuries after it, proposes an ox capable of human-like, multistep strategic action. Echoing the natural histories of Pliny and Aelian and the philosophical reflections of Plutarch and Porphyry, the Palestinian Talmud imagines a purposive ox.

The background for the Palestinian Talmud's discussion is Mishnah Shabbat 13:3, which legislates that only labor that is productive is prohibited on the Sabbath. If labor is destructive (*meqalqel*), it does not fall into the category of prohibited Sabbath labor. The Palestinian Talmud features a dispute regarding two destructive acts: injuring a person and setting something on fire. Are these two acts exceptions to the general principle that prohibited Sabbath labor be productive such that these acts, despite being destructive, still incur liability? Or are they included in that principle such that one is liable for them, just as for all other labors, only if there is some productive component? That is the crux of the dispute.

A rabbi-named Ben Pedaya takes the first position that injuring a person and igniting an object do in fact constitute prohibited Sabbath labor even though they are destructive acts:

Ben Pedaya said: All those who destroy are exempt, except for the one who sets fire and the one who makes a wound.[61]

בן פדייא אמ' כל המקלקלין פטורין חוץ מן המבעיר והעושה חבורה

---

[60] On the introduction of shame into rabbinic laws of personal injury, see Jonathan A. Pomeranz, "The Rabbinic and Roman Laws of Personal Injury," *AJS Review* 39, no. 2 (2015): 303–31.

[61] Palestinian Talmud Bava Qamma 3:10 (3d); Leiden manuscript. In parallels in Palestinian Talmud Pesahim 6:1 (33b) and Shabbat 2:5 (5a), the teaching appears as a baraita, and the position here attributed to Ben Pedaya is attributed there to Bar Kappara.

Disagreeing with him, the early Palestinian amora Rabbi Yohanan narrows the application of Ben Pedaya's position:

Rabbi Yohanan said: With respect to the one who sets fire, he is not liable until he needs to for the ash, and for the one who makes a wound, he is not liable until he needs to for the blood.

אמ' ר' יוחנן במבעיר אינו חייב עד שיהא צריך לאפר והעושה חבורה אין חייב עד שיהא צריך לדם

In Rabbi Yohanan's revision of Ben Pedaya, liability for Sabbath violation is incurred only when one ignites for the purpose of using the ashes or injures for the purpose of using the injured's blood. Rabbi Yohanan is arguing, in effect, that even these two acts must have some productive component associated with them for a person to become liable for them as Sabbath violations. Igniting and injuring are not exceptions to the general exemption for destructive labors. These acts fully comport with the principle that prohibited Sabbath labor be productive.

The dispute bears no discernible relationship to animal torts, and one would have good reason to wonder why the Palestinian Talmud speaks of it in connection with Mishnah Bava Qamma 3:10. A seasoned reader might anticipate that the point of overlap will be the ox or person who sets fire to a stack of grain on the Sabbath, the last of the four cases in Mishnah Bava Qamma 3:10 ("His ox who set fire to a stack of grain on the Sabbath, he is liable, but he who set fire to a stack of grain on the Sabbath, he is exempt because he is judged with his life"). In a brief back-and-forth, the Palestinian Talmud uses that case from Mishnah Bava Qamma 3:10 to address the dispute about injuring and setting fire on the Sabbath:

But we teach "his ox"!

והתנינן שורו

A number of assumptions are built into this clipped challenge to Rabbi Yohanan's position about injuring and setting fire on the Sabbath.[62] The first is that the ox who sets fire to a stack of grain on the Sabbath mentioned by Mishnah Bava Qamma 3:10 cannot possibly be doing so because he needs some by-product of the fire. Oxen, it is assumed, are incapable of such strategic action. Second, the person who sets fire to a stack of grain on the Sabbath, also mentioned by Mishnah Bava Qamma 3:10, must be acting in a fashion parallel to the ox, since the Mishnah

---

[62] The challenge is more fully spelled out in the parallel on Shabbat 2:5 (5a).

groups the two. If that is the case, then the person, like the ox, cannot be setting fire to a stack of grain on the Sabbath for some productive purpose such as generating ashes. All this being the case, the person of this mishnah would appear to incur capital punishment ("he is judged with his life") for setting a fire on the Sabbath *for which he has no need –* in other words, for a purely destructive act. This runs against Rabbi Yohanan's position that setting a fire on the Sabbath, like any other act, must have a productive dimension associated with it for it to constitute prohibited Sabbath labor. Mishnah Bava Qamma 3:10 seems to imply, on the contrary, that the act of lighting a fire is indeed the exception that Ben Pedaya claims it to be. It is a purely destructive act that violates the Sabbath, even though in almost all other cases purely destructive acts are not considered Sabbath violations.

The final flourish of the Palestinian Talmud passage either puts Rabbi Yohanan's position out of commission or, if read declaratively rather than interrogatively, rescues Rabbi Yohanan from being overturned by the Mishnah:[63]

"His ox" – he needs the ash.

שורו צריך את האפר

Read interrogatively or rhetorically ("he needs the ash?!?"), the Palestinian Talmud reiterates its skepticism that an ox can act with purpose. Surely an ox does not have the mental wherewithal to set something aflame with the express purpose of producing ashes. If so, neither must the person be acting with such an aim in mind. All the same, the Mishnah holds that person fully liable for Sabbath violation. Ben Pedaya's exception stands. Read declaratively, however, the ox's capacity to light a fire with productive purpose is affirmed rather than denied.[64] In this reading, the ox who sets a fire on the Sabbath featured in Mishnah Bava Qamma 3:10, just like the person who sets a fire on the Sabbath in Ben Pedaya's legislation, does so because "he needs the ash." Setting a fire on the Sabbath, like any other Sabbath labor, must have some constructive dimension to it if it is to be prohibited. The person – and in this case the ox as well – must be

---

[63] I thank Marc Hirshman for alerting me to the interrogative reading and to Yisrael Levi's commentary on Yerushalmi Bava Qamma, which is the source of it. See Israel Lewy, *Introduction and Commentary to the Talmud Yerushalmi: Bava Qamma Chapters 1–6* (Jerusalem: Kedem, 1969).

[64] The declarative reading is the one offered in the Pnei Moshe commentary by Moshe Margoliot, though I have not imported the Babylonian Talmud's language as he does.

engaging in the activity in order to create something he can use. Rabbi Yohanan's position is the one that stands.

The talmudic challenge starts with a presumption – a "we all know" gesture – that an ox is incapable of a strategic, multiphase plan of action based on his perception of his needs ("But we teach "his ox"!"), the example being lighting a fire in order to produce ashes that might be used for healing or other purposes. The ox would have to sense that he has some need for ash and understand that lighting a fire would produce it. The talmudic editor, if read declaratively, simply reverses course to reject these limitations on animal cognition ("He needs the ash"). One could attribute the editor's approach to his interest in supporting Rabbi Yohanan's legal stance on Sabbath labor, but the editor could conceivably have found other means of doing so. Moreover, he clearly considered this solution, which claims expansive animal cognition, to be persuasive to his audience.

BABYLONIAN TALMUD BAVA QAMMA
34B–35A: THE CLEVER OX

The passage in the Babylonian Talmud builds on these core materials in the Palestinian Talmud to explore broader themes of animal intelligence and intentionality. The Babylonian Talmud also produces a new representational scheme that exists neither in the relevant mishnah, which features a stark divide between human being and animal, nor in the Palestinian Talmud passage, which offers an intriguing parallelism between human beings and animals regarding their respective needs and abilities to pursue them. The Babylonian Talmud introduces the figure of the suffering animal (for more on animal suffering, see Chapter 4).

The Babylonian Talmud's discussion begins with the same dispute about destructive lighting on the Sabbath, though in the Babylonian Talmud the dialogue is cast between Rabbi Yohanan and Rabbi Abahu:

Rabbi Abahu teaches before Rabbi Yohanan: All those who perform a destructive act are exempt except for the one who injures and the one who sets a fire.

He said to him: Go out and teach it outside![65] The one who injures and the one who sets fire is not a mishnah.

[65] Besides a parallel passage in Shabbat 106a, this expression appears also in several other passages (Betzah 12b; Yevamot 77b; Sanhedrin 62a). According to Rashi's commentary on the expression in Betzah, the speaker is claiming that the teaching at hand "was never taught in the study house" or, in other words, is a corrupt, fraudulent, or otherwise incorrect tradition.

And if you want to say it is a mishnah – one who injures refers to one who needs to for his dog; one who sets a fire refers to one who needs to for its ash.

תני רבי אבהו קמיה דרבי יוחנן כל המקלקלין פטורין חוץ מחובל ומבעיר

א"ל פוק תני לברא חובל ומבעיר אינה משנה

ואם תימצי לומר משנה חובל בצריך לכלבו מבעיר בצריך לאפרו[66]

Rabbi Yohanan takes the same position here that he is represented as taking in the Palestinian Talmud, but here in the Babylonian Talmud he is shown offering two rationales for considering igniting and injuring under the rubric of normal Sabbath labors: (1) the teaching that holds igniting and injuring to be exceptions is inauthentic; (2) that teaching should be understood as referring to igniting and injuring only when they include some constructive component. That second rationale matches up with Rabbi Yohanan in the Palestinian Talmud, though the injurer here is one who "needs to for his dog" rather than "needs the blood," as in the Palestinian Talmud.[67] The one who sets fire stays the same from one Talmud to the other, as a person who "needs its ash," and it is that case that will become the inspiration for the passage's reflections on animal resourcefulness.

The Babylonian Talmud passage continues along the same lines as the one in the Palestinian Talmud. The mishnah comparing human and animal liabilities is brought to bear on the dispute between Rabbi Abahu and Rabbi Yohanan. This mishnah is at first said to challenge Rabbi Yohanan, since it would appear to be describing a purely destructive act that nevertheless incurs full liability for Sabbath labor. Then the passage reverses the initial assumption about animal behavior to claim instead that the ox – and person – described by the mishnah are acting constructively or strategically, setting a fire with the conscious intention of producing ashes:

We teach [in a mishnah]: His ox who sets fire to a stack of grain on the Sabbath, he is liable; but he who sets fire to a stack of grain on the Sabbath, he is exempt.

And he teaches – "he" is comparable to "his ox": just as his ox does not need it, so too he does not need it, and it teaches "exempt because he is judged with his life."

No! "His ox" is comparable to him: just as he does need it, so his ox needs it.

---

[66] The manuscripts and early printing for this passage found in the Lieberman transcriptions feature very little variation from the standard printing.

[67] The medieval Talmud commentator Meiri explains: "he needs the blood that flows out of the wound for his dog or for some other purpose" (*Bet ha-Behirah* s.v. *le-inyan issur*).

תנן שורו שהדליק את הגדיש בשבת חייב והוא שהדליק את הגדיש בשבת פטור

וקתני הוא דומיא דשורו מה שורו דלא קבעי ליה אף הוא נמי דלא קבעי ליה וקתני פטור מפני שהוא נדון בנפשו

לא שורו דומיא דידיה מה הוא דקבעי ליה אף שורו דקבעי ליה

The passage creates an analogy between the ox and the person ("'he' is comparable to his ox,'" *hu dumya de-shoro*). What is known about the person must come from what is known about the ox. Since one knows that an ox cannot act strategically, presumes the dialectic, setting a fire with the express purpose of producing ashes (in the passage's language, "his ox does not need it" (*lo qa-va'e leh*), neither must the person be acting strategically ("so too he does not need it").

As in the Palestinian Talmud, the passage proceeds to simply reverse the claim, arguing instead that it is perfectly plausible for the animal to light a fire with the intention of producing the ashes ("so his ox needs it," *qa-va'e leh*). The Babylonian Talmud differs from the Palestinian Talmud, however, by highlighting the conceptual processes of which an animal is capable – yes, an animal can plan out behaviors in order to address his or her needs – as well as the conceptual processes by which "we" rabbinic scholars, the Talmud's human authors and audiences, define such capacities. The Babylonian Talmud's initial proposal instructs readers to extrapolate from animal behavior to human behavior, but the rebuttal asks readers to move in the reverse direction, to extrapolate from the human being to the animal: "No! 'His ox' is comparable to him" (*la! shoro dumya dideh*). Readers are invited into an imaginative exercise in anthropomorphism.[68] If readers move in epistemological terms from people to animals instead of the other way around, a different set of assumptions emerges about what is or is not possible for an animal to accomplish.[69]

The passage goes on to probe the new and expansive claim about animal capacity:

"His ox" – How do you find it?
Rav Ivya said to him: What are we dealing with here? With a clever ox who has received a bite on his back, and he needs to burn it in order to roll himself in the ash.

---

[68] For a parallel in contemporary thinking, see the distinction between animal-centric and anthropocentric anthropomorphism in de Waal, *The Ape and the Sushi Master*. For further discussion, see Chapter 1.

[69] One could argue, on the other hand, that behavior with a productive purpose has less emotional complexity than purely destructive behavior, which Maimonides and his commentators interpret as an attempt to assuage one's anger (Hilkhot Shabbat 12:1).

And how do we know?

Since after he burned it, he rolls in the ash.

And is there such a case?

Yes, for there was an ox in Rav Pappa's household whose teeth[70] were hurting him; he went and burst open the cask and drank the beer and was healed.

שורו היכי משכחת לה

א"ל רב אויא הכא במאי עסקינן בשור פקח שעלתה לו נשיכה בגבו וקא בעי למקלייה ואיגנדר בקוטמא

ומנא ידעינן

דלבתר דקלייה קמגנדר בקוטמא

ומי איכא כי האי גוונא

אין דההוא תורא דהוה בי רב פפא דהוה כיבין ליה חינכיה עייל ופתקיה[71] לנזייתא ושתי שיכרא ואיתסי

Apparently expecting some resistance, the talmudic editorial voice asks for a concrete example of animal behavior of this sophisticated type. Rav Ivya, a relatively obscure fourth-generation Babylonian rabbi, provides it: the animal has been bitten on his back and seeks ashes as a remedy for the bite.[72] Rav Ivya describes this ox as a *shor piqe'ah*, which the Babylonian Talmud commentator Rashi interprets to mean a particularly clever ox, a *shor hakham*.[73] Now that this example has been furnished, the editorial voice questions once again the evidence for high-level animal behavior, asking how it is possible to prove that the animal was acting with relatively elaborate intentions when he lit the fire ("And how do we know?"). The sequence of events, replies the editorial voice, is sufficient evidence to assign a causal link between them ("Since after he burned it,

---

[70] According to Rashi, *hinkheh* refers to his teeth. According to Rabbenu Hananel, the word refers to his gums. That second understanding is followed by the medieval Talmud dictionary, the Arukh, s.v. *h-n-kh*.

[71] The Munich manuscript has *pasqeh* instead of *patqeh*, which can have the same meaning of "divide" or "split open."

[72] Gittin 69a uses similar language to describe rolling various substances in ash and inserting it into the nostril in order to stop a nosebleed.

There are linguistic breaks in Rav Ivya's statement from Aramaic to Hebrew and back, suggesting that the original statement consisted only of "with a clever ox who has received a bite on his back."

[73] *Piqe'ah* is often used as an antonym to *heresh* (deaf), *shoteh* (mentally unsound), and *qatan* (a minor) and refers not to high intelligence but to "normal" adult (human) intelligence. Here I believe Rashi is correct that the adjective refers to extraordinary intelligence, which it does in some talmudic texts; see entry 3, s.v. *piqe'ah*, in Marcus Jastrow, "Dictionary of the Targumim, the Talmud Babli and Yerushalmi, and the Midrashic Literature," 1208, accessed July 13, 2017, www.tyndalearchive.com/TABS/Jastrow/. Mishnah Teharot 3:8 uses the adjective for dogs when it claims that "it is not his habit to leave food and go after water." There the Mishnah is describing dog intelligence as superior to that of other animals, who do not guard their food as effectively.

he rolls in the ash"). If the animal is seen first to light a fire and then to roll in the ashes, it can be safely presumed that he did the first *in order* to do the second. Additional evidence for purposive animal behavior is supplied in the form of a particular ox once owned by Rav Pappa. Rav Pappa's ox, it is told, was driven to drink by a toothache. He broke open the lid of a vat of a beer and helped himself so that he could get relief for his pain.[74]

The ox owned by Rav Pappa may be intended to reflect the greatness of Rav Pappa himself. Who but a well-known rabbi would own an animal aware that a swig of beer would make him feel better? Moroever, Rav Pappa is described within the Talmud as a profitable brewer, making his ox's affinity for beer particularly apt, and his ox's access to it easy.[75] The passage does not explicitly deny the same perspicacity to the normal run of oxen, but neither does it leave the impression that these capacities are typical.

The concluding section of the passage clearly defines the limits of animal consciousness. An ox, it is argued, cannot intend to cause shame:

Our rabbis said before Rav Pappa: Can one say that his ox is comparable to him? Behold he teaches: His ox who embarrasses [a person], he (the ox's owner) is exempt [from paying compensation for shame], but he who embarrasses, he is liable. His ox is comparable to him! He (the ox) intended to embarrass – how do you find it?!

For example, he intended to injure, as the master said [in a baraita]: He intended to injure even if he did not intend to embarrass.

אמרו רבנן קמיה דרב פפא מי מצית אמרת שורו דומיא דידיה והא קתני שורו שבייש
פטור והוא שבייש חייב שורו דומיא דידיה נתכוון לבייש היכי משכחת לה
כגון שנתכוון להזיק דאמר מר נתכוון להזיק אע"פ שלא נתכוון לבייש

Rav Pappa's students push back on the passage's claims about purposive animal behavior as well as the epistemological pathway by which those claims are derived. Surely the imaginative exercise in anthropomorphism

---

[74] On the role of narrative within the Babylonian Talmud's legal discussion, see Wimpfheimer, *Narrating the Law*. Rav Pappa's ox also recalls the tradition in Greek and Roman natural histories of "remarkable animal" anecdotes; see French, *Ancient Natural History*, 206–7. An article in the *New York Times* suggests that the story of Rav Pappa's ox seeking out alcohol to soothe pain may have scientific plausibility; see Benedict Carey, "Male Fruit Flies, Spurned by Females, Turn to Alcohol," *The New York Times*, March 15, 2012, www.nytimes.com/2012/03/16/health/male-fruit-flies-spurned-by-females-turn-to-alcohol.html.

[75] For statements about Rav Pappa's career as a brewer, see Berakhot 44b, Pesahim 113a, and Bava Metzia 65a.

has its limits, they point out ("Can one say that his ox is comparable to
him?"). That limit is shame. The students refer to another part of this
mishnah, that which differentiates the shame payment for the ox from
the shame payment for his owner. In another "we-all-know" gesture, the
passage asserts that an ox cannot intend to cause shame ("He intended to
embarrass – how do you find it?!").[76] If so, the interpretive strategy that has
so far been adopted for this mishnah, whereby the behavior of animals is
derived from that of humans, is upset, since a person's desire to humiliate
another cannot possibly be replicated in the ox, so goes the logic. Whereas
earlier the passage simply backtracked from its initial "we-all-know" about
animals and permitted some far-reaching claims about animal capacities,
here the passage adheres to the limitations on animals that it initially presumes. The passage goes on to reconsider its assumptions not about animal
intelligence but about the legal import of the Mishnah. The shame spoken
of here, claims the editorial voice basing itself on an early rabbinic teaching,
is shame caused by the intention strictly to injure, not the intention also to
shame ("He intended to injure even if he did not intend to embarrass").
As such, intention to shame is off the table and a more minimal parallel
between human and animal – both of whom can intend to injure, it is presumed – is left to stand. This passage defines the scope of animal thinking and feeling with the outer limits marked by shame, perhaps because
shame is understood to be so fundamentally shaped by consciousness of the
Other (unlike the self-soothing of the animal anecdotes) and because it is
the trait understood to be quintessentially human going back to the account
of human origins in Genesis. It is also a quintessentially rabbinic trait, the
fuel of rabbinic hierarchy and discourse, and the flip side of rabbinic honor.
Withholding shame from animals keeps them not only outside the circle of
humanity but also outside the doors of the rabbinic academy.

The Babylonian editors take the Palestinian Talmud's lead and link
the mishnah's materials about animal liability with an amoraic Sabbath
labor dispute, but they have injected into the discussion a new interest
in epistemology as they weave the amoraic materials into a new and distinctive composition.[77] How do we know what we know about animals?

---

[76] As the commentator Rashba puts it: "Behold 'he intended to shame' is not relevant to his
ox" (s.v., *kegon she-nitkaven*).

[77] While they appear to be responding to Rabbi Yohanan's position on setting fire on the
Sabbath, the rabbinic (amoraic) voices featured here, Rav Ivya, the students of Rav Pappa,
and later Rava, are more likely responding directly to Mishnah Bava Qamma 3:10. The
Amoraim appear to be bothered by the inexactitude of the Mishnah's parallel between
the person and the ox. When the Mishnah speaks of the ox who lights a stack of grain,

The editors' persistent skepticism – "How do you find it?" "How do we know?" – is typical of talmudic discourse, but distinctive to this passage is that the subject itself is knowledge. How do *we* know what *animals* know? The Amoraim and Stammaim of this Babylonian Talmud passage also contribute to the discussion a new portrait of the animal in pain. In the case of the ox with a bite on his back or an ache in his teeth, cognitive potential is actualized by suffering. While the mishnah at hand highlights difference and limitation, the Babylonian Talmud leans toward identification and empathy, not least in its nearly comic characterization of the animal who appreciates alcoholic beverages. At the same time, the Talmud may be assuming that it is only something like pain, as a physiological sensation, that could spur an animal to greater cognitive complexity. So even while the passage fosters admiration for the clever ox, it may also be invoking some of the same binary thinking that structures this mishnah. Moreover, the talmudic passage explicitly puts some experiences – the intention to shame – beyond the animal's ken.

CONCLUSIONS: ANIMAL LESSONS

As I write this chapter about what the Talmud knew about animals, I ignore what my computer's grammarcheck "knows" about animals in its efforts to change "who" to "that" and "he" to "it" when I use them in reference to animals. Somehow the spellcheck "knows" that animals should be grouped with objects rather than with living beings.[78] Like the talmudic passages that start with what we all know animals cannot

for example, it probably has in mind something similar to the dog it describes in Mishnah Bava Qamma 2:3, who drags a charcoal-baked cake to a stack of grain and accidentally lights it. The person lighting the fire, on the other hand, is flagrantly violating the Sabbath – and that is the point: a person can violate the Sabbath, but an animal cannot.

The later Rabbis assume that the Mishnah's contrast between people and animals is built on some implicit similarity within each case, however. If the person causes shame or knocks out the tooth of his slave, and so forth, the animal's act must be comparable. Rav Ivya addresses the problem with respect to igniting a fire and comes up with the "clever ox" as a solution. Rav Pappa's students address the problem with respect to shame, and as a solution the passage draws upon an alternative understanding of shame payments that links them to intention to injure rather than intention to shame. Rava, whom I have not discussed and whose position is cited later in the passage, addresses the problem in a different way, arguing that the person described by this mishnah is not in fact acting with full conscious intention.

[78] See the exchange from late June 2012 on H-animal, the animal studies list-serv, about grammar-checking and copy editing that refuse to use "human" grammar for animals: http://h-net.msu.edu/cgi-bin/logbrowse.pl?trx=lx&list=H-Animal&user=&pw=&month=1206. On similar grammar problems in the area of gender, see Julie Abbou and

do, think, or feel, our grammar reflects and instills our sense of animal/ human difference.

Like others in antiquity, Rabbis called attention to this difference in order to bring into relief what makes man man, and, more specifically, a rabbi a rabbi. Rabbinic knowledge of the animal's knowledge became a way for rabbis to know rabbis, Jews, and other humans. According to that knowledge, nonrabbis, non-Jews, and nonmen frequently recede to the margins of the human, just as barbarians do in relation to Rome, and pagans, Jews, and sectarians do in relation to the Church. But the discussion of the clever ox harnesses notions of human/animal difference not only to reinforce certain kinds of difference – between humans and other species, and among humans – but also to upend other kinds. The clever ox of this talmudic passage is not alone. Scattered throughout the Talmuds are companions who rival him with their ingenuity and purpose: the snake of the House of Akhbore who topped off a wine cask with water so that the wine inside would spill out (Avodah Zarah 30a); the donkey of Rabbi Pinhas ben Yair who was too pious to eat untithed food (Hullin 7b); the "prophetess" rat who hoards bread knowing that Passover is about to arrive (Pesahim 9b); the "wicked" mice who call over their friends when they happen upon a stash of produce (Palestinian Talmud 3:7 [9b]).[79] Knowledge about animals, like knowledge about various human others, combined that which was taken for granted with imaginative challenges to it. Thus did the project of knowing animals – especially trying to know what they knew – populate the margins of late ancient reality with its fantastic others, creatures unusual or impossible, like the flying camels and massive snakes of the Mishnah, along with somewhat more imaginable yet still extraordinary animals like the Babylonian Talmud's clever ox.

Fabienne H. Baider, eds., *Gender, Language and the Periphery: Grammatical and Social Gender from the Margins* (Philadelphia: John Benjamins Publishing Company, 2016).

[79] On that snake, see Wasserman, *Jews, Gentiles, and Other Animals*, 139–45. On that donkey, see also Shabbat 112b, and discussion in Ofra Meir, "The She-Ass of R. Pinhas ben Yair," *Folklore Research Center Studies* 7 (1983): 117–37; Louis Jacobs, "The Story of R. Phinehas Ben Yair and His Donkey in B. Hullin 7a-B," in *A Tribute to Geza Vermes: Essays on Jewish and Christian Literature and History*, ed. Philip R. Davies and Richard T. White (New York: Bloomsbury, 1990), 193–205; Leib Moscovitz, "'The Holy One Blessed Be He... Does Not Permit the Righteous to Stumble': Reflections on the Development of a Remarkable BT Theologoumenon," in *Creation and Composition: The Contribution of the Bavli Redactors (Stammaim) to the Aggada*, ed. Jeffrey L. Rubenstein (Tübingen: Mohr Siebeck, 2005), 125–80; Tal Ilan, *Massekhet Hullin: Text, Translation, and Commentary* (Tübingen: Mohr Siebeck, 2017), 126–8; Kulp and Rogoff, *Reconstructing the Talmud*, 289–336. Thanks to Moulie Vidas for references to the last two texts.

3

Animal Morality

Sanhedrin 55a–b

TRYING ANIMALS

"What happens when we include other species in our understanding of subjectivity?"[1] That is the question that Colleen Glenney Boggs sees at the core of critical animal studies. For the "identity theorists" I described in Chapter 1, inclusion of animals in subjectivity means having them join the ranks of liberal subjects, along with women, African Americans, LGBTQs, and other historically marginalized groups. But for the "difference theorists" and the branch of animal studies rooted in continental philosophy, the liberal subject is not expanded, but exploded. Animal studies deconstructs subjectivity rather than redefining it.[2]

In this chapter I will argue that a talmudic passage on Sanhedrin 55a–b that asks whether an animal who has sex with a non-Jew should be tried and executed – does both. In the earlier literary strata, the passage expands subjectivity to include the animal, but the passage also, in the course of the talmudic editors' argumentation, destabilizes the schemas of subjectivity. The passage does so by introducing "a fundamental plurality to the very notion of subjectivity," bringing "us to the limits of our own self-certainty and certainty about the world."[3] The passage not only decenters the human, but it also destabilizes the coherence of the subjective self.

---

[1] Boggs, *Animalia Americana*, 3.
[2] For a fuller description of critical animal studies with reference to the identity theorists and difference theorists, see the Introduction.
[3] Boggs, *Animalia Americana*, 17, 7.

While rabbinic animal trials have received minimal attention, scholarly or otherwise, and this particular passage about gentile-animal sex even less, animal trials in medieval and early modern Europe have attracted legal historians, social scientists, dramaturgs (I was in the audience for a staging of "The Tragical-Comical Trial of Madame P and Other 4-Legged and Winged Creatures"), and filmmakers (Colin Firth stars as the lawyer Barthélemy de Chassanée who defends a pig accused of homicide in "The Advocate").[4] By trying and sentencing animals, courts appear to be treating them as though they possessed the same moral culpability as people. Scholars ask: Were these courts, quite literally, insane?[5]

[4] The play was staged at John Jay College, 2010. The film with Colin Firth was released in the United Kingdom in 1993 as "The Hour of the Pig" and released in the United States by Miramax under the other title. It was written and directed by Leslie Megahey.

With its copious collection of evidence and lively interpretive style, the touchstone for scholarship is Edward Payson Evans, *The Criminal Prosecution and Capital Punishment of Animals* (New York: Dutton, 1906). An expansion of essays he had published in *The Atlantic Monthly* in 1884, it can be found on line at multiple sites. At least one of the trial accounts featured in Evans, the famous sow of Falaise, has since been revealed as highly embellished by the various people who retold it; see Paul Friedland, *Seeing Justice Done: The Age of Spectacular Capital Punishment in France* (Oxford, UK: Oxford University Press, 2012), 1–20. For a treatment of Evans' work that claims him as an early animal rights thinker, see Piers Beirnes, 'The Law Is an Ass: Reading EP Evans' The Medieval Prosecution and Capital Punishment of Animals,' *Society & Animals* 2, no. 1 (1994): 27–46.

Animal punishment in the Bible and rabbinic literature earns only brief and sporadic mention in the scholarship on the European phenomenon. The classic work on the ancient Israelite sources remains that of Jacob J. Finkelstein. His work was published first as Jacob J. Finkelstein, "The Goring Ox: Some Historical Perspectives on Deodands, Forfeitures, Wrongful Death and the Western Notion of Sovereignty," *Temple Law Quarterly* 46, no. 2 (1972): 169–290. An Assyriologist at Yale, Finkelstein was unable to complete the research project due to his sudden death at age fifty-two. Using Finkelstein's notes, an editor posthumously published an expansion of his work as Jacob J. Finkelstein, *The Ox That Gored*, vol. 71 (Philadelphia: American Philosophical Society, 1981). The classic treatment of The topic in rabbinic texts is Victor Aptowitzer, "The Rewarding and Punishing of Animals and Inanimate Objects: On the Aggadic View of the World," *Hebrew Union College Annual* 3 (1926): 117–55.

Plato and Aristotle both mention animal trials (Plato in *Laws* IX.12, at 873d–874a; Aristotle in *Athenian Constitution* Chapter 57, Section 4). Starting with the Twelve Tables and later in the Digest of Justinian (Book 9, Section 1), Roman law developed an institution called pauperies in which animals who had committed homicide were to be surrendered to the victim's family. It is unclear whether this was originally conceived of as a punishment to the animal or as compensation to the victim. See discussion of the Greek and Roman sources in Philip Jamieson, "Animal Liability in Early Law," *Cambrian Law Review* 19 (1988): 45–68, pages 46–7.

[5] For example, Peter T. Leeson, "Vermin Trials," *Journal of Law and Economics* 56, no. 3 (2013): 811–36, on p. 812: "One interpretation of vermin trials is that the judicial officials who conducted them were mad. Examining these trials' records it's tempting to conclude as much." Or Esther Cohen, "Law, Folklore and Animal Lore," *Past & Present*,

Insanity not being a persuasive scholarly explanation, scholars have tried almost every thinkable approach to animal trials: jurisprudential (animal trials impressed upon audiences the severity of a particular crime); Foucauldian (they impressed upon audiences the omnipotence of the court); economic (the trials reinforced people's sense of obligation to pay taxes to the sovereign); psychological (they furnished an explanation for tragedies); cultural anthropological (they served as public storytelling and rituals of healing); biblical (they restored the hierarchy of creation articulated in Genesis); popular religious (they exorcised demons); functional (they removed a dangerous animal from society and deterred negligence among animal owners); evolutionary atavistic (they were a holdover from a primitive, vengeful, and cognitively confused age); carefully contextualizing (on the reasonable assumption that every animal trial has its own particular explanations); and sprawling multidisciplinary (on the equally reasonable assumption that any complex cultural phenomenon is multivectored).[6] The rich range of explanations – and the tendency of scholars writing on the topic to move into metadiscussions about explanation – points to the problem that animal trials pose to the authority of law itself, whose rationality and gravitas are called into question by the specter of a rat or a pig sitting on the stand.[7]

no. 1 (1986): 6–37, on p. 15: "The very existence of animal trials in Europe poses severe problems for the historian of western culture. The practice runs counter to all commonly accepted conceptions of justice, humanity and the animal kingdom; and yet it survived and flourished for centuries."

[6] The earlier writers like Evans are the ones who tend toward the evolutionary perspectives. For explanations oriented toward jurisprudential concerns like deterrence, see survey in Jamieson, "Animal Liability," p. 58. Leaning toward the anthropological and psychological are Nicholas Humphrey, *The Mind Made Flesh: Essays from the Frontiers of Psychology and Evolution* (New York: Oxford University Press, 2002), 235–54; Jesse Elvin, "Responsibility, 'Bad Luck', and Delinquent Animals: Law as a Means of Explaining Tragedy," *The Journal of Criminal Law* 73, no. 6 (2009): 530–58; Paul Schiff Berman, "Rats, Pigs, and Statues on Trial: The Creation of Cultural Narratives in the Prosecution of Animals and Inanimate Objects," *New York University Law Review* 69 (1994): 288–326. Finkelstein, *Ox That Gored*, and Cohen, "Law, Folklore, and Animal Lore," stress the biblical, theological, and cosmological. Leeson, "Vermin Trials," is on the side of economics, while Jen Girgen, "The Historical and Contemporary Prosecution and Punishment of Animals," *Animal Law* 9 (2003): 97–133, highlights the "simple primal power for *revenge*" (p. 129). A multidisciplinary perspective is advocated by Peter Dinzelbacher, "Animal Trials: A Multidisciplinary Approach," *Journal of Interdisciplinary History* 32, no. 3 (2002): 405–21.

[7] See William Ewald, "Comparative Jurisprudence (I): What Was It Like to Try a Rat?," *University of Pennsylvania Law Review* 143, no. 6 (1995): 1889–2149, riffing on Thomas Nagel's "What Is It Like to Be a Bat?": "So far I have been writing as though the principal task were to understand the animal trials; but this last line of inquiry raises an uneasy question, namely, how well we understand our own legal rituals" (p. 1917).

Modern philosophers, clerics, and other intellectuals found animal trials to be impious, barbaric, or just plain ridiculous, and the trials more or less fell into desuetude.[8] In a strange twist of fate, contemporary animal law activists appear to be inviting a return to the medieval in advocating that animals once again stand trial.[9] A rising tide of animal lawyers argue that putting animals on trial is not barbaric – *denying* them that opportunity is. Since only an individual with legal standing can bring a case – that is to say, only someone who can show a direct connection to the action or law in question is permitted to challenge it – many cases brought on behalf of animals never make it into the courtroom.[10] Legal scholar-activists Steven M. Wise, Joyce Tischler, David Favre, and Gary Francione argue that animals should be defined as legal "persons" fit to bring a case to court.[11] If corporations can be considered persons, why not animals too?[12] Wise

---

[8] On objections to animal trials and literary satires of them, see Jan Bondeson, *The Feejee Mermaid and Other Essays in Natural and Unnatural History* (Ithaca, NY: Cornell University Press, 1999), 148–53.

[9] At the forefront of these efforts are the Animal Legal Defense Fund, founded in 1979 (modeled on the NAACP Legal Defense Fund), and the Nonhuman Rights Project, founded in 2007. The academic home is the Center for Animal Law Studies at Lewis and Clark Law School in Portland, Oregon. For a readable history of the people and organizations involved in gaining legal rights for animals, see David Grimm, *Citizen Canine: Our Evolving Relationship with Cats and Dogs* (New York: PublicAffairs, 2014), 133–257. For a profile of Steven Wise, see Charles Siebert, "Should a Chimp Be Able to Sue Its Owner?," *The New York Times*, April 23, 2014, www.nytimes.com/2014/04/27/magazine/the-rights-of-man-and-beast.html; Chris Hegedus and D. A. Pennebaker, *Unlocking The Cage*, Documentary (HBO Documentary Films, 2016). For further discussion of these legal efforts, see Chapter 6.

[10] The classic work on legal standing for nonhuman entities is Christopher D. Stone, *Should Trees Have Standing? Law, Morality, and the Environment* (New York: Oxford University Press, 2010).

[11] On Tischler, Favre, and Wise, see Grimm, *Citizen Canine*, 161–75; on Francione, see 248–57. According to Grimm's account, Francione was inspired by an incident at the U.S. Supreme Court when Francione was clerking for Justice Sandra Day O'Connor. A dog was struck by a car in front of the Supreme Court building, and Francione brought the dog into the court, apparently to the consternation of Justice Rehnquist. The dog did not survive, but the animal control officer who came to the court happened to be Ingrid Newkirk, who with her boyfriend had just founded PETA. Francione and Newkirk got to talking, Francione invited the couple over for dinner, and they proceeded to dump the milk and eggs in Francione's refrigerator and to convince him on the spot to become vegan. Francione was involved in PETA's first animal rights cases, though he eventually became disillusioned with PETA for being too sensationalist in its strategies (Grimm, *Citizen Canine*, pp. 250–2).

[12] On the link between legal personhood of animals and that of corporations, see "When Animal 'Legal Personhood' Gets Personal," *Advocate Magazine, Lewis & Clark Law School*, Summer 2014, https://law.lclark.edu/live/news/26010-when-animal-legal-personhood-gets-personal.

differentiates contemporary advocacy from earlier animal trials, however, which, according to Wise, left intact the fundamental status of animals as property (for further discussion of animals as legal things, see Chapter 6).[13]

The area of animal law I treat in this chapter – that governing sexual intercourse between animals and people ("bestiality") – is uniquely fraught. In early America, a person who had sex with a member of another species was thought to have sunk to the level of "beast" or even past that. The animal too was thought to have become "more unclean and beastly than it was."[14] Bestiality created entirely new categories of corporeality, with animal love being "queer beyond queer."[15] In tracing the criminalization of bestiality among the Puritans to the bestialization of Iraqi detainees at Abu Ghraib (among other topics in her book), Boggs says she is "trying to retell the story of modern subject formation."[16] Building on Boggs, the discussion of talmudic texts in this chapter suggests that subject formation in antiquity has its own story, and that the criminalization of bestiality and its operation as a "site of biopolitical regulation and resistance" play a role in that story.[17] This chapter will show that bestiality laws in the Talmud operate along similar lines to the Puritan laws in their delineation of personhood. The talmudic laws challenge in some ways and reinforce in others the binaries of personhood (human/animal, man/woman, child/adult, Jew/non-Jew, animate/inanimate) that dominate Jewish legal discourse.

I will first discuss the passages in the Bible and Mishnah that criminalize bestiality, paying particular attention to a digression within the Mishnah about animal moral consciousness. The chapter will then turn to a passage on Babylonian Talmud Sanhedrin 55a–b about gentile bestiality. The combination of two marginal subjects in this violation, the animal and the gentile human, and the absence of a fully subjective Jew, make it a boundary case ripe for refining categories. I will argue that it is difficult to determine whether the animal or the gentile is the passage's

---

[13] See Steven M. Wise, *Rattling the Cage: Toward Legal Rights for Animals* (Cambridge, MA: Perseus Books, 2000), 35–48.

[14] Boggs, *Animalia Americana*, 55, citing Samuel Danforth in 1674; see Boggs, 59, on John Winthrop in 1645 describing men who have sex with animals as becoming more bestial than beasts.

[15] Ibid., quoting Alice Kuzniar, "'I Married My Dog': On Queer Canine Literature," in *Queering the Non/Human*, ed. Myra J. Hird and Noreen Giffney (Burlington, VT: Ashgate, 2012), 208.

[16] Boggs, *Animalia Americana*, 25.

[17] Ibid., 15.

central interest, and that the ambiguity appears to be strategic. In offering a variety of answers to the question of whether the animal should be executed, the rabbinic voices featured in the passage – early rabbinic (tannaitic), later rabbinic (amoraic), and editorial (stammaitic) – stake out a spectrum of approaches to animal and human subjectivities.

BESTIALITY, THE BIBLE, AND BAD WRITING

All the major law collections in the Pentateuch condemn sexual intercourse between a person and an animal.[18] Only one of those passages, Leviticus 20:15–16, discusses the consequences for the animal:

> If a man has sexual relations with an animal, he must be put to death, and you shall kill the animal. If a woman approaches any animal to mate with her, you shall kill the woman and the animal; they must be put to death – their bloodguilt is upon them.

וְאִישׁ אֲשֶׁר יִתֵּן שְׁכָבְתּוֹ בִּבְהֵמָה מוֹת יוּמָת וְאֶת-הַבְּהֵמָה תַּהֲרֹגוּ. וְאִשָּׁה אֲשֶׁר תִּקְרַב אֶל-כָּל-בְּהֵמָה לְרִבְעָה אֹתָהּ וְהָרַגְתָּ אֶת-הָאִשָּׁה וְאֶת-הַבְּהֵמָה מוֹת יוּמָתוּ דְּמֵיהֶם בָּם.

When a man or woman has sex with an animal, both sexual partners, the human and the animal, shall be put to death.[19] That the animal's fate is discussed at all is striking given that in the only other extant ancient Near Eastern law code that prohibits sexual relations with animals – that of the Hittites, which prohibits sex with a sheep, pig, cow, or dog on pain of death or banishment – the animal's fate goes unmentioned (except in one relatively late tablet, which calls for veiling the offending animal like a bride and sending her out as though she were being divorced).[20]

---

[18] Exodus 22:23; Leviticus 18:23, 20:15–16; Deuteronomy 18:22.

[19] Leviticus 18 implies that the person's punishment for sex with an animal is, on an individual level, excision (*karet*), and on the collective level, being vomited out of the land. See Baruch J. Schwartz, *The Holiness Legislation: Studies in the Priestly Code (Torat ha-Qedushah: Iyunim ba-Huqah ha-Kohanit sheba-Torah)* (Jerusalem: Magnes Press, 1999), 141.

[20] See Harry Hoffner, "Incest, Sodomy, and Bestiality in the Ancient Near East," in *Orient and Occident: Essays Presented to Cyrus H. Gordon on the Occasion of His Sixty-Fifth Birthday*, ed. Harry Hoffner (Neukirchen-Vluyn, Germany: Neukirchener Verlag, 1973), 81–90. See pp. 82–3, 85. The relevant material in the Hittite laws is 187–8 and 199–200A. While the person who had sex with an equid was not punished, certain restrictions did thereafter apply: he could not approach the king or become a priest (p. 85). Hoffner says that "there is no indication in the Hittite laws that the life of the animal involved was ever spared" (p. 83), though his argument seems to be based on silence in the text. Later in the same essay Hoffner published a newly discovered tablet, which he argues comes from a later period, that requires the animal offender to be treated as a bride, veiled

Shifts in language in the course of Leviticus 20:15–16 make it difficult to say how the animal should be killed. In Verse 15, the man is to
"be put to death" (*mot yumat*), but the instruction for the animal is to
"kill" (*taharogu*) her. Since *mot yumat* is standard language for judicial
execution and *harag* is not used this way, one might safely conclude that
the human being is killed by judicial execution while the animal is killed
summarily.[21] That conclusion gets upended in the next verse, however,
where the root *harag* governs the punishment of both the animal and
the person, in that case a woman. One might legitimately conclude at
that point that a woman who has sex with an animal is, like the animal
but not like the man, deprived of judicial process and punished with dis-
patch.[22] That conclusion is in turn upended, however, by the closing of
Verse 16, which uses *mot yumatu* for the woman and the animal, suggesting that both of them are given a judicial execution, just as the man is.

The ambiguities lead to a range of scholarly views on the animal's fate.
Jacob Milgrom reads the animal execution in Verse 16 as the product
of a scribe with a strong sense of justice but weak set of writing skills.[23]
Milgrom's suggestion is that the early textual tradition called for judicial
execution for the man but not the woman. Uncomfortable with the ineq-
uity, the transmitting scribe appended to Verse 16 the language of *mot
yumatu demeham bam* ("they must be put to death – their bloodguilt is
upon them") in order to apply the same judicial procedure to women
that is used for men. The phrasing accidentally caught the animal up
into the judicial procedure too. Milgrom calls it "a lame attempt" "if
not an outright error" and concludes that "in any case, the result is a
jarring grammatical and illogical construction."[24] Along similar lines, J.J.
Finkelstein calls Leviticus 20's penalty for the animal "purely ancillary to

before she is sent away and, as in a divorce, to have her "dowry" be paid back, though
it is not clear how and to whom. Hoffner argues that the greater leniency toward the
animal and the offending person were the result of Hurrian influence.
[21] See Jacob Milgrom, *Leviticus 17–22: A New Translation with Introduction and
Commentary*, vol. 3A, The Anchor Bible (New York: Doubleday, 2000), 1752. The only
other place in the Pentateuch that *h-r-g* is used prescriptively is Deut. 13:10, where it
almost certainly refers to killing the instigator of apostasy without delay. This is how
Rabbi Eliezer in Tosefta Sanhedrin 3:1 understands the verb *taharogu* in Leviticus 20:15,
since he cites the verse as the basis for depriving all homicidal animals except the ox of
the right to a trial.
[22] This reading is given by Jan Joosten, *People and Land in the Holiness Code: An Exegetical
Study of the Ideational Framework of the Law in Leviticus 17–26* (Leiden: Brill,
1996), 51–2.
[23] Milgrom, *Leviticus 17–22*, 3A:1751–3.
[24] Ibid., 3A:1752–3.

the execution of the human culprit."[25] By contrast, Baruch Levine reads the punishment of the animal in Leviticus 20 as a direct and intentional avowal of the animal's culpability: "the punishment in this case derives from the notion that animals, like humans, also bear guilt."[26] Jonathan Burnside reads the shifting verbs as a reflection of the category collapse precipitated by bestiality: "The woman who acts like a man and like a beast is punished *both* like a man *and* like a beast. The beast that acts like a man is punished *both* like a beast *and* like a man. The confusion between the parties is so great that it is impossible to distinguish between the two of them. Both parties thus receive the same punishment."[27]

It is not important for my purposes to decide among Milgrom, Finkelstein, Levine, and Burnside on whether Leviticus intends to hold the bestial animal accountable in the same way that it does the human partner. My interest is rather in the text's susceptibility to multiple readings. On the one hand is the verb *h-r-g*'s implication that the animal, unlike the man, is simply slaughtered. On the other hand is the final clause *mot yumatu demeham bam* ("they must be put to death – their bloodguilt is upon them"), which groups the animal with the human being and considers the death of both of them to be potential sources of bloodguilt. Whether a reader chooses to emphasize the language of judicial execution or that of summary killing may very well depend as much on her assumptions about animal difference as on her understanding of biblical syntax and sources. The ambiguity in the biblical passage leads to multiple readings not only in modern scholarship but also in the Mishnah, to which I now turn.

CAN AN ANIMAL SIN? THE MISHNAH'S RHETORICAL QUESTION

When Mishnah Sanhedrin Chapter Seven reaches bestiality in its list of sins that incur the execution of stoning, it takes a detour to ask about the animal:

And these are those who are stoned:

… The one who has sexual intercourse with the male, or with the animal, or the woman who causes the animal to have sexual intercourse with her.

---

[25] Finkelstein, *The Ox That Gored*, 71:71.

[26] Baruch A. Levine, *Leviticus = Va-Yiqra: The Traditional Hebrew Text with the New JPS Translation* (Philadelphia: Jewish Publication Society, 1989), 138.

[27] Jonathan Patrick Burnside, *God, Justice, and Society: Aspects of Law and Legality in the Bible* (New York: Oxford University Press, 2011), 366.

If a person sinned, did the animal sin?

Rather, since an obstacle came to the person through her, therefore the verse said she should be stoned.

Another proposal: so that the animal will not pass in the market, and they will say, "This is the one whom person Ploni (i.e., John Doe) was stoned on account of."

ואילו הן הניסקלים... הבא על הזכור ועל הבהמה והאישה מביאה את הבהמה

אם אדם חטא מה חטאת הבהמה

אלא לפי שבאת לאדן תקלה על ידיה לפיכך אמ' הכתוב תיסקל

דבר אחר שלא תהא הבהמה עוברת[28] בשוק ויאמרו זו היא שניסקל איש פל על על ידיה.[29]

The Mishnah's question – "Did the animal sin?" – is rhetorical. The implied answer is that only a human being and no other animal is capable of sin. The Mishnah is interested in the problems, both logical and moral, that the question raises. If animals are not capable of sin, then how can they be punished? Leviticus, however, says that they are.

The Mishnah makes sense of the animal's punishment in two ways. The first explanation – "Rather, since an obstacle came to the person through her, therefore the verse said she should be stoned" – is that the animal is punished for being the instrument of human sin in the way that a dagger might be destroyed for serving as the weapon in a murder. The second explanation – "so that the animal will not pass in the market, and they will say, 'This is the one whom person Ploni was stoned on account of'" – also makes the animal's punishment dependent on the human sin, but here it is the aftermath of the sin, not the sin itself, for which the animal is held responsible. The animal's public appearance recalls the sin, along with the shame of the sinner.

The Mishnah does not tend to offer explanations, say two things when it can say one, or take off on tangents. What might be inspiring the verbosity here? Colleen Glenney Boggs suggests that in "… criminalizing crossing of the species barrier, the law tries to establish and naturalize ontological categories that it simultaneously reveals to be highly unstable."[30] When a legal code prohibits and punishes sex between a human being and an animal, the code recognizes the collapsibility of the species divide at the same time that the code tries to reinstate it. The

[28] In the talmudic quotation, the verb appears as *mehalekhet*.

[29] Mishnah Sanhedrin 7:4 (Kaufmann manuscript). Tosefta Sanhedrin 10:2 specifies that the penalty applies whether the sexual relations are *ke-darkah* ("in its [usual] way" or, in other words, vaginal intercourse) or *she-lo ke-darkah* ("not in its [usual] way" or, in other words, anal intercourse) but does not include the discussion of animal sin.

[30] Boggs, *Animalia Americana*, 55.

instability in the criminalization of bestiality is particularly troublesome in the Mishnah, since earlier, the Mishnah requires a full criminal trial for the animal:

Death-penalty cases are [judged] with twenty-three [judges].

The [animal] who plays the penetrative role in sexual intercourse [with a human being] and the [animal] who plays the penetrated role in sexual intercourse is with twenty-three, as it is said, "You shall kill the woman and the animal" (Lev. 20:16), and it says "And you shall kill the animal" (Lev. 20:15).

The stoned ox is with twenty-three, as it is said, "The ox shall be stoned and its owner, too, put to death" (Exod. 22:29) – like the execution of the owners, so too is the execution of the ox.

דיני נפשות בעשרים ושלשה

והרובע והנירבע בעשרים ושלשה שנ והרגת את האשה ואת הבהמה ואומ ואת הבהמה תהרוגו

שור ניסקל בעשרים ושלשה שנ השור יסקל וגם בעליו יומת כמיתת הבעלים כך מיתת השור[31]

This mishnah first lays out a twenty-three judge requirement for all criminal cases, and it then lays out that requirement also for the two animal "criminal" cases that appear in scripture: bestiality and homicide. An animal is tried in the same way that a person is, suggesting equivalence in their moral culpability. The parallel Tosefta strengthens that equivalence by applying to both the person and the animal the same execution method (the odd combination of pushing and stone-dropping that characterizes the early Rabbis' understanding of biblical stoning).[32] The

---

[31] Mishnah Sanhedrin 1:4 (Kaufmann manuscript). This text is discussed also in Chapter 5.

[32] Tosefta Sanhedrin 3:2; text from Moses Samuel Zuckermandel, ed., *Tosephta; based on the Erfurt and Vienna codices (Tosefta al-pi Kitve-yad 'Erfurt Vinah)* (Jerusalem: Wahrman, 1970):

The stoned ox is with twenty-three, as it is said, "The ox shall be stoned and its owner, too, put to death" (Exod. 22:29) – like the execution of the owners, so too is the execution of the owners. Just as the execution of the owners is with stoning, pushing, and twenty-three, so too the execution of the owner is with stoning, pushing, and twenty-three.

השור יסקל וגם בעליו יומת כמיתת בעלים כך מיתת השור מה מיתת בעלים בעשרים ושלשה שנ ובדחייה ובעשרים ושלשה אף מיתת השור בסקילה ובדחייה ובעשרים ושלשה

The Tosefta goes on (3:3) to articulate key differences in the judicial treatment of the person and the animal, whose criminal trial is not tipped toward acquittal as a person's is:

What difference is there between the ox and the human being? For the ox, they open his case in the daytime and may close even at night; they may open and close his case on the same day whether it is for acquittal or for conviction; they incline on the basis of one [witness's word] whether it is for acquittal or for conviction; anyone may argue for

Mishnah's procedures suggest that the animal is an independent agent with his own culpability and right to trial.

These procedures would seem to be part of a larger legal shift in the treatment of animal homicide from the Bible to the early rabbis. The partner to Sanhedrin 1:4, Mishnah Bava Qamma 4:5, imposes a monetary payment for the negligent human owner of an animal who has committed homicide. That legislation goes against the grain of Exodus 21:29–30, which offers a monetary payment as a secondary option but makes clear that the human owner in such a case deserves the death penalty:

When an ox gores a man or a woman to death, the ox shall be stoned and his flesh shall not be eaten, but the owner of the ox is not to be punished. If, however, that ox has been in the habit of goring, and his owner, although warned, has failed to guard it, and he kills a man or a woman – the ox shall be stoned and his owner, too, shall be put to death. If ransom is laid upon him, he must pay whatever is laid upon him to redeem his life.

וְכִי-יִגַּח שׁוֹר אֶת-אִישׁ אוֹ אֶת-אִשָּׁה וָמֵת סָקוֹל יִסָּקֵל הַשּׁוֹר וְלֹא יֵאָכֵל אֶת-בְּשָׂרוֹ וּבַעַל הַשּׁוֹר נָקִי. וְאִם שׁוֹר נַגָּח הוּא מִתְּמֹל שִׁלְשֹׁם וְהוּעַד בִּבְעָלָיו וְלֹא יִשְׁמְרֶנּוּ וְהֵמִית אִישׁ אוֹ אִשָּׁה הַשּׁוֹר יִסָּקֵל וְגַם-בְּעָלָיו יוּמָת. אִם-כֹּפֶר יוּשַׁת עָלָיו וְנָתַן פִּדְיֹן נַפְשׁוֹ כְּכֹל אֲשֶׁר-יוּשַׁת עָלָיו.

The early rabbis seem to have been uncomfortable with the severity of the penalty for the human owner given that there is no direct, intentional commission of a crime. Exodus 21:29–30 itself seems to waver on culpability when it permits the human owner of the animal to pay his way out of the crime ("If ransom is laid upon him..."). The rabbinic understanding of Exodus 21:29 goes further in that direction, removing the death penalty entirely from the human owner and placing all criminal procedures and outcomes on the shoulders of the animal. The human owner is left to bear strictly civil law consequences.

While the recalibration of penalties solves one problem – the lack of parity between the human owner's crime, which is negligence, and his punishment, execution – it creates another problem: robust animal culpability. Mishnah Sanhedrin 7:4 would appear to be addressing this new problem. When Mishnah Sanhedrin 7:4 poses its question about whether animals can sin, it might be read as a response to the procedures that

---

either acquittal and conviction; one who argues for acquittal may reverse and argue for conviction. [All this] is not the case for a human being.

מה בין שור לאדם שהשור פותחין את דינו ביום וגומרין אף בלילה פותחין וגומרין דינו בו ביום בין בזכות בין לחובה. בין לחובה מטין על פי אחד בין לזכות בין לחובה הכל מלמדין בין לחובה בין לזכות המלמד זכות יכול לחזור וללמד חובה מה שאין כן באדם

presuppose such capacity. Mishnah Sanhedrin 7:4 denies not once but twice the possibility of animal moral subjectivity, even while the legal procedures all seem to be pointing in that direction. The Mishnah's rhetorical question ("If a person sinned, did the animal sin?") turns out to be not so rhetorical after all.

THE QUESTION OF GENTILE BESTIALITY

This tension in the Mishnah, and in the Bible before that, is the backdrop for the talmudic passage to which I now turn. On the one hand are procedures that reflect moral culpability on the part of the animal, who is tried and punished like a person. On the other hand are explicit denials of any such parallelism. The talmudic passage starts with a question whose aim is to explore this tension:

> They asked Rav Sheshet: A non-Jew (*goy*)[33] who has sexual intercourse with an animal – what is it (i.e., the law)?[34]

> בעו מיניה מרב ששת גוי הבא על הבהמה מהו

Leviticus says that both the human and animal partner in a sexual union must be killed. But does the animal's penalty pertain if the human partner is not Jewish? Is an animal who has sex with a non-Jew still executed?

The formula that introduces this question – *be'u mineh...mahu* – tends to feature a question designed to flesh out ambiguities in the law. In this case, the ambiguity is itself ambiguous. The question could be read as pressing Rav Sheshet, the Babylonian amora to whom the question is posed by the anonymous students of the study house, to take a position on animal moral culpability. On the assumption that the gentile's sin does not count, so to speak, as sin, the case of animal-gentile sex could be a way of determining whether guilt can be borne by an animal. If it is determined that the animal is still executed, then a clear statement is being made that an animal can be "guilty." On the other hand, the assumption about gentile sin might be the very thing that the question is designed to address. Perhaps it is the animal's sin that clearly does not "count." If so, the case of animal-gentile sex would determine whether a gentile can

---

[33] On the emergence of the idea of the goy, see Ishay Rosen-Zvi and Adi Ophir, "Goy: Toward a Genealogy," *Dine Israel* 28 (2012): 69–122.

[34] Sanhedrin 55a.

bear guilt. If the animal is still executed in such a case, then the statement being made is not that animal sin holds weight, but that gentile sin does.

It is difficult to discern whether the question of gentile-animal sex is designed to explore animal or gentile moral capacity, since both animals and gentiles are, in the rabbinic perspective, variables with respect to a human Jewish constant. The ambiguity in the question makes it a Rorschach test for all who come to answer it. The later rabbis (amoraim) and talmudic editors (stammaim) featured in the passage vary not only on the positions they take but even on what they think the question is asking in the first place.

RAV SHESHET: PROXIMITY TO SIN

The first answer is from Rav Sheshet. He excerpts a passage from the Sifra, an early rabbinic collection of legal exegesis:

Rav Sheshet said[35]: You have learned it [from an early rabbinic tradition]: Since trees, which neither eat nor drink nor smell, the Torah said, "Destroy, burn, and decimate!" If an obstacle came to the person through them, one who leads his friend astray from the paths of life to the paths of death,[36] how much the more so.

אמר רב ששת תניתוה מה אילנות שאין אוכלין ואין שותין[37] ואין מריחין אמרה תורה השחת שרוף וכלה הואיל ובא[38] לאדם תקלה על ידן המתעה את חבירו מדרכי חיים לדרכי מיתה על אחת כמה וכמה

The passage Rav Sheshet pulls from the Sifra does not exactly answer the question about gentile-animal sex. The passage speaks of people and plants, not animals, and it is not interested in gentiles. The interest of the passage is in the evils of luring a man into sin. If the Torah is so rigorous about sin that it calls for the utter eradication of an inanimate object like a tree for playing a passive, unconscious part in a person's downfall, then one can only imagine, so goes the Sifra's logic, how severely God must judge a man who purposely leads his friend down the wrong path.

Where do animals fit in? Are they more like the unknowing tree worshipped by the wayward sinner, or the treacherous friend who persuades him into it? Rav Sheshet would seem to have been drawn to this passage because it uses the same phrase "if an obstacle came to the person through them" found in the mishnah about bestiality ("Rather, since an obstacle

---

[35] Other manuscripts: "Rav Sheshet said to them."
[36] Munich 151 omits "to the paths of death."
[37] Karlsruhe manuscript omits "neither drink."
[38] Other manuscripts have the feminine verb.

came to the person through her, therefore the verse said she should be stoned"). Since that phrase is used in the Sifra with respect to the tree, and in the Mishnah with respect to the animal, and neither a tree nor an animal would seem to be capable of consciously corrupting a person, that would suggest that Rav Sheshet is associating the one (the animal) with the other (the tree) and contrasting both with human beings.

But the tree is described in the Sifra as something that does not eat or drink or smell in contrast to the human. This characterization would point instead toward grouping the animal with the human, not the plant. The animal may not be an intention-filled agent of corruption like the human, it is true, but neither is the animal the agency-free instrument that the tree is understood to be. Rav Sheshet's legal ruling is clear either way: the animal should be executed. If even the tree is destroyed, and based on that the person too, then it should not matter whether the animal more greatly resembles the tree or the person. Her fate is the same as both: total destruction, for having participated even tangentially in a person's downfall.

Immediately prior to the passage cited by Rav Sheshet in the Sifra is a parallel to the mishnah on bestiality:

"You shall kill the woman and the animal" (Lev. 20:16): If a person sinned, did the animal sin? Rather, since an obstacle came to the person through her, therefore the verse said she should be stoned. Reasoning from the major to the minor: Since an animal, who does not know to distinguish between good and evil, if an obstacle came to the person through her, the verse said, "She should be stoned"; a person who causes his friend to veer from the path of life to the path of death, how much the more so should the Place (i.e., God) cause him to pass from the world.

והרגת את האשה ואת הבהמה אם אדם חטא מה חטאה בהמה אלא לפי שבא לאדם תקלה על ידיה
לפיכך אמר הכתוב תסקל ק"ו ומה אם בהמה שאינה יודעת להבחין בין טוב לרע על שבאת תקלה על
ידה לאדם אמר הכתוב תסקל אדם שגורם לחבירו להטותו מדרך החיים לדרך המות עאכ"ו שיעבירנו
המקום מן העולם

Why did Rav Sheshet cite the subsequent passage that obliquely addresses animal penalties rather than this passage that does so explicitly? If Rav Sheshet had cited this passage, he would have found himself facing the same tension in the Mishnah that his students' question was designed to resolve. In fact, the Sifra goes further than the Mishnah in accentuating the animal's innocence ("Since an animal, who does not know to distinguish between good and evil..."). The Sifra, like the Mishnah, makes clear that animals cannot sin and that their punishment is not a function of their own moral agency. The moral drama in the Mishnah, and even more so in the Sifra, is that the animal is punished for being merely prox-imate to the human sin. The passage in the Sifra that goes uncited rein-states the same paradox found in the Mishnah: animals cannot bear sin but are punished as though they could.

The passage Rav Sheshet chooses to cite, by contrast, opens up new possibilities for thinking about the animal's relationship to human sin. Notice my language – "human" sin. The entire section in the Sifra speaks in universalist terms of the righteous and the wicked. The section nowhere implies any ethnic or religious identities with which righteousness and wickedness are associated (for instance, that the righteous = Israel, and the wicked = the nations). In order for Rav Sheshet to arrive at an answer based on this passage, he has to see a gentile in the Sifra instead of a wayward Jew who worships trees. Rav Sheshet is doing just that, and we barely notice it, because the Jew/gentile binary is not his interest, just as it is not the Sifra's. The *animal* is Rav Sheshet's interest, along with the question of consequences for contribution to somebody else's sin.

Rav Sheshet stakes a claim for animal consciousness that is modeled on human consciousness, both of which are rooted in a bodily porous-ness – eating, drinking, smelling[39] – said not to be possessed by vegeta-tion.[40] Rav Sheshet says that consciousness is not, in the end, the hinge on which rests the burden of punishment for being proximate to sin. The point Rav Sheshet makes, following in the footsteps of the Sifra, is that human sin is such serious business that any facilitation, no matter how passive or unconscious, incurs punishment. But at the same time Rav Sheshet suggests that if punishment for being proximate to sin *did* hinge on consciousness or culpability, animals might not escape it. Animals, like people, interact with the world with a depth and dynamism absent in plants. Animals can sway people from the ways of life, as the Sifra puts it, toward the ways of death. Not so plants, which serve as a foil for a con-sciousness that Rav Sheshet attributes only to animate species. The gen-tile's sin may or may not carry the same gravity as a Jew's – Rav Sheshet does not address this – but the fact that the animal led him into that sin with some degree of awareness, however minimal that awareness may be, is more than sufficient to subject the animal to punishment.

---

[39] "Eat, drink, smell" is echoed in "destroy, burn, decimate." The matching trio of verbs seems designed to emphasize the harshness with which proximity to sin is treated by the Torah.

[40] One could certainly argue that plants do eat, drink, and smell, but that is not the assump-tion in this passage.

ABAYE: GENTILE MORAL CONSCIOUSNESS

The second answer to the question of gentile bestiality, offered by the later rabbi Abaye, is interested not like Rav Sheshet's answer in the person, animal, or plant who is proximate to the sin, but in the sinner himself:

Abaye said: This one – his disgrace is great; but that one – his disgrace is minimal.

אמר אביי זה קלונו מרובה וזה קלונו מועט

Medieval Talmud commentaries debate the meaning of Abaye's vague statement. My view is that when Abaye says "this one" and "that one," he is referring to the gentile and the Jew, and he is claiming for the Jew a greater capacity for humiliation.[41] Abaye is not saying – we should note because the talmudic editors will say otherwise – that gentiles cannot experience humiliation, but only that the Jew experiences more. The question remaining is Abaye's ruling on the matter at hand. In Abaye's perspective, is the humiliation experienced by the gentile sufficient to cause the animal to be condemned to death? Does the gentile's sin qualify the animal for stoning?

I would argue that Abaye is saying no, the human sin here does not "count," and the animal should not be executed.[42] This would put Abaye at odds with Rav Sheshet on the legal outcome, making for a neat dispute between the two. But Abaye and Rav Sheshet also dispute the stakes of the legal question. For Rav Sheshet, the question addresses the moral culpability of the animal (even though his answer will assert that moral consciousness is ultimately irrelevant, since any contribution to human sin, no matter how unconscious, merits punishment). For Abaye, the question relates only to the moral culpability of the person. In Abaye's understanding, at stake in the question about sex between a gentile and an animal are the scope and significance of gentile moral consciousness.

[41] I follow Rashi's explanation that Abaye is comparing the Jew's level of humiliation to the gentile's when each has sexual intercourse with an animal. The Tosafists on the printed Talmud page argue against Rashi, proposing that Abaye is comparing the Jew who has sexual intercourse with an animal to the Jew who commits idolatry, who would experience less humiliation for his sin than the Jew who commits bestiality. Rabbenu Hananel, Nahmanides, and Tosfot ha-Rosh take the same approach as the Tosafists.

[42] This follows Rashi's first understanding (Rashi offers two possibilities for the legal implications of Abaye's position) that the gentile's humiliation is too negligible to merit execution of the animal.

RAVA: ANIMAL MORAL CONSCIOUSNESS

The passage adds a third voice to the mix, that of Rava. Rava's position, like the first position (Rav Sheshet) but unlike the second (Abaye), understands the question to be addressing the animal. Whereas the first view is interested in the animal in so far as he or she has served as an accomplice to human sin, Rava's interest is the animal's own capacity to sin:

Rava said: The Torah said: An animal derives pleasure from sin, she should be executed.

רבא אמר אמרה תורה בהמה נהנית מעבירה תיהרג

In Rava's approach to the question of gentile bestiality, the gentile's culpability is irrelevant, as is the animal's collaborationist or instrumentalist role.[43] The question is whether the animal deserves punishment for her own act.

Rava presumes that enjoyment of sin is what makes it punishable. Rava claims that animals (at least some – whether he is speaking of all animals or certain individuals is ambiguous) are capable of enjoying sin.[44] If animals can enjoy sin, Rava says they can be punished for it too.[45] Rava comes close to Rav Sheshet in his legal stance as well as in his approach to animal moral capacities. Both rabbis hold animals responsible for sin

---

[43] Rava is also the key figure in the passage in Bava Metzia 32a–33a that is the locus classicus in Jewish law for the prohibition, prevention, and minimization of animal suffering. See discussion in Chapter 4. There also Rava roots his claim in scripture.

[44] In other words, is Rava claiming that "an animal, who by definition enjoys sin, should be executed" or "an animal who happens to be an individual who enjoys sin, that animal should be executed (but an animal who is not of this more human-like moral character should not be executed)"? The syntax and logic lean in the first direction, but the second understanding, that only some animals are executed, would create a clean three-way dispute, with Rav Sheshet legislating that all animals are executed, Abaye legislating that none are, and Rava legislating that some are. The Karlsruhe manuscript, which has *behemah ha-nehenet* ("the animal who enjoys...") might suggest the second reading.

    Rava might be recognizing human rape of animals as a phenomenon in suggesting that not every instance of bestiality will bring pleasure to the animal. On whether sexual relations between a person and an animal should legally constitute rape of the animal and therefore an act of animal abuse, see discussions in Anthony L. Podberscek and Andrea M. Beetz, eds., *Bestiality and Zoophilia: Sexual Relations with Animals* (Oxford, UK: Berg, 2005); Marcela Iacub, "Paternalism or Legal Protection of Animals? Bestiality and the French Judicial System," in *French Thinking about Animals*, ed. Louisa Mackenzie and Stephanie Posthumus, The Animal Turn (East Lansing: Michigan State University Press, 2015), 121–34.

[45] When Rava says "an animal derives pleasure from sin," Rava may be saying either that the animal derives pleasure from an act that the Torah happens to consider a sin, or that

and stake a claim for animal moral capacity. The difference is that Rav Sheshet holds the animal responsible for the human sin while Rava holds the animal responsible for her own sin.

GOD'S (SOMETIME) COMPASSION FOR ANIMALS

Thus far, I have surveyed the answers of three named Babylonian rabbis to the question of whether an animal who has sex with a gentile is executed just as they would be if their sexual partner had been Jewish. Those answers look very different once the talmudic editors have reframed them. From the start, the talmudic editors assume that gentiles do not experience sin in a morally significant way:[46]

We require "obstacle" (*taqalah*) and "disgrace" (*qalon*), and here there is obstacle but there is no disgrace, or perhaps [the animal is executed when there is] obstacle even though there is no disgrace?

תקלה וקלון בעינן והכא תקלה איכא קלון ליכא או דילמא תקלה אע"פ שאין קלון[47]

The editors start with an assumption that gentiles would not experience disgrace or humiliation (*qalon*) from having sex with an animal. They are just as prohibited as Jews, however, from doing so. The idea of prohibition is embodied in the editors' term "obstacle" (*taqalah*), which refers to the animal's operating as an obstacle to the person's rectitude. One might say that sex with an animal adds to a person's commandment rap sheet. For the editors, then, the question is whether the animal should be executed in a case in which "obstacle," i.e., a legal prohibition, is relevant, but "disgrace," i.e., the experience of shame or humiliation, is not. Perhaps, ruminates the talmudic editor, the Torah calls for execution for an animal only when both "obstacle" and "disgrace" are in play, as is the case when a Jew engages in bestial relations. The Torah may not call for the same severity in the case of the gentile, which involves "obstacle"

---

the animal enjoys the *sinfulness* of the sin rather than simply the sex that constitutes the sin, as humans do when they seek the thrill of the forbidden. The first reading may seem more likely but perhaps imposes upon Rava an assumption about animal moral consciousness (or lack thereof) that is more our own than Rava's.

[46] The editor considers gentile sin to possess objective legal reality (*taqalah*) but not a subjective, experiential component (*qalon*).

[47] The editor plays with two conceptual categories, "obstacle" (*taqalah*) and "disgrace" (*qalon*). While the editor constructs a binary out of the two categories, they are in fact linguistically similar to each other; both would appear to come from the root *qalah* or *qalal*.

alone. On the other hand, speculates the editor, "obstacle" may be the only condition necessary for the animal to incur punishment.

In framing the amoraic statements through these notions of "obstacle" and "disgrace," the talmudic editors paradoxically make the earlier rabbinic statements either redundant or anomalous. Since the talmudic editors assume from the outset that being an accomplice to sin is just as bad as being the sinner, Rav Sheshet's position becomes unnecessary to state. The editors steal Abaye's thunder, and even contradict him, when they say outright that a gentile who sins does not experience disgrace. Rava's position is also precluded by the editors, whose focus on gentile culpability implies that animal moral capacity is a closed question. The main questions the three earlier rabbis played with – the facilitation of sin (Rav Sheshet), the gentile's experience of sin (Abaye), the animal's experience of sin (Rava) – are, for the editors, already decided. For the editors, then, the question worth asking is not whether animals possess moral consciousness, or whether gentiles do; we already know that they do not.

What then do the talmudic editors think this legal question tests, if not animal moral capacity, or gentile? What ambiguity does it clarify? The task of the question, as it emerges from the discourse of the editors, is to test God. The question according to the editors is whether, *despite* the fact that animals lack moral culpability and that gentiles lack shame, animals' status as living, animate beings is sufficient to move God to offer them special dispensation such that they, unlike trees, should not be wantonly destroyed for unknowingly inspiring a human being to violate a divine decree.

The editors are divided on how to answer this version of the question. The first half of the talmudic passage answers in the affirmative. God gives special care to animals, whom God places in a different category from plants:

And behold trees, for whom disgrace (experienced by the person who worships a tree) is not great, yet the Torah said, "Destroy, burn, and decimate"! We are speaking about living creatures, for whom God has compassion...

... And behold trees, who do not derive pleasure from sin, yet the Torah said, "Destroy, burn, and decimate"! We are speaking about living creatures, for whom God has compassion.

והרי אילנות דאין קלונן מרובה ואמרה תורה השחת שרוף וכלה בבעלי חיים קאמרינן דחס רחמנא
עלייהו...

...והרי אילנות דאין נהנין מעבירה ואמרה תורה השחת שרוף וכלה בבעלי חיים קאמרינן דחס רחמנא
עלייהו

Like the tree, the animal deserves total destruction for the part they play in human sin, even if that human sin is, in this case, "defective" due to the absence of any humiliation experienced on the part of the gentile sinner. But God, like the president issuing a pardon, gives a reprieve to the animal because of the animal's status as a living creature ("We are speaking about living creatures, for whom God has compassion"). One would not expect such a pardon were the animal to have sex with a Jew, in which case the law in the Torah and Mishnah is explicit that the animal must be executed. In the Talmud's boundary case of gentile bestiality, however, God extends mercy.

The talmudic editors flip-flop in the second half of the passage, where, using the same language that they did in the first, the editors deny special dispensation for animals:

Since she (a girl the age of three years and a day and under, who has sex with an animal) is an intentional violator, there is also "obstacle" (the animal has facilitated the violation), and it is God who has compassion for her (and exempts her from punishment). On her, He has compassion; on the animal, He does not have compassion (and the animal is executed).

… Since he (the boy the age of nine years and a day and under, who has sex with an animal) is an intentional violator, there is also "obstacle" (the animal has facilitated the violation), and it is God who has compassion for him (and exempts him from punishment). On him, He has compassion; on the animal, He does not have compassion (and the animal is executed).

כיון דמזידה היא תקלה נמי איכא ורחמנא הוא דחס עלה עלה דידה חס אבהמה לא חס

כיון דמזיד הוא תקלה נמי איכא ורחמנא הוא דחס עילויה עליה דידיה חס רחמנא אבהמה לא חס רחמנא

According to the editors' claim here, God gives special consideration only to human beings and denies His mercy to animals ("On her/him, He has compassion; on the animal, He does not have compassion"). In the part immediately prior, two Babylonian rabbis (Rav Yosef and Rava) bring passages from Mishnah Niddah (5:4–5) to answer a question that another Babylonian rabbi, Rav Hamnuna, had raised regarding whether the animal is still executed in the case of sexual intercourse with a Jew who has committed the act unwittingly (the Rav Hamnuna text is cited in the subsequent section of this chapter). Just what is involved in an unwitting act of bestiality deserves further consideration (!), but the rabbis offer one possible scenario: the case of a child, presumably on the assumption that a child may not understand the sinful nature of the act. The talmudic editors here reject the initial claim that the child in such a case should be considered "unwitting": "s/he is an intentional violator (*mezidah*/*mezid*)." The editors conclude that in the case of the child who has sex with an animal, the child deserves to be executed because he or she is a knowing sinner. God pardons the child, however, sparing them from punishment. The editors go on to contrast God's pardon for the child with God's strict judgment of the animal. While in the first half of the talmudic passage, God is described as offering special mercy to animals, here in the second half, only the child receives merciful treatment, and the animal is left to suffer due punishment.

THE UNWITTING JEW AND OTHER PARTIAL SUBJECTIVITIES

As is usually the case with the Babylonian Talmud, the point lies less in answering the question than in exploring the problems and tensions it raises. That is certainly the case here, since the structure of the passage is surprisingly circular. The passage's latter half, which introduces the case of the unwitting Jew, opens with a reading of the Mishnah that is patently absurd. The reading begs to be rejected, and it ultimately is. The proposed reading is that the first explanation of animal execution in the Mishnah ("since an obstacle came to the person through her, therefore the verse said she should be stoned") embodies a case of "disgrace" (*qalon*) without "obstacle" (*taqalah*):

The *resha* (the first segment of the Mishnah), this teaches us that even [in a case of] disgrace without obstacle, they hold [the animal] liable.

רישא הא קמ"ל⁴⁸ דאפילו קלון בלא תקלה נמי מיחייבי

The segment of the Mishnah that the editors here claim to represent a case of "disgrace" but no "obstacle" actually uses the word "obstacle" (*taqalah*) to justify the animal's punishment! The medieval Talmud commentator Rashi is forced into hermeneutical gymnastics to make sense of the Talmud's proposal:

"Disgrace without obstacle," for example, the unwitting Jew who thinks it is permitted [to have sex with an animal]. For there is disgrace, since he disgraces himself with a thing that is disgraceful, but there is no obstacle. But what is the obstacle that [the Mishnah] teaches, "since an obstacle came to the person through her"? It speaks of the *obstacle of* disgrace. And it is appropriate to interpret it thus, and

---

48 The Jerusalem manuscript reverses the first part (*resha*) and second part (*sefa*) in this line (and then later again in the conclusion), likely for the reasons I am laying out here, that the claim about the second part (*resha*) is problematic.

not for the *resha* (the first part of the mishnah) to be interpreted as referring to a non-Jew, and the *sefa* (the second part of the mishnah) to a Jew.

קלון בלא תקלה כגון ישראל שוגג כסבור מותר דאיכא קלון שגינה עצמו בדבר מגונה ותקלה ליכא
ומאי תקלה דקתני שבאת לאדם תקלה ע"י תקלת קלון קאמר וניחא לאוקמה הכי ולא תוקמא רישא
בגוי וסיפא בישראל

When the Talmud proposes that this part of the mishnah deals with an instance of disgrace, it really means the *obstacle of* disgrace, claims Rashi. Rashi goes on to explain why the Talmud would offer so tenuous an interpretation of the Mishnah. The Talmud would rather have both segments of the mishnah deal with the same category of person (either Jew or non-Jew, but not a switch from one to the other). One can tell from Rashi's grapplings that this moment in the talmudic passage is a purely discursive one designed to produce discussion rather than to present a plausible position.

The passage ultimately circles back from the question about the unwitting Jew to Rav Sheshet's question about the gentile. Whether the passage ever answers that question about gentile bestiality – I would say it offers several answers – it does succeed in exploring instabilities in the nature of subjectivity and agency. The shift from the first half of the passage to the second on whether animals are more like trees or more like people highlights the relative character of subjectivity. Comparisons throughout the passage are constant: the adult with the child, the boy child with the girl child, the child with the animal, the animal with the tree, the tree with the man, the Jewish man with the gentile man. The passage creates a spectrum of subjectivities or selves that take their departure from the full subjectivity of the adult male Jew, who appears only in the interstices of the passage.

Other features of the passage enhance the impression that subjectivity and agency are not inherent, fixed attributes but vary based on circumstance and perspective. The little boy and little girl of Mishnah Niddah, cited in the passage, may be unwitting at this stage of development but knowing at a later one.[49] They may be considered unwitting for bestiality but not for other acts such as eating tithes, transmission of impurity, and disqualification from the priesthood, which are the other legal areas that appear in the cited teachings. Another figure in the passage, the unwitting adult Jew, is presumed unwitting for the purposes of bestiality but is

[49] For discussion of that mishnah, see Leib Moscovitz, "'The Actions of a Minor Are a Nullity'? Some Observations on the Legal Capacity of Minors in Rabbinic Law," ed. Berachyahu Lifshitz, *Jewish Law Annual* 17, no. Part I (2008): 92–5.

likely considered to be in full possession of his wits with respect to other acts. The passage's interest is in all kinds of partial subjectivities. It creates a laundry list of figures who are not fully there, whose accountability for their actions and exercise of moral judgment are unstable since they depend on context, on the type of act for which they are being judged, and on who is doing the judging. The only potentially stable subjectivity is that of God, though even that shifts in the course of the passage, with God's compassion showered upon animals in the first half of the passage but withheld from them in the second. It is clear from the first half that God does not have mercy on trees, and from the second half that God has mercy on children, but whether He pities animals seems to depend on whom they are being compared with. Perhaps one is meant to conclude that while God's subjectivity might be stable, the human perspective on it is not.

It is likely that the question of the unwitting Jew inspired the passage in the first place, since the parallel in the Palestinian Talmud features only him and not the gentile:

Rabbi Ba bar Memel asked: Imagine (literally: your self has arrived at) that one who has sexual intercourse [with an animal] unwittingly, behold she is stoned on account of him, but he is exempt.

Rabbi Shimon asked: Imagine that he plows on the Sabbath, behold he is stoned on account of her, but she is exempt.

רבי בא בר ממל בעי הגע עצמך שבא עליה שוגג הרי היא נסקלת על ידיו והוא פטור

ר' שמעון בעי הגע עצמך שחרש בשבת הרי הוא נסקל על ידה והיא פטורה[50]

Rabbi Ba bar Memel is bothered by the discrepancy in punishment when the unwitting Jew has sex with an animal: the animal is executed, but the person goes scot free. The converse is true for plowing on the Sabbath, the subject of Rabbi Shimon's question. The person is executed, but the animal goes unpunished. The rabbis featured in this Palestinian Talmud passage believe that there should be some parity between the animal's

[50] The answer to Rabbi Shimon's question offered by Palestinian Talmud Sanhedrin 7:7 (36a) is less than clear:

You have only that which Rabbi Shmuel bar Rav Yitzhak said: "Of their silver and gold, they have made themselves images, to his own undoing" (Hosea 8:4): "to their own undoing" it is not written here, but "to his own undoing." It is like a person who says, "May so-and-so's bones be ground!" and his son goes out to wicked activity.

לית לך אלא כהדא דמר ר' שמואל בר רב יצחק כספם וזהבם עשו להם עצבים למען יכרתון אין כתיב כאן אלא למען יכרת כאינש דמר שחוק טימייה דפלן דאפיק בריה לעבדא בישא

punishment and the person's, yet these cases yield outcomes with gross disparity.

The Babylonian rabbis do not appear to have the same concerns. The case of the Jew who "unwittingly" has sex with an animal is presented by Rav Hamnuna in judicially neutral terms. It is a difficult question requiring serious deliberation ("The Jew who has intercourse unwittingly with an animal, what is the law?" in contrast to Rabbi Ba bar Memel's "Imagine that ...!"). The Babylonian rabbis also conjure up a parallel case, that of the gentile ("The gentile who has intercourse with an animal, what is the law?"). By adding the question of the gentile to that of the unwitting Jew and neutralizing the tone, the Babylonian rabbis shift the terms of the question away from the problem of parity and toward the problem of moral agency, culpability, and consciousness.

The talmudic editors, in one last step, string the two questions together to produce a full-scale exploration of subjectivity, sin, and shame:

They asked Rav Sheshet: A non-Jew who has sexual intercourse with an animal – what is it? We require "obstacle" and "disgrace," and here there is obstacle but there is no disgrace, or perhaps [we hold liable when there is] obstacle even though there is no disgrace?

As Rav Hamnuna asked: A Jew who has sexual intercourse with an animal unwittingly – what is it? We require "obstacle" and "disgrace," and here there is disgrace but there is no obstacle, or perhaps [we hold liable when there is] disgrace even though there is no obstacle?

בעו מיניה מרב ששת גוי הבא על הבהמה מהו תקלה וקלון בעינן והכא תקלה איכא קלון ליכא או דילמא תקלה אע"פ שאין קלון

דבעי רב המנונא ישראל הבא על הבהמה בשוגג מהו תקלה וקלון בעינן והכא קלון איכא תקלה ליכא או דילמא קלון אע"פ שאין תקלה

The unwitting Jew is described by the talmudic editors as possessing shame but no legal accountability, while the gentile is described as possessing legal accountability but no shame. The two halves of the passage are meant to mirror each other, with the editors presenting the unwitting Jewish man (shame but no legal accountability) as the precise inverse of the gentile man (legal accountability but no shame). While the named Babylonian rabbis likely would have seen the two figures as loosely parallel, for the anonymous editors, the two figures have become precise opposites.

CONCLUSIONS: ANIMAL MIRRORS

The mirror structure in this talmudic passage evokes Dina Stein's discussion in *Textual Mirrors*, which explores moments in rabbinic literature when characters see themselves in the mirror and rabbinic authors reflect upon themselves as authors.[51] The subject of the talmudic discussion that immediately precedes the one I have been discussing takes self-reflection to an extreme:

Rav Ahadboy bar Ami asked Rav Sheshet: One who has the first stage of sexual intercourse with himself, what is it (the law)?

He said to him: You have insulted us!

Rav Ashi said: Why would you ask? It is not found when [the penis] is erect. When it is found, it is when he has sex [when the penis is] limp (literally, "he has sexual intercourse dead"). According to the one who says that one who has sex limp with forbidden partners is exempt, here he is exempt. And according to the one who says he is liable, here he is liable twice: he is liable for being the active partner and he is liable for being the passive partner.[52]

בעא מיניה רב אחדבוי בר אמי[53] מרב ששת המערה בעצמו מהו

אמר ליה קבסתן

אמר רב אשי מאי תיבעי לך בקושי[54] לא משכחת לה כי משכחת לה[55] במשמש מת למאן דאמר משמש מת בעריות פטור הכא פטור ולמאן דאמר חייב הכא מיחייב תרתי מיחייב אשוכב ומיחייב אנשכב

Rav Ahadboy's name is a compound of the number one (*ahad*) and the verb for sexual intercourse (*ba*, here *boy*), reflecting his interest in a man who seeks to have sexual intercourse with, as we might say today, number one or, in other words, himself. Rav Sheshet believes Rav Ahadboy's question to have gone beyond the boundaries of good taste and legal discourse altogether.[56] Rav Ashi, on the other hand, takes the case seriously, in fact so seriously that he attaches to it not one but two death penalties.

One may read this brief discourse about sex with the self as a precursor and parallel to the discussion of gentile bestiality that follows. Both discussions explore the boundaries of culpability and challenge the coherence of the self. Whereas Rav Sheshet brushes off the question about male self-penetration, he answers the one about animal-gentile sex and, in so doing, launches the passage's reflections on the varieties of subjectivity and the scope of moral consciousness. Perhaps the question on

---

[51] Dina Stein, *Textual Mirrors: Reflexivity, Midrash, and the Rabbinic Self* (Philadelphia: University of Pennsylvania Press, 2012), 6, 8. See also Mira Balberg, Ishay Rosen-Zvi, Joshua Levinson, Jonathan Schofer, and Elana Stein on notions of self and subjectivity within rabbinic literature; references can be found in the Conclusion.

[52] Sanhedrin 55a.

[53] "Bar Ami" absent in Karlsruhe-Reuchlin 2.

[54] Karlsruhe-Reuchlin 2 mistakenly has *be-qodshi* instead of *be-qoshi*.

[55] "When it is found" absent in Florence II-I-9.

[56] Rashi: "you have pained me by asking me a question about something that is impossible."

self-sex is meant to prime readers for the one about animal-gentile sex so that by the time it is reached, the question no longer seems as outrageous as it once might have.

In the talmudic passage I have here examined, the animal plays a critical role in the passage's broader inquiry into the nature of culpability and consciousness. Glenney Boggs proposes that "the law does not simply apply to a subject that exists a priori; it constructs the humanity of that subject (or his lack thereof)."[57] This talmudic legal passage constructs the humanity of the subject, or lack thereof, by imagining animal partners for it and playing out the legal consequences for the animal. But the subject being constructed here is not only a human one. The animal subject is being constructed as well, along with a variety of other shifting, unstable, or partial subjectivities.

[57] Boggs, *Animalia Americana*, 55.

4

Animal Suffering

Bava Metzia 32a–33a

THE RACCOON IN THE KITCHEN

The landlord of their Brooklyn apartment building dismissed their complaints when the couple, Will and Malya, told him about the crying that they could hear inside their walls. So Will and Malya took matters into their own hands. One night when the crying got bad, Will took a hammer, moved the stove, and started to hack away at the wall. He made a hole a little larger than the size of his hand. Wanting to capture whatever it was that was going to happen, Malya videoed Will as he put on a rubber kitchen glove and plunged his hand into the dark space behind the wall. Will's glove emerged from the hole clasping a baby raccoon, like a rabbit being pulled out of a magician's hat. Will's first instinct was, for some reason, to bring the shocked raccoon to the bathroom mirror so that the two of them could look at their reflection. Will went over to the bathtub, apparently to wash off the raccoon from the drywall dust, but that is when Malya stopped the video. When they posted the video on YouTube, it went viral, bringing CBS News and local fame to the Brooklyn couple.[1] The juxtaposition of forest critter and urban kitchen, the couple's quirky Brooklyn vibe, and the adorableness of the baby raccoon drew people to the story.

The reader of Peter Singer's *Animal Liberation* may find it strange when, a little way into the book, Singer considers whether animals are

---

[1] For the YouTube video, see www.youtube.com/watch?v=CodWq8lRBfU. For the coverage on CBS local news, see www.youtube.com/watch?v=x-Abp9QZYOE.

capable of suffering.[2] Watching the video of Will and Malya and the raccoon, one wonders how anyone could doubt the capacity of an animal to suffer. Yet doubt is to be found even in the events inside Will and Malya's apartment, at the heart of which was an animal's suffering so palpable that it compels the couple to break through their kitchen wall. But then there is the landlord who cannot be bothered to answer Will and Malya's calls, and the joking of the CBS news anchors, who when they wrap up the story laughingly remark that the outcome could have been different: "That sucker could have come out angry." One of the anchors pretends to be a giant scary raccoon baring his claws.

A fine line distinguishes responses to the raccoon. If the cry had been from a rat instead of a raccoon, the couple might have called the exterminator instead of hacking through the wall. If the raccoon had died immediately when she fell from her family's den in the roof (which it turns out is what happened), the couple would have been disgusted by the stench of her decaying corpse rather than saddened by her crying.[3] But this baby raccoon, with her black bandit mask already visible and her tiny paws splayed out on the two sides of Will's kitchen glove, got a new home in the woods of upstate New York where the wildlife service relocated her. Her suffering touched the lives of Will and Malya and the many YouTube and news viewers who gasped, along with Malya, when the raccoon emerged from the hole behind the stove. In the end, though, if one follows the comments on YouTube, it was Will's bushy beard and shirtless chest that drew more attention than anything else.

This chapter deals with the complexity of human reactions to animal suffering. In some cases that suffering activates empathy and curiosity, while in other cases, that suffering is feared, ignored, repressed, or ridiculed. The same instance of suffering more often than not invokes conflicting responses, as was the case for the raccoon in Will and Malya's kitchen. A good illustration from the Jewish scriptural tradition is the Hebrew Bible's commandment to send the mother bird from the nest before taking her fledglings or eggs, known in later Jewish traditions as

---

[2] Singer notifies readers who do not require any persuasion to skip ahead, but he clearly considers it a plausible enough position to give attention before proceeding to his main arguments about the philosophical flaws of speciesism. For an argument that other animals actually suffer more than human beings, see Sahar Akhtar, "Animal Pain and Welfare: Can Pain Sometimes Be Worse for Them than for Us?," in *The Oxford Handbook of Animal Ethics*, ed. Tom L. Beauchamp and Raymond Gillespie Frey (New York: Oxford University Press, 2011), 495–518.

[3] The raccoon turned out to be female.

shilu'ah ha-qen, "the sending of the nest."[4] Deuteronomy 22:6–7 promises prosperity and long life for the one who heeds this instruction:

If, along the road, you chance upon a bird's nest, in any tree or on the ground,
with fledglings or eggs and the mother sitting over the fledgling or on the eggs, do
not take the mother together with her young. Let the mother go, and take only
the young, in order that you may fare well and have a long life.

כִּי יִקָּרֵא קַן־צִפּוֹר לְפָנֶיךָ בַּדֶּרֶךְ בְּכָל־עֵץ אוֹ עַל־הָאָרֶץ אֶפְרֹחִים אוֹ בֵיצִים וְהָאֵם רֹבֶצֶת עַל־הָאֶפְרֹחִים
אוֹ עַל־הַבֵּיצִים לֹא־תִקַּח הָאֵם עַל־הַבָּנִים. שַׁלֵּחַ תְּשַׁלַּח אֶת־הָאֵם וְאֶת־הַבָּנִים תִּקַּח־לָךְ לְמַעַן יִיטַב לָךְ
וְהַאֲרַכְתָּ יָמִים.

Commentators going back to antiquity have observed this commandment's links to a number of other ones: the admonition to keep an ox,
goat, or sheep with the mother for the first seven days of life (Leviticus
22:27); the prohibition on slaughtering an animal and his young on the
same day (Leviticus 22:28); and the prohibition on cooking a kid in his
mother's milk (Exodus 23:19, 34:26; Deuteronomy 14:21).[5] These commandments all seem to demand respect for the parent-child bond among
animals.

The question is why.[6] A major line of interpretation understands
shilu'ah ha-qen to stem from a concern with animal suffering.[7] One
should not make the mother bird suffer by stealing her children out from

[4] A recent discussion of this commandment, with focus on its interpretive trajectory among
German Jewish pietists, can be found at the beginning of Shyovitz, "'How Can the
Guilty Eat the Innocent?'" See also the discussions of Rachel Muers, "Setting Free the
Mother Bird: On Reading a Strange Text," *Modern Theology* 22, no. 4 (2006): 555–76;
Eliezer Segal, "Justice, Mercy and a Bird's Nest," *Journal of Jewish Studies* 42, no. 2
(1991): 176–95; Joseph Tabory, "שילוח הקן: על היחס בין טעם המצווה לבין דינה," in *(Studies in
Halakhah and Jewish Thought)* חקרים בהלכה ובמחשבת ישראל : מוגשים לכבוד הרב מנחם עמנואל רקמן
בהגיעו לגבורות, ed. Moshe Beer (Ramat Gan: Bar-Ilan University, 1994), 121–41; Jordan
D. Rosenblum, *The Jewish Dietary Laws in the Ancient World* (New York: Cambridge
University Press, 2016), 22–4.

[5] See discussion of the "animal family" commandments in Jacob Milgrom, *Leviticus
1–16: A New Translation with Introduction and Commentary*, vol. 3, The Anchor Bible
(New York: Doubleday, 1991), 738–9; Milgrom, *Leviticus 17–22*, 3A:1883–5. See also
Noah J. Cohen, *Tsa'ar Ba'ale Hayim–The Prevention of Cruelty to Animals: Its Bases,
Development and Legislation in Hebrew Literature* (Washington, DC: Catholic University
of America Press, 1959), 76–101.

[6] On the project of explaining commandments, see Yonatan Yisrael Brafman, "Critical
Philosophy of Halakha (Jewish Law): The Justification of Halakhic Norms and Authority"
(PhD diss., Columbia University, 2014).

[7] Haran opts for this explanation and gives a brief survey of others who have; see
Menahem Haran, "Seething a Kid in Its Mother's Milk," *Journal of Jewish Studies* 30, no.
1 (1979): 29–30. For classical rabbinic traditions that take this route, see references in
Shyovitz, "'How Can the Guilty Eat the Innocent?'"

under her. The animal suffering imagined here is not physiological but emotional and relies on a presumption of fairly strong continuity between human and animal experience. Since we can imagine what we would feel like were our children torn away from us, we should not put the animal in such a position. But if animal suffering is the issue, the commandment does not seem to go far enough, as commentators have noted.[8] If the Bible's commandment is concerned with the avian mother's psychological distress and predicated on our empathy with her, why not prohibit taking her young in the first place? The other commandments that feature the parent-child bond among animals are even more resistant to being read in light of a concern with animal suffering. Surely cooking a kid in some other goat's mother's milk, or in water or oil, saves neither that mother nor that kid any suffering. The same can be said of slaughtering parent and child animals on different days.

Another common explanation of this prohibition, put forth by Maimonides and Nahmanides, is that it is virtue training.[9] The fifth of the Ten Commandments (Exodus 20:12; Deut. 5:16), "honor your father and your mother," promises prosperity and long life with the same language that the mother bird commandment does, suggesting that the commandments related to animal families might be designed to reinforce "family values." The philosophical tradition associated with Immanuel Kant explains cultivation of kindness to animals along these lines, as habituating people into proper treatment of other people.[10] According to this approach, the mother bird commandment is not concerned with animal suffering per se but with human socialization and moral education.

The practice of Sumatran hunters described by Jet Bakels in her anthropological work helps to grasp the paradox of a commandment that seems to want to avoid animal suffering at the same time as condoning it. The Sumatrans studied by Bakels show respect for the personhood of the animal at precisely the moment that they kill the animal: "Dear pig, do not feel angry because we now have to kill you ... please remember

---

[8] See criticism of the humanitarian explanation in Milgrom, *Leviticus 1–16*, 3:739.

[9] See Shyovitz, "'How Can the Guilty Eat the Innocent?'" and references there, which include Kasher, "Animals as Moral Patients in Maimonides' Teachings"; Roslyn Weiss, "Maimonides on 'Shilluaḥ Ha-Qen,'" *Jewish Quarterly Review* 79, no. 4 (1989): 345–66.

[10] For a brief discussion of this tradition, see Calarco, *Thinking Through Animals*, 10. For more detailed treatment of Kant's animal ethics, see Christine M. Korsgaard, "Interacting with Animals: A Kantian Account," in *The Oxford Handbook of Animal Ethics*, ed. Tom L. Beauchamp and Raymond Gillespie Frey (New York: Oxford University Press, 2011), 91–118.

how well we fed you all your life."[11] The Sumatrans' apologetic slaughter suggests that the paradoxes surrounding animal suffering apparent in the biblical laws may be widespread, cross-cultural, and deeply rooted. A perspective on animal suffering that is less tied to rational logic and more amenable to paradox, that tries to tangle with what has been called the schizophrenia in human relationships with other species, can countenance the simultaneous avoidance and infliction of animal suffering in the mother-bird commandment and in the other animal-related commandments of Jewish scriptural traditions.[12]

The argument of this chapter is that the Babylonian Talmud offers such a perspective in the classic talmudic treatment of animal suffering on Bava Metzia 32a–33a. The case addressed by this passage is a donkey struggling underneath his burden (Exodus 23:5; Deuteronomy 22:4). Like the raccoon stuck in the wall – Is it pet or pest? Cute critter or nasty intruder? – the burdened pack animal is subject to double viewing. The pack animal on the one hand evokes empathy, since everyone knows what it feels like to be too tired to continue with a difficult task. On the other hand, he or she may be viewed as little more than the iron-age version of a pick-up truck broken down by the side of the road. The Talmud plays with the double character of the burdened animal so as to highlight the contradictions regarding animal suffering in the inherited sources. The suffering animal in this situation could not be more clearly in view, even more so than it was for Will and Malya, who could hear but not see the helpless raccoon. But is the suffering of the animal really the problem, asks the Talmud? To what extent does animal suffering – in this scenario where an animal is, to all eyes, doing just that – matter at all? Are the Bible and the Mishnah in fact concerned with that suffering? These are the questions posed by the talmudic commentary.

This chapter frames the talmudic commentary with the work of Peter Singer and his critics. I consider the insufficiencies in Singer's rationalist utilitarianism that have been pointed out especially by his feminist readers. I rely upon that feminist critique as I read the talmudic back-and-forth. I first discuss the biblical and early rabbinic material on which the talmudic back-and-forth is based, considering whether animal

---

[11] Jet Bakels, "Animals as Persons in Sumatra," in *The Politics of Species: Reshaping Our Relationships with Other Animals*, ed. Raymond Corbey and Annette Lanjouw (New York: Cambridge University Press, 2013), 158. See my discussion of Bakels also in Chapter 6.

[12] On the term schizophrenia applied to human-animal relationships, see n. 71, Chapter 6.

suffering motivates the early legislations. I then cover highlights of the talmudic commentary, which offers several testing grounds for the concern for animal suffering: the financial interests of the Jewish animal owner, the relationship of the Jewish animal owner to non-Jews, and the relationship of the Jewish animal owner to fellow Jews. These testing grounds feature the major forces that the Talmud understands to compete with or eclipse a concern for animal suffering. My goal is to show how in the eyes of the Talmud, and still for us, animal suffering can seem urgent, it can exert a powerful demand, yet at the same time, when looked at in the same events with the same eyes, can also seem trivial or invisible.

PETER SINGER AND HIS CRITICS

Animal suffering was at the heart of Peter Singer's 1975 *Animal Liberation*. Animal suffering was the thing that allowed one to speak of animals as having interests that could be recognized, and the thing that the animal liberation movement could dedicate itself to minimizing. Animals might not be able to voice or reflect upon their suffering in the same way that human beings do, but they could experience it in a way that, in Singer's example of a schoolboy kicking a rock, the rock cannot. Singer brought new prominence to a line from the utilitarian philosopher Jeremy Bentham: "… The question is not, Can they reason? nor, Can they talk? but, Can they suffer?"[13]

Some of the problems in Singer's arguments are apparent already in the line he cites from Bentham, which implies that despite the fact that animals can neither reason nor talk, their suffering qualifies them for equal consideration (which Singer distinguishes from equal treatment – granting a pig's interest in being cage-free makes sense in a way that granting a pig the right to vote does not). Ethologist pioneers like Jane Goodall, Marc Bekoff, and Frans de Waal (see discussion in Chapter 1), now joined by many a Nova special and Animal Planet, reveal that animals exercise a great deal of reason and speech if reason and speech are expanded to include the kinds that other species are capable of. Other species are in fact much better than human beings at certain forms of communication or processing. The question is no longer "Can they suffer?" but, rather, how could anyone have ever thought that they did not.

[13] Peter Singer, *Animal Liberation: The Definitive Classic of the Animal Movement* (New York: Ecco, 2009), 7.

For animal liberationist thinkers today, the question is neither can they suffer, nor can they reason, nor can they talk, but does how the fact that animals can clearly do all these things shape the moral claims that they make.

More recent philosophers correct the problems in Singer's utilitarianism or question its utilitarian premise altogether.[14] Tom Regan's rights-based approach, or Martha Nussbaum's orientation toward "capabilities," offer alternatives to utilitarianism as a philosophical ground for animal liberation.[15] Other thinkers inspired by Freudianism and feminism advocate modifying the rationalist framework to give greater attention to affective, irrational, and unconscious forces.[16] Instead of asking in Singer-like style – if we must choose to kill a "retarded" human baby or a brilliant border collie, whom should we choose? – let us ask what makes it hard or easy for us to kill either one, and why we are posing such an unsettling question to begin with. Cora Diamond asks why, if by all philosophical accounts a vegetarian is justified in eating a cow struck by lightning, would many vegetarians still not eat that steak?[17] Because, Diamond observes, drawing upon children's ditties and poems rather than Bentham or other philosophical tracts, a vegetarian may think of

---

[14] Frey argues that Singer's approach is deficient in utilitarian rigor; see Raymond Gillespie Frey, "Utilitarianism and Animals," in *The Oxford Handbook of Animal Ethics*, ed. Tom L. Beauchamp and Raymond Gillespie Frey (New York: Oxford University Press, 2011), 172–97. Visak takes up probably the most controversial part of Singer's argument, that husbandry and slaughter that treats animals well while they are alive is morally justified: Tatjana Višak, *Killing Happy Animals: Explorations in Utilitarian Ethics* (Basingstoke, Hampshire: Palgrave Macmillan, 2013). Palmer extends Singer's discussion of suffering to cases of "wild" animals, asking whether people have an obligation to mitigate, avoid, or prevent the suffering of animals over whom human beings do not exercise direct control: Clare Palmer, *Animal Ethics in Context: A Relational Approach* (New York: Columbia University Press, 2010).

[15] Non- or anti-utilitarian approaches to animal rights include Tom Regan, *Defending Animal Rights* (Urbana: University of Illinois Press, 2001); Regan, *The Case for Animal Rights*; Martha Craven Nussbaum, "The Moral Status of Animals," in *Animal Rights: Current Debates and New Directions*, ed. Martha Craven Nussbaum and Cass R. Sunstein (New York: Oxford University Press, 2004), 30–6; Martha Craven Nussbaum and Cass R. Sunstein, eds., *Animal Rights: Current Debates and New Directions* (New York: Oxford University Press, 2004); Martha Craven Nussbaum, *Frontiers of Justice: Disability, Nationality, Species Membership* (London: Belknap, 2007).

[16] On the feminist critique of logocentrism, see Calarco, *Thinking Through Animals*, 22–3.

[17] Cora Diamond, "Eating Meat and Eating People," in *Animal Rights: Current Debates and New Directions*, ed. Martha Craven Nussbaum and Cass R. Sunstein (New York: Oxford University Press, 2004), 96. For a discussion of eating animals (and other sorts of things, including other people) from a feminist sociological perspective, see Elspeth Probyn, *Carnal Appetites: FoodSexIdentities* (New York: Routledge, 2003).

that cow as a "fellow creature."[18] A vegetarian would no more think of eating that cow than they would their aunt. Feminist care philosophy criticizes the classic analytic tradition for its demotion of affective forces, which are frequently associated pejoratively with the feminine and kept outside the realm of the ethical and political.[19] Feminist animal ethicists tend to get personal and talk about their own experiences with individual animals (and sometimes to thank those animals in their acknowledgments), at the same time that they take note of the larger structures of domination that shape the most intimate of relationships.

A different critique of Singer comes from theology and religious studies. Singer's *Animal Liberation* portrays western religion as responsible for much of animal suffering.[20] One need not be an apologist for western religions to point out – as Peter Singer himself does in subsequent work – that

[18] On the "literary turn" among Anglo-American animal ethicists, see Tzachi Zamir, "Literary Works and Animal Ethics," in *The Oxford Handbook of Animal Ethics*, ed. Tom L. Beauchamp and Raymond Gillespie Frey (New York: Oxford University Press, 2011), 932–56.

[19] On the feminist ethic of care as it applies to animals, see Carol J. Adams and Lori Gruen, eds., *Ecofeminism: Feminist Intersections with Other Animals and the Earth* (New York: Bloomsbury Publishing USA, 2014); Donovan and Adams, *The Feminist Care Tradition in Animal Ethics*. I am associating this orientation with feminism but one can see the emphasis on affect in many animal ethics works – for instance, Michael Allen Fox and Lesley McLean, "Animals in Moral Space," in *Animal Subjects: An Ethical Reader in a Posthuman World*, ed. Jodey Castricano (Waterloo, ON: Wilfrid Laurier University Press, 2008), 145–75; Kathy Rudy, *Loving Animals: Toward a New Animal Advocacy* (Minneapolis: University of Minnesota Press, 2011).

Singer says outright that animal ethics is not about experiencing emotions but about being logically consistent. In the preface to his original 1975 edition, Singer offers an anecdote about a woman who invited him and his wife over for lunch in order to talk about animals; Singer, *Animal Liberation*, xx–xxi. As she served them ham sandwiches, she asked Singer and his wife whether they owned pets and expressed great surprise when told that they did not: "But you are interested in animals, aren't you, Mr. Singer?" Singer speaks dismissively of the woman's inconsistency and sentimentality.

The dismissal of emotion and elevation of rationality continues in, for example, Andrew Linzey, *Why Animal Suffering Matters: Philosophy, Theology, and Practical Ethics* (New York: Oxford University Press, 2009), 6–7, in the final section of the preface, which is called "Towards Impartiality." This is faced on the opposite page by the title of Part I, which is "Making the Rational Case." Linzey says on page 3:

While not decrying the importance of emotional reactions, I judge them insufficient to determine the rightness or wrongness of a given action. Feelings are often good in themselves and much to be emulated in some regards, but the assumption that mere feeling ("love of animals") does the case for animals justice must be jettisoned absolutely.

[20] Singer's treatment of Hebrew scriptures claims to represent its "basic position," but he dedicates to the matter no more than a paragraph (Singer, *Animal Liberation*, 188.).

some Abrahamic traditions are sensitive to animal suffering.[21] Recent religious studies work points out, moreover, that the positive/negative binarizing of religious traditions misses the complexity of those traditions. The talmudic tale of Judah the Patriarch taking pity on a family of weasels is a case in point:

The sufferings of Rabbi Elazar ben Rabbi Shimon were preferable to those of Rabbi, for those of Rabbi Elazar ben Rabbi Shimon came through love and left through love, [while those] of Rabbi came through an incident and left through an incident.

"Came through an incident" – what was it?

There was a calf[22] that was being brought to slaughter. He went and hung[23] his head in Rabbi's lap and cried.

He said to him, "Go![24] For this you were created."

They say: Since he had no compassion, let sufferings come upon him.[25]

"And left through an incident" –[26]

One day Rabbi's slavewoman was sweeping the house. She cast aside[27] the children of a weasel and was sweeping them.

He said to her, "Leave them alone! It is written,[28] 'His compassion is over all his creatures' (Psalms 145:9)."

They say: Since he had compassion, let us be[29] compassionate to him.[30]

---

[21] For subsequent discussion from Singer on religion and animal liberation that takes a subtler approach, see Peter Singer, "Animal Protection and the Problem of Religion," in *A Communion of Subjects: Animals in Religion, Science, and Ethics*, ed. Paul Waldau and Kimberley Patton (New York: Columbia University Press, 2006), 616–28.

[22] In some manuscripts: "There was a calf *in the house of Rabbi* that was being brought to slaughter."

[23] In one manuscript: "He went and folded his head into Rabbi's lap and cried." Another manuscript: "He went before him and buried his head in Rabbi's lap" (the crying is omitted).

[24] "Go" is missing in one version.

[25] In some versions, this sentence is abridged, and "They say: 'Since he had no compassion ...'" is absent. This version does not thematize compassion and also does not feature the anonymous "they" pronouncing Rabbi's fate.

[26] In some manuscripts, the symmetry is complete, with the Talmud asking, as before: "What was it?"

[27] Some manuscripts: "There were some children of a weasel living there (*shari* instead of *shadi*), and she was sweeping them."

[28] "It is written" is absent in some versions.

[29] Most other versions have *rahamu* ("be compassionate").

[30] Bava Metzia 85a (text from standard printed edition). In some versions, this last line is absent, and instead it says: "His sufferings left him." One manuscript uses the same verb, "leave alone," to describe Rabbi's sufferings, that Rabbi himself used in his comment to the slavewoman.

See my discussion of this text, with Marion Katz, in Beth A. Berkowitz and Marion Katz, "The Cowering Calf and the Thirsty Dog: Narrating and Legislating Kindness to Animals

יסורי דר' אלעזר בר' שמעון עדיפי מדרבי דאילו ר"א בר"ש מאהבה באו ומאהבה הלכו דרבי ע"י
מעשה באו וע"י מעשה הלכו

ע"י מעשה באו מאי היא

דההוא עגלא דהוו קא ממטו ליה לשחיטה אזל תלא לרישיה בכנפיה דרבי וקא בכי

אמר ליה זיל לכך נוצרת

אמרי הואיל ולא קא מרחם ליתו עליה יסורין

וע"י מעשה הלכו

יומא חד הוה קא כנשא אמתיה דרבי ביתא הוה שדיא בני כרכושתא וקא כנשא להו

אמר לה שבקינהו כתיב ורחמיו על כל מעשיו

אמרי הואיל ומרחם נרחם עליה

Judah the Patriarch is known as perhaps the most prominent of the founding fathers of rabbinic Judaism because of his status, wealth, and influence as a patriarch representing the Jews of Palestine to its Roman rulers, and because of his putative role in editing the Mishnah. The routines of animal slaughter are problematized by this story, and compassion is introduced as the antidote to suffering, the suffering of the animals and of Judah the Patriarch himself. Only after Judah learns the importance of attending to animal suffering is his own suffering relieved.

The story invites contrast between its two halves. In the first half, Judah the Patriarch comes across as heartless when he ignores the cries of the calf who seeks refuge in the folds of his clothing. In the second half, Judah takes pity on animals who are basically pests that any good exterminator – like the slavewoman doing her job – would remove. In the first half, Judah quotes a teaching in Mishnah Avot 2:9: "If you

in Jewish and Islamic Texts," in *Islamic and Jewish Legal Reasoning: Encountering Our Legal Other*, ed. Anver M. Emon (London: Oneworld, 2016), 61–111.

Parallels to the story can be found in Palestinian Talmud Kilayim 9:4 (32b), Ketubbot 12:2 (35a), and Genesis Rabbah 33:1 (Theodor-Albeck edition). Key differences between the Babylonian Talmud's version and those in the Palestinian Talmud and Genesis Rabbah include: Rabbi is studying Torah before the Babylonian synagogue in Sepphoris when the calf approaches him (GR); the calf seems to speak to Rabbi, pleading to be saved (GR) or lowing (PT), while in the BT he hides in the folds of Rabbi's cloak; Rabbi seems more sympathetic to the calf, asking "What can I do for you?" (GR); Rabbi's sufferings are more specific – he has a toothache for thirteen years – and women in that period of time are described as not suffering the normal pain of childbirth and miscarriage (GR); the last part of the story involves Rabbi's daughter (GR) or unnamed figures (PT) rather than a slave girl, and a generic pest (*sheretz*) (GR) or nest of mice (PT) rather than a family of weasels; she is poised to kill the animal (GR and PT) rather than sweep them away; the setting is not specific to Rabbi's house as it is in BT. Overall, the distinctive elements of the Babylonian Talmud's version, especially when compared to the Genesis Rabbah version, make the Babylonian Talmud's telling more of a domestic drama, set in Rabbi's household and with consequences only for that household, with more of a transformation in Rabbi from the first part of the story to the second, and with the calf a less active but more pitiful figure.

have learned much Torah, do not take it as merit for yourself, since *for this you were created*." While the original phrase in Mishnah Avot 2:8 teaches humility for the Torah scholar, Judah twists its meaning to justify his cruelty. In the second half, Judah cites a biblical verse, Psalm 145:9, in praise of God's kingship, now acknowledging the true source of power – God – and showing appropriate humility. Later that same psalm describes "all flesh" (Verse 21) praising God. These contrasts between the first and the second half of the story dramatize the character change that Judah the Patriarch undergoes in his relationship to animals.

The story, on one level, argues for the importance of showing compassion to animals, and one can understand why it is a favorite of Jewish vegetarians.[31] But upon closer inspection, the moral of the story is not so clear. Judah the Patriarch moves from one extreme to the other in the course of the story, from cold dismissal of an almost humanized lamb, to welcoming embrace of the pests that live in the corner of his home. Neither of these postures seems all that viable or compelling for the "average person," which surely Judah the Patriarch is not anyway intended to represent. One guesses that the story does not mean to argue for an end to animal slaughter or to extermination of pests, yet it seems to critique those behaviors even while perhaps ultimately reinforcing them, the "I'm sorry" said to the pig (here, calf) before killing him. The story shows, when read with Singer and his critics, that responses to animal suffering are not reducible to a single stance. Analytic logic, affective bonds, structures of domination, and religion all play a role. This is an insight that the Babylonian Talmud will furnish as its editors discuss the biblical and early rabbinic traditions to which I now turn.

THE RESTING DONKEY (EXODUS 23:5) AND THE EXHAUSTED OX (DEUTERONOMY 22:4)

Exodus 23:5 appears to require a person to assist his enemy if he should come across him on the road in need of assistance:

When you see the ass of your enemy lying under its burden and would refrain from raising it, you must nevertheless raise it with him.

כִּי-תִרְאֶה חֲמוֹר שֹׂנַאֲךָ רֹבֵץ תַּחַת מַשָּׂאוֹ וְחָדַלְתָּ מֵעֲזֹב לוֹ עָזֹב תַּעֲזֹב עִמּוֹ.

[31] On this story, see David Charles Kraemer, *Responses to Suffering in Classical Rabbinic Literature* (New York: Oxford University Press, 1994), 108; Gross, *The Question of the Animal and Religion*, 167–71; Rosenblum, *The Jewish Dietary Laws in the Ancient World*, 109–10.

One might picture a man who happens upon a neighbor with whom he has had some spat, and that neighbor's donkey has collapsed underneath his cargo. The question facing the man is: Help out, or ignore the neighbor's plight, given the bad blood that exists between them. The verse says – Do not ignore him. Help out, and put aside the grudge.

That understanding runs according to the Jewish Publication Society (JPS) translation, but JPS is forced to fudge a few things to get there.[32] The verb associated with the enemy's ass, *rovetz*, is understood by JPS to refer to the donkey "lying" or struggling beneath his load ("the ass of your enemy lying under its burden"), but the semantic range of the verb – it is the same verb used to describe the mother bird roosting in her nest in the mother-bird commandment – suggests that the donkey is merely taking a rest.[33] A still more problematic translation is "raise" to describe the core instruction of the verse, *azov* ("you must nevertheless raise it with him"). JPS relies on a rare usage in Nehemiah and a parallel in Ugaritic or, alternatively, on an amendation that changes *a-z-v* to the similar *a-z-r*, which refers to assistance or help. Normally *a-z-v* refers to leaving, however, not assisting (which in this case entails raising). JPS also is forced to supply a direct object for the verb, "you must nevertheless raise *it* with him," and to ignore the befuddling shift in preposition from the *lamed* of the previous clause (*azov lo*, "raising it") to *im* (*azov ta'azov imo*, "raise it with him") in the closing clause.

With these problems in mind, Alan Cooper suggests that the root *a-z-v* be read in the more typical way, as referring to leaving rather than raising, and that the addressee is being instructed not to *help* but to *walk on*:[34]

When you see the ass of your enemy lying under his burden and would refrain from leaving it/him, you must nevertheless leave [with] it/him.

According to this reading, the verse features a true sworn enemy against whom the passerby wishes harm, and a donkey merely taking a break. When the addressee happens upon the donkey, he is tempted to take advantage of the donkey's resting state and to grab either his enemy's

[32] Marc Zvi Brettler and Adele Berlin, eds., *The Jewish Study Bible: Featuring the Jewish Publication Society Tanakh Translation* (New York: Oxford University Press, 2004).

[33] See the entry for *r-v-tz* in Francis Brown, *The Brown, Driver, Briggs Hebrew and English Lexicon: With an Appendix Containing the Biblical Aramaic: Coded with the Numbering System from Strong's Exhaustive Concordance of the Bible* (Peabody, MA: Hendrickson, 1996). The root is translated there as "stretch oneself out, lie down, lie stretched out."

[34] Alan Cooper, "The Plain Sense of Exodus 23:5," *Hebrew Union College Annual* 59 (1988): 1–22.

donkey or the cargo atop the donkey or, worse, to assault the man, assuming he is nearby. The verse is intervening to say: Leave him, his donkey, and his cargo well enough alone. This understanding not only solves the problem of *a-z-v*'s usage but also avoids reading Exodus through a Christianizing lens according to which people are being instructed, in effect, to turn the other cheek. The lesson in Exodus is not to be nice to a person whom one despises, argues Cooper, but to hold oneself back from theft or assault and battery.

This reading raises other problems, however, such as what the verse means at the end when it instructs the person to "leave *with* it/him." Cooper suggests that the verse is instructing the man to leave the cargo with the donkey – "leave [it, the cargo] with him" – but this requires reading a direct object into the verse. These cruxes must have been the motivation for Deuteronomy to clarify the scenario.[35] According to Deuteronomy 22:4's version, the animal is clearly stuck rather than resting, and the addressee is being instructed to help:

You shall not see your fellow's ass or ox fallen on the road and ignore them; you must surely raise up with him.

לֹא-תִרְאֶה אֶת-חֲמוֹר אָחִיךָ אוֹ שׁוֹרוֹ נֹפְלִים בַּדֶּרֶךְ וְהִתְעַלַּמְתָּ מֵהֶם הָקֵם תָּקִים עִמּוֹ.

In Deuteronomy's reformulation, the verb associated with the animal is *noflim* ("fallen") rather than *rovetz* ("lying"), making clear that the animal is in distress. The final verb is *haqem taqim* ("raise up"), which, unlike *azov ta'azov*, refers indisputably to helping. The prepositional phrase *imo* ("with him"), which is the last word in both the Exodus and Deuteronomy verses, plays an unambiguous role in Deuteronomy, where one visualizes the addressee generously cooperating with his fellow.

Deuteronomy creates its own new ambiguities, however. Are the two men working together to raise up the animal or the load? One would think the animal, since no load is mentioned in Deuteronomy's formulation. Deuteronomy's expansion of the scenario from only a donkey – the standard pack animal – to include the ox – the standard work animal – suggests that the scenario in Deuteronomy need involve no load at all. The likely reading, then, is that the two men raise the animal back up to his feet. If one reads Deuteronomy with the assumptions of Exodus in place, however, as the Rabbis will, one

---

[35] On Deuteronomy's reworkings of Exodus, see Bernard M. Levinson, *Deuteronomy and the Hermeneutics of Legal Innovation* (New York: Oxford University Press, 1997).

would understand the Deuteronomy verse instead as an instruction to help raise the cargo, with the animal expected to scramble back up to his feet on his own. Deuteronomy is more straightforward than Exodus also regarding what *not* to do. Deuteronomy unequivocally commands the addressee not to "ignore them" (*ve-hitalamta mehem*), while Exodus hypothesizes an addressee tempted to "refrain from raising it" (*ve-hadalta me-azov lo*). Deuteronomy's shift from enemy to friend similarly helps clarify the intent of the verse, which is to require a person to go out of his way to assist a fellow in need. Deuteronomy's impulse to clarify Exodus begins already in the first word, the imperative "you shall not see" (*lo tireh*), rather than the Exodus verse's casuistic "when you see" (*ki tireh*).

Is there animal suffering in these verses? Could the donkey or ox be just as easily replaced with a tractor and the verses would carry the same essential message? Could the person himself have stopped on the road, to take a nap, or having sprained his ankle? Because Exodus 23:5 is a more ambiguous verse overall, it is difficult to determine the role of the animal within it. If Cooper is correct that the command of the verse is, in effect, "do not steal from your enemy or commit assault and battery against him when given a good opportunity to do so," then animal suffering does not feature in the scenario at all, and the addressee is meant to assist neither the person nor the animal. The animal is present not because he is suffering or requires assistance, but only because he makes his owner vulnerable to attack by anchoring him to a particular location and tempting the enemy with a valuable cargo ripe for theft. In updating the scenario, one could replace the animal with an expensive car loaded up with purchases and still maintain the spirit of the verse. This reading accords with the broader concern of Exodus 23 to prevent injustice, especially toward tempting targets like the poor, or in tempting situations like this one.

The animal plays a less replaceable role in Deuteronomy. The inclusion of the ox in addition to the donkey and the absence of cargo suggest that the animal is not strictly a vehicle that an owner would wish not to have stolen from him or to be forced to abandon. Other features of the Deuteronomy verse also suggest that the creatureliness of the animal is integral to the scenario: the verb *noflim* ("fallen") used to describe the condition of the animal; the instruction not to ignore "them," the person and the animal; the replacement of "your enemy" with "your brother," which might be making the point that one is obligated to help not only one's brother but even one's brother's animal. One should not draw the conclusion, however, that animal suffering is the Deuteronomy verse's main concern. The main concern is incontrovertibly the relationship between the two men. The final word of the verse speaks to that relationship: "raise up *with him.*" The animal in the Deuteronomy verse is not utterly fungible as he seems to be in the Exodus verse, but neither is he irreplaceable.

MISHNAH BAVA METZIA 2:10: SADISTIC, SICK, AND ELDERLY DONKEY DRIVERS

The Mishnah does not follow Alan Cooper's reading of the Exodus verse in which the donkey is a tempting target ("Walk on!") but instead presumes the JPS translation of a donkey in distress ("Stop and help!"):

One unloaded [the animal] and reloaded, one unloaded and reloaded, even four or five times, one is [still] obligated [to help unload again], as it is said, "You must nevertheless raise [it]" (Exodus 23:5).

He (the animal owner) went and sat himself down [and] said to him, "Since the commandment is upon you, if you want[36] to unload, unload" – one is exempt, as it is said, "with him" (Exodus 23:5). [If] he (the animal owner) was old or sick, one is obligated.

It is a commandment from the Torah to unload, but not to load.

Rabbi Shimon says: Even to load.

Rabbi Yose the Galilean says: [If] there was upon him (the animal) more than his [appropriate] burden, one is not bound with respect to him – as it is said, "under his burden" (Exodus 23:5) – a burden that he is able to withstand.[37]

פרק וטען פרק וטען אפילו ארבעה וחמשה פעמים חייב שנ' עזוב תעזוב

הלך וישב לו אמ לו הואיל ועליך מצוה אם רציתה לפרוק פרוק פטור שנ עמו היה זקן או חולה חייב

מצוה מן התורה לפרוק אבל לא לטעון

ר שמעון אומ אף לטעון

ר יוסה הגלילי או היה עליו יתר ממסואו אינו זקוק לו שנ תחת מסאו מסוי שהוא יכול לעמוד בו

This mishnah has a peculiar structure. The section reads like legal midrash but does not follow the sequence of the Exodus verse, since it starts with the end of the verse and ends with the beginning. The Deuteronomy verse is not mentioned at all. One would expect the general statement about the commandment ("It is a commandment from the Torah to unload ...") to come first or last but not to be sandwiched in the middle

---

[36] Printed edition: "If your wish (*retzonakh*) is to unload ..."
[37] Text from the Kaufmann manuscript.

of the somewhat unusual situations that the laws depict. The overall placement of the material is also puzzling, since it is itself sandwiched in the middle of a discussion of lost objects.[38]

A number of rulings can be distilled from this mishnah:

1. One must repeatedly fulfill the obligation to unload the animal if need be.
2. One is exempt from the obligation if the owner of the animal does not himself makes reasonable efforts.
3. All authorities agree on a fundamental scriptural obligation to unload, but they disagree over whether loading is also a scriptural obligation.
4. According to one authority (Yose the Galilean), one is exempt from the obligation (to unload, presumably) if the owner has placed upon the animal an unreasonably heavy load.

This mishnah's aim seems to be a mutually satisfying and socially constructive cooperation between the two men caught in this situation. The man called upon to assist must do so repeatedly. The man requiring assistance must himself make good-faith efforts and must not land himself in this situation through his own bad judgment or greed. By raising these possibilities, the Mishnah seems bent on assuring the person giving the assistance that his generosity will not be exploited, and the person given the assistance that he will receive as much as he needs.

The securing of trust between the two men comes at the expense of the animal in a couple of the cases. The repeated help required by Ruling 1 would benefit the animal, but if the owner is lazy as he is in Ruling 2, the animal suffers for it, since the owner's cavalier attitude means that his animal does not receive assistance. Ruling 4 is similar in that the owner who has loaded too much cargo onto the animal ends up depriving the animal of aid, according to Yose the Galilean. That animal is in fact the one who needs help the most, yet the passerby is not obligated to help and is possibly even discouraged from doing so, presumably because it would undermine the cooperative spirit that this set of laws is meant to foster.

The role of animal suffering is more difficult to sort out with respect to Ruling 3: "It is a commandment from the Torah to unload, but not

---

[38] The topics are coupled together in both Exodus and Deuteronomy, but that does not explain why the topic of fallen pack animals is featured as an interruption of the discussion of lost objects.

to load. Rabbi Shimon says: Even to load."[39] This ruling differentiates
the status of loading from unloading and will suggest to its talmudic
interpreters that the Mishnah possesses a concern for animal suffering,
since the requirement to unload the animal presumes that harm will

[39] This ruling clearly involves some disagreement over scripture, but it hard to say defini-
tively what is the nature of the disagreement. The Tosefta features the same legislation
word-for-word but includes exegetical elaboration:

It is a commandment from the Torah to unload, but not to load.
Rabbi Shimon says: Even to load, as it is said, "with him."
"With him" – on the back of the donkey, the words of Rabbi Shimon.
And the Sages say: "with him" – you are, with a fee.

מצוה מן התורה לפרוק אבל לא לטעון
ר שמעון או אף לטעון שנ עמו
עמו על גבי החמור דברי ר שמעון
וחכמים או עמו אתה בשכר

Tosefta Bava Metzia 2:28; Saul Lieberman, ed., *Tosefta according to Codex Vienna*, vol.
The Order of Nezikin (New York: The Jewish Theological Seminary of America, 2001),
71–2. Rabbi Shimon would seem to be referring to the Deuteronomy verse, not the Exodus
one (both end with the word "with him," but midrash halakhah and talmudic commentaries point to Deuteronomy 22:4 as the lemma). Rabbi Shimon's interest is in resolving
the ambiguity in Deuteronomy 22:4's final instruction which, I mentioned earlier, could
be read as referring to the two men raising up either the animal (I see this as more plausible), or the load (Rabbi Shimon sees this as more plausible, probably because it resolves
the redundancy between the two verses). Rabbi Shimon thus understands Exodus 23:5 to
refer to unloading and Deuteronomy 22:4 to refer to this reloading, a position that appears
repeatedly in the Mekhilta; see Horovitz and Rabin, *Mechilta d'Rabbi Ismael*, 326.
The Tosefta's presentation of the Sages' position is explained by the commentary
Hasdei David (authored by David Samuel ben Jacob Pardo, 1718–90) and, in his footsteps, Saul Lieberman, as permitting the passerby to ask for a fee for his services when he
loads. The passerby is obligated to help reload but need not do it for free. One can infer
that for Rabbi Shimon the passerby cannot ask for money; he must help for free.
This understanding of the Sages and Rabbi Shimon, which is adopted by standard
commentaries on the Mishnah, has one big problem as I see it, which is that it contradicts
the legislation it is intended to explain. One must read the Sages' position in the following way: "It is a commandment from the Torah to unload [for free], but not to load [for
free, though for a fee one is obligated]." According to this reading, the Tosefta's claim is
that when the Sages said "commandment from the Torah," they meant it in a Kantian
sense in which one does the commandment purely for its own sake and not for reward.
Describing a behavior as a "commandment from the Torah" (*mitzvah min ha-Torah*) is
rare in early rabbinic texts, appearing in only one other place (Sifre Deuteronomy 166,
with reference to appointing a king), and its import is unclear, which may help to explain
why the commentators read the line counter-intuitively. The main motivation for this
reading is likely to harmonize the Sages' position with the positions found in midrash
halakhah, all of which claim loading to be a scriptural obligation.
It makes more sense, however, to understand the Sages in the Tosefta to be reading
Deuteronomy 22:4 as a reference to unloading (like Exodus 23:5), with loading entirely
absent from the Torah in the Sages' view. Deuteronomy 22:4's legislative contribution, in

otherwise befall him in a way that the requirement to load the animal does not. If the animal is struggling under the weight of his cargo, he might sustain injury or even die. Reloading, by contrast, is a pressing need of the animal owner but not of the animal himself, who if anything might prefer a little extra time unsaddled. All that being the case, might not the Sages' privileging of unloading over reloading suggest that they believe Scripture to evince a concern for animal suffering and, taking this possibility a step further, for that concern to be at the core of this entire set of legislations?

I would say, with some assurance – no. First, the exclusion of loading from the Torah's sphere of command exists only in the Mishnah and Tosefta and not in the Mekhilta, where loading is considered to be at least derived through logic from scripture and at most explicit in scripture. Second, while it is not impossible to see animal suffering at stake in these rulings, there is still no reason to think that animal suffering is an independent concern that transcends the interpersonal stakes of the commandment. As the Talmud will point out, animal suffering and human loss are co-extensive in the case of a burdened pack animal. If the animal is injured under the burden of his load, the owner incurs damage to a valuable piece of property.[40] If one wants to determine whether mitigation of animal suffering is the driving force behind the commandment, one would need a test case in which the animal's welfare is at odds with either the material flourishing of the owner or the desired relationship between owner and passerby. In fact, the Mishnah already has that. The other rulings in this mishnah are all too tolerant of animal suffering when helping to alleviate it contravenes the interpersonal aims of the commandment.

Finally, it is doubtful that avoidance of even human suffering is the motivation for Ruling 3. The chief motivation for the Sages' preference for unloading may well be the maddening relationship between the Exodus and Deuteronomy passages. When the Sages say, "It is a commandment from the Torah to unload, but not to load," they could be taken at face

---

the Sages' view, is to permit the taking of a fee for assisting in unloading should one be forced to take off from other productive activities while one is engaged in this commandment. The Tosefta's representation of the Sages' position, according to this approach, is: "It is a commandment from the Torah to unload, but not to load. If so, what is the unique teaching of Deuteronomy 22:4, since the commandment to unload is already found in Exodus 23:5? Deuteronomy 22:4 permits a person under certain circumstances to demand a fee for helping to unload."

40 As Rashi points out, s.v., *"periqah it bah hesron kis."*

value to be making an exegetical claim. Rabbi Shimon along with many other early rabbis understands Deuteronomy 22:4 to be obligating a passerby to help reload the animal. But as noted earlier, Deuteronomy 22:4 does not mention a load at all. The Sages, who read both Exodus 23:5 and Deuteronomy 22:4 as a reference to unloading (though the Talmud understands their view differently – see footnote 39), offer a more natural reading of the verses. Their reading does violate one major principle of rabbinic exegesis, however, which is scriptural conservation of language. It is that problem of redundancy that likely led to the approach taken by Rabbi Shimon and the rabbis mentioned in the Mekhilta.

The Mishnah features a suffering animal, to be sure, but there is no moment when one can say that the animal's suffering makes any claim that goes beyond the person whom that suffering most affects. The larger set of interests in this section of the Mishnah, which deals with obligations generated by lost objects, reinforces the sense that the animal here is little more than an example of valuable property, along with the coins, food, clothing, utensils, and books that appear also in the chapter. Yet there are a couple laws in the Tosefta and Mekhilta that betray a glimmer of interest in the animal qua animal. One of those is in the Tosefta, when it links treatment of someone else's animal to treatment of one's own:

Just as is the commandment on his own animal, so too is the commandment on one's fellow's animal.[41]

וכשם שמצוה על בהמת עצמו כך מצוה על בהמת חבירו

In this section, the Tosefta is speaking of two animal-related commandments, and it is difficult to say whether this line refers to assisting with unloading an animal (*Hasdei David*'s reading), returning a lost animal (Lieberman's reading), or perhaps to all animal-related commandments. Whatever the referent may be, the Tosefta is speaking of some obligation that one has directly to an animal that does not seem to hinge on human interpersonal dynamics. If anything, the obligations that apply interpersonally are presented as secondary or derivative to the obligations that one has directly to one's own animal. *Hasdei David* proposes that the text is incorrect and reverses the order: "Just as is the commandment on one's fellow's animal, so too is the commandment on one's

[41] Tosefta Bava Metzia 2:12. Lieberman, *Tosefta*, The Order of Nezikin:72, note 71. See expanded commentary in Saul Lieberman, *Tosefta Ki-Fshuṭah: A Comprehensive Commentary on the Tosefta*, vol. Parts IX–X: Order Nezikin (New York: The Jewish Theological Seminary of America, 2001), 168.

own animal."[42] Lieberman likewise argues that the text is mistaken, a slip from a similar passage further on, and he also proposes that the word "commandment" is used atypically here to refer to habitual behavior rather than to formal legal obligation. Lieberman acknowledges, though, that the text is constant in all major versions of the Tosefta, both manuscript and printed. One wonders whether the idea of an independent obligation to one's animal is implausible to these later commentators but perhaps not so unthinkable to the ancient authors.

That thinkability is suggested also in the Mekhilta when it asks about an obligation to help the animal herself:

"You must raise with him" (Exodus 23:5). Why was it said? Since it says "Raise up with him" (Deut. 22:4), I have only unloading and reloading. An animal herself from where [do we know]? Scripture teaches, "Raise up with him" (Deut. 22:4).

עזוב תעזוב עמו למה נאמר לפי שהוא אומר הקם תקים עמו אין לי אלא פריקה וטעינה בהמה עצמה
מנין ת"ל הקם תקים עמו

The exegetical argument here seems circular, since the same phrase from scripture ("Raise up with him") both generates and resolves the question.[43] One suspects a textual error, but my interest is the passage's assumption that somewhere in scripture must be an obligation that applies directly to the animal herself. The same language of self (*behemah atzmah*, "the animal herself") is used in this passage as in the Tosefta (*behemat atzmo*, "his own animal") to raise the specter of a more direct relationship between person and animal.

RAVA'S REVOLUTION

One is sometimes tempted to read the history of interpretation as a comedy of errors, and Rava's claim in the Talmud about animal suffering is one such time (if suffering can be comic). That "error" begins with Deuteronomy 22:4's rewriting of Exodus 23:5. While Exodus 23:5 (read according to Cooper) features neither a person in need of assistance nor an animal suffering under his load, Deuteronomy 22:4 introduces both,

---

[42] *Hasdei David* understands the extension of obligations to someone else's animal to one's own animal as motivated by a concern with animal suffering.

[43] The version in Midrash Tannaim is only slightly less enigmatic:

"Raise up with him" (Deut. 22:4): "You must raise with him" (Exodus 23:5): I have only unloading and reloading. An animal herself from where [do we know]? Scripture teaches, "You must raise with him" (Exodus 23:5).

הקם תק עמו עזב תע' עמו אין לי אלא פריקה וטעינה בהמה עצמה מנ ת"ל עזב תע עמ

probably in the interests of greater clarity and out of a different ethical orientation. The Mishnah produces a second "error": the suffering animal "travels" from the second verse (Deut. 22:4) to the first (Exod. 23:5). Reading Exodus 23:5 through the lens of Deuteronomy 22:4, the Mishnah sees in Exodus 23:5 an animal struggling under his burden and in Deuteronomy 22:4 an animal who is ready for reloading.[44]

The next "error" is Rava's reading of the Mishnah, to which I now turn. According to a comment attributed to the Babylonian rabbi Rava, who was purported to have lived in the early fourth century CE, the dispute about these two verses that is featured in the Mishnah is a sign that scripture is concerned with animal suffering:

Rava said: From the words of both of them it can be learned: The suffering of living creatures is from the Torah.[45]

אמר רבא מדברי שניהם נלמד צער בעלי חיים דאורייתא

The language here, "from the words of both of them it can be learned," appears only two other times in the Babylonian Talmud, is attributed to Rava in all three cases though it has the hallmarks of the talmudic editors, and relies upon an opaque logic.[46] The idea seems to be that the combination of the two positions in the Mishnah yields some datum. I would venture to guess that Rava's logic hinges on an easily missed word in the Mishnah, "even" (*af*): "It is a commandment from the Torah to unload, but not to load. Rabbi Shimon says: *Even* to load." While Rabbi Shimon holds reloading (where no animal suffering is at stake) to be just as much of a scriptural obligation as unloading (where animal suffering is at stake), he still presents reloading as the less likely obligation ("*even* to load"). Even the disputant who holds that assistance where no animal suffering is entailed is just as scripturally mandated as assistance where animal suffering is entailed, concedes that it is a little bit surprising – a little less obvious – that assistance would be required

<hr>

[44] The Talmud reads the Sages as being in accordance with Rabbi Shimon in understanding Deut. 22:4 as an obligation to reload; see my note above on this complicated question.
[45] Bava Metzia 32a–b.
[46] Keritot 22b and Menahot 104b (the sentence may have originated in this second context, where the statement is all in Hebrew and begins the talmudic discussion of the Mishnah). Rava uses the same language in both these cases with respect to an extended dispute in the Mishnah between Rabbi Tarfon and Rabbi Akiva. In a parallel for Keritot in Zevahim 84a, the statement appears without *midivre shenehem* ("from the words of both of them"). Similar language appears once in Palestinian Talmud Peah 6:6 (19d), though the verb *nilmad* ("it can be learned") is added in the Leiden manuscript by a scribe.

where no animal suffering is involved. Thus does Rava infer that all early rabbinic parties take the Torah to evince a concern for animal suffering.

This reading strategy of Rava's is, in my view, radical, since, as I have discussed, the Mishnah hardly seems preoccupied with animal suffering. The very language of Rava's claim reflects its inventive character. Neither the biblical verses nor the Mishnah speak explicitly of distress of any sort, except perhaps in the verb *noflim* ("fallen") in Deuteronomy, which is at any rate a more physiological description than is Rava's *tza'ar* ("suffering"). "Suffering" is, by contrast, an emotion-laden and normally human term in the Babylonian Talmud.[47] Rava's term for animals, "possessors of life" (*ba'ale hayim*), is also distinctive, a largely Babylonian invention, used only once or twice in midrash halakhah and the Yerushalmi yet about twenty-five times in the Bavli.[48] Rava's complete phrase, literally "the suffering of possessors of life," normally and here translated as "animal suffering," is used in a number of other talmudic passages, always within redactional strata, to alternatively query, legitimate, or elaborate upon norms of behavior or a particular rabbi's practice with respect to animals.[49] Rava's declaration about animal suffering is, in sum, revolutionary, not only in his inferring it from a mishnah that is highly resistant to such a reading, but also in its very formulation and conceptualization,

---

[47] Shulamit Valer, *Sorrow and Distress in the Talmud*, trans. Sharon Blass (Boston: Academic Studies Press, 2011), 17–53, Chapter 1. The root is associated frequently not just with the human but with the distinctively rabbinic, such as with sages who experience emotional distress over their Torah study.

[48] Mishnah and Tosefta use the rich language of *davar she yesh bo ruah hayim* ("a thing that has within it the spirit of life").

[49] See Betzah 26a; Hullin 7b; Avodah Zarah 13a; Shabbat 117b, 154b. The contexts vary – transmission of impurity, Sabbath and festival observance, superstition of evil animals, counteracting idolatry – but "suffering" in all these cases refers either to the maiming or the starving of an animal (all belonging to the category of livestock). The phrase is used, on the one hand, to challenge behavior that flagrantly disregards the well-being of an animal, such as in Shabbat 154b, where Rabban Gamliel's donkey dies after Rabban Gamliel refuses to unload him; Avodah Zarah 13a, which refers to the purposeful disabling of an animal so that it will not be used for idolatry; and Hullin 7b, which also refers to purposeful maiming of an animal, in this case in a narrative in which white mules standing outside of Rabbi Judah the Patriarch's home are thought to be an evil omen. The phrase is used, on the other hand, to explain or justify some behavior or legislation that contravenes the expected norm, such as in Bava Batra 20a, where the Talmud explains why a person would not cut off an animal's already partially severed limb that is blocking the transmission of impurity from one room to another, or in Shabbat 128b, where the Talmud justifies Rav's override of the Sabbath prohibitions of *muktzeh* and *melakhah* in the event that an animal falls into a stream on the Sabbath.

which marks a watershed in rabbinic thinking regarding animals, suffering, and the capacity of the one for the other.[50]

The next set of "errors" belongs to the talmudic redactors, the Stammaim, in the long discussion that follows Rava's claim.[51] In that discussion, the redactors bring a series of early rabbinic traditions that alternately substantiate or rebut Rava's claim that animal suffering is a concern of scriptural status ("Know that animal suffering is a scriptural concern ..."; "Know that animal suffering is not a scriptural concern ..."; "In fact, animal suffering is a scriptural concern ..."). The manner in which the redactors choose to fill in the blanks is not what one would expect. The passage might have first launched a challenge from the biblical laws of animal sacrifice, which obligate a person to inflict animal suffering, and then the passage could have offered a rebuttal based on the biblical prohibition against muzzling an ox, which seems designed to prevent animal suffering.[52] The passage might have then gone back and forth between biblical laws that cause animal suffering and those laws that limit it. That is not the sort of dialectic the Talmud offers. The dialectic instead understands Rava to be making a much narrower claim about *this* commandment, that of the burdened pack animal.[53] All the proofs that appear in the dialectic relate to this scenario and this scenario only. One emerges from the dialectic with a fair sense of the role played by animal suffering in the early rabbinic laws treating the burdened pack animal, but with no sense of whether scripture more generally evinces a concern for animal suffering. While Rava would appear to be making a broad claim about scripture's treatment of animals, the redactors take him to be making a far more limited claim about this particular commandment.

The other error one might speak of at the level of the editors is the binary of *de-oraita* (scriptural status)/*de-rabbanan* (rabbinic status) that is

---

[50] The anomalous character of Rava's claim and heavily stammaitic character of the larger passage is likely why the Rif (Alfasi, Isaac of Fez, born 1013) in his codification of this passage omits the entire discussion about animal suffering, leaving just one short mention of it at the end of the section.

[51] Bava Metzia 32b–33a.

[52] While the animal threshed, they would normally have stopped to eat some of the grain. Some owners might have stopped the animal from doing so either to save grain or to maximize the animal's work time. "Deuteronomy forbids such pettiness"; see Jeffrey H. Tigay, *Deuteronomy = [Devarim]: The Traditional Hebrew Text with the New JPS Translation* (Philadelphia: Jewish Publication Society, 1996), 231.

[53] This is pointed out by Dov Linzer, "Tza'ar Ba'alei Chaim (Animal Suffering): A Case Study in Halakha and Values," in *Mishpetei Shalom: A Jubilee Volume in Honor of Rabbi Saul Berman*, ed. Yamin Levy (Riverdale, NY; Jersey City, NJ: Ktav, 2010), 4–5.

implicit in Rava's comment and that runs through the larger talmudic passage.[54] The activation of that binary is in fact misleading, because when the talmudic dialectic repeatedly considers whether animal suffering is *de-oraita* or *de-rabbanan*, what it really seems to be asking is whether animal suffering is a concern *at all*.[55] *De-rabbanan* becomes code for nonexistent, which is not, I would hazard to say, how that status is generally intended to operate within the Talmud.[56] The redactors treat Rava's claim as a rather crude one about whether animal suffering matters at all, and as a rather limited one about whether it matters *here*. The "error" of subsequent Talmud interpreters is in nevertheless treating this passage as the locus classicus within rabbinic literature for animal suffering.

THE TALMUD'S TESTING GROUNDS

In this closing section, I want to suggest that the redactors' choices, if not motivated by the wish to illustrate the "error" of Rava's ways, at least had the impact of doing so. In other words, the talmudic dialectic leads its reader to see the ingenuity of Rava's claim and, along with that, the difficulties of reading animal suffering back into the sources as Rava wishes to do. The passage accomplishes this by setting up several testing grounds for animal suffering: (1) financial loss to the Jewish animal owner; (2) relationships between Jewish animal owners or users and non-Jewish animal owners or users; (3) ethical self-cultivation. On each testing ground, the Talmud weighs whether animal suffering is determinative of early rabbinic teachings, discarded by them or, in a third option, whether it is impossible to tell where the early rabbinic teachings stand

---

54 Surprisingly, only once in the passage does the term *de-rabbanan* explicitly appear. Otherwise, the binary is presented as *de-oraita* versus "not *de-oraita*" (e.g., "Know that animal suffering is not *de-oraita*!" rather than "Know that animal suffering is *de-rabbanan*").

55 As the Tosafot observe with respect to the recurring question within the passage of whether one may ask for a wage for assisting with the other person's animal (s.v., *mikhlal*, on Bava Metzia 32b): "the entire passage presumes that if animal suffering is not of scriptural status, one is not obligated to assist him even with a wage." In other words, the passage presumes that if animal suffering is of *de-rabbanan* status, one is not obligated to do anything to relieve it.

56 The binary makes more sense in another talmudic context where the question of animal suffering surfaces, that of Rabban Gamliel's donkey on Shabbat 154b. In that passage animal suffering is a concern competing with other concerns such as Sabbath observance; see Joshua Cahan, "Tza'ar Ba'alei Ḥayim in the Marketplace of Values," *Conservative Judaism* 65, no. 4 (2014): 33–4. Even in that case, however, *de-rabbanan* seems synonymous with lacking legal significance.

on the question of animal suffering. That final possibility is ultimately, in my reading, the impression that the talmudic passage wishes to convey, but I will also consider other readings of the passage offered by Joshua Cahan, Dov Linzer, and Aaron Gross.

On the first testing ground, the talmudic dialectic shows itself to be unable to disentangle the animal owner's concern for his animal as property (i.e., the owner's economic interests) from the animal owner's concern for his animal qua animal (i.e., animal suffering):

And if [for] loading, where there is no financial loss, one is obligated, then unloading, where there is financial loss, [should not one be obligated] all the more so?

But is there no financial loss with loading? Are we not dealing with where he loses time from the marketplace in the meantime? Or, alternatively, thieves come and take everything he has with him?

ומה טעינה דלית בה חסרון כיס חייב פריקה דאית בה חסרון כיס לא כ"ש

וטעינה אין בה חסרון כיס מי לא עסקינן דאדהכי והכי בטיל משוקיה אי נמי אתו גנבי ושקלי כל מה דאיכא בהדיה

This section challenges Rava's inference from the Mishnah. Perhaps the Mishnah's preference for unloading over loading (in the sense that the Sages consider unloading but not loading to be a scriptural obligation) stems from the financial loss that the owner incurs when his animal sustains injury in the course of bearing her burden. The passage is pointing out that animal welfare and economic interests, when they converge, become indistinguishable. Who is to say whether the obligation to unload the animal stems from the one or the other? Why not assume that human interests are uppermost?

Why not indeed, retort the redactors. The dialectic retracts in the next step not by reasserting the moral significance of animal suffering but rather by admitting to the ubiquity of human economic interests. Unloading the animal simply entails a different kind of economic stress than loading does which, if delayed, causes the owner to lose valuable transaction time in the marketplace or to become a target for thieves. The passage proposes that human economic interests will always pervade human interactions with animals. The pervasiveness of property interests ironically frees the argument to return to the moral significance of animal suffering. If financial concerns are a factor in every interaction, then they cancel out and allow other kinds of concerns to become visible.[57]

[57] As the Ritba (Yom Tov ben Abraham Ishbili, Spain, 1250–1330) in his commentary says (s.v. *u-mehedrinan*): "That is to say that with respect to loading there is also financial

The second testing ground for animal suffering is the relationship between Jews and non-Jews:

Say that [the following early rabbinic teaching] supports him (Rava): The animal of a gentile – one must care for her like the animal of an Israelite. If you say, this is well if animal suffering is a scriptural concern, that is why one must care for her like the animal of an Israelite. But if you say that animal suffering is not a scriptural concern, why must one care for her like the animal of an Israelite? There [it is] because of enmity.

לימא מסייע ליה בהמת גוי מטפל בה כבהמת ישראל⁵⁸ אי אמרת בשלמא צער בעלי חיים דאורייתא
משום הכי מטפל בה כבהמת ישראל⁵⁹ אלא אי אמרת צער בעלי חיים לאו דאורייתא אמאי מטפל בה
כבהמת ישראל התם משום איבה

The early rabbinic teaching obligates a Jew to attend to a non-Jew's animal in the same way that he would attend to a fellow Jew's.⁶⁰ Of all the early rabbinic teachings featured in the talmudic discussion, this would seem to be the one that speaks most directly to a concern for the animal, propose the talmudic editors. Obligations to non-Jews are few and far between in rabbinic literature.⁶¹ If a rabbinic teaching requires a Jew to attend to a non-Jew's animal, then that obligation – so goes the Talmud's logic – must stem from a concern for the animal. It cannot be the non-Jewish human owner who is the object of concern.

The redactor handily refutes the evidence, however, with the oft-cited principle "because of enmity." One must help gentiles not because of any obligation toward them but because they might retaliate were they to get

---

loss, and the essence of the a fortiori argument that we formulated earlier (the Ritba refers here to an earlier segment of the dialectic that uses a similar a fortiori argument) is animal suffering, and this other matter [of financial loss] is *snifin be-alma* (merely a side issue)."

⁵⁸ See the parallel to this teaching in Tosefta Bava Metzia 2:27 and in Palestinian Talmud Bava Metzia 2:11 (8d).

⁵⁹ Escorial G-1-3, Hamburg 165, and Vatican 117 have missing "If you say, this is well if animal suffering is a scriptural concern, that is why one must care for her like the animal of an Israelite" and pick up immediately after the baraita with "But if you say that animal suffering is not a scriptural concern," which does not materially change the logical flow.

⁶⁰ The verb used, *metapel*, would seem more naturally to be referring to the care one must offer a lost animal while their owner seeks to recover them (see Tosefta Bava Metzia 2:23). The passage nevertheless considers the baraita to be relevant to the case of unloading.

⁶¹ On the "double standard" for Jew and non-Jew within early rabbinic law, see "Navigating the Anomalous: Non-Jews at the Intersection of Early Rabbinic Law and Narrative," in Steven D. Fraade, *Legal Fictions*, vol. 147, Supplements to the Journal for the Study of Judaism (Leiden: Brill, 2011), 345–64.

shabby treatment from Jews.[62] The requirement to help the gentile is thus shown to rebound back to the Jewish – not to mention, human – self. The Jewish self becomes even more central in the subsequent discussion (not cited here), which articulates the "suffering of Israel" as the grounds for action.[63] The expression that the Talmud uses, "because of the suffering of Israel" (*mishum tza'ara de-yisrael*), echoes, on the one hand, the earlier principle "because of enmity" (*mishum evah*) and, on the other hand, the main subject of the passage, "the suffering of animals" (*tza'ar ba'ale hayim*). The rhetoric suggests an alignment of sufferings – the Jew's, the gentile's, the animal's – even as the Jew's suffering comes to take center stage. The aphorism that the redactors invoke at the end of the discussion also points to this alignment: "the assumption is that a person goes after his donkey" (*stama de-milta inish batar hamareh azel*).[64] The aphorism is brought as evidence that animal owners hire animal drivers of the same ethnicity as their own, but the poetics speak to a broader correlation between person and animal. The aphorism also subtly subverts the normative hierarchy of being: the person "goes after" the animal rather than the other way around.

The third testing ground of animal suffering is the inner world of the self:

Come and learn: [One's] friend (literally, "lover") is to be unloaded, and [one's] enemy to be loaded, it is a commandment with respect to the enemy, in order to compel his (i.e., the bystander's) *yetzer*. And if it arises to your mind that animal suffering is a scriptural concern, this (the obligation to unload the friend's animal)[65] would be preferable for him! Even so, in order to compel his *yetzer* is preferable.

ת"ש אוהב לפרוק ושונא לטעון מצוה בשונא כדי לכוף את יצרו[66] ואי סלקא דעתך צער בעלי חיים דאורייתא הא עדיף ליה אפ"ה כדי לכוף את יצרו עדיף

Faced with a choice between helping unload the animal of a friend or loading the animal of an enemy, which obligation should one fulfill first?

---

[62] See Michael Matthew Pitkowsky, "Mipnei Darkhei Shalom ('Because of the Paths of Peace') and Related Terms: A Case Study of How Early Concepts and Terminology Developed from Tannaitic to Talmudic Literature" (The Jewish Theological Seminary of America, 2011). Pitkowsky discusses this passage on pp. 198–204.

[63] In this section, the editor plays with the identities of the owner of the animal, the owner of the cargo, and the driver of the animal in order to determine the role played by animal suffering.

[64] Escorial G-1-3 and Hamburg 165 have *inish* two times in a row, which would best be translated as: "the assumption of a person is that a person goes after his donkey."

[65] The word "to unload" is explicit in Escorial G-1-3.

[66] See the parallel in Tosefta Bava Metzia 2:26. There the language is *lishbor et libo* rather than *lakhof et yitzro*.

Even though the friend is a worthier recipient of aid and the friend's animal more in need of it, the early rabbinic teaching prioritizes the enemy, explaining that the value of overcoming hatred of one's enemy – the hatred is embodied by the *yetzer* – is greater than meeting the needs of one's friend.[67] In its commentary, the Talmud raises the problem of animal suffering only to claim that it is less pressing than conquering the *yetzer*.

Here at the end of the passage, Rava's claim about animal suffering is undone, yet again, as it meets other interests. The editor never outright rejects Rava's claim and, with it, the significance of animal suffering. On the contrary, the passage closes with an affirmation of Rava and a marginalization of early rabbinic teachings that do not seem to support him (those teachings are assigned to the dissenting opinion of Yose the Galilean). Yet the passage raises serious questions regarding whether animal suffering can ever be isolated as *the* ground of obligation and, even when it can, whether it carries real force when compared with other concerns within rabbinic culture. Each of the testing grounds within the talmudic dialectic reveals the revolutionary character of Rava's claim and the challenge of identifying animal suffering as a substantive concern within authoritative rabbinic traditions.[68]

CONCLUSIONS: COMPETING CONCERNS, LAW AND
ETHICS, SLIPPERY SLOPES

This talmudic passage has in modern times been buried under an apologetic reading that reduces it to Rava's statement – usually saying that animal suffering is a "Jewish value" – and that loses sight of the literary complexities that I have here tried to untangle.[69] Recent readings of the passage have moved past the apologetics, however, and I wish to showcase their contributions before situating my own reading among them.

---

[67] This usage conforms to Rosen-Zvi's characterization of the Rabbi Ishmaelan *yetzer* as an internal demonic force that impedes a person from worshipping God and acting rightly (even though only the Talmud and not the Tosefta here uses the term *yetzer*); see Ishay Rosen-Zvi, *Demonic Desires: Yetzer Hara and the Problem of Evil in Late Antiquity* (Philadelphia: University of Pennsylvania Press, 2011).

[68] My reading parallels in many ways Kraemer's reading of a passage in Bava Qamma 83b–84a, which he claims "communicates discontinuity in spite of its final formal support of the contrary"; see David Charles Kraemer, *Reading the Rabbis: The Talmud as Literature* (New York: Oxford University Press, 1996), 34.

[69] A quick google search on animal suffering in Judaism produces a plethora of websites that feature this type of approach.

Joshua Cahan reads this passage and a short parallel on Shabbat 154b as an exercise in weighing competing goods.[70] "…[H]ow do we adjudicate the tension between this and other principles, both in explaining why we do things and in deciding what we should do?"[71] Cahan reads the talmudic passage on animal suffering as a demonstration of the processes by which a person selects one value over another. Cahan also considers the medieval legal traditions that accumulated around this passage and related ones, showing that over time the concern for animal suffering diminishes and almost entirely drops out, leading to a less dynamic Jewish legal stance surrounding animal suffering. Published in *Conservative Judaism* journal, Cahan's essay is aimed at restoring what he perceives to be the lost legal dynamism of talmudic and early medieval Jewish law. While animal suffering may seem like a modern concern, Cahan argues that it is in fact native to Jewish law. Cahan sees the narrative of Jewish law as one in which "the rabbis fit that value into the real-life challenges of Jews in different eras."[72] Avoidance or prevention of animal suffering is one value that rabbis tried to balance with other ones as they faced the challenges of their time.

Dov Linzer similarly sees the talmudic and medieval traditions on animal suffering as a juggling act of sorts.[73] Whereas for Cahan the balance is among competing values, each vying with the other for dominance and together contributing to the dynamism of Jewish law, for Linzer the dialectic is between "Torah value" and "halakhah" (Jewish law). Coming from an open-Orthodox perspective, Linzer explores how a value considered to be based in the Torah might inform the shaping of law. Linzer's question, he himself points out, is not the one often asked of whether there are values *outside* the Torah that might influence the interpretation of Torah. Rather, Linzer is interested in whether there are values *inside* the Torah that can be read *back* into the Torah in order to shape its interpretation. Animal suffering is a fitting case for Linzer's inquiry since it is a "value" whose biblical status is explicitly affirmed by the Talmud.[74] Linzer therefore uses the case of animal suffering to gauge the extent to which Jewish legal decisors give weight to Torah values in the

---

70 Cahan, "Tza'ar Ba'alei Ḥayim in the Marketplace of Values."
71 Ibid., 36.
72 Ibid., 31.
73 Linzer, "Tza'ar Ba'alei Chaim."
74 Whether animal suffering is in fact a concern resident within the Bible is, I have tried to show, a separate and complicated question. Because Rava says that it is, the scriptural status of animal suffering is turned into a rabbinic "fact."

course of determining halakhah. Linzer characterizes a variety of medieval commentators with respect to how each configures the relationship between the "value" of avoiding animal suffering and the commandment of unloading the pack animal. Linzer argues that some commentators (Rashi and Tosafot) see value and law as autonomous sectors, while others (Ritva, Rabbenu Peretz, and Ra'avad) understand values to have power in shaping the scope of the law.

For Linzer and Cahan, the talmudic passage on animal suffering illustrates a larger dialectic within Jewish law. For Aaron Gross, it illustrates a larger dialectic within Jewish ethical culture, between what Gross calls "ascendancy" and "kindness" in the Jewish relationship to other species, which together produce something Gross conceptualizes as the "humane subject."[75] Gross sees in the talmudic passage on animal suffering the jostling of "ascendancy" with "kindness." The parts of the talmudic dialectic that oppose the Torah-status of animal suffering are on the side of "ascendancy," a stance in which human beings see themselves as ascendant over other creatures. The parts of the passage that support Rava are aligned with "kindness," when human beings see themselves as kindred spirits with other species and as having obligations toward them that flow from that similarity in kind. Gross understands the talmudic passage to be expressing anxiety about the broader ramifications of "kindness."[76] Were animal suffering to be recognized as a concern of scriptural status and "kindness" fully ensconced as a legal principle, the entire scaffolding of Jewish practice might falter, with animal husbandry, slaughter, and sacrifice all seemingly out of sync with a key scriptural concern. The resistance in the talmudic passage about animal suffering to recognizing its scriptural status stems not just from the familiar ascendancy model, speculates Gross, but from an awareness that animal suffering can never be uprooted. "Kindness" can only go so far before it hits the very heart of Judaism.

For Cahan, Linzer, and Gross, the passage represents an irresolvable conflict between poles: between one value and another, between value and law, between ascendancy and kindness. In these readings, the fundamental question posed by the talmudic passage is: What values does a concern for animal suffering compete with, what laws can a concern for animal suffering be read into, or what practices does the concern for animal suffering challenge? In my reading, the fundamental question is,

[75] Gross, *The Question of the Animal and Religion.*
[76] Ibid., 165–7.

rather, *Is animal suffering there at all?* Rava stakes a claim for animal suffering that is undone by the passage, time after time, when tested against the sources in the different scenarios that those sources imagine. In my reading, this passage is less about the slippery slope of law and practice than about the slipperiness of animal suffering itself. Like the story of Judah the Patriarch and the calf, this talmudic passage wants, first and foremost, to make animal suffering visible. Its ultimate aim, however, is to identify how very normal and normative is the invisibility of animal suffering within rabbinic discourse.

5

Animal Danger

Bava Qamma 80a–b

DANGEROUS ANIMALS

It used to be bloodhounds that people feared. Harriet Beecher Stowe's best-selling *Uncle Tom's Cabin* did not feature any, but when producers staged the novel, they added a pack of snarling bloodhounds to chase Eliza across the frozen Ohio River, and audiences loved it.[1] Because of their size, strength, and excellent noses, bloodhounds had become popular guard dogs and trackers. To make them aggressive, they were confined and abused. Once the monster was unleashed, it was hard to control. Bloodhounds attacked the wrong people – neighbors, children – in a rash of tragic incidents in the late 1800s and early 1900s. The bloodhound became larger than life, a mythic figure around whom terrors and anxieties converged.

It did not last long. Newfoundlands and Saint Bernards replaced the bloodhound, Great Danes and German shepherds replaced Newfoundlands and Saint Bernards, and Dobermans and Rottweilers replaced the breeds that preceded them. The pit bull is the most recent dangerous dog. The breed name comes from a sixteenth-century English ritual in which a bull was tied down, and whichever dogs managed to

---

[1] This discussion is based on David Grimm, *Citizen Canine: Our Evolving Relationship with Cats and Dogs* (New York: PublicAffairs, 2014), whose account draws from Karen Delise, *The Pit Bull Placebo: The Media, Myths and Politics of Canine Aggression* (Sofia, Bulgaria: Anubis Publishing, 2007). See now also Susan Hunter and Richard A. Brisbin, *Pet Politics: The Political and Legal Lives of Cats, Dogs, and Horses in Canada and the United States* (West Lafayette, IN: Purdue University Press, 2016), 313–350; Bronwen Dickey, *Pit Bull: The Battle Over an American Icon* (New York: Knopf Doubleday, 2017).

hold onto the terrified and angry bull without being thrown off or injured were considered to be the best hunters of large game.[2] Bulldogs were the dogs who won the contest most often. Pit bulls were prized for their courage and tenacity, but, as it happened with bloodhounds, their strengths turned into liabilities as owners intensified their traits, abusing them if they were not aggressive enough and training them for dog fights. Pit bulls came to be associated with an underworld of illegal gambling, drugs, and guns, with vicious attacks, and with African-American men.[3] Features were attributed to the pit bull that were thought to make the dog inherently aggressive: a locking jaw, a powerful bite, an inability to feel pain, killer instincts. After some dramatic attacks by pit bulls, breed-specific legislations emerged in the 1980s and 1990s. Denver outlawed pit bulls in 1989 and allowed police to enter people's homes to take their dogs. More than two hundred cities followed suit with "dangerous dog" laws.[4] The entire United Kingdom banned pit bulls in 1991. The consequences of these laws for pit bulls and their owners have been predictably dire. The dogs can be confiscated and "euthanized" at will, sometimes by the very humane societies or anticruelty organizations whose mission is to protect dogs.[5]

This chapter deals with species-specific legislations in the Mishnah and Talmud. I first discuss passages from the Mishnah whose purpose, I argue, is to develop an epistemology in which normal animal behavior can be distinguished from abnormal and animal danger can be accurately anticipated. According to the Mishnah's epistemology, some "wild" species are *ab initio* dangerous, while various domestic species are said to require restriction or confinement. I then turn to a talmudic story about these sorts of species-specific legislations. In that story, several rabbis

[2] Grimm, *Citizen Canine*, 187.
[3] See Meisha Rosenberg, "Golden Retrievers Are White, Pit Bulls Are Black, and Chihuahuas Are Hispanic: Representations of Breeds of Dog and Issues of Race in Popular Culture," in *Making Animal Meaning*, ed. Linda Kalof and Georgina M. Montgomery (East Lansing: Michigan State University Press, 2011), 113–26. See also, passim, Colin Dayan, *With Dogs at the Edge of Life* (New York: Columbia University Press, 2015). For more on the intersection of race, species, and danger, see Kim, *Dangerous Crossings: Race, Species, and Nature in a Multicultural Age*.
[4] For discussion of "dangerous dog" laws, see Joan Schaffner, *An Introduction to Animals and the Law* (New York: Palgrave Macmillan, 2011), 123–9. The New York City Housing Authority instituted a ban on pit bulls in April 2009; see Dayan, *With Dogs at the Edge of Life*, 4.
[5] See Dayan, *With Dogs at the Edge of Life*, 53–110: "And they kill them after rescuing them – kill them while speaking the language of salvation" (p. 76).

attend the celebration of a baby boy. While the rabbis jostle each other in the doorway, arguing about who should enter the room first, a cat attacks the baby and mutilates his hand. In reaction, one of the rabbis issues a series of prohibitions on cats that evoke the pit bull bans of our day. I propose that in juxtaposing this story with the laws, the Talmud is offering a critical perspective on discourses of animal danger.

The talmudic discussion asks us not to take the legislations about animal danger at face value, and this chapter will follow suit. That is not to say that animals do not sometimes pose very real threats to people. When an American dentist allegedly paid 50,000 dollars to bag a lion in Zimbabwe and outrage erupted, an op-ed in *The New York Times* observed that the people of the villages of Zimbabwe are not exactly lion fans: lions kill people, and people are terrified of them.[6] Nevertheless, discourses of animal danger have a habit of selecting certain features of reality to emphasize (e.g., a particular attack), mixing those features with elements of fantasy (e.g., alleged biological characteristics of an animal, as has been the case with the pit bull), suppressing features of reality that do not conform to the discourse (e.g., aggressive non-pit bulls, friendly pit bulls), and channeling that fear for a variety of ends.[7] The discourse of animal danger constructs a knowledge about animals, and it casts certain figures as the appropriate managers of risk. Knowledge about animal danger takes on a life of its own such that the behavior of real, individual animals can become irrelevant. Note the decision of a Maryland appeals court: "When an attack involves pit bulls, it is no longer necessary to prove that the particular pit bull or pit bulls are dangerous."[8] The constructed quality of the danger is apparent in the killing of puppies whose eyes are barely opened on the grounds that they are "threats to the public."[9] This chapter will explore the knowledge about animal danger that the Mishnah offers and will consider, first, how the early rabbinic

[6] Goodwell Nzou, "In Zimbabwe, We Don't Cry for Lions," *The New York Times*, August 4, 2015, www.nytimes.com/2015/08/05/opinion/in-zimbabwe-we-dont-cry-for-lions.html.

[7] This chapter follows the general approach to risk perception found in John Tulloch and Deborah Lupton, *Risk and Everyday Life* (Thousand Oaks, CA: Sage, 2003): "Risk knowledges are ... historical and local. What might be perceived to be 'risky' in one era at a certain locale may no longer viewed so in a later era, or in a different place. As a result, risk knowledges are constantly contested and are subject to disputes and debates over their nature, their control and whom is to blame for their creation" (p. 1).

[8] See Dayan, *With Dogs at the Edge of Life*, 5. Also in Dayan: "A suspected 'innate character' or 'vicious propensity' stands in handily for actual wrongdoing" (p. 74).

[9] Ibid., 54. And see also pp. 79, 80–1.

authors position themselves through that knowledge as assessors of risk and as arbiters of the household, and, second, how the talmudic materials then reflect on that rabbinic self-positioning.

The most common criticisms of breed-specific legislations resonate with the talmudic materials. Chief among those criticisms is that animals are not to blame for the dangers they pose – people are. One study of pit bull temperament shows them to be as docile as golden retrievers are thought to be. The talmudic story likewise suggests that animals are not inherently dangerous but become so through circumstance and context. Critics also point to the race and class associations with so-called dangerous animals. "Canine profiling" follows the same logic as racial profiling in presuming an individual to be dangerous based on his belonging to a particular category, and the two kinds of profiling work in tandem to create a cluster of cultural assumptions about danger (e.g., poor, black, male, pit bull, violent).[10] Along similar lines, the talmudic discussion points to the cultural specificity of the notion of cat danger. Critics also argue that pit bull legislations are ineffective. They fail to keep the public safer from dog attacks, and they generate large public costs related to animal control and enforcement, kenneling and veterinary care, euthanasia and carcass disposal, DNA testing, and litigation.[11] The pit bull legislations may also be unconstitutional. People must have clear enough information about a law so that they can take appropriate precautions not to violate it, yet the definition of a pit bull is far from clear. The breed is typically defined as "American Pit Bull Terrier, American Staffordshire Terrier, and Staffordshire Terrier," but the American Kennel Club does not recognize pit bull itself as a breed.[12] As a result, the bans tend to sweep under their scope any dog that looks in some way like a pit bull.[13] These criticisms – about the effectiveness and economics of species-specific legislations, and the inaccuracy and confusion that arise in trying to define a species – emerge also from the talmudic materials.

---

[10] The term "canine profiling" is found on ibid., xv. For discussion of non-Jews being associated by talmudic texts with dangerous animals, see Conclusion, and also Wasserman, *Jews, Gentiles, and Other Animals*, 145–9. Worth pointing out in Wasserman's discussion of the Talmud's clustering of danger, snakes, and gentiles is the combination of fear and attraction entailed in depictions of danger; see p. 146.

[11] That list is from Schaffner, *An Introduction to Animals and the Law*, 125.

[12] Grimm, *Citizen Canine*, 198. On the emergence and evolution of the notion of dog breed, see Chapter 2 in Susan McHugh, *Dog* (Chicago: University of Chicago Press, 2004).

[13] See discussion in Claire Molloy, "Dangerous Dogs and the Construction of Risk," in *Theorizing Animals: Re-Thinking Humanimal Relations*, ed. Nik Taylor and Tania Signal (Leiden: Brill, 2011), 124.

If dangerous animal discourses are something more than strictly rational, instrumental responses to risk, then how are they best explained? David Grimm understands the purpose of pit bull legislations to be protecting the myth that dogs are furry children. The demon dog is the doppelgänger for the good dog who can be embraced as a beloved family member.[14] Karen Delise similarly sees pit bull legislation as a placebo for public anxiety about dog aggression.[15] Drawing upon moral panic theory, Claire Molloy considers the United Kingdom's media discourse about dog danger in light of various social and economic crises in the late 1980s and early 1990s.[16] Sigmund Freud understood animal phobias – famous cases he discussed were Little Hans, the Wolf Man, and the Rat Man – to be displacement for a boy's fear of his father's castrating anger. In Julia Kristeva's revision of Freud's theory, fear of the animal expresses the young child's ambivalence toward the maternal body.[17] This chapter will not adopt one of these interpretive models so much as see the Babylonian Talmud as making a contribution to them. At the same time, I will draw from these modern approaches to animal danger – animal as protector of myth, as placebo, as generator of moral panic, as symbol, as displacement – to enrich my reading of the rabbinic materials.

ABNORMAL OXEN

Mishnah Bava Qamma 1:4 can be read as a form of animal profiling. It sets forth claims about the nature of animals and bases torts liability upon those claims:

[There are] five innocent [sources of damage] and five attested [sources of damage].

An animal is not attested [as a source of damage with respect to]: (1) goring (2) butting (3) biting (4) squatting or (5) kicking.

(1) The tooth is attested with respect to eating all that is appropriate to it.

(2) The foot is attested with respect to smashing as it walks.

(3) The attested ox.

---

[14] "Pit bulls became the demon dog du jour just as pets were turning into full-fledged family members." Grimm, *Citizen Canine*, 195.

[15] Delise, *The Pit Bull Placebo*.

[16] Molloy, "Dangerous Dogs." My general framing of the discussion here relies on Molloy.

[17] Kelly Oliver, "Little Hans's Little Sister," *Philosophia* 1, no. 1 (2011): 9–28; Alison Suen, "From Animal Father to Animal Mother: A Freudian Account of Animal Maternal Ethics," *Philosophia* 3, no. 2 (2013): 121–37.

(4) The ox who causes damage in the domain of the one damaged.
(5) And the human.

The wolf and the lion and the bear and the leopard and the panther and the serpent: these are attested.

Rabbi Elazar says: When they are domesticated they are not attested.

And the serpent is always attested.

What is there between innocent and attested?

Only that the innocent pays half of the damage, and from its own body, while the attested pays full damage from the upper story.

חמשה תמים וחמשה מועדים

הבהמה אינה מועדת לא ליגח ולא ליגוף ולא לישוך ולא לירבוץ ולא לבעוט

השן מועדת לאכל כל[18] את הראוי לה

והרגל מועדת לשבור כדרך הילוכה

ושור המועד

ושור המזיק ברשות הניזק

והאדם

הזאב והארי והדוב והנמר והפרדלס והנחש הרי אילו מועדים

ר אלעזר אומ בזמן שהן תרבות אינן מועדים

והנחש מועד לעולם

מה בן תם למועד

אלא שהתם משלם חצי נזק ומגופו

והמועד משלם נזק שלם מן העליה[19]

This mishnah distinguishes between animal tort cases in which the owner must pay full compensation (what the Mishnah calls "attested," to be paid out of the owner's possessions kept in the "upper story" of his domicile) and cases in which the owner need pay only half-compensation (what the Mishnah calls "innocent," for which the owner need not dip into his savings but pays only out of the value of the goring ox himself). A variety of peculiar elements make this mishnah difficult to parse: its strange organizing binary of "innocent" and "attested"; the asymmetry between the first simple list of five innocent categories, the second complex list of five attested ones, and a third unnumbered list of six "wild" species (i.e., wolf, lion, etc.); its use of animal body parts, "tooth" and "foot," to stand in for categories of damage; its redundant claim that the attested ox is attested;

[18] The word *kol* ("all") is absent in the Parma manuscript, which is not surprising given that the two letters of the word repeat the last two letters of the verb "eating" (*le'ekhol, lokhal* in Parma) and could therefore be easily accidentally skipped by a scribe.
[19] Kaufmann manuscript, and for all subsequent mishnahs cited.

its brief interest in location ("in the domain of the one damaged"); and the appearance of the human being in a list of animal torts. My explanation of this mishnah, which I will proceed through step-by-step, is that its obscure language and structure are designed to create a new discourse about animal nature, and that the peculiarities are a product of the mishnah patching this discourse together out of prior traditions that do not entirely lend themselves to the project.

This mishnah begins with the five *tam*s, or innocent sources of damage, and five *muad*s, attested sources of damage. The biblical verses on which this mishnah relies, Exodus 21:28–32, 35–6, and 22:4, do not use these terms. Exodus 21:29 uses a word that is similar to *muad*, the past tense verb *huad*, which means "warned" or "testified":

If, however, that ox has been in the habit of goring, and his owner, though warned (*ve-huad*), has failed to guard it, and he kills a man or a woman—
the ox shall be stoned and his owner, too, shall be put to death.

וְאִם שׁוֹר נַגָּח הוּא מִתְּמֹל שִׁלְשֹׁם וְהוּעַד בִּבְעָלָיו וְלֹא יִשְׁמְרֶנּוּ וְהֵמִית אִישׁ אוֹ אִשָּׁה הַשּׁוֹר יִסָּקֵל וְגַם-בְּעָלָיו יוּמָת.

If an ox displays aggressive tendencies, his owner must be warned about it.[20] If the owner has received such a warning and does not exercise care in restraining his ox, then the owner possesses a greater degree of liability if his ox attacks again. While the owner of an ox with no such warning on his head is completely free of penalty if his ox kills a person, and he must pay only half the cost if his ox gores another ox, the owner of the goring ox who does carry such a warning must pay the full cost if his ox gores another ox, and he pays with his *life* if his ox kills a person. Many have marveled at the severity of the ox owner's punishment in such a case given that the homicide was, after all, both accidental and indirect.[21]

---

[20] As commentaries point out, if the ox had previously killed a person, he would have already been executed. Therefore, the ox would have had to show aggression either toward other oxen, or toward human beings but short of a homicidal attack. The passive *hu'ad* leaves unclear who is charged with warning the owner about the ox and what constitutes a warning.

[21] Greenberg argued that the severe punishment of the owner reflects the Hebrew Bible's distinctive valuation of life; see "Some Postulates of Biblical Criminal Law," in Moshe Greenberg, *Studies in the Bible and Jewish Thought* (Philadelphia: Jewish Publication Society, 1995), 25–42, and response by "Reflections on Biblical Criminal Law," in Bernard S. Jackson, *Essays in Jewish and Comparative Legal History* (Leiden: Brill, 1975), 25–63. I argue in Chapter 3 that the Mishnah reinterprets these biblical materials out of a discomfort with the severity of the punishment.

The Mishnah transforms the meaning of *muad* from its usage in Exodus. The word no longer refers, as it does in Exodus, to whether a particular owner has been warned about a particular ox. The Mishnah partners *muad* ("attested") with the antonym *tam* ("innocent"), a term that the Mishnah fabricates whole cloth, and uses the pair to refer to whether an animal is exhibiting normal or abnormal behavior. When the Mishnah declares the *behemah* – note the shift to a generic term for "animal" from Exodus's "ox" – to be unattested (i.e., not *muad*) for the five activities it lists (goring, butting, etc.), the Mishnah means that it is *not normal* for an animal to do them. Because goring, butting, and so forth are said by the Mishnah to be atypical behaviors, the owner is not considered negligent if his animal causes damage by doing them. The owner is fully liable only for that which he can reasonably anticipate, and these animal behaviors could not be reasonably anticipated. The Mishnah ultimately follows the same principle of liability found in Exodus – namely, that if an owner cannot predict the animal's injurious behavior, he is less liable for the harm the animal causes. But whereas for Exodus, that predictability hinges on particular information the owner may or may not receive, for the Mishnah it hinges on a scheme of behavioral norms that the Mishnah produces. The Babylonian Talmud in its commentary on the Mishnah makes the Mishnah's thinking explicit, applying to the Mishnah the Aramaic phrases *urheh* and *lav urheh*, literally "his way" and "not his way," or normal and not normal.[22]

The Mishnah contrasts the animal's abnormal aggressive behavior – these are the five *tams* – with an animal's normal behavior, the *muads*. The *muads* are those behaviors that an animal owner should be able to anticipate and for which he is consequently fully liable should his animal cause damage through them. The first two on this list of five are "the tooth" and "the foot." The Mishnah uses the body parts of the animal, tooth and foot, to represent the animal's normal behaviors of eating and walking. As the Mishnah will go on to explain, an animal can be expected to eat fruits and vegetables that he comes upon or to break small objects that lie in his path.[23] Since the owner of the animal can easily anticipate such damages, he is held fully liable for them. These delineations once again display a shift in thinking from Exodus to the Mishnah. While "attestation" refers in Exodus to an instance in which an animal has

---

[22] Bava Qamma 16a–b.
[23] Mishnah Bava Qamma 2:1–2.

exhibited aggressive behavior, in the Mishnah it refers to cases where an animal is up to his everyday activities, humdrum walking and eating.

Number three on the list of *muads* seems oddly redundant: the *shor muad* is *muad*, the "attested ox" is "attested." This would appear to refer to an ox who has exhibited abnormally aggressive behavior, and the owner has been apprised of this behavior. For this particular ox, the abnormal has become the normal; he has shown himself to typically act atypically. This case is exactly the one that Exodus had in mind, the ox whose owner has been warned about him. The return to the language of ox (*shor*) rather than animal (*behemah*) should cue the audience into that biblical connection. The apparent redundancy, however – "the attested ox is attested" – points to the Mishnah's departure from the framework of Exodus such that Exodus's conception, when it now appears, is the one that seems anomalous.

The fourth and fifth items on the list of *muads*, the ox who causes damage on private property and the human being, are also anomalous, each in his or her own way. The sudden injection of location as a relevant criterion for damage assessment raises all sorts of questions about the assumptions that have so far been in place. When the Mishnah spoke of goring and biting, did it have private or public property in mind? When the Mishnah spoke of the animal's leg breaking an object in his path, or the animal's eating a plant, which kind of property was being assumed? Are the owners of objects – and not just the owners of animals – expected to take appropriate precautions to protect their possessions within a bustling urban marketplace?[24] The invocation of place complicates the epistemology of danger that the Mishnah has so far constructed by showing danger to be dependent on context and shaped by expectation. People adjust their sense of risk based on where they are. The *adam*, the human being, is last on the list of five and functions as the connective between this first hodge-podge list of *muads* and the subsequent list of six "wild" species. It is hard to know what to make of the human being's appearance here, whether he or she is meant to be seen as similar to the benign cow eating grass on the first *muad* list or the wolf and lion on the second. Either way, the human is presented as just another species to watch out for, capable of causing harm.

WILD ANIMALS

"Attested" is not the best translation for the six animal species on the final list; *dangerous* is. Unlike the domesticated animal, for whom aggressive

---

[24] These questions are raised in Bava Qamma 15b–16a.

behavior is considered abnormal, for these species (i.e., wolf, lion, bear, leopard, panther, serpent), aggressive behavior is said to be normal.[25] An owner of any member of these *muad* animal species (exactly why a person would own one of these "wild" animals is not addressed; perhaps exotic animals were objects of fascination or status symbols) is expected to pay full damages whether his animal has a track record of injury or not.[26] An exception is made by Rabbi Elazar for cases where the animal has been domesticated or trained ("Rabbi Elazar says: When they are domesticated they are not attested"). Rabbi Elazar's exception is said not to apply to the snake, who is declared incorrigible, *muad le-olam*, "forever dangerous," which is no surprise given biblical associations with the snake and their pervasiveness in the ecology of Palestine.[27]

That same list of dangerous animals occurs in other early rabbinic traditions.[28] Mishnah Sanhedrin 1:4 features a debate over whether the dangerous animal species deserve the same due process of law as domesticated animals when they commit a "crime" (see Chapter 3 for further discussion of animal trials):

The lion and the bear and the leopard and the panther and the snake: Their execution is with twenty-three [judges].

Rabbi Eliezer says: Anyone who advances to kill them, he has acted properly.

Rabbi Akiva says: Their execution is with twenty-three.

הארי והדוב והנמר והפרדלס והנחש מיתתן בעשרין ושלשה

ר' אליעזר או' כל הקודם להורגן זכה

ר' עקיבה או' מיתתן בעשרין ושלשה

[25] On stereotypes of some of these species as dangerous, see the cultural histories in Robert E. Bieder, *Bear* (Chicago: University of Chicago Press, 2005); Drake Stutesman, *Snake* (Chicago: University of Chicago Press, 2005); Deirdre Jackson, *Lion* (Chicago: University of Chicago Press, 2010); Garry Marvin, *Wolf* (Chicago: University of Chicago Press, 2012); Desmond Morris, *Leopard* (Chicago: University of Chicago Press, 2014).

[26] On keeping lions and bears as status symbols, see Gilhus, *Animals, Gods and Humans*, 30.

[27] For a broad cultural and natural history of the snake, see Stutesman, *Snake*. On their prevalence in contemporary Israel, see Kochva Elazar, "Venomous Snakes of Israel: Ecology and Snakebite," *Public Health Reviews* 26, no. 3 (1998): 209–32.

[28] The toseftan parallel does not give the list of wild animals but instead presents positions as additions of particular species to a presupposed list. Rabbi Meir adds the hyena, and Rabbi Elazar adds the snake, suggesting that the snake was not originally on the Tosefta's version of the list. See the argument about the relationship between these mishnah and tosefta passages in Judith Hauptman, *Rereading the Mishnah: A New Approach to Ancient Jewish Texts* (Tübingen: Mohr Siebeck, 2005), 173–88. Hauptman proposes that the Tosefta had an original list of wild species and that this list was the original list of five muads. The Mishnah then changed the number and type of lists as a means for organizing its subsequent material.

Whereas Mishnah Bava Qamma takes the dangerous nature of these species to be justification for full compensation in a tort case in which a member of these species is the culprit, Mishnah Sanhedrin sees their danger as a reason to potentially deprive them of the right to a trial in a homicide case. That is Rabbi Eliezer's opinion, though the anonymous consensus position and then Rabbi Akiva, recapitulating it, would apply the same judicial trials for dangerous species who kill a human being as for a member of any other species that does.[29]

Rabbi Eliezer's opinion might be read as giving people license to attack a wild animal who has not yet committed a crime: "Anyone who *advances* to kill them…"[30] If so, then this mishnah and the one from Bava Qamma are portraying these species as, in effect, walking weapons. That is how Mishnah Avodah Zarah 1:7 explicitly describes bears and lions when it prohibits a Jew from selling to a gentile a bear, lion, "or anything that has in it [the capacity to wreak] harm on the multitudes." These species are shown to present a situation of dire crisis from which nothing can be saved or survive, not unlike what modern insurance companies call an act of God. In the Sifra, dangerous animals are understood literally to be an act of God. They are God's emissaries sent to carry out a fatal punishment.[31] One suspects that the same assumption is behind the Mekhilta's exemption from liability for the guardian of an animal who is attacked and killed by any of the dangerous species.[32] The phenomenon of dangerous animals also holds out the possibility of miraculous escape, such as when Tosefta Bava Metzia 2:2 permits the person who saves a lost object from "the mouth of the lion, or from the mouth of the wolf, or from the mouth of the bear" to keep it, on the grounds that the owner would have despaired of recovering it. Tosefta Berakhot 1:11 presents the

---

[29] In Tosefta Sanhedrin 3:1, Rabbi Eliezer advises summary killing not just for dangerous animals, but for any other animal besides the ox:

> An ox who killed: Whether [it be] an ox who killed or another domesticated animal, or a wild animal, or fowl who killed him, their execution is with twenty-three. Rabbi Eliezer says: An ox who killed, his execution is with twenty-three, but for another domesticated animal, or a wild animal, or fowl who killed him, anyone who advances to kill them, he has acted properly regarding the heavens, as it is said, "You shall kill the woman and the animal" (Lev. 20:16), and it says "And you shall kill the animal" (Lev. 20:15).

[30] This question is raised on Sanhedrin 15b, where Rabbi Yohanan and Resh Lakish debate whether the animal has to already have killed a person.

[31] Sifra Emor Parashah 8, beginning of Pereq 9; the passage mentions bears, lions, tigers, venomous serpents, and scorpions.

[32] Mekhilta de-Rabbi Yishma'el Mishpatim 16.

story of a man who survives an encounter with a wolf bragging about his escape, only to subsequently encounter a lion and to replace the old story with the new more dramatic one, and so on with a snake. That story similarly presumes that it is possible to survive an encounter with one of these dangerous animals, however unlikely.

Other invocations of the dangerous animal list make refinements within it, suggesting that there is more to its seemingly homogenous representation of dangerous animals than initially meets the eye. Like the Mekhilta passage mentioned earlier, Mishnah Bava Metzia 7:9 declares an attack by one of the dangerous animals to be a situation of *ones*, or utter lack of control, exempting from liability the guardian of an animal who is preyed upon by one of these species. This mishnah distinguishes, however, between a wolf and other dangerous species, between one wolf and two wolves, between packs of wolves and lone wolves, between dogs and wolves, between animals coming from one direction and animals coming from two, and between animals coming on their own devise and animals whom people approach. The details of the attack clearly make a difference, and the level of danger should be assessed according to those details. Tosefta Berakhot 1:11, mentioned earlier, also makes distinctions with regard to danger level: a wolf is less dangerous than a lion, a lion less so than a snake.[33] Tosefta Bekhorot 1:10, by contrast, lumps all the dangerous species together, attributing to them the same gestation period of three years (and adding to that list also the elephant, monkey, and ape). These different species are shown to share a fundamental biological link that undergirds the discourse of danger that groups them, which does so likely because their danger seems much more dramatic than the workaday danger posed by the ox (whose threat, precisely because of its frequency, may in fact be more worth worrying about).[34]

Taking these early rabbinic traditions together, one emerges with the following set of assumptions: Domesticated animals are normally not aggressive on the level of species, though individually they may be; some animal species are inherently aggressive, though individually they may not be; some

[33] See also Mishnah Hullin 3:1, which attributes varying degrees of danger to wolves and lions.
[34] See Tulloch and Lupton, *Risk and Everyday Life*, 8.: "… people tend to see familiar or voluntary risks as less serious than risks that are new or imposed upon them, and … they are more likely to be concerned about risks that are rare and memorable than those that are seen as common but less disastrous." But Tulloch and Lupton also take a critical perspective on experts who "represent lay people as deficient in their abilities, drawing on 'irrational' assumptions when making judgements about such phenomena as risk" and who see their own assessment of risk as neutral and strictly rational.

animal species are incorrigibly aggressive, possibly including the human species. Drawing on biblical legal motifs, the early rabbinic texts create a new discourse about the nature and norms of other species. This discourse is by no means wrinkle-free. It organizes animals into a binary of domesticated and wild even while complicating the binary at every turn, with domesticated animals constantly causing unwitting damage as they walk and eat, some domesticated animals turning unpredictably aggressive, and some "dangerous" animals proving not always as dangerous as they would initially seem, such as if they are trained, or in the cases where people and objects miraculously escape from their jaws, or when they are in their own habitats. The various species on the list, while they may have in common key biological features, at the same time do not pose equal danger to each other or the same level of danger in all circumstances, and the rabbinic majority holds that they deserve the same due process of law that other species (including the human) do.

ANIMALS IN THE HOUSE

These rabbinic traditions purport to describe animal nature and to predict animal danger. Other teachings try to get rid of certain species altogether or to strictly limit their numbers, such as Mishnah Bava Qamma 7:7:

One may not raise small cattle in the land of Israel, but one may raise [them] in Syria and in the wilderness of the land of Israel.

One may not raise chickens in Jerusalem because of the sacrifices, and priests [may not raise them] in the land of Israel because of the pure things.

An Israelite may not raise pigs anywhere.

And a person may not raise a dog unless he is tied up by a chain.

One may not set traps for pigeons unless it is thirty *ris* from the inhabited area.[35]

אין מגדלים בהמה דקה בארץ יש׳ אבל מגדלים בסוריה ובמדברות שבארץ יש׳

אין מגדלים תרנגלים בירושלם מפני הקדשים ולא כהנים בארץ יש׳ מפני הטהרות

לא יגדל יש׳ חזירים בכל מקום

ולא יגדל אדם את הכלב אלא אם כן היה קשור בשלשלת

אין פורסין נשבים ליונים אלא אם כן היה רחוק מן היושב[36] שלושים רוס[37]

35 Mishnah Bava Qamma 7:7.
36 Other versions have *yishuv* ("habitation" or "settlement") instead of *yoshev* ("inhabitant" or "settler").
37 The length measurement in other versions is spelled with a yud, *ris*.

This mishnah targets small cattle (i.e., sheep and goats), chickens, pigs, dogs, and pigeons. The rhetoric of the Mishnah is resoundingly negative, even if certain permissions are granted by the legislations. Each line starts with either *eyn* or *lo* ("not"), posting a veritable "Keep out" sign before these species.

The problems these animals pose are left largely implicit. One might be surprised to find an outright restriction on small cattle, i.e., sheep and goats, in ancient Palestine, but in fact, these farm animals were likely not very convenient within the nuclear village paradigm of Roman Palestine and would have uncomfortably crowded residential space and picked apart good agricultural land.[38] The problems posed by small cattle, and especially by the people whose job it was to watch them, i.e., shepherds, took on a decidedly moral tone in the early rabbinic texts. The Tosefta declares shepherds to be invalid witnesses, along with

---

[38] On the nuclear village in Roman Palestine, see Zeev Safrai, "Agriculture and Farming," in *The Oxford Handbook of Jewish Daily Life in Roman Palestine*, ed. Catherine Hezser (New York: Oxford University Press, 2010), 257.

Given scripture's positive portrait of shepherds, Gulak finds surprising the condemnation of shepherds in rabbinic literature, which he associates with the prohibition on raising small cattle; see Asher Gulak, "Shepherds and Breeders of Domestic Cattle after the Destruction of the Second Temple," *Tarbiz* 12 (1940–1941): 181–9. He finds insufficient the common explanation that shepherds would sometimes pasture their flocks in fields that they weren't supposed to, pointing out that Exodus 22:4 had already addressed that problem; see ibid., 182, 184. Gulak mentions that the story of Shimon Shazuri in Tosefta Bava Qamma 8:14 does support this explanation, since his flock is depicted as crossing through someone else's field and trampling it, but Gulak sees this as a later elaboration of the story. Gulak finds unpersuasive the hypothesis that these restrictions were an attempt on the Rabbis' part to discourage commerce and to promote agriculture; see pp. 184–5.

Gulak suggests that these rabbinic legislations be understood in light of the *boukoloi*, shepherd rebels in Egypt at the time of Marcus Aurelius, desperate and marginal figures looking to escape from the ruling eye. Gulak argues that a similar set of conditions pertained in Palestine, where at the time of the Roman revolt people might have fled to the desert areas and hills for similar reasons and with a similar profile to the *boukoloi*. The rabbinic legislations against shepherds and the raising of small cattle, which emerged at the time of the great revolt against Rome according to Gulak, represented an attempt on the part of the Rabbis to preserve agricultural production, to prevent people from taking on a nomadic and dangerous existence, and to stem the tide of rebellion against Rome. After the revolt, these concerns dissolved, and the rabbis became more lenient on these matters, and their concern shifted to the more prosaic one of shepherds trespassing on people's fields. The more lenient legislations, says Gulak, can be explained as a product of this period.

While Gulak's proposal is creative, the methodological problems with it include his dating these rabbinic traditions as precisely as he does, his seeing them as policy responses to political and social problems, and his extrapolating from Egypt to Palestine.

For a comprehensive cultural history of sheep and goats, see Joy Hinson, *Goat* (Chicago: University of Chicago Press, 2015); Philip Armstrong, *Sheep* (Chicago: University of Chicago Press, 2016).

robbers, extortionists, and all who are "suspect in matters of money" (*ha-hashudin al ha-mamon*), suggesting a snooty disdain for shepherds.[39] In Mishnah Demai 2:3, Rabbi Yehudah makes one of the criteria for being counted as a *haver* (a person who adheres to the stringencies of purity and tithing laws) to be refraining from raising small cattle.[40] The Tosefta tells a number of tales in which the lives of righteous men were marred by the one grievous "sin" of raising small cattle or in which shepherds "repent" of pasturing animals.[41] These tales attest not only to the moral judgments that attached to the possession of small cattle but also to what must have been a widespread disregard or ignorance of those judgments, as corroborated by the plentiful faunal evidence of sheep and goats in Roman Palestine as well as by other rabbinic teachings that simply presume the presence of flocks and shepherds.[42] Some of the rabbinic traditions describe sheep or goat being tied to the pillows of the bed, which is declared preferable to having the animals graze out in the fields, yet which also suggests a startling intimacy between people and their

---

[39] Tosefta Sanhedrin 5:5. Mishnah Bava Qamma 10:9 implies that shepherds may have stolen their wares from others when it prohibits buying wool, milk, or goats from them. Tosefta Yevamot 3 seems to present as controversial the requirement to save a shepherd from a wolf's attack. Tosefta Bava Metzia 2:33 groups shepherds, those who raise sheep and goats, and gentiles, and instructs a person not to save a person who falls into these categories from a pit into which they have stumbled but also not to purposely lower them into one. See discussion in Saul Lieberman, *Tosefta Ki-Fshuṭah: A Comprehensive Commentary on the Tosefta*, vol. Parts VI–VII: Order Nashim (New York: The Jewish Theological Seminary of America, 1995), 23–4; Gulak, "Shepherds and Breeders."

[40] In Tosefta Sukkah 2:5, those who raise small cattle are numbered among the causes of the stars being stricken. In Tosefta Bikkurim 2:16, those who raise small cattle are among those who will never see a sign of blessing. On the *haver* in early rabbinic literature, see discussion in Yair Furstenberg, "Am ha-Aretz in Tannaitic Literature and its Social Contexts," *Zion* 78, no. 3 (2013): 287–319.

[41] The story of Yehudah ben Bava's "sin" is in Tosefta Bava Qamma 8:17 (and parallels in Palestinian Talmud Sotah 9:10 [24a]; Babylonian Talmud Bava Qamma 80a; Temurah 15b). The repentant shepherd is in Tosefta Bava Qamma 8:15. In Tosefta Bava Qamma 8:14, Rabbi Shimon Shazuri attributes his family's downfall to their raising small cattle (and to judging civil cases singly).

[42] On the faunal evidence, see Ann E. Killebrew, "Village and Countryside," in *The Oxford Handbook of Jewish Daily Life in Roman Palestine*, ed. Catherine Hezser (New York: Oxford University Press, 2010), 201.
  Many early rabbinic texts speak of shepherds and presume the prevalence of their hiring. Quite a few also speak of sheep (*kevasim*) and goats (*izim*) and more generally of flocks and herds (*tzon, eder*). Sheep and goats are a strong presence within the Bible, so to some extent the rabbinic texts cannot avoid them and should not be read as simply reflecting the realities of animal life in Roman Palestine. The Tosefta explicitly recognizes the tension between the Bible's presumption of sheep and goats and the rabbinic prohibition; see Tosefta Bava Qamma 8:10.

livestock.⁴³ In one of the more memorable moments of the Tosefta, a sick Yehudah ben Bava buys a goat after being told by his doctor that fresh milk is his only cure; Yehudah ben Bava ties the goat to his bed and proceeds to suckle from her in the hopes of getting well. When his rabbinic colleagues come for a visit, they balk at the "robber" that they declare Yehudah ben Bava to be harboring in his house.⁴⁴ Upon his deathbed, Yehudah ben Bava confesses to this violation, his sole sin.⁴⁵ The Tosefta asks more than once about the reason for the prohibition on small cattle and offers a number of exceptions and accommodations to it, as well as an alternative position that overturns the prohibition altogether, and a position that permits keeping certain dogs and cats and other animals "who clean the house" (this last teaching will come up in the talmudic materials I discuss later in this chapter).⁴⁶ In Tosefta Yevamot 3, the prohibition on raising small cattle (and on raising dogs, pigs, and chickens) is one of a long series of legal questions posed to Rabbi Eliezer that he

⁴³ Tosefta Bava Qamma 8:11 requires that small cattle be tied to the bed rather than pastured. Mishnah Kelim 19:2 speaks of tying the paschal lamb to the bed. On tying animals to the bed, see Lieberman, *Tosefta Ki-Fshuṭah*, Parts VI–VII: Order Nashim:23; Lieberman, *Tosefta Ki-Feshuṭah*, 2001, Parts IX–X: Order Nezikin:87.
⁴⁴ Shepherds are coupled with robbers also in Mishnah Bava Metzia 7:9, cited above.
⁴⁵ His confession presents the sin as a violation of the legislation of his colleagues. For discussion of exactly how Yehudah ben Bava violated rabbinic precedents (Did he follow a dissenting opinion? Was it a case of insufficient medical danger to override a standing prohibition?), see Lieberman, *Tosefta Ki-Feshuṭah*, 2001, Parts IX–X: Order Nezikin:88.
⁴⁶ The Tosefta permits the raising of chickens under certain conditions (8:10); raising first-born small cattle for limited time periods (8:10, see parallel in Mishnah Bekhorot 4:1 and Tosefta Bekhorot 3:2); and raising small cattle before festivals or celebrations (8:11). The Tosefta permits a person who owns small cattle and other small animals to gradually sell them off rather than to do so all at once (8:15). The Tosefta permits raising village dogs, porcupines, cats, and monkeys (8:17, with parallel in Tosefta Avodah Zarah 2:3). Tosefta Shevi'it 5:9 prohibits trade of these animals with non-Jews. Mishnah Kilayim 1:6 addresses the speciation of the dog and village dog, while Mishnah Kilayim 8:5–6 classifies a number of animals that include porcupines, monkeys, dogs, and pigs according to whether they are considered domesticated or wild; see later discussion.
  See discussion of the laws about dogs and cats in Joshua Schwartz, "Cats in Ancient Jewish Society (The Place of Domesticated Animals in Everyday Life and the Material Culture of 2nd-Temple Judaism and Ancient Palestine)," *Journal of Jewish Studies* 52, no. 2 (2001): 225–6; Joshua Schwartz, "Good Dog-Bad Dog: Jews and Their Dogs in Ancient Jewish Society," in *A Jew's Best Friend: The Image of the Dog Throughout Jewish History*, ed. Phillip Ackerman-Lieberman and Rakefet Zalashik (Portland, OR: Sussex Academic Press, 2013), 52–89. For discussion of Tosefta Shevi'it's prohibition on trade of these species with gentiles, with emphasis on later codification, see Saul Lieberman, *Tosefta Ki-Fshuṭah: A Comprehensive Commentary on the Tosefta*, vol. Part II: Order Zera'im (New York: The Jewish Theological Seminary of America, 2001), 552–3.

evades answering likely because he saw the legislation as controversial or without proper precedent.[47]

More clearly articulated in the Mishnah is the threat posed by chickens, which is said to be to the sacrifices in Jerusalem and to the priestly pure foods anywhere outside.[48] This problem does not seem to have been considered that serious, since rabbinic sources elsewhere presume that people are raising chickens.[49] The problem with pigs may have been more obvious and thus unnecessary for the Mishnah to state, which is that the pig since the time of the Second Temple was considered the impure animal par excellence.[50] It was also the animal that most distinguished Jews in the Roman Empire from their neighbors, since pigs were the most popularly farmed animals within the empire. The power of the pig to differentiate Jews from others may explain why the Kaufmann and Parma manuscripts of the Mishnah at that point introduce "Israelite" as the

---

[47] See discussion of this passage in Lieberman, *Tosefta Ki-Fshuṭah*, Parts VI–VII: Order Nashim:22–3.

[48] See parallel Tosefta Bava Qamma 8:10. According to Rashi, the chickens eat impure insects, and then when they feed upon pure or sacred food, they mix particles of the impure food with the pure or sacred.

Mishnah Taharot 3:8 speaks of *neqirat tarnegolim*, the pecking of hens, and suggests that the problem posed to purity by chickens may be their drinking impure liquid and then pecking at pure food without first drying their beaks. There the Mishnah makes chicken pecking habits seem somewhat less threatening to pure foods, however, since it maintains the purity of dough that has been pecked near impure liquids so long as there was enough distance between the liquid and the dough for the chicken to have a chance to dry their beak on the ground. Also, the Mishnah there does not make a significant distinction between the threat posed to pure dough by chickens and the threat posed by all other animals.

Mishnah Nedarim 5:1 prohibits joint courtyard owners who have vowed not to derive benefit from each other not to use even their own part of the space for raising chickens, apparently presuming that the impact of chickens is hard to contain and will spill over into the shared space. Tosefta Nedarim 2:9 extends the prohibition in this case to small cattle. A similar presumption about the negative impact of cattle and chickens on a courtyard, and the need for their strict containment, is found in Mishnah Bava Batra 3:5.

On chickens in ancient Jewish households, see Schwartz, "Cats in Ancient Jewish Society," 215–20. For a general natural and cultural history of chickens see Annie Potts, *Chicken* (Chicago: University of Chicago Press, 2012).

[49] Safrai, "Agriculture and Farming," 257.

[50] See discussion of pork's symbolism for Jews in David Charles Kraemer, *Jewish Eating and Identity through the Ages* (New York: Routledge, 2007), 30–3. See also Safrai, "Agriculture and Farming," 258. On the origins of the pork taboo in the Hebrew Bible, see Marvin Harris, "The Abominable Pig," in *The Sacred Cow and the Abominable Pig: Riddles of Food and Culture* (New York: Simon & Schuster, 1987), 67–87. On the controversial status of the pig in modern Israel, see Daphne Barak-Erez, *Outlawed Pigs: Law, Religion, and Culture in Israel* (Madison: University of Wisconsin Press, 2007). For a general natural and cultural history of the pig, see Brett Mizelle, *Pig* (Chicago: University of Chicago Press, 2011).

subject of the sentence (and shift the subject to the more generic *adam* ["person"] in the subsequent law restricting dogs). The problem with the dog would seem to be a fear of attack, as suggested by the Mishnah's requirement to keep him chained, yet the Tosefta passage that compares the person who raises dogs to the person who raises pigs suggests a moralizing of the dog restriction as well.[51] The problem posed by pigeons is less from the animal itself than from the property conflict that might start when people trap them.[52] The real danger is not *from* the bird but *to* it. When the Tosefta returns to pigeons at the end of its discussion of domestic animals, it introduces the theme of hunting and the question of which species people can freely pursue for hunting purposes and where.[53]

The Mishnah's rules about small domestic animals vary depending on where you are, who you are, and the animal breed, but a general distrust of these animals pervades the laws. The traditions about large domesticated animals present them as a more serious danger, with their capacity to gore and their habit of breaking and eating things, but the traditions about the small animals that inhabit the household are in fact less hospitable. The usefulness of the large animals for farm work (done by cows and oxen) and for carrying loads (done by donkeys) clearly outweighed whatever dangers they posed, while the wool and milk that came from sheep and goats do not seem to have offered enough justification, in the Mishnah's eyes, for their presence.[54] Mishnah Betzah 5:7 develops a vocabulary for these household animals, calling them *bayatot*, an adjective fashioned out of the noun *bayit*, house. The Mishnah explains that these are animals who spend the night in town. The Mishnah contrasts the *bayatot* animals with those who are *midbariyot*, an adjective made out of the noun *midbar*, wilderness. The Mishnah defines those animals as the ones who spend the night in *efer*, or pasture.[55] Elsewhere,

---

[51] Tosefta Bava Qamma 8:17. On the relationship between this mishnah and this tosefta, see Hauptman, *Rereading the Mishnah*, 34–6. Elsewhere the Tosefta compares the one who raises bees to the one who raises dogs; Bava Batra 1:9.

[52] See parallel Tosefta Bava Qamma 8:9. According to Safrai, raising pigeons was not very popular in Roman Palestine; see Safrai, "Agriculture and Farming," 257.

[53] Tosefta Bava Qamma 8:17.

[54] Tosefta Shevi'it 3:13 explains that the public must be capable of implementing a rabbinic decree, and that the prohibition on small cattle is manageable, but a prohibition on large cattle would not be. The parallel on Bava Qamma 89b adds that small cattle are relatively easily imported.

[55] The parallel Tosefta Betzah 5:11 makes the same distinction but defines it differently:

These are the *midbariyot*: these are the ones who leave at Passover and return by the first rainfall. *Bayatot*: these are the ones who spend the night within the *tehum* (the area of

the Mishnah organizes species of animals according to whether they are a domesticated species (*min behemah*) or wild (*min hayah*).[56] The development of an explicit vocabulary for domestic and domesticated animals would seem to reflect a robust conception of them and a sensitivity to their contribution to the identity of the household. While elite Romans were embracing animals as members of their households, elite Rabbis can be found, by contrast, tightening the boundaries of the household and creating a more rigorous dividing line between nature and culture even while recognizing the realities of their blurring.[57]

BAD CATS AND BAD RABBIS

The early rabbinic discourse presents a spectrum of animal danger that runs from mildly annoying, to morally questionable or ritually polluting, to instantly fatal. The teachings represent animals attacking both from within and without, either predictably or erratically, preying upon persons and property, within domestic as well as public space. A story recounted in the Babylonian Talmud illuminates the threat posed by animals to the most intimate spaces of the household and the most vulnerable of its members:[58]

human habitation). Rabbi Meir says: Both of these leave the *tehum*. Even though they enter the *tehum* only at nightfall, it is permitted to slaughter them on the festival (because they are *bayatot*). These are *midbariyot*: those who pasture in the meadow all the time.

[56] Mishnah Kilayim 8:5–6; parallel in Tosefta Kilayim 5:7–8.
[57] On pet-keeping in the Roman world, see Michael MacKinnon, "Pack Animals, Pets, Pests, and Other Non-Human Beings," in *The Cambridge Companion to Ancient Rome*, ed. Paul Erdkamp (New York: Cambridge University Press, 2013), 116–17.

  A famous example of Romans' affection for their pets is the funerary frieze of a dog and accompanying inscription that reads: "To Helena, foster daughter, incomparable and praiseworthy soul" (150–200 CE). See MacKinnon, p. 117.

  MacKinnon warns against imposing modern notions of the pet onto ancient Rome, however, where he sees more blurring among animal roles (an animal could be seen as a pet but also as a work or military animal). Gilhus recommends the term "personal animal" so as "to avoid identifying these human-animal relationships too closely with modern culture"; see also Gilhus, *Animals, Gods and Humans*, 29.

  For more on Romans' affective relationships with their animals, see the discussion on Mary Beard, "A Don's Life," *A Pig's Epitaph*, March 15, 2015, http://timesonline.typepad .com/dons_life/2015/03/the-pigs-epitaph.html.

  On how pet-keeping practices are "part of the social control of nature" and how they emerge from the "'loss of boundaries' between the realms of nature and culture," see Molloy, "Dangerous Dogs," 109. For analysis of "commensal" animals (animals who cohabit with people) more generally, see Terry O'Connor, *Animals as Neighbors: The Past and Present of Commensal Species* (East Lansing: Michigan State University Press, 2013).
[58] That a cat is at the center of this narrative about threats to the household may be due to the fact that cats are the most boundary-crossing of domestic animals; see Schwartz, "Cats in Ancient Jewish Society," 220, n. 48.

Rav, Shmuel, and Rav Asi happened to come to the house of a "week of the son" (i.e., a circumcision), or some say [it was] the house of a "salvation of the son" (i.e., a *pidyon ha-ben*, redemption of a first-born son). Rav would not enter before Shmuel, and Shmuel would not enter before Rav Asi, and Rav Asi would not enter before Rav. They said, "Who will go behind?" Shmuel should go behind, and Rav and Rav Asi should go [ahead]. But Rav or Rav Asi should have gone behind! Rav was only making a gesture on Shmuel's behalf. Because of that incident where he cursed him, Rav gave him precedence over himself.[59] In the meanwhile, a cat came and bit off the hand of the child. Rav went out and expounded: "It is permitted to kill a cat and forbidden to raise him. Theft does not apply to him, nor does the obligation to return a lost item to its owners."[60]

רב ושמואל ורב אסי[61] איקלעו לבי שבוע הבן ואמרי לה לבי ישוע הבן רב לא עייל קמיה שמואל לא עייל קמיה דרב רב אסי לא עייל קמיה דרב אמרי מאן נתרח[62] נתרח שמואל[63] וניתי רב ורב אסי ונתרח רב או רב אסי[64] רב מילתא בעלמא הוא דעבד[65] ליה לשמואל משום ההוא[66] מעשה דלטייה אדבריה רב[67] עליה אדהכי והכי אתא שונרא קטעיה לידא[68] דינוקא[69] נפק רב ודרש חתול מותר להורגו ואסור לקיימו ואין בו משום גזל ואין בו משום השב אבידה לבעלים

This story is composed of six elements:

1. Rav, Shmuel, and Rav Asi arrive at the celebration of a baby boy.
2. They cannot decide who should enter first (entering first is a greater honor).
3. They finally decide who should hang back and who should proceed.
4. The narrator interrupts the story to ask a question about this decision and to give background for it.

---

59 The translation of the last part of the sentence is from Michael Sokoloff, *A Dictionary of Jewish Babylonian Aramaic of the Talmudic and Geonic Periods* (Baltimore: Johns Hopkins University Press, 2002), 313, s.v. *d-v-r*.

60 Bava Qamma 80a–b. One can find brief discussion of this narrative in Schwartz, "Cats in Ancient Jewish Society," 223.

61 Rav Asi is mistakenly absent in his first appearance in Munich 95.

62 Escorial G-I-3, Florence II-I-8, and Munich 95 spell "go behind" or "hang back" with a *tet* instead of a *taf*, referring to the root *t-r-h* (with a *tet*), to take the trouble or make an effort, instead of the root *t-r-h* (with a *taf*), to remain, delay, wait.

63 Munich 95 first says, "Rav should go behind!" (*natrah Rav*) before it says "Shmuel should go behind!" (*natrah Shmuel*).

64 Escorial G-I-3 and Hamburg 165 have the word "they say" (*omri*) before Rav: "They say Rav was only making …"

65 Escorial G-I-3 has *de-avad* ("making") twice.

66 Florence II-I-8 omits *hahu* ("that") before *ma'aseh* ("incident").

67 Escorial G-I-3, Florence II-I-8, and Munich 95 omit "Rav."

68 Escorial G-I-3 has *yatza* instead of *yeda* ("hand") in what seems to be a scribal error. Florence II-I-8 omits the word altogether in what also appears to be a scribal error.

69 Escorial G-I-3 has *hahu yenuqa* ("that baby"), making clear that the baby attacked by the cat is the same one being celebrated.

5. A cat bites off the hand of the child being celebrated.
6. Rav issues four legislations about cats.

The story nearly gets derailed at the start. Three rabbis are going to a celebration for a baby boy, and the story pauses to consider what kind of celebration it is, a circumcision, or a celebration that happens somewhat later after the boy's birth, a *pidyon ha-ben*, here called the "salvation of the son."[70] From an audience perspective, the appropriate response would seem to be – who cares? The pause's purpose, one might speculate, is to focus attention on the baby and to contrast the attention that the story showers upon the baby with the relative lack of attention given to him by the rabbis who are the protagonists of the story. There is also an irony in the types of celebration mentioned. The son will be anything but saved at the "salvation of the son," and the possibility that the celebration was a circumcision foreshadows the cat's attack upon the baby's body part.

The main characters, the three rabbis, are concerned not with the baby who is the figure being celebrated but with the rituals of honor that govern their relationships. According to the rules of the rabbinate, no rabbi should enter a room before a rabbi of greater honor. In this case, the rules bring them to a comic standstill. Rav refuses to enter before Shmuel, Shmuel refuses to enter before Rav Asi, and Rav Asi refuses to enter before Rav, his teacher. No one, in short, can move. Realizing the predicament in which they find themselves, the three rabbis ask each other: "Who will hang back?" In posing the question this way, the rabbis portray themselves not as bent on giving the other appropriate honor but each as being unwilling to give up on his own.

The rabbis determine that Shmuel should defer to the others. A challenge to that decision is interjected by the editorial voice ("But Rav or Rav Asi should have gone behind!"). The narrator goes on to explain that Rav had been compensating for a prior incident in which Rav had cast a curse

[70] Both are rare idioms in rabbinic literature. Rashi explains that "week of the son" refers to a circumcision since it occurs after the first seven days of the baby boy's life. Commentators disagree over the second celebration mentioned within the passage, the "salvation of the son." My translation follows Rashi, who understands it to be referring to the redemption of the first-born son. Rashi's explanation is that the Hebrew word *yeshu'a*, salvation, is standardly translated into Aramaic as *purqan*, which was then associated with the Hebrew *pidyon*, the word for redemption. According to the Tosafot, however (s.v. *le-ve yeshu'a ha-ben*), the salvation in the word *yeshu'a* refers more logically not to the redemption of the first-born from the priest but to the "salvation" or escape of the baby boy from the danger of childbirth. If so, then "salvation of the son" would seem to be a reference to a party to celebrate a healthy baby being born.

upon Shmuel. That incident is narrated in full elsewhere in the Talmud.[71] In that story, Rav gets a terrible stomachache, and Shmuel "cures" Rav by feeding him great amounts of food and then, rather sadistically, preventing him from using the bathroom. Rav's response at the time, unsurprisingly, was to curse Shmuel. The editorial interruption explains that Rav's initial impulse to enter behind Shmuel was a product of his regret over having cursed him ("Because of the incident where he cursed him, Rav gave him precedence over himself").[72] Technically, however, Rav's greater honor dictated that Rav should have entered first ("Rav was only making a gesture on Shmuel's behalf"), which is why the three rabbis ultimately decided that Rav should enter first.[73] Again, one might ask about the rhetorical function of the editorial interruption, which mentions an incident that it does not bother to fully rehearse and which seems not entirely necessary to justify the plot developments here. As before, the interruption seems designed to alert the audience to an important theme they are soon to encounter in the story. In this case, the theme is Rav's fierce anger and his lack of restraint in expressing it. The interruption also points to the dark side of rabbinic honor, which is rabbis' hostility toward one another.[74] The honorific gestures, one learns, turn quickly into curses.

While these negotiations are occurring – *adehakhi ve-hakhi* ("in the meantime") – a cat sneaks up on the baby and attacks him, biting off his hand.[75] The rabbinic personages are too preoccupied with their honor, as are, one imagines, the gathered family and guests, to notice when a cat attacks the baby who is the very object of celebration. Rav emerges from the encounter issuing a set of legislations that permit a person to kill or steal a cat and that prohibit giving provisions to a cat. The severity of the legislations is brought home by the editorial treatment, which questions why Rav needed to state as many legislations as he did:

---

[71] Shabbat 108a. For story cues where the full story never appears, see Daniel Rosenberg, "Short(hand) Stories: Unexplained Story Cues in the Babylonian Talmud" (PhD diss., New York University, 2014).

[72] The commentator Meiri goes into a lengthy explanation here of the dynamics of honor, insult, regret, and compensation, s.v. *talmid*.

[73] The Meiri explains that the presence of a third party suspended the promise that Rav had made to compensate for cursing Shmuel.

[74] On shame and violence among Babylonian rabbis, see Rubenstein, *The Culture of the Babylonian Talmud*, 54–79.

[75] A story on Bava Qamma 84a uses the same language to describe a donkey who bites off a baby's hand, which is followed by the story of an ox who bites off (using the verb *alas* instead of *qata)* a baby's hand. There the problem is the assessment and collection of personal injury payments by the baby's father.

And since you say "it is permitted to kill him," why is there further "it is forbidden to raise him"?

What is it that you would have supposed from "it is permitted to kill him"? There is no prohibition! He teaches us [otherwise].

They say [another challenge], that since you say "theft does not apply to him," why is there further "nor does the obligation to return a lost item to its owners"?

Ravina said, "For his (the cat's) skin" (which one need not return to the owner).

וכיון דאמרת מותר להורגו מאי ניהו תו אסור לקיימו

מהו דתימא מותר להורגו⁷⁶ איסורא ליכא קמ"ל

אמרי⁷⁷ וכיון דאמרת אין בו משום גזל מאי ניהו תו⁷⁸ אין בו משום השב אבידה לבעלים

אמר רבינא לעורו

The talmudic commentary portrays Rav's legislations as redundant. The question asked twice by the editorial voice, "why is there further...," highlights Rav's overenthusiasm. Rav's zeal results in cats not *even* reaching the legal status of property, much less the status of a living thing.⁷⁹

The introduction to Rav's legislations, "Rav went out and expounded," is a signal that Rav's legislations should be understood in light of his role in the preceding events.⁸⁰ The narrative serves, as is often the case in the Talmud, to provide a counterpoint to the law and to offer a critical stance with respect to it.⁸¹ Rav steps in as an authoritative legislator precisely when he and his rabbinic colleagues seem most impotent. They are literally paralyzed by their preoccupation with the micropower struggles within their hermetic world. Rav's legislation seems designed to shift attention

---

⁷⁶ "It is permitted to kill him" (*mutar le-horgo*) absent in Escorial G-I-3, Florence II-I-8, Hamburg 165, and Munich 95.

⁷⁷ "They say" (*omri*) absent in Escorial G-I-3, Hamburg 165, Florence II-I-8, and Munich 95, the last two of which also omit *qa mashma lan* ("he teaches us").

⁷⁸ "Further" (*tu*) absent in Escorial G-I-3.

⁷⁹ Rav's legislation forms a contrast with the discussion in my next chapter, where property is the inferior status to persons; here, cats are not *even* property, such that if one steals, loses, or kills a cat the act does not legally register.

The severity of the legislation is observed by the Tosafot, s.v. *mutar*, who contrast it with the materials in Sanhedrin that deal with the dangerous animal species list and that are in fact less severe. The Tosafot offer a creative solution to the discrepancy, which is that perhaps Rav sees cats as even more dangerous than lions and tigers because people do not typically perceive them to be as dangerous, so they are less on guard around them. The other hypothesis that the Tosafot offer, which relies on a similar logic, is that people typically tie up dangerous species but do not tie up cats.

⁸⁰ Despite the Tosafot's explanation that these legislations had in fact been issued beforehand; s.v. *nefaq*. The rationale of the Tosafot is that the Talmud would not challenge the legislation from an early rabbinic teaching if they were clearly issued as a context-specific decree.

⁸¹ See discussion of legal narrative in Wimpfheimer, *Narrating the Law*.

away from the Rabbis' impotence by generating a moral panic around the figure of the cat. As Molloy observes in her study of pit bull laws in the United Kingdom, it is usually a key event that turns the tone to one of crisis, and it is almost always an event that involves the victimization of a child.[82] Far from being presented as a rational response to animal danger, Rav's legislations appear, through their juxtaposition to the narrative, to be disproportional, with their purpose being the displacement of Rav's guilt.[83] Rav would rather blame the entire cat species than consider his own accountability or alternative legislative possibilities.

RABBIS, THEIR WIVES, AND THEIR ANIMALS

The flaws of rabbinic authority are apparent also in the surrounding literary materials. Prior to the story is another one in which rabbis behave badly and children pay the consequences. That story features Rav Huna in conversation with an obscure rabbi-named Ada bar Ahavah. The story is predicated on another "animal-phobic" legislation issued by Rav. In that legislation, Rav extends the prohibition on raising small cattle from Palestine to Babylonia:

Rav Yehudah said that Rav said: We have made ourselves in Babylonia like the land of Israel with respect to small cattle.
Rav Ada bar Ahavah said to Rav Huna, "Yours – what [is the case]?"
He (Rav Huna) said to him (Rav Ada bar Ahavah), "Ours – Hovah[84] watches them."
He (Rav Ada bar Ahavah) said to him (Rav Huna), "Hovah will bury her sons!"
All the years of Rav Ada bar Ahavah, Rav Huna never had a child from Hovah.

אמר רב יהודה[85] אמר רב עשינו עצמנו[86] בבבל כארץ ישראל לבהמה דקה

א"ל רב אדא בר אהבה לרב הונא דידך מאי

---

[82] "Within a moral panic extant analyses have shown that there is usually a key event that shifts the panic to the status of a crisis ... in each case study, we find the death of children or young people to be a powerful signifier of crisis." Molloy, "Dangerous Dogs," 123.

The Babylonian Talmud portrays the danger of dogs also as a threat to children (or, rather, potential children). In Bava Qamma 83a (and parallel on Shabbat 63b), a dog's bark is said to scare a pregnant woman into miscarrying, with the catastrophic consequences of causing God's presence to withdraw from Israel. Another story follows of a woman miscarrying because of a dog's bark. See discussion in Schwartz, "Good Dog-Bad Dog," 69–70.

[83] On disproportionality as a critical feature of moral panic, see Molloy, "Dangerous Dogs," 127.

[84] In Escorial G-I-3 and Munich 95, her name is *Hibah*, which means love, esteem, or honor (making her a perfect match with her husband, "son of Love").

[85] In Munich 95 it is Rav Huna and not Rav Yehudah.

[86] "We have made ourselves" (*asinu atzmenu*) is absent in Hamburg 165, which features the expression later in an alternative version of the tradition (I do not here discuss that segment).

א"ל[87] דידן[88] קא מינטרא להו חובה

א"ל חובה[89] תקברינהו לבנה

כולה שניה דרב אדא בר אהבה לא אקיים זרעא לרב הונא מחובה

Putative founder of the Babylonian rabbinic movement, Rav grants to the land of Babylonia a status equal to that of the land of Israel. If Israel needs to be protected from small cattle, then so too does Babylonia. Rav's language, "we have made ourselves," is one of self-empowerment and thematizes Rav's judicial assertiveness in the face of competition between Palestine and the new rabbinic center in Babylonia.[90]

Rav's legislation is contravened by none other than Rav's most famous student, Rav Huna, who appears to have his own small herd. Rav Ada bar Ahavah challenges Rav Huna, calling him out for his hypocrisy: "Yours – what [is the case]?" How do you, Rav Huna, justify your own keeping of small cattle despite your master's ban on them? Rav Huna's response only makes things worse. Rav Huna announces that it is not he, but his wife Hovah, who watches over the herd. Thus Rav Huna, *technically*, has committed no violation. Rav Huna's wife named Hovah, which ironically is the word for legal obligation, allows Rav Huna to evade his *hovah*, or legal obligation.[91] Rav Ada bar Ahavah has no patience for Rav Huna's rerouting of blame and puts a curse on him and his household: "Hovah will bury her sons!" This terrible curse, the story's narrator relates, comes true, and the sheep-herding couple never produce a "herd" of their own in what seems to be a measure-for-measure punishment. Hovah's activity as a shepherd ultimately prevents Rav Huna from fulfilling his "hovah" to reproduce. This story has the same key elements as the subsequent story about Rav, the circumcision, and the cat: a legislation about animals, rabbis competing, one rabbi curses another, a tragedy befalls a child, and a disproportionate punishment.

The medieval commentators on this story are horrified by Rav Ada bar Ahavah's venom. To soften the portrait of Rav Ada bar Ahavah, some

---

[87] "He said to him" (*amar leh*) is missing in Hamburg 165.

[88] "Ours" (*didan*) is absent in Munich 95.

[89] *Hovah* is absent here in Hamburg 165.

[90] Though that expression is not in every version; see earlier note. Rav is described in Gittin 6a with the same language; there he is extending to Babylonia power over divorce agreements. For a discussion of Rav's judicial assertiveness in the context of the competition between Palestine and Babylonia, see Isaiah Gafni, *Land, Center and Diaspora: Jewish Constructs in Late Antiquity* (Sheffield, UK: Sheffield Academic Press, 1997), 116.

[91] It makes for a strange name, which is why Rashi feels compelled to explain that it is a name; s.v. *Hovah*.

read his words – "Hovah will bury her sons!" – to be not a curse but a caution. If Hovah spends all her time raising sheep, she will have no time remaining to raise her children.[92] But in a parallel story elsewhere in the Talmud with the same characters, the same words are uttered, and there it is clear that they are intended as a curse.[93] One is left to wonder at the level of spite that leads one rabbi to wish upon another the death of a child. There is irony not only in Hovah's name but also in Rav Ada bar Ahavah's. Ada refers to a person who sets traps for other people's animals in order to steal them, which is appropriate here, since Ada essentially sets a trap for Rav Huna, who himself maintains prohibited animals.[94] Ahavah means love, a quality noticeably absent from Ada bar Ahavah the man. The greatest danger appears to be not from the animals that people harbor in their homes but from the rabbis who tolerate neither the animals themselves nor any challenges to their legislations about them.

BLACK AND WHITE WORLD-VIEWS

The Talmud's deconstruction of the discourse of animal danger continues after the story about Rav at the circumcision. The talmudic dialectic challenges Rav with an early rabbinic tradition that is a good deal more accepting of cats than Rav is:

They challenge [based on an early rabbinic teaching]: Rabbi Shimon ben Elazar says: One may raise village dogs, cats, monkeys, and porcupines because they go around[95] cleaning the house.[96]

This is not difficult: One is [speaking of] black [cats], and the other of white.

But the incident of Rav was a black cat!

That was a black the offspring of a white.

But Ravina [already] asks that question, as Ravina asks: A black the offspring of a white, what is [the law]?

---

92 Rashi's comment: "'will bury her sons': "since you are relying upon her, and she is unable to watch [them]."

93 Nazir 57b. See discussion in Tosafot, s.v., *Hovah*.

94 Jastrow, s.v. *Ada*: "equivalent to biblical Hebrew *tzodeh*, 'fowler,' 'one who puts up baits, snares &c. for other people's doves."

95 "Go around" is a loose translation of *asu'i*, which Jastrow translates as "spend time, tarry" or as "forced," either of which may be in play in here, since the house animals catch mice and rats and other critters, probably out of some combination of entertainment and hunger.

96 Parallel in Tosefta Bava Qamma 8:17. See discussion of this part of the passage in Schwartz, "Cats in Ancient Jewish Society," 224.

When Ravina asks, it is about a black the offspring of a white who is the offspring of a black. The incident of Rav was a black the offspring of a white who is the offspring of a white.

מיתיבי⁹⁷ רבי שמעון בן אלעזר אומר מגדלין כלבים כופרין⁹⁸ וחתולין וקופין⁹⁹ וחולדות סנאים¹⁰⁰ מפני שעשויין לנקר את הבית¹⁰¹

לא קשיא הא באוכמא הא בחיורא¹⁰²

והא מעשה¹⁰³ דרב אוכמא הוה

התם¹⁰⁴ אוכמא בר חיורא הוה

והא מבעיא בעיא ליה רבינא דבעי רבינא¹⁰⁵ אוכמא בר חיורא מהו¹⁰⁶

כי קמבעיא ליה לרבינא באוכמא בר חיורא בר אוכמא מעשה¹⁰⁷ דרב באוכמא בר חיורא בר חיורא¹⁰⁸ הוה

The Talmud proposes that the permissive tradition attributed to Rabbi Shimon ben Elazar ("One may raise village dogs, cats, monkeys, and porcupines because they go around cleaning the house") relates to one kind of cat, the black cat, presumably a "good" cat who mouses within the house, while Rav's legislation relates to another kind of cat, the white cat, who is a dangerous creature to be destroyed at all costs.[109]

---

[97] Florence II-I-8 and Munich 95 incorrectly write *metiv* instead of *metivi*. Vatican 116 has *motivi*.

[98] "Village" (*qufrin*) absent in Escorial G-I-3.

[99] Munich 95 mistakenly has *zequfin* instead of *ve-qofin*.

[100] The *huldot sena'im* ("porcupines") are missing from Hamburg 165 and Vatican 116.

[101] Escorial G-I-3 and Hamburg 165 add "they say" (*omri*) before "it is not difficult" (*la qashya*).

[102] Vatican 116 reverses this line to: "One [is speaking] of white, and the other of black."

[103] Escorial G-I-3 and Vatican 116 use the Aramaic *uvda* instead of the Hebrew *ma'aseh*. Hamburg 165 omits the word altogether.

[104] Instead of "there" (*ha-tam*), Escorial G-I-3 has "[the incident] of Rav." Hamburg 165 and Vatican 116 omit the word altogether.

[105] "As Ravina asks" (*de-ba'ey Ravina*) absent in Florence II-I-8 and Hamburg 165.

[106] Escorial G-I-3, Hamburg 165, and Vatican 116 have *may* instead of *mahu*.

[107] Word *ma'aseh* ("incident") absent in Hamburg 165.

[108] Escorial G-I-3 and Hamburg 165 curiously add the word *le-olam* ("after all" or "always") after the final *hivra* ("a white"). Vatican 116 is missing the last "offspring of a white one," so that it reads only as "the incident of Rav was a black the offspring of a white."

[109] Rashi uses the earlier vocabulary of the tractate, *muad*, to describe the white cat, knitting together the discourse of danger; s.v. *hivra*.

Berakhot 6a features the placenta of a "black female cat the offspring of a black female cat, the first-born offspring of a first-born," in its magical formula for a potion that can allow a person to see normally invisible demons. That text associates protective though also potentially dangerous magical powers with the black cat. See discussion of the Berakhot passage in Hillel Athias-Robles, "'If The Eye Had Permission to See No Creature Could Stand Before the Mezikin': Demons and Vision in the Babylonian Talmud" (MA thesis, Columbia University, 2015).

The picture of good and bad cats, black versus white, soon becomes nebulous. The editorial voice claims first that the "bad" cat in the Rav story was in fact black and not white, thus muddling the simplicity of the initial equation of black = good and white = bad. To restore that equation, the talmudic dialectic plays with permutations of ancestry. The cat in the Rav story, it is claimed, was really white after all. It only looked black because it was "black the offspring of a white." That cannot be the case either, however, it is said in the next turn of the dialectic, since the later rabbi Ravina appears to have asked about precisely such a case, which he would not have, according to the norms of rabbinic discourse, if the case had already been decisively treated by a prior rabbinic teaching. That claim is itself corrected, however, when the Talmud explains that Ravina's question was not actually about that case (i.e., black offspring of white), but rather about the more complicated case of a black cat born of a white cat who was himself born of a black one. Which ancestry wins out in determining the character of that cat: black or white? That question is never answered, but one does find out the proper treatment for a black cat born of a white cat who was in turn born of a white cat. Such a cat, the dialectic concludes, was precisely the type featured in the story with Rav – the kind that bites off a baby's hand and that should be dispatched on sight.

But how does one know which kind of cat one is dealing with? According to the talmudic logic, a black cat may be a white cat in disguise, and vice versa. The equation of black with good and white with bad seems simple enough, but applying it to any particular cat seems nearly impossible without the help of a professional geneticist.[110] As is the case with pit bulls, danger ends up detached from empirical reality. Any

In Persian literature, the black cat is associated with powerful magic, sometimes protective, sometimes harmful; see Mahmud Omidsalar, "Cat I: In Mythology and Folklore," *Encyclopaedia Iranica* (Winona Lake, IN: Eisenbrauns, 1990), www.iranicaonline.org/articles/cat-in-mythology-and-folklore-khot. On sacral associations with black cats in Egyptian Isis worship, see Donald W. Engels, *Classical Cats: The Rise and Fall of the Sacred Cat* (New York: Routledge, 1999), 123–4. The black cat in Bava Qamma is claimed to be protective in a far more prosaic way than is the Egyptian or Persian black cat. On black versus white cats in rabbinic literature see also Schwartz, "Cats in Ancient Jewish Society," 223, n. 65.

[110] The Tosafot make this observation, s.v. *mutar*, discussed in footnote above: "... people do not know if he is the offspring of a black or the offspring of a white, for [people] do not know their (i.e., the cats') fathers." The Meiri describes Rav, before making his decree, going and checking the particular species of cat; s.v. *yesh*.

individual can be subject to suspicion, and the suspicion seems circular: if a black cat misbehaves, he must really be of white stock, etc. I therefore read the dialectic not the way commentators have typically done, as a straightforward exercise in determining the parameters of danger laws, but rather as a *reductio ad absurdum*, since the flaws in the logic of cat danger are so readily apparent, and the attempts to apply it so dizzying (one needs a Punnett square to keep track of the cat lineages in the passage).[111] In the vein of Holger Zellentin's and Daniel Boyarin's understandings of certain passages of Talmud as parodic or satiric, I read this material as a parody of discourses of animal danger.[112] The parody brings to light the constructedness and malleability of assertions about animal danger and ridicules how "black and white" those discourses try to make the danger seem.

The parody is also meant to mediate the clash of cat cultures that these traditions represent. Rav's harsh legislation rings of the *xrafstar* category of Middle Persian texts, which considers certain animal species to be utterly repulsive and cosmically dangerous. These species are considered the product of demonic forces and are understood to deserve instant destruction. Felines fall into this category.[113] The severity of Rav's legislations would seem to reflect this kind of dualistic, moralistic, cosmic demonization of cats, whom Zoroastrians considered "restive and perfidious." In a story reminiscent of the one with Rav, the last great Sasanian king Kosrow II is described as charging one of his governors with destruction of all the cats in the city.[114]

---

[111] On attempts by codifiers of the Talmud to flesh out the practical implications of this passage, see discussion in Schwartz, "Cats in Ancient Jewish Society," 223–4, n. 67. Maimonides, the Tur, and the Shulchan Arukh limit Rav's legislation to "evil cats" that kill or harm children.

[112] Boyarin, *Socrates and the Fat Rabbis*; Holger M. Zellentin, *Rabbinic Parodies of Jewish and Christian Literature* (Tübingen: Mohr Siebeck, 2011). One of Zellentin's chapters treats a passage in Bava Metzia that also, curiously, features cats being killed; see pp. 27–50.

[113] Omidsalar, "Cat"; Macuch, "Treatment of Animals," 167; Moazami, "Evil Animals," 302, 314–15. See n. 4 on p. 167 in Macuch for discussion of the ambiguity in the vocabulary for cats in Persian texts. The quotation about perfidy is from Moazami, p. 315. According to Boyce, current Zoroastrian belief holds that even if one washes a bowl seven times after a cat has eaten from it, the bowl remains unclean, that eating food that has touched a cat's whiskers will cause one to waste away, and that a cat's glance will cause demons to enter a corpse; see Mary Boyce, *A Persian Stronghold of Zoroastrianism* (Oxford, UK: Clarendon Press, 1977), 163, n. 51.

[114] See Omidsalar, "Cat." That story is told in the *Shahnameh*, Moscow edition, Vol. IX, pp. 192–3, vv. 3082–3102.

By contrast, "to the cats ... the Roman Empire represented something of a golden age of peace, prosperity, and civil society."[115] Colonies of cats seem to have spread to all corners of the late Roman Empire, where they were generally considered useful members of the household who ate up disease-spreading, supply-destroying rats (the down side was that they also ate domestic birds).[116] Mosaics from Pompeii display cats hunting and climbing; one marble relief now in the Museo Capitolino depicts a cat learning to dance.[117] A Latin tombstone from second-century Rome commemorates a woman named Calpurnia Felicla, whose second name means "kitten," and below the inscription is a picture of an eponymous small cat. Hundreds of inscriptions can be found from all over the Empire in which women have some form of the nickname "kitten."[118] Cats are depicted as household hunters, playmates, and pets.[119] The Third Legion Cyrenaica, stationed in Arabia Nabatea after the year 123 CE, had a cat as its mascot.[120] The immense popularity throughout the Roman Empire of the Egyptian cult of Isis, who was frequently shown accompanied by her sacred cat companion Bubastis or actually identified with the cat, would have contributed to the cat's embrace by Roman audiences (except by Roman pagan and Christian intellectuals, who satirized Egyptian cat worship).[121] One might see the permissive rabbinic teaching cited in the talmudic passage in light of this cultural context in which the cat was, generally speaking, a figure of favor.

In the next chapter I will argue that the meeting of Zoroastrian laws about animals with Graeco-Roman ones may have inspired the talmudic

---

[115] Engels, *Classical Cats*, 95.

[116] The spread was possibly not before the first century; see John Percy Vyvian Dacre Balsdon, *Life and Leisure in Ancient Rome* (New York: McGraw-Hill, 1969), 151. On the patterns in osteological cat remains, see Engels, *Classical Cats*, 107–8. On cats and public health, see Engels, *Classical Cats*, 108–14. A cat buried and preserved in the Roman Red Sea port city of Quseir el-Qadim, probably in the first or second century CE, had the remains of six rats found in his belly; see p. 136. On cats eating farmyard hens, see Schwartz, "Cats in Ancient Jewish Society," 215–20.

[117] Engels, *Classical Cats*, 97–8.

[118] Ibid., 99.

[119] Even if the rabbinic texts never embrace the cat as a pet or playmate; see general argument in Schwartz, "Cats in Ancient Jewish Society." For more on Roman cultural representations of cats – as clean, swift, useful, of "big cats" as exotic status symbols, as pets, as signs of the divine – see Malcolm Drew Donalson, *The Domestic Cat in Roman Civilization* (Lewiston, NY: Edwin Mellen Press, 1999). For a general cultural history of the cat that includes ancient Egypt and Rome, see Katharine M. Rogers, *Cat* (Chicago: University of Chicago Press, 2006).

[120] Engels, *Classical Cats*, 107.

[121] Ibid., 115–28. On the critique of cat worship, see pp. 123, 132–3.

editors to think critically about the legal categorization of animals. Here I am proposing that the encounter between the cat-demonizing tendencies of the Zoroastrians and the cat tolerance of the Romans facilitated for the talmudic editors a reflective distance on both. The diametrically opposed rabbinic traditions featured in this passage, on the one side Rav's severe legislation, on the other the early rabbinic teaching's permissiveness, represent competing cultures of animal danger.[122] The passage's interest is less in promoting one of these discourses of danger over the other than in exploring and exposing the processes of production that lie behind such discourse. The passage pursues this interest by presenting Rav's legislations alongside the story that purportedly led to them, and by juxtaposing those legislations with the more tolerant teachings that preceded them.

CONCLUSIONS: MACHO RABBIS AND QUEER ANIMAL-LOVERS

According to Freud, the fear of being eaten, and concomitant wish to be eaten, is primal.[123] A sense of the uncanny arises when the prey becomes the predator, the passive turns active, and the domesticated animal goes wild.[124] One can view dangerous animal laws as a response to the uncanny, a restoration of order, the promise of protection from being eaten, and the continual domestication of that which threatens to go wild. The authorities who make these laws demonstrate their expertise in managing risk, their power to regulate human/animal relations, and their capacity to control.[125] Identification or empathy with animals, in this scheme, becomes legally unprotected if not prohibited, and is associated with the female and the infantile. This set of associations – [men, control of animals, maker of laws] vs. [women and children, consumption by

---

[122] Molloy speaks of competing authorities on animal danger and risk; see Molloy, "Dangerous Dogs," 107, 111.

[123] See Oliver, p. 11: "In a certain sense, all fear is linked to the fear of being eaten, the fear of becoming the eaten rather than the eater, becoming passive rather than active ... In the case of the animal phobias and the fear of being devoured by the father, Freud sees a hidden wish; namely, the desire to be in the feminine or passive position in relation to the father in a sexual way."

[124] See Oliver, pp. 13–14: "An uncanny sensation is produced when something that should be passive becomes active or something domesticated becomes wild, whether that something is a girl or an animal."

[125] This borrows from the formulation in Molloy, "Dangerous Dogs," 108–9.

animals or compassion toward them, subject to laws] – helps to explain why the male animal activists described by Alison Suen are vilified by their opponents as queers.[126] To reject control and consumption of animals, and aggression toward them, is to reject masculinity itself as it is normatively configured, as Carol Adams argues in her *Sexual Politics of Meat*.[127] Through Rav's harsh legislations, Rav tries to resolve the crisis of rabbinic masculinity posed by the cat's attack upon the baby and by the rabbis' paralysis precipitating the attack. The cat legislations aim to protect the myth of the rabbi as protector. The cat externalizes and embodies danger so that rabbinic law can master it (the cat, and the danger).

Protection, Derrida observes, is a bargain made with the law.[128] The law insulates from fear, but it creates fears of its own.[129] Dangerous animal laws may assuage people's fears, but they also put on display the sovereign's own fearsome power over life and death and, as is the case in the story of Rav and the cat, the harm caused by the exercise of that power. Echoing the critics of the pit bull legislations, the talmudic materials ask whether it is possible to tell which animal is dangerous and which is not and whether the real risk is from the animal at all. The moral panic that runs through the talmudic texts, the risk to baby boys and to male lines (the baby boy at the bris, the curse on Rav Huna's household), is shown to be rooted not, in the end, in the aggressiveness of animals but in the cruelty and competitiveness of rabbinic culture. Rabbinic machismo turns out to be the problem, not the solution. What destroys the household are not the odd sheep, goats, cats, dogs, chickens, or pigeons who roam around it, but the rabbis who regulate them. Standing before his cat naked, as he describes himself in a famous essay, Derrida never really wondered what his cat was thinking.[130] Neither

---

[126] See Suen, p. 132: "One man described how hunters called him an 'animal rights queer' during a protest against hunting."

[127] Carol J. Adams, *The Sexual Politics of Meat: A Feminist-Vegetarian Critical Theory* (New York: Bloomsbury USA, 2015).

[128] *The Beast and the Sovereign*, discussed by Suen, p. 124. "'I protect you' means for the state, I oblige you, you are my subject, *I subject you*."

[129] "The law is instituted out of fear (of losing one's life), and the law is sustained out of fear (of punishment)"; Suen, p. 124.

[130] Derrida does at several points reflect on his cat's point of view, but he is ultimately more interested in how his cat's stare affects his perception of himself. For his references to the cat's point of view, see Jacques Derrida, "The Animal That Therefore I Am (More to Follow)," trans. David Wills, *Critical Inquiry* 28, no. 2 (January 1, 2002): 377, 380, 382.

For a critique of the thinness of Derrida's reflection on his cat, see Donna Jeanne Haraway, *When Species Meet* (Minneapolis: University of Minnesota Press, 2008),

do these talmudic texts. The texts do illuminate, however, what rabbis might be thinking when they make their laws about cats and other household animals.

19–27: "He came right to the edge of respect ... Somehow in all this worrying and longing, the cat was never heard from again ... But with his cat, Derrida failed a simple obligation of companion species; he did not become curious about what the cat might actually be doing, feeling, thinking, or perhaps making available to him in looking back at him that morning" (p. 20).

6

Animals as Livestock

Sukkah 22b–23b

Schoolhouse Rock imprinted upon a generation of children, me among them, the definition of a noun:

Well, every person you can know,
And every place that you can go,
And anything that you can show,
You know they're nouns.

Where do animals fit in? They aren't places, so they must be either person or thing. "Person" normally means human, however, while "thing" suggests inanimate object. For Schoolhouse Rock, animals are anomalous. The term "livestock" captures this anomaly. On one hand, the animal is part of the "stock" or merchandise owned by the farmer. On the other hand, the animal is as "live" as the farmer. To address the anomaly, some grade-school teachers have inserted "animal" into the lineup of categories that constitute a noun: "person, place, thing, or animal."[1]

The anomaly of the animal – Person or thing? Subject or object? – is the concern of this chapter. The talmudic passage I will examine, Sukkah 22b–23b, plays with the status of animals as things, exploring the ways

---

[1] This is one teacher's question on a website for teachers: "I teach first grade and have for 13 years. There are two fresh out of college teachers who are teaching that nouns are people, places, things and animals. When did the category of animals get added to the list? I was taught that animals were "things" and not a subcategory of their own. I don't want to seem behind the times and I am willing to include animals as a group for nouns if this is now what is being done. Help someone … set me straight! Thanks!" See www .proteacher.net/discussions/showthread.php?t=2619

that animals exceed the category. The passage begins with an odd legal question. Can one use an animal as the floor or wall of a sukkah (the fall festival booth), as the stake or boards for an eruv (the Sabbath boundary marker that permits carrying), as the closure for a grave (normally a stone), or as the "parchment" for a divorce decree (the divorcing husband would theoretically write the agreement somewhere upon the living animal, such as on his horn)? In all these cases, the animal substitutes for some inanimate object: wood, stone, paper. Rabbi Meir is said to prohibit such substitution. The talmudic commentary's question is why. In the course of answering the question, the passage considers what differentiates animals from things and makes animals "bad" property.

The classification of animals as things – objects to own, benefit from, and argue over, along with other kinds of property – can be traced back to the earliest legal systems.[2] Biblical and other ancient Near Eastern law codes contain clauses covering ownership, renting, and theft of animals and their products, as well as compensation for harm or loss.[3] Biblical law takes for granted the necessity and propriety of animal labor, consumption, and sacrifice. The last of the ten commandments, "Thou shalt not covet thy neighbor's house, thou shalt not covet thy neighbor's wife, nor his manservant, nor his maidservant, *nor his ox, nor his ass, nor anything that is thy neighbor's*," shows how embedded was the idea of the animal as property.[4]

Roman law made similar assumptions about animals: "The legal thinghood of nonhuman animals was a Roman legal axiom."[5] The

---

[2] The following discussion will more or less equate the concepts of "property" and "thing" even though there are differences between them (e.g., many "things" are unowned). The ancient texts I discuss here take it as a given that animals are property and are more interested in the problem of their thingness. Since contemporary animal rights debates frame the problem in terms of person vs. property (see later discussion), however, I have adopted that language as well.

[3] On the status of the animal in the Bible and in other ancient Near Eastern laws, see Steven M. Wise, "The Legal Thinghood of Nonhuman Animals," *Boston College Environmental Affairs Law Review* 23, no. 2 (1996): 477–88.

[4] Exodus 20:17; parallel in Deuteronomy 5:21. Wife and slave, also mentioned in the verse, occupy a similarly ambiguous status as both living being and a form of household property. On the ambiguous status of slaves and women in rabbinic law, see Judith Romney Wegner, *Chattel or Person? The Status of Women in the Mishnah* (New York: Oxford University Press, 1988); Paul Virgil McCracken Flesher, *Oxen, Women or Citizens? Slaves in the System of the Mishnah* (Atlanta, GA: Scholars Press, 1988).

[5] Wise, "Legal Thinghood," 492. On animal status in Roman law, see ibid., 492–505. On the occupation of wild animals, see the Digest of Justinian 41.1.14, citing Neratius, and Digest 41.2.3.14, citing the Sententiae of Paul. See also Digest 41.1.5, 41.1.44.

Institutes of Gaius introduced a taxonomy of persons, things, and actions within which animals were classified as things. Animals were protected from harm insofar as they belonged to a person who possessed rights and duties, but animals themselves could possess neither. Late antique Roman law understood the property status of animals to flow from their "occupation" (*occupatio*, obtaining title by seizing possession of a previously unowned object), originally when the animal was wild. The title was thought to then be passed down from generation to generation in an extending sequence of occupations.[6] The greatest medieval common law treatise, Henry de Bracton's *Tractatus de Legibus et Consuetudinibus Angliae*, hewed to the categorization of animals found within Roman law, with William Blackstone's *Commentary* following suit, anchoring the idea of animal ownership in the cosmology of the Bible. James Kent's *Commentaries on American Law* classified domesticated animals as absolute property, subject to all the laws of private property, and classified *ferae naturae* ("wild animals") as qualified, or temporarily held, property. The general statement from the *Corpus Juris Secundum*, an encyclopedia of US law, captures this long line of legal thinking: "Domestic animals, as you would expect, are as much subject to property rights as an inanimate object such as a chair or ring."[7] While neither the US Constitution nor the US Supreme Court has expressly defined personhood, it is fair to say that American legal traditions take for granted that it does not attach to animals.[8]

Some lawyers would like that to change. As legal things and not persons, animals "are invisible to civil law," argues Steven Wise, founder of the Nonhuman Rights Project, "and exist solely for legal persons."[9]

---

[6] The most famous American court case to address animal "occupation" and possession is the 1805 *Pierson v. Post*. It was a trivial-seeming case about who was the rightful owner of a cheap fox pelt, but it made its way to the US Supreme Court because it raised fundamental questions about how something attains the status of property. See the introduction in Chad Luck, *The Body of Property: Antebellum American Fiction and the Phenomenology of Possession* (New York: Fordham University Press, 2014).

[7] C.J.S. Animals 4, at 475 (1973); discussed in Wise, "Legal Thinghood," 538.

[8] Jessica Berg, "Elephants and Embryos: A Proposed Framework for Legal Personhood," *Hastings Law Journal* 59 (2007): 371.

[9] Steven M. Wise, "The Capacity of Non-Human Animals for Legal Personhood and Legal Rights," in *The Politics of Species: Reshaping Our Relationships with Other Animals*, ed. Raymond Corbey and Annette Lanjouw (New York: Cambridge University Press, 2013), 241. See also Steven M. Wise, "Legal Personhood and the Nonhuman Rights Project," *Animal Law* 17 (2010): 1–11.

On legal personhood for animals, see also Maneesha Deckha, "Critical Animal Studies and the Property Debate in Animal Law," in *Animal Subjects 2.0*, ed. Jodey Castricano and Lauren Corman (Waterloo, ON: Wilfrid Laurier University Press,

Legal persons, unlike legal things, have legal rights, including rights of action, and as potential plaintiffs possess "standing," which permits them to pursue a lawsuit against a defendant for harm caused to them. As long as humans do not cause "unnecessary suffering" to other species, and as long as the harm they cause has "legitimate purpose," it will be considered legal as long as animals are classified as property rather than persons.[10] The human interests themselves – consumption, entertainment, research, labor, transportation, and so forth – cannot be challenged, argues Gary Francione.[11] Others like Cass Sunstein point out that there are perks that

2016); Tomasz Pietrzykowski and Visa A. J. Kurki, eds., *Legal Personhood: Animals, Artificial Intelligence and the Unborn* (New York: Springer, 2017). For a short history of the concept of person, legal and otherwise, see Kurt Danziger, "Historical Psychology of Persons: Categories and Practice," in *The Psychology of Personhood: Philosophical, Historical, Social-Developmental, and Narrative Perspectives*, ed. Jack Martin and Mark H. Bickhard (New York: Cambridge University Press, 2012), 59–80; Bartosz Brożek, "The Troublesome 'Person,'" in *Legal Personhood: Animals, Artificial Intelligence and the Unborn*, ed. Tomasz Pietrzykowski and Visa A. J. Kurki (New York: Springer, 2017), 3–13.

[10] On the test of unnecessary suffering, see Mike Radford, "'Unnecessary Suffering': The Cornerstone of Animal Protection Legislation Considered," *Criminal Law Review* 9 (1999): 702–13. A debate about the usefulness of this principle as well as of the standard of legitimate purpose can be found in Gary L. Francione and Robert Garner, *The Animal Rights Debate: Abolition or Regulation?* (New York: Columbia University Press, 2010). Garner is for these standards and tests, Francione against.

[11] In the cases that Wise and other animal lawyers are presently pursuing in American courts, they tend to take a more restrained approach than the one found in Gary Francione that argues for a total overhaul of the legal categorization of animals as property. The lawyers bring cases on behalf of "intelligent" species like great apes, and they argue for animals to be granted limited or implicit legal personhood. This more conservative approach can be found in Susan Berg's suggestion that animals be considered, like corporations, "juridical persons," and that this distinction takes place at the state level, and in David Favre's proposal that animals retain the status of property but that they be granted the power to own themselves. See Berg, "Elephants and Embryos"; her discussion of animal personhood is on pp. 402–6. Favre's arguments can be found in David Favre, "A New Property Status for Animals: Equitable Self-Ownership," in *Animal Rights: Current Debates and New Directions*, ed. Cass R. Sunstein and Martha Craven Nussbaum (New York: Oxford University Press, 2004), 234–50.

On the "stepping-stone" or "backdoor" approach to expanding the legal protection of animals, see David S. Favre, "Judicial Recognition of the Interests of Animals: A New Tort," *Michigan State Law Review* 2005 (2005): 333–67; Richard L. Cupp Jr., "Dubious Grail: Seeking Tort Law Expansion and Limited Personhood as Stepping Stones toward Abolishing Animals' Property Status," *Southern Methodist University Law Review* 60 (2007): 3; Seps, "Animal Law Evolution." As Richard Cupp points out in arguing for the moderate approach, were animals to be given legal standing as plaintiffs in the United States, the number of potential plaintiffs in the country would grow from around three-hundred million (the human population) to over twenty-five billion (to include the vast number of animals raised by the food industry, kept as pets, and used for research, and that is not taking into account wild animal populations). Favre envisions a similarly

come with being classified as property. One is not permitted by law to burn down one's house, blow it up, or play the stereo as loud as one wants.[12] Owners cannot treat their animals in whatever way they wish.[13] Even Sunstein admits that the language of property has its problems, however: "I think that in the end Francione is right to object that this way of talking does violence to people's most reflective understandings of their relationships with other living creatures."[14] In a rejoinder to Sunstein, Francione adds that categorizing animals as property is not only incompatible with the moral idea that animals have intrinsic value, but it also does not in the real world result in their greater protection except perhaps in the case of companion animals, and that it will always cause animals to lose in the weighing of interests.[15]

THE PERSONHOOD OF ANIMALS

Along with grade-school teachers, Steven Wise, and Gary Francione, a new wave of critical animal studies conceives of animals as persons, agents, and subjects. In his ethnography of a dog assistance agency, Avigdor Edminster considers how staff, volunteers, and clients relate to the assistance dogs as "persons." He argues that his "informants' relationships uniquely draw on and shape possibilities regarding personhood and sociality."[16] Disabled clients who use the agency's services see a parallel between their own "questionable or imperiled full personhood" and that of their assistance dogs. The clients frequently describe the relationship between them and their dog as one where the two figures "save"

---

untenable outcome were animals suddenly to be given full legal rights; see the opening section of Favre, "A New Property Status for Animals."

[12] Cass R. Sunstein, "Slaughterhouse Jive: Introduction to *Animal Rights: Your Child or the Dog?* By Gary L. Francione," *New Republic*, January 29, 2001, 44. A similar argument can be found in Favre, "Judicial Recognition." Favre points out that the property status of animals has not stopped them from receiving a variety of legal protections and rights (he points to the anti-cruelty statutes and the Federal Animal Welfare Act as examples).

[13] Sunstein, "Slaughterhouse Jive."

[14] Sunstein, "Slaughterhouse Jive."

[15] Gary L. Francione, "Equal Consideration and the Interest of Nonhuman Animals in Continued Existence: A Response to Professor Sunstein," *University of Chicago Legal Forum*, no. 1 (2006): 231–52.

[16] Avigdor Edminster, "Interspecies Families, Freelance Dogs, and Personhood: Saved Lives and Being One at an Assistance Dog Agency," in *Making Animal Meaning*, ed. Linda Kalof and Georgina M. Montgomery (East Lansing: Michigan State University Press, 2011), 128.

each other. Their narratives suggest that personhood is not something separately and individually attained but is a shared pursuit and experience.[17]

Nik Taylor's ethnography of two animal shelters in the United Kingdom considers the means by which shelter workers construct the personhood of the rescued animals: naming them, assessing their "personalities," assuming care for them, and showing suspicion for the level of care that potential adopters will offer.[18] Taylor considers these practices to be "technologies of person production." Taylor notes that the shelter workers consistently explain aggressive or difficult behavior on the part of the animals as the fault of human beings and interpret their experiences with the animals so as to maximize the personhood of the animals.[19]

In her and her husband's work with the Mentawai hunting tribe on an archipelago off the west coast of Sumatra, Jet Bakels describes tribal norms that attribute personhood to animals.[20] Animals must not be ridiculed or laughed at. Behavior around animals must be appropriate – no burping or farting. Animals' souls must be treated well after they die so that they will maintain good relations with their living relatives. Mentawai tribespeople adhere to a pact that they believe their ancestors to have made with the animals and spirit beings of the forest. Animals are thought of "as thinking agents," who "can be addressed and placated, influenced and appeased."[21] The animal they most fear, the crocodile, is thought to attack only those people who have violated traditional rules and evaded human punishment. Animals are "moral persons."[22]

Philosopher Elisa Aaltola argues that the personhood of people depends on the personhood of animals. Withholding personhood from animals implies something amiss in our own.[23] While some ethicists

---

[17] See especially p. 131.

[18] Nik Taylor, "'Never an It': Intersubjectivity and the Creation of Animal Personhood in Animal Shelters," *Quantitative Sociology Review* 3, no. 1 (April 2007): 59–73.

[19] Ibid., 68.

[20] Bakels, "Animals as Persons in Sumatra." See further reference to Bakels in Chapter 4.

[21] Ibid., 160.

[22] Ibid., 162.

[23] "In rethinking the basis of personhood, we have to face the possibility that defining others as 'persons' and 'things' has implications for our own personhood. Something seems to be amiss in our moral character, if animals are treated as mere mechanisms." (p. 190). Or, later, citing Juan Carlos Gomez's discussion of apes: "I am a person insofar as I and another perceive and treat each other as persons" (p. 192). See Juan Carlos Gomez, "Are Apes Persons? The Case for Primate Intersubjectivity," in *The Animal Ethics Reader*, ed. Richard George Botzler and Susan Jean Armstrong (New York: Routledge, 2003), 138–43.
    The same reciprocal relationship seems not to hold true for juridical personhood, argues Berg: "There is little evidence, for example, that failing to recognize animals as

object to the notion of animal personhood, claiming that the concept of personhood is fuzzy, restrictive, elusive, "mystical," or that it simply requires too much expansion beyond its normal meaning to encompass animals, others argue that as a concept with the power to define moral significance and to establish a "serious moral right to life," personhood is indispensable for animals.[24] Whether personhood should hinge on the individual's possession of certain attributes, and which attributes those should be, remains a vexed question. Attributes offered by philosophers as possible criteria for personhood include theoretical reason (Aristotle), rationality and propositional language (Descartes), autonomy (Kant, Rousseau), and continuity of consciousness (Locke). Michael Tooley counts at least fifteen more criteria that have been suggested, including the capacity to experience pleasure and pain, have desires, have intention, have social interactions, remember past events, anticipate future events, be aware of time, and be aware of oneself.[25] The debates are part of a larger problematizing of personhood posed also by embryos and fetuses, people who are severely impaired in their functioning, and artificial intelligence. The practical implications are vast (e.g., if animals are persons with a moral right to life, where does that leave the slaughter industry?).

juridical persons, or failing to give them particular rights, harms the exercise of those rights for human persons." See Berg, "Elephants and Embryos," 405.

[24] Tooley, being cited by Aoltola, p. 177. The "mystical" is from Aoltola, p. 178, referring to David deGrazia.

Notable arguments against conceiving of animals as persons are Raymond Gillespie Frey, *Interests and Rights: The Case against Animals* (New York: Oxford University Press, 1980); Jan Narveson, "A Defense of Meat Eating," in *Animal Rights and Human Obligations*, ed. Peter Singer and Tom Regan (Englewood Cliffs, NJ: Prentice Hall, 1989), 192–5.

Notable arguments on behalf are Mary Midgley, *Utopias, Dolphins, and Computers: Problems of Philosophical Plumbing* (New York: Routledge, 1996); David Sztybel, "Animals as Persons," in *Animal Subjects: An Ethical Reader in a Posthuman World*, ed. Jodey Castricano (Waterloo, ON: Wilfrid Laurier University Press, 2008), 241–57. See the narrative bibliography at the end of Martha Craven Nussbaum and Cass R. Sunstein, eds., *Animal Rights: Current Debates and New Directions* (New York: Oxford University Press, 2004), 321–4, though it does not focus on the vocabulary of personhood and is also in need of updating.

[25] Michael Tooley, "Are Nonhuman Animals Persons?," in *The Oxford Handbook of Animal Ethics*, ed. Tom L. Beauchamp and Raymond Gillespie Frey (New York: Oxford University Press, 2011), 339. For discussion of criteria for moral personhood from a bioethics perspective, see Bonnie Steinbock, *Life before Birth: The Moral and Legal Status of Embryos and Fetuses* (New York: Oxford University Press, 1992); Mary Anne Warren, *Moral Status: Obligations to Persons and Other Living Things* (Oxford, UK: Clarendon Press, 1997).

Some philosophers advocate that personhood be extricated from debates about criteria; see arguments in Elisa Aaltola, "Personhood and Animals," *Environmental Ethics* 30, no. 2 (2008): 175–93.

Religion is also being reimagined to accommodate animal personhood. Invoking J. Z. Smith's famous quip that "there is no data for religion," Aaron Gross observes that the exclusion of animals as religious persons is a choice that the scholar makes based on her own normative assumptions and commitments and not simply on "the facts" of religion.[26] Given how central animals are to religion as we know it, the denial of animal personhood is, if anything, the choice that requires greater justification.[27] Gross takes up the work of Tim Insgold on the Cree tribe of northeastern Canada, which argues that for the Cree, "personhood ... is open equally to human and nonhuman animal (and even nonanimal) kinds."[28] Gross argues that Insgold's study of the Cree "points us toward a way of thinking a religious actor that is no longer strictly a human (or divine) subject."[29] Donovan Schaefer is likewise interested in how animal personhood challenges standing notions of religion. If religion is associated with affective experience rather than with, say, canonical texts, then animals – whom cognitive ethology has shown to possess a wide emotional range – can be thought of as capable of religion. Other recent works in religious studies demonstrate the myriad ways that animals operate as "persons" across the world's religions.[30] Animals are not just "good to think with," though they are that too, but they are also agents and actors within human experience and within their own.

These studies across disciplines point to all the problems with animals being categorized as property or things. The categorization of animal as thing and not person results in maltreatment of animals; it inaccurately reflects the way people really relate to animals; it inaccurately reflects the way animals themselves exist in the world.[31] The rabbinic texts to which I now turn are preoccupied with these problems that arise from thinking of animals as things. I will take readers through the selected

---

[26] Gross, *The Question of the Animal and Religion*, 116.

[27] Ibid., 118.

[28] Ibid., 107. (See n. 43 for reference in Insgold.)

[29] Ibid., 114.

[30] Waldau and Patton, *A Communion of Subjects*; Deane-Drummond and Clough, *Creaturely Theology*; Deane-Drummond, Clough, and Artinian-Kaiser, *Animals as Religious Subjects*; Moore, *Divinanimality*; Dalal and Taylor, *Asian Perspectives on Animal Ethics*.

[31] At the same time, one still finds scholarly works that seem unaware of debates about animal personhood; this is the impression one gets from, for example, the editors' introduction in Jack Martin and Mark H. Bickhard, eds., *The Psychology of Personhood: Philosophical, Historical, Social-Developmental, and Narrative Perspectives* (New York: Cambridge University Press, 2012).

materials from tractate Sukkah and consider how they problematize the thingness of animals, much as contemporary thinkers are doing. I will close with discussion of the new thinking about things ("thing theory"), and Zoroastrian laws about animals, to consider how both help to make sense of the notoriously peculiar talmudic passage that this chapter addresses.[32]

TRAVEL SUKKAHS IN THE MISHNAH

Mishnah Sukkah 2:3 describes several sukkahs that a person might build if they are in the midst of a journey as the festival of Sukkot arrives:

One who makes his sukkah on top of a wagon or on top of a ship, it is fit, and one may ascend it on the festival.

[One who makes his sukkah] on top of a tree or on the back of a camel, it is fit, but one may not ascend it on the festival.

העושה סוכתו בראש העגלה או בראש הספינה כשירה ועולים לה ביום טוב

בראש האילן או על גבי הגמל כשירה ואין עולין לה ביום טוב[33]

Four sukkah structures are depicted, each built on top of something else: a wagon, a ship, a tree, and a camel. The sukkahs are grouped by twos. The first two may be ascended on all days of the festival, while the second two may be ascended only during the intermediate days. Mishnah Betzah 5:2's interdiction against climbing trees and riding animals on the Sabbath and festivals would seem to be the source of Mishnah Sukkah's prohibition on ascending the treetop and "camel-back" sukkahs on the festival days.

The Mishnah still calls the treetop and camel-back sukkahs fit even though a person cannot enter them on the festival, suggesting that the Mishnah may be going out of its way to encourage travelers to build sukkahs during an inconvenient time rather than to dismiss the obligation. Or, alternatively, if one imagines an especially pious traveler rather than a lax one, the Mishnah's message may be that the traveler need not interrupt his trip in order to celebrate the festival. He can take it with him, so to

---

[32] The peculiarity of this passage is likely what inspired an Israeli organization called Pshita to make an animated version of it. See discussion and link in Shai Secunda, "Talmud and the Absurd: The Elephant in the Sukkah," *The Talmud Blog*, October 10, 2011, https://thetalmudblog.wordpress.com/2011/10/10/talmud-and-the-absurd-the-case-of-the-elephant-sukkah/.

[33] Kaufmann manuscript.

speak, on the road.[34] The only sukkah "floor" that does not conform in an obvious way to the travel theme is the treetop, though one could imagine a treetop being an appealing spot in which to build one's sukkah if one were traveling in unknown territory and wanted protection from malevolent people or animals.[35] The parallels in Tosefta Sukkah mention only the treetop sukkah (1:3) and the wagon-top sukkah (1:11). If the toseftan parallels are earlier, they point to the possibility that the Mishnah's redactor brought together the two cases of the treetop and wagon-top sukkahs and added two more in order to create a new theme of travel-sukkahs.[36]

ANIMALS AS ARCHITECTURE IN TALMUDIC TRADITIONS

A baraita (i.e., a purportedly early rabbinic tradition) in the Babylonian Talmud reconfigures these traditions in order to explore still another theme: the use of animals as ritual objects.[37] The first segment of the baraita is essentially a restatement of the camel-back sukkah, this time as the subject of a legal dispute:

One who makes his sukkah on the back of an animal:
Rabbi Meir validates, but Rabbi Judah disqualifies.[38]

העושה סוכתו על גבי בהמה ר"מ מכשיר ורבי יהודה פוסל

---

[34] That one should build one's sukkah while on the road resonates with rabbinic texts that adjure Torah study while on the road, which is understood to protect the traveler from danger; see discussion in Ruth Haber, "Rabbis on the Road: Exposition En Route in Classical Rabbinic Texts" (PhD diss., University of California, 2014). On travel more generally in Roman Palestine, see Catherine Hezser, "Travel and Mobility," in *The Oxford Handbook of Jewish Daily Life in Roman Palestine*, ed. Catherine Hezser (New York: Oxford University Press, 2010), 210–26.

[35] Mishnah Berakhot 2:4 and Tosefta Berakhot 2:8 discuss the treetop as a potential site for prayer recitation so that workers will not have to take off time from their labors to descend the tree that they are pruning or picking. Perhaps Mishnah Sukkah 2:4 has such work considerations in mind, rather than or in addition to secure travel accommodations, when it permits the sukkah to be built on a treetop. I thank Michal Bar-Asher Siegal for this suggestion.

[36] Contra Saul Lieberman, *Tosefta Moed* (New York: The Jewish Theological Seminary of America, 2002), 259, n. 35. The treetop appears in the Tosefta probably because it, like the bed with which it is grouped, provides a convenient scaffolding on which to build a sukkah.

[37] The tannaitic tradition can either be viewed as a single baraita with stammaitic interruptions or as two closely related baraitot. I take the former approach, since the disputants and subject stay relatively consistent throughout.

[38] Sukkah 23a.

Aside from presenting the status of this sukkah as disputed rather than simply permitted, this baraita differs from the Mishnah in that it generalizes to all animals. (How many domesticated species have backs large enough to sustain a valid sukkah is another question; medieval Talmud commentator Rashi's fanciful image is a sukkah whose flooring is formed out of doors placed atop two horses.)[39]

The second segment of the baraita goes further in its generalizations, moving from the case of the sukkah to a variety of other instances in which an animal might be used as a ritual object:

He made out of an animal the wall of the sukkah:
Rabbi Meir disqualifies, but Rabbi Judah validates.

For Rabbi Meir used to say: Anything that has in it the breath of life, one does not make it either the wall for a sukkah, the stake for an alley [to mark a Sabbath enclosure],[40] the boards for wells [to mark a Sabbath enclosure],[41] or the closure [*golel*] for a grave.[42]

In the name of Rabbi Yose the Galilean they said: One does not even write upon it divorce agreements for women.

עשאה לבהמה דופן לסוכה

ר"מ פוסל ור' יהודה מכשיר

שהיה רבי מאיר אומר כל דבר שיש בו רוח חיים אין עושין אותו לא דופן לסוכה ולא לחי למבוי ולא פסין לביראות ולא גולל לקבר

משום רבי יוסי הגלילי אמרו אף אין כותבין עליו גיטי נשים

There are a number of differences between the previous dispute and this one. First, the architectural use of the animal within the sukkah has shifted from floor to wall. Second, the positions of Rabbi Meir and Rabbi Judah are reversed. Rabbi Meir validates and Rabbi Judah disqualifies the animal-*floor* sukkah, but it is Rabbi Judah who validates and Rabbi Meir who disqualifies the animal-*wall* sukkah. Finally, the dispute is extended to other cases that are related to that of the sukkah only by

---

[39] Rashi borrows the image from Mishnah Parah 3:2/Tosefta Parah 3:2, cited in Sukkah 21a.

[40] The stake (*lehi*) is a device used to create a fictive private space in which people are permitted to carry on the Sabbath; see Mishnah Eruvin 1.

[41] The boards for wells are a variation on an eruv (the Sabbath boundary marker) that permit animals to drink from public wells on the Sabbath; see Mishnah Eruvin 2:1–4.

[42] On the *golel*, see Mishnah Ohalot 2:4. The Tosafot on Sukkah 23a, s.v. *ve-lo*, discuss at length what the *golel* is. The order of the boards and the gravemarker is reversed in the London manuscript.

their common use of living creatures for purposes normally served by
inanimate objects.[43]

A survey of related Mishnah passages suggests that this baraita
was composed through recombining and expanding a variety of exist-
ing traditions, either by a relatively late tannaitic composer or by the
Babylonian Talmud editors.[44] The main inspiration for this baraita
appears to have been Mishnah Eruvin 1:7, which contains several of the
same components:[45]

One may make the stakes [for the eruv, i.e., Sabbath boundary marker] with anything, even with something that has in it the breath of life.

Rabbi Yose declares impure [something that has in it the breath of life] as a closure for a grave; Rabbi Meir declares pure.

One writes on it divorce agreements for women; Rabbi Yose the Galilean
disqualifies.

בכל עושין לחיים אפילו בדבר שיש בו רוח חיים

ר יוסה מטמא משם גולל ר מאיר מטהר

כותבין עליו גיטי נשים ר יוסה הגלילי פוסל

Like the talmudic "super-baraita," this mishnah brings together the
diverse legal areas of the Sabbath boundary stake, the grave closure, and
the divorce agreement. Like the Sukkah baraita, this mishnah's main

---

[43] The section of the baraita featuring Rabbi Meir's extended position appears in Eruvin 15b,
where the focus of the commentary is Rabbi Yose the Galilean's position about divorce
agreements (that material repeats on Sukkah 24b). The baraita appears without the extension to other cases, featuring just the case of the sukkah, in a parallel on Eruvin 44a.

   The passage in Eruvin 44a–b is worth its own discussion, since its interest is in the
problems of treating *people* as things. The passage considers it legitimate (in the sense
that the outcome is considered legally valid) to use a person as a thing only if the person,
paradoxically, is *aware* of his being treated as a thing. The question in the Eruvin passage, which does not seem to be operating in the early rabbinic texts I have been discussing, is whether, if the regular wall has fallen, reconstituting it out of an animal or person
or vessel would count as prohibited labor on the festival or on the Sabbath. The question
is whether rebuilding the wall in this way might be legitimate as a loophole around the
prohibition on building a regular wall.

[44] On the liberties that the Babylonian Talmud takes with baraitot, see Shamma Friedman,
"Towards a Characterization of Babylonian Baraitot: 'Ben Tema' and 'Ben Dortai,'" in
Neti'ot Le-David: Jubilee Volume for David Weiss Halivni, ed. Yaakov Elman, Ephraim
Bezalel Halivni, and Zvi Aryeh Steinfeld (Jerusalem: Orhot, 2004), 195–274.

[45] The manuscript variations for this mishnah are significant. This translation is based on
the Kaufmann manuscript, whose text is featured above. The standard printed edition
reads: "One may make the stakes with anything, even with something that has in it the
breath of life. And Rabbi Yose prohibits. And he declares impure as a closure for a grave,
and Rabbi Meir declares it pure ..."

concern is the use of living creatures for these purposes, and it uses the same terminology of "anything that has in it the breath of life." Finally, both passages cite Rabbi Meir and Rabbi Yose the Galilean as taking positions on these questions. But Mishnah Eruvin 1:7 is likely an inchoate form of the baraita in Sukkah, since it mentions neither the sukkah nor the boards for wells and, more tellingly, has not harmonized the purity language associated with the grave closure with the language of prohibition and permission associated with the other legal areas.

Most striking about the baraita in Sukkah 23a is its legal perspective, which runs counter to Mishnah Eruvin 1:7. Whereas in Mishnah Eruvin 1:7 the consensus position permits the use of living creatures for Sabbath boundary stakes and divorce documents, the featured position in the baraita is Rabbi Meir's prohibition. The same divergence can be found in the other early rabbinic traditions upon which the talmudic super-baraita has drawn. One of these is Mishnah Ohalot 15:9, which treats the case of an animal's being used to seal off a grave. While the consensus position there holds that one who touches such an animal contracts impurity just as though one had touched a conventional gravestone, Rabbi Meir's dissenting opinion is that the person would not contract impurity. (Rabbi Meir does not explicitly prohibit animal use for such purpose; that is an innovation of the baraita.) The super-baraita seems possibly to have drawn from Mishnah Ohalot 15:9 – perhaps indirectly through Mishnah Eruvin 1:7, whose cluster of themes comes from far-flung parts of the Mishnah corpus – but the super-baraita spotlights Rabbi Meir and omits the consensus (or Rabbi Yose, in Mishnah Eruvin 1:7). Another early rabbinic tradition is Mishnah Gittin 2:3, where the consensus position, as in Mishnah Ohalot 15:9 and Mishnah Eruvin 1:7, permits the use of living creatures.[46] The Gittin case permits a man to write his divorce contract on the horn of a cow. He simply delivers the entire cow to his wife in order to divorce her (just as he might, according to this mishnah, write the divorce agreement on the hand of a slave and then give his wife the slave to effectuate the divorce). Rabbi Yose the Galilean's position prohibiting the writing of divorce agreements on living creatures (and on foods, he adds) is presented in Mishnah Gittin as the dissenting view.

---

[46] See parallel in Tosefta Gittin 2:4, where the consensus position and Rabbi Yose the Galilean's position both appear, but not juxtaposed as tightly as in the Mishnah. If the Mishnah is reworking the Tosefta, it would seem to be thematizing live animal use more than does the Tosefta. The two other relevant mishnahs, Eruvin 1:7 and Ohalot 15:9, do not have toseftan parallels.

A bird's-eye view of the Mishnah suggests that the creator of the talmudic super-baraita followed in the steps of the author of Mishnah Eruvin 1:7, which is itself a kind of super-mishnah whose interest is the translegal theme of using animals as legal or ritual objects. The author of the Sukkah super-baraita (whether tannaitic, amoraic, or stammaitic) added the case of the animal-walled sukkah (perhaps based loosely on the camel-back sukkah in Mishnah Sukkah 2:3, where travel rather than animal use is the unifying theme) and the boards for wells, shifted the emphasis from the permissive to the prohibitive position, and attributed that prohibitive position consistently to Rabbi Meir (except for the final case of divorce documents).[47]

The outstanding question is why. What is the thinking behind the baraita's positions and the manner in which they have been presented?[48] Is Rabbi Meir's objection to using animals based on practical concerns? The animal might very well not cooperate, creating all kinds of legal problems as a consequence. Is the prohibition on live animal use, alternatively, based on a sense of propriety? Perhaps Rabbi Meir does not think it shows sufficient respect for the dead, for the Sabbath and festivals, or for the law itself, to use animals to seal graves or to construct sukkahs and Sabbath boundary markers. Or might the motivating concern be the welfare of the animal forced to stand in a fixed position for an extended period of time?

---

[47] Palestinian Talmud Eruvin 1:7 (19b) features a different baraita, with fewer themes clustered together and Rabbi Meir a less consistent figure:

> Anything that has in it the breath of life, one may make into a wall but may not make into a stake (for the eruv); the words of Rabbi Meir. But the sages say: One may not make it into a wall, but one may make it into a stake.

כל דבר שיש בו רוח חיים עושין אותו דופן ואין עושין אותו לחי דברי ר"מ וחכ"א אין עושין אותו דופן אבל עושין אותו לחי

> Here the sukkah and eruv themes are combined, as in the Babylonian Talmud super-baraita, but without the full set of themes from Mishnah Eruvin, and with Rabbi Meir here permitting rather than prohibiting an animal-walled sukkah. The status of the baraita and the logic of the positions are discussed by Palestinian amoraim within the Palestinian Talmud passage in which it appears. One possible reconstruction (among others) is that the Babylonian Talmud redactors knew of the Palestinian Talmud baraita or some version of it, they drew upon its juxtaposition of the sukkah and the eruv, combined it with the other themes from Mishnah Eruvin, and ironed out Rabbi Meir's position in the process, perhaps inspired by amoraic criticism featured in the Palestinian Talmud.

[48] Tosefta Gittin 2:4 presents Rabbi Yose the Galilean's position as having an exegetical basis: "Just as *sefer* does not have in it the breath of life, [so] is excluded anything that has in it the breath of life." Yose the Galilean gives a strict reading of the word *sefer* ("bill" or "certificate") in Deuteronomy 24:1's description of divorce. For parallels, see Lieberman, *Tosefta Moed*, 250, notes on lines 18–19.

FLIGHT AND DEATH AMONG THE RABBIS: WHAT
MAKES ANIMALS BAD "THINGS"

The rabbis featured in the talmudic passage address precisely this question:

What is the reason of Rabbi Meir?
Abaye said:[49] Lest she die.
Rabbi Zera said: Lest she flee.[50]

מ"ט דר' מאיר
אביי אמר שמא תמות
רבי זירא אמר שמא תברח

Many of the manuscripts, and the subsequent passage in the standard printed text, feature the word *gezerah* ("it is a decree") in both of these rabbis' explanations, indicating that they think Rabbi Meir's prohibition on live animal use is a legal stringency designed to ensure that commandments do not end up violated or procedures bungled.[51] Rabbi Zera's understanding of Rabbi Meir is the more straightforward. Any animal in good mental and physical health when placed in a fixed position would, at some point in the not distant future, decide to move. The animal's departure would pose serious problems for the purpose it had served: the sukkah would fall, the Sabbath boundary marker (eruv) would vanish, the grave would lie open. Abaye's understanding of Rabbi Meir, which attributes to him a concern with the animal's dying, is harder to parse. The case of the grave closure, which seals off the cave or tomb in which the corpse is decaying, could well be complicated by the animal's death during the long period of decomposition.[52] But the cases of the eruv and the sukkah turn Rabbi Meir, in Abaye's view, into the most acute of pessimists. Need one worry that an animal in the course of a single day

[49] The attribution to Abaye is missing in NY – JTS Rab. 1608 (ENA 850), but that manuscript has a different presentation of materials in general. In Oxford – Bodl. heb. e. 51 (2677), only Abaye is mentioned, and "it is a decree lest she flee" is attributed to him instead of "lest she die." This would seem to be a case of homoteleuton from the first appearance of the word *gezerah* to the second.

[50] NY – JTS Rab. 1608 (ENA 850) features *tifrah* with a *peh* rather than *tivrah* as in all the other versions.

[51] The positions attributed to Abaye and Rabbi Zera are perhaps reactions to the super-baraita, but they alternatively could be reactions to any one or more of the early rabbinic traditions in which animal use appears.

[52] On ancient Jewish burial practices (focusing on the period right before the Rabbis), see Rachel Hachlili, *Jewish Funerary Customs, Practices and Rites in the Second Temple Period* (Leiden: Brill, 2005).

(the eruv on the Sabbath), or even in the course of a single week (the seven-day period of the Sukkot festival), is going to die?

Yes, if one is a talmudic rabbi with a taste for the improbable, especially if it creates a fertile legal dilemma. Moreover, one might interpret Abaye's understanding of Rabbi Meir as worried less about the sukkah, the eruv, and the grave than about the *animal*. Stationing an animal at a burial cave or as part of a sukkah or eruv might create a situation of great physical hardship for the animal, bringing about the animal's untimely death. The pessimistic Rabbi Meir is probably a more persuasive portrait than the animal lover, however, since animal welfare is not a characteristic concern of the rabbis, but rigorous observance of commandments and procedures is.[53] The talmudic redactors see him certainly in the pessimist mode. Abaye's position becomes the jumping-off point for an extended discussion of whether "death is frequent" or, in other words, whether death should be considered, from a legal principles perspective, an imminent threat that legal procedures must take into account.

Both Abaye and Rabbi Zera, in their explanations of Rabbi Meir, would seem to be pointing out why it is a bad idea to substitute a living thing for a rock or piece of wood or parchment. For Abaye, mortality sets animals apart from other kinds of "things." In taking this approach, Abaye may be reacting to the language in which Rabbi Meir's position is couched. "Anything that has in it the breath of life" at some point, inevitably, no longer will. Rabbi Zera points to a different problem that arises from treating animals the way one would treat inanimate property. Animals have will or agency. You can position an animal as the wall of a sukkah, but you can't make him stay, at least not without a good deal of coercion (the passage will speak more about coercion later). While rocks and stakes of wood are relatively easy to manipulate, fellow creatures are not, as anyone who has a dog or cat or other kind of companion animal knows. "Domesticated" animals are routinely distinguished from "wild" ones, but domestication remains a relative term. Control of other living beings is never complete.

Abaye's emphasis on mortality and Rabbi Zera's on agency together demonstrate what makes animals bad property. It is generally undesirable to have one's property die or disobey. While animals are valuable property because of their labor, milk, wool, or flesh, they also pose unique problems as property. The rabbis would seem to be reflecting on these

---

[53] The outlier is Rava (or, perhaps more accurately, Rava as the redactors portray him). See my discussion in Chapter 4 of the passage on animal suffering that features Rava.

problems here because these are boundary cases. While animals are frequently grouped with inanimate property, here they are substituted for inanimate property and treated as such. But these extreme cases bring to light a paradox within the norm. It is the paradox that I mentioned at the start of this chapter captured in the word "livestock," which combines the attribute of life with the "stuff-ness" of stock, and that is also reflected in the Mishnah's expression "a *thing (davar)* that has in it the breath of life." In the case of the animal-walled sukkah and in the other scenarios addressed, Abaye and Rabbi Zera suggest that the animal owner has upset the precarious balance within the normal terms, overemphasizing the "stock" and ignoring, at his peril, the "live."[54]

THE SEARCH FOR A STABLE SUKKAH

At this moment when the conceptual paradox of animal property is most laid bare, the talmudic editors try to overcome it in what can appropriately be called a fantasy of total animal domination. This fantasy is never entirely fulfilled, and the animal, ultimately, evades the use that his owner wishes him to serve. The interpretation I offer here of the dynamics of the dialectic is to some extent my own fantasy, since one could easily read the back-and-forth as an entirely unremarkable display of talmudic argumentation. I will first discuss the passage in these more typical terms, as a piece of legal argumentation, taking readers through the various steps, and I will then offer a reading of the passage that takes it to be dealing not just with the formal principles of law but with the deeper dilemmas those principles pose.

Let me first clarify three assumptions in the talmudic material, which focuses on Rabbi Meir's prohibition on using an animal for a sukkah wall: (1) There are in fact cases where Rabbi Meir would *not* prohibit such a sukkah; (2) How one defines those cases depends on how one explains Rabbi Meir, whether one adopts Abaye's or Rabbi Zera's explanation for him; (3) There must be at least one case where it makes a difference, from the perspective of practical law, whether Rabbi Meir is explained according to Abaye or according to Rabbi Zera. In other words, there must be an animal-walled sukkah for which Abaye would think that Rabbi Meir would hold one way, whereas Rabbi Zera would

---

[54] Both Rabbi Zera and Abaye are supplanted when in a later discussion (Sukkah 24a) it is proposed that the question of whether a partition that "stands by means of breath" is a valid partition lies behind the debate between Rabbi Meir and other sages.

think that Rabbi Meir would hold the opposite. The purpose of the talmudic passage is to find that one case. The broader assumption within
the passage is that Amoraim (here: Rabbi Zera and Abaye) do not explain
early rabbinic positions (here: Rabbi Meir) merely to satisfy intellectual
curiosity but also to generate practical law. Different explanations ("lest
she flee"; "lest she die") must in some case entail different legal positions.
The other general assumption that fuels the talmudic dialectic is that
each Amora would have fully considered the other Amora's position and
incorporated it into his thinking.

The talmudic redactors present a sequence of three animal-walled sukkahs, only the last of which satisfies the passage's objective:

With respect to a bound elephant, no one disagrees,[55] for even if the elephant dies,
his corpse is at least ten [hand-breadths][56] high.

When they disagree, it is with respect to an elephant that is not bound. According
to the one who says "lest she die," we are not concerned.

According to the one who says "it is a decree lest she flee," we are concerned.

According to the one who says "lest she die," let him be concerned lest she flee!

Rather, with respect to an elephant that is not bound no one disagrees. When they
disagree, it is with respect to a bound farm animal [*behemah*].

According to the one who says "it is a decree lest she die," we are concerned.[57]

According to the one who says "it is a decree lest she flee," we are not concerned.[58]

But according to the one who says "it is a decree lest she flee," let him be concerned lest she die!

Death is not frequent.[59]

בפיל קשור כולי עלמא לא פליגי דאי נמי מיית יש בנבלתו י'

כי פליגי בפיל שאינו קשור

למאן דאמר שמא תמות לא חיישינן

למאן דאמר גזרה שמא תברח חיישינן

למאן דאמר גזרה שמא תמות ניחוש שמא תברח

---

55 The argumentational structure and terminology are used atypically here; see Tosafot s.v.
   be-pil.
56 The word *tefahim* is absent in the printed edition but appears in London – BL Harl. 5508
   (400), Munich 140, and Oxford Opp. Add. fol. 23 (all as transcribed and listed on the
   Henkind Talmud Text Databank). A *tefah* is the width of a hand.
57 This sentence is absent in NY – JTS Rab. 1608.
58 "According to the one who says 'it is a decree lest she flee,' we are not concerned" is
   absent in Munich 95, but that appears to be a scribal error since the absence disrupts the
   symmetry, and the repetition of the same phrases throughout the argumentation would
   make copying errors likely.
59 Vatican 134: "death is different, for it is not frequent."

אלא בפיל שאינו קשור כולי עלמא לא פליגי

כי פליגי בבהמה קשורה

למ"ד גזרה שמא תמות חיישינן

למ"ד גזרה שמא תברח לא חיישינן

ולמאן דאמר גזרה שמא תברח ניחוש שמא תמות

מיתה לא שכיחא

The first case is the bound elephant, the second is the unbound elephant, and the third is the bound farm animal. The first case is presented as a backdrop for the latter two, since the dialectic states explicitly that Abaye and Rabbi Zera would agree on Rabbi Meir's position on the first case, and the goal of the passage is to find a case where the two Amoraim would disagree. The first case – the bound elephant – is considered a clear point of agreement between Abaye and Rabbi Zera, since whether one thinks Rabbi Meir's concern is flight (i.e., Rabbi Zera), or one thinks Rabbi Meir's concern is death (i.e., Abaye), this sukkah would satisfy Rabbi Meir's concern. The dialectic does not bother to articulate why Rabbi Zera would think that Rabbi Meir would permit such a sukkah since it is patently obvious: a bound animal cannot flee. The dialectic does make explicit why Abaye would think that Rabbi Meir would permit this sukkah, since the thinking here is less obvious. Were the animal to die, which is Rabbi Meir's fear according to Abaye's view, the death is not necessarily "fatal" to the sukkah structure so long as the animal's corpse is large enough – as is no doubt the case with an elephant, who is the large animal par excellence – to sustain the sukkah.[60]

The problem here is not one of legal logic, which is impeccable, but of ritual reality. Is one meant to take seriously the prospect of a sukkah being held up on one side by a tied-up, decaying elephant corpse? Is the dialectic so removed from real people's festival observance that it would imagine anyone of sound mind celebrating in such a sukkah? Or is the exoticism of the elephant and the gruesomeness of his decaying body potentially an attraction, a sort of fun-house sukkah, or imperialist

---

[60] See, for example, Basil of Caesarea: "Why does the elephant have a trunk? Because the animal is large, the largest of land animals, and, made to inspire fear in those who meet it, had to have a weighty and compact body." Or in Isidore of Seville: "The Greeks think the elephant was named after the size of its body, which surpasses a mountain in size, for Greeks call a mountain *lophos*." In Grant, *Early Christians and Animals*, 105, 132. For a general cultural history of the elephant, with discussion of its enormous size in Chapter 2, see Dan Wylie, *Elephant* (Chicago: University of Chicago Press, 2009).

spectacle like the animals imported from afar and put on display in the Roman arena?[61] The passage seems to take talmudic logic to an absurdity.

The second case, the unbound elephant, is the passage's first stab at finding a practical legal difference between Abaye and Rabbi Zera. Drawing implicitly on the logic of the first case, the passage argues that Abaye would hold that Rabbi Meir would permit a sukkah one of whose walls was constituted by an unbound elephant, because, if the elephant died, the corpse would be large enough to sustain the sukkah. The passage proceeds to argue that Rabbi Zera, on the other hand, would hold that Rabbi Meir would prohibit such a sukkah: "According to the one who says 'it is a decree lest she flee,' we are concerned." An unbound animal is likely to run away and pull down the sukkah in the process. Because, according to Rabbi Zera, that is precisely Rabbi Meir's fear, this sukkah would be invalid in Rabbi Meir's view. The passage goes on to reject the first half of the proposal ("according to the one who says 'lest she die,' we are not concerned"), however, on the grounds that even Abaye would have to recognize that flight is always a risk when it comes to animals: "According to the one who says 'lest she die,' let him be concerned lest she flee!" The passage concludes that even Abaye would concede that Rabbi Meir would prohibit such a sukkah: "Rather, with respect to an elephant that is not bound no one disagrees." The passage has forced Abaye, in effect, to adopt Rabbi Zera's position.

The third case – the bound farm animal – is the charm. For this case, Abaye would imagine Rabbi Meir to prohibit, while for Rabbi Zera, Rabbi Meir would permit: "According to the one who says 'it is a decree lest she die,' we are concerned. According to the one who says 'it is a decree lest she flee,' we are not concerned." For Abaye's approach to Rabbi Meir, this sukkah would pose serious problems, since were the animal to die, her corpse would not be large enough to sustain the sukkah. For Rabbi Zera's approach, on the other hand, the sukkah would be valid, because a bound animal cannot flee. The remaining question, which the symmetry of the argument begs to be asked, is whether Rabbi Zera would concede the validity of Abaye's concerns and follow suit in seeing a prohibition. That question is posed, ("But according to the one who says 'it is a decree lest she flee,' let him be concerned lest she die!"), and the answer

---

[61] On the Roman fascination with exotic animal species like the elephant, see Chris Epplett, "Roman Beast Hunts," in *A Companion to Sport and Spectacle in Greek and Roman Antiquity*, ed. Paul Christesen and Donald G. Kyle (Hoboken, NJ: Wiley Blackwell), 505–19.

given is: "Death is not frequent." While flight is a serious risk that even Abaye must acknowledge, death is not, and Rabbi Zera does not have to concede to Abaye regarding this concern. Their theoretical disagreement stands, and the talmudic dialectic has found the case it was seeking.

FANTASIES OF CONTROL IN THE CODA

In the redactors' eyes, the animal's will proves to be the more serious obstacle to objectifying them. Dead animals can still be useful, but runaway animals cannot. Moreover, animals do not in the course of daily events die, but they do flee. It would seem, then, that as long as one ties down an animal, one can successfully use him as a sukkah wall, at least according to Rabbi Zera. But the coda to the passage suggests that such success is hard-won:

But there is a space in between![62]
Where he fills it with palm and laurel leaves.[63]
But perhaps she[64] will lie down![65]
Where she is pulled by ropes from above.[66]
But according to the one who says, "it is a decree lest she die," [say] also that she is pulled by ropes from above!

---

[62] London – BL Harl. 5508 (400) and Vatican 134 have "between his legs." The coda is prefaced in Munich 95 with "with respect to an unbound farm animal," which may be intended to clarify the flow of logic or, alternatively, serves as the final words of the previous claim about death's infrequency.

[63] *Havtza vedafna* is used together frequently in the Talmud to refer to the leaves of palm and laurel trees woven together to make a fence.

[64] My translation adheres to the gender of the Aramaic grammar: the person is male, while the animal is female.

[65] The verb root, *r-v-a*, has associations in rabbinic literature with animals and is used for the animal who has sexual intercourse with a human being. It is also used for intercourse between two men (e.g., Sanhedrin 9b). For a discussion of the nexus between bestiality and male homosexuality in one cultural context, see Jens Rydström, *Sinners and Citizens: Bestiality and Homosexuality in Sweden, 1880–1950* (Chicago: University of Chicago Press, 2003). The Hebrew Bible groups the prohibitions on sex with other men and sex with animals (Leviticus 18:22–3), and the English term buggery encompasses both sodomy and bestiality. Contemporary conservative public discourse continues to group the two kinds of sex; see discussion of Rick Santorum, Jerry Falwell, and Bill O'Reilly in Cynthia Chris, "Boys Gone Wild: The Animal and the Abject," in *Animals and the Human Imagination: A Companion to Animal Studies*, ed. Aaron S. Gross and Anne Vallely (New York: Columbia University Press, 2012), 169, n. 1.

[66] The order of arguments is reversed in NY – JTS Rab. 1608 (ENA 850), NY – JTS Rab. 218 (EMC 270), and Oxford Bodl. heb. e. 51 (2677): first the lying down is mentioned, then the space in between the legs.

Sometimes he places [the animal][67] less than three [hand-breadths] from the *sekhakh* [sukkah roofing],[68] and when she dies, she shrinks, and it is not on his mind [to check it and to fix it].

והאיכא רווחא

דביני ביני דעביד ליה בהוצא ודפנא

ודלמא רבעה

דמתיחה באשלי מלעיל

ולמאן דאמר גזרה שמא תמות נמי הא מתיחה באשלי מלעיל

זמנין דמוקים בפחות משלשה סמוך לסכך וכיון דמייתא כוותא ולאו אדעתיה

While binding the animal, in the main section of argumentation, seems simple enough, the coda shows it to require further adjustments. The animal's body, her shape with a trunk and limbs, does not make for a very good wall ("But there is a space in between!"). The awkward spaces must be stuffed so that the animal body forms a continuous surface ("Where he fills it with palm and laurel leaves."). The animal's body poses a different kind of problem in the next step of the passage: "But perhaps she will lie down!" The dialectic would appear to be speaking at this point about a bound farm animal. The dialectic points out that even the bound animal, with her legs stuffed with leaves, would still be able to crouch or lie down. She cannot run away, the passage has determined, but she can still move, even if in a very limited way. This problem is solved by tying up the animal so that she becomes completely immobilized: "Where she is pulled by ropes from above." In both turns of the dialectic, the tension that arises from the animal's objectification is overcome rather than resolved. The animal's body shape is artificially modified, and the animal's need to rest is deprived rather than eliminated. Rabbi Meir's prohibition on objectifying animals is also overcome, as the passage continues its search for the sukkah that would slip through the cracks of his prohibition.

The dialectic at this point has found such a sukkah, but in fact the dialectic has succeeded too well. The sukkah that has been imagined – with its wall constituted by a bound, suspended, stuffed farm animal – is so secure that Abaye's reservations would now seem also to vanish. Remember that the objective of the passage is to find a sukkah that Abaye would think

---

[67] Vatican 134 and Oxford Opp. Add. fol. 23 insert before the verb "he places" (*moqi*) the added verb *mekaven* ("he positions/directs/aims").

[68] From the sekhakh" (*samukh le-sekhakh*) is absent in London – BL Harl. 5508 (400), Munich 140, Munich 95, NY – JTS Rab. 1608 (ENA 850), NY – JTS Rab. 218 (EMC 270), Oxford Bodl. heb. e. 51 (2677), Oxford Opp. Add. fol. 23, and Vatican 134.

Rabbi Meir prohibits, but Rabbi Zera would think Rabbi Meir permits. Such a sukkah has been found, since in Rabbi Zera's view, Rabbi Meir could not possibly find any threats to the stability of the animal-wall. It has already been concluded that in Abaye's view the animal would have to be the size of an elephant for the corpse to sustain the sukkah, and the sukkah under discussion is made out of a farm animal, not an exotically large one. The problem now is that this animal-wall has been imagined in such a way that even death no longer matters: "But according to the one who says, 'it is a decree lest she die,' [say] also that she is pulled by ropes from above!" As Rashi explains, "if she were to die, she would not fall." The size of the corpse matters, one now realizes, only with a normal death, when a creature slumps down and no longer occupies the same height that they did while alive and standing. But now that the animal has been completely immobilized, whether she is living or dead becomes legally immaterial. Abaye's view would now cohere with Rabbi Zera's in picturing a permissive Rabbi Meir.

The final flourish of the passage resuscitates Abaye's fears: "Sometimes he places less than three from the *sekhakh*, and when she dies, she shrinks, and it is not on his mind." The concern attributed to Abaye relies on a legal concept, developed elsewhere in the Babylonian Talmud, called *lavud*. If the sukkah wall comes within three hand-breadths of the roof, it is considered to be reaching it and thus to constitute a valid wall.[69] If in the case of the suspended and stuffed animal wall, the owner of the sukkah had relied on this concept, placed the animal just barely within three hand-breadths of the roof, and the animal then died during the subsequent days of the festival, the animal's corpse would slightly shrink, just enough to fall short of the requisite three hand-breadths, but also just enough to mislead the owner into thinking that his sukkah wall continued to be valid.[70] It is fear of this eventuality that would lead Abaye to believe that Rabbi Meir would prohibit such a sukkah. Rabbi Zera, however, who believes Rabbi Meir to be concerned with flight rather than death, would maintain a permissive position for Rabbi Meir.

The creativity and complexity of the logic are typical of the talmudic redactors, but what seems unusual here is the disgusting and downright

---

[69] On *lavud*, see Sukkah 6a; 14a; Eruvin 9a; Eruvin 25a.

[70] The redactor may have drawn inspiration from the discussion in the Palestinian Talmud Eruvin passage mentioned earlier about the animal becoming loose and the person who used him "not feeling [it]" (*eyno margish*), but the meaning of that phrase is unclear and debated by commentators and therefore difficult to connect to this passage.

weird character of the final image. We have a *behemah*, let us assume it is a cow, her legs stuffed with leaves, her body bound to the ground and to the other walls of the sukkah as well as suspended with cords from above, dead, shriveling up, the sukkah builder somehow not noticing. I suggest reading this strange image as a fantasy of animal control that at the same time recognizes itself as such. It is a fantasy that contains the seeds of its own unraveling, the perfectly controlled animal that in her death evades the purposes to which her owner has put her. The final image of the shrinking corpse that falls just a little bit short of the requisite length captures the suspense within the passage. In this fantasy that fails, an animal can be turned into good property. In the course of overcoming rather than resolving the problems that arise from using an animal in this way – problems that stem from the animal's body, her sentience, her will, her movement, her mortality – the passage is at once pursuing the ultimate "propertizing" of animals while acknowledging why it will never work.

CONCLUSIONS: THE PERSONHOOD OF THINGS

These rabbinic traditions about animals suggest that even in antiquity, when animals were incontrovertibly considered "mere property," there was recognition of the tensions involved in this categorization.[71] The passage in tractate Sukkah explores the various ways that animals constitute bad things. The early rabbinic materials feature an extreme objectification – in the literal sense – of animals. That objectification becomes the grounds for the later rabbis, the Amoraim, to consider the practical problems entailed in treating animals this way, and it inspires the talmudic redactors to imagine animals in the sadistic bindings and stuffings that such objectification would ultimately require. One might see this passage as an outlier, a ridiculous extreme with little connection to the "normal" uses of animals described in, for example, tractate Bava Qamma's animal torts, or tractate Bava Metzia's loading and unloading animals, or tractate Shabbat's saddled and accessoried animals. But I suggest reading the extreme as shedding light on the mean. The *reductio ad absurdum* casts doubt on cultural givens and exposes the paradox at the heart of animal status, what Francione calls the "moral schizophrenia" in human relationships to other species.[72]

---

[71] That formulation is from Sunstein, "Slaughterhouse Jive," 45.
[72] In the title of Chapter 1, Francione, *Introduction to Animal Rights*.

The passage evokes current approaches to thingness that question whether anything is really a "thing."[73] In "The Secret Life of Things," Bill Brown describes what happens when a person "misuses" a tool, putting it to some purpose other than the one for which it was meant.[74] If one uses a knife as a screwdriver, in the example he offers, one sees the knife suddenly in a new way. One notice aspects of it that one never did before:

we have the chance (if just a chance) to sense its presence (its thinness ... its sharpness and flatness ... the peculiarity of its scalloped handle, slightly loose ... its knifeness and what exceeds that knifeness) as though for the first time. For the first time, perhaps, we thus also sense the norms by which we customarily deploy both knife and screwdriver.[75]

By misusing the knife, one experiences it anew, and comes to some awareness of the norms that govern how one usually sees it. One recognizes in that moment of misuse "not a life behind or beneath the object but a life that is its fluctuating shape and substance and surface, a life that the subject must catalyze but cannot contain."[76] One is drawn to notice "... the excess of the object (a capacity to be other than it is) ..."[77] Elsewhere Brown uses an example, borrowed from William James, of turning a painting upside-down and seeing texture and colors that one had not before.[78] That new perspective depends on "disorientation, both habit and its disruption."[79]

One might read the passage I have been discussing in similar terms, as featuring a moment of "misuse" in which the "excess of the object" is experienced. The object is the cow or elephant being "misused" as the wall of a sukkah. The elephant as sukkah-wall is a disorientation; it disrupts one's habitual ways of seeing sukkahs, animals, and walls. The strange sukkah in this passage "reminds us ... that things might be other than they are."[80] The Babylonian Talmud is doing its own version

---

[73] For a brief history of these approaches, see the survey in Ileana Baird, "Introduction: Peregrine Things: Rethinking the Global in Eighteenth-Century Studies," in *Eighteenth-Century Thing Theory in a Global Context: From Consumerism to Celebrity Culture*, ed. Ileana Baird and Christina Ionescu (Burlington, VT: Ashgate, 2013), 1–16.

[74] Bill Brown, "The Secret Life of Things (Virginia Woolf and the Matter of Modernism)," *Modernism/modernity* 6, no. 2 (1999): 1–28. Baird speaks, alternatively, of "misplacement"; see Baird, "Introduction," 15.

[75] Brown, "The Secret Life of Things," 3.

[76] Ibid.

[77] Ibid., 2.

[78] Ibid., 6.

[79] Ibid., 7.

[80] Ibid., 10.

of "thing theory" as it reflects on what it means to be material.[81] The problem with which it is engaged is, to some extent, one that arises from trying to reduce *anything* material to static thinghood.

Let me speculate, in closing, that the Babylonian Talmud's reflection is inspired by its authors' exposure to two very different ways of thinking about animals. While Roman law, as discussed earlier, divides the world into persons and property and puts animals clearly into the second category, classical Zoroastrian law organizes animals according to a different set of binaries.[82] As I have discussed in previous chapters, the *Videvdad*, part of the Avesta scriptures, divides animals into two types, beneficent or noxious.[83] Beneficent animal species are thought to have been created by the good deity Ahura Mazda and to descend from the primordial bull of creation. They include cattle and dogs and some undomesticated animal species such as the otter and weasel. Beneficent animal species sometimes participated in religious ritual and could themselves be the subject of religious ritual. Dogs accompanied priests in funeral processions, for example, and were given their own funerals.[84] Noxious species, by contrast, are thought to have been created by the evil deity Ahriman. They include insects, reptiles, rodents, and predators like lions and tigers who harm people or crops.

Standards of behavior flow from these categories. It is meritorious to kill a noxious creature but prohibited to harm a beneficent one unless one adheres closely to the rules of slaughter. And, vice versa, it is meritorious to promote the welfare of a beneficent creature and prohibited to do so for a noxious animal. Rewards and punishments in the here-and-now as well as in the afterlife follow this logic. Offenses against animals are frequently classified by Zoroastrian law as sins "pertaining to the soul" rather than as "sin regarding opponents," which are the two categories into which Pahlavi texts organize offenses.[85] Harm against that which we would typically call an object, such as walls, clothing, and property, could fall into the category of sins pertaining to the soul, but so could harm to

---

[81]   On thing theory, see the introductory essay in Bill Brown, ed., *Things* (Chicago: University of Chicago Press, 2004).

[82]   This discussion is based on Macuch, "Treatment of Animals." See also Foltz, "Zoroastrian Attitudes toward Animals." I discuss Zoroastrian views also at the end of Chapter 5.

[83]   On the evolution of the concept of noxious creature (*xrafstar*) in Zoroastrian literature, see Moazami, "Evil Animals."

[84]   Foltz, "Zoroastrian Attitudes toward Animals," 370–1; Moazami, "A Purging Presence: The Dog in Zoroastrian Tradition."

[85]   Sometimes an offense could fall into both categories.

poor people, suggesting that the foundational Roman binary of property versus person is alien to the Zoroastrian legal tradition, in which the lines dividing people, animals, and objects are more fluid.

Zoroastrian law's classification of animals came to be a trademark element. Maria Macuch says that the "moral obligation to protect beneficent animals" became "*one of the characteristic features of Zoroastrian jurisprudence*" (her italics).[86] Mahnaz Moazami similarly says that "the partition of animals as beneficial or maleficent represents one of the most important and original aspects of the ancient Iranian religious worldview."[87] Herodotus and other ancient writers took this feature of Persian culture to be its most distinctive.[88] The Babylonian Talmud composers would surely have noted the striking contrast between Persian law, which held animals and behavior toward them to be morally charged and cosmologically significant, and the law of the Romans, which relegated animals to the realm of things.

Perhaps it was this excess of legal cultures in late antique Babylonia that allowed the talmudic editors to see the excess of the thing in so far as thingness adhered to animals. The talmudic passage's final image of the shrinking, stuffed animal corpse speaks to the power of the thing to come to life, to blur the boundary between fantasy and reality, and to threaten the status of the subject.[89] The thing's "what-is-it-ness," as Ileana Baird puts it, troubles schemes of classification, pointing to their insufficiencies.[90] The escaping elephant of the Sukkah passage is one such thing with the power to break free from the sukkah builder's – and rabbinic law's – confinement.

[86] Macuch, "Treatment of Animals," 188.
[87] Moazami, "Evil Animals," 301.
[88] Herodotus, *Histories* 1:140; Plutarch, *Isis et Osiris*; for references, see ibid., 304, n. 17 and 18.
[89] For this formulation of the power of the thing, see Baird, "Introduction," 5.
[90] Ibid., 6.

7

Conclusion

Jewish Animals

Two immigrants, old friends from the Old World, encounter each other after many years. They get to talking about this and that, all with an eye toward figuring out just how American and modern each other has become. "Do you keep Shabbos?" one asks the other. "Nah," comes the response. "How about keeping kosher?" "Nope." Eventually it becomes clear that friend No. 1 maintains very few, if any, Jewish rituals, prompting friend No. 2, to ask him, in exasperation, how it is that he still considers himself a member of the tribe. "Well," he retorts, "I'm still afraid of dogs."[1]

ANIMALS AND THE RABBINIC SELF

The chapters of this book have introduced a number of characters into the rabbinic imaginary: the clever ox, the weary donkey, the vicious cat, the escaping elephant. Here in the conclusion, I review current conceptions of the rabbinic self and consider how these talmudic animalities might push the boundaries of what we have come to think of as that self.[2] I consider the role of the animal also in making various rabbinic Others and as one such Other. Looking at contemporary Jewish pet rituals like animal funerals and "bark mitzvahs," I close with reflection on the long road that the animal has taken from the Temple to the Talmud to the contemporary Jewish household.

---

[1] Joke told by Jenna Weissman Joselit, "Jews and Animals, A Very Modern Story," *The Forward*, March 3, 2010, http://forward.com/culture/126414/jews-and-animals-a-very-modern-story/.

[2] On approaches to the self in antiquity, with emphasis on Michel Foucault and Pierre Hadot, see David Brakke, Michael L. Satlow, and Steven Weitzman, eds., "Introduction," in *Religion and the Self in Antiquity* (Bloomington, IN: Indiana University Press, 2005), 1–11.

The animals who populate the rabbinic world can never, of course, *be* rabbis. They cannot sit in the study hall, hear cases, or do anything quintessentially rabbinic. But the talmudic passages examined here show animals who are capable of being selves, even if not distinctively rabbinic selves. These animals strategize; they soothe themselves; they thrill to the forbidden; they break down from exhaustion; they attack the vulnerable; they long for freedom. They possess subjectivity. They experience things and have interests. They are actors under the law, themselves held responsible for sin, and others are held accountable for their suffering. They are perhaps most often the law's victims, punished with death when raped (that is one reading of the Sanhedrin passage), tortured by Jewish ritual (the Sukkah passage), and scapegoated for human failings (the story of Rav in Bava Qamma). These animal selves illustrate the ways that all selves, even rabbinic selves, fall prey to the law and are compelled to live under its empire.

There is no one rabbinic self. A survey of current work in rabbinics yields multiple selves: the sensory self; the suffering self; the cultivated self; the emerging self; the relational self; the self-reflective, reflexive, or split self; the public self.[3] Work on "the sensory self" is that which considers how selves interact with the world and with other selves through sensory experience: hearing, smelling, seeing, tasting.[4] With its bleeding wounds, pounding aches, profuse sweats, or writhing intestines, "the suffering self" is one sort of sensory self; the suffering body makes claims to authority, differentiates communities, and produces powerful rhetoric.[5]

---

[3] One might include the "gendered self," and no doubt there are many other possible selves that could enrich the discussion.

[4] As the primary medium for rabbinic instruction, hearing has long been central to the study of rabbinics; the most influential work in recent years on rabbinic orality has been Martin S. Jaffee, *Torah in the Mouth: Writing and Oral Tradition in Palestinian Judaism, 200 BCE–400 CE* (New York: Oxford University Press, 2001). On smell: Deborah A. Green, *The Aroma of Righteousness: Scent and Seduction in Rabbinic Life and Literature* (University Park: Pennsylvania State University Press, 2011). On sight: Rachel Neis, *The Sense of Sight in Rabbinic Culture* (New York: Cambridge University Press, 2013). On taste/food: Kraemer, *Jewish Eating and Identity through the Ages*; Jordan Rosenblum, *Food and Identity in Early Rabbinic Judaism* (New York: Cambridge University Press, 2010). I do not know of any recent work that focuses on the sense of touch.

[5] While justification of suffering in light of belief in a good God, i.e., theodicy, is a classic concern of monotheistic religion, recent work in rabbinics, inspired by scholarship on suffering in early Christianity, looks at the suffering self not only as a theological problem but also as a strategy of self-representation. Work from the last decade or so includes: Daniel Boyarin, *Dying for God: Martyrdom and the Making of Christianity and Judaism* (Palo Alto, CA: Stanford University Press, 1999); Jeffrey L. Rubenstein, *Rabbinic Stories* (Mahwah, NJ: Paulist Press, 2002), 207–28; Ra'anan S. Boustan, *From Martyr to Mystic: Rabbinic Martyrology and the Making of Merkavah Mysticism*

The "cultivated self" resists desires, consorts with the proper companions, studies the proper teachings, and labors daily to transform itself into the right kind of self.[6] Related to the always vigilant cultivated self is the "emerging self," gestating in the womb, maturing in childhood and aging as an adult, shaped by rabbinic temporalities.[7] Work on "the relational self" shows that for the rabbis, the self and the "stuff" that surrounds it are not as separate and discrete as one might have expected.[8] Work on "the self-reflective self" looks at phenomena in rabbinic literature such as what Belser calls "performative perception," the self's ability to influence its own experience through its interpretive choices; the self's reckoning with its epistemological limitations; the self's capacity to deceive itself; and the impact of the self's state of mind upon the legal status of an object or act.[9] One can also speak, anachronistically, of "the subconscious self," of split selves and multiple selves; these occur in the discourse of the *yetzer*, and in the projection of rabbinic cultural concerns onto heretics or gentiles, and in rabbinic dream interpretation.[10] In contrast to

(Tübingen: Mohr Siebeck, 2005); Valer, *Sorrow and Distress in the Talmud*. On rabbinic asceticism: Eliezer Diamond, *Holy Men and Hunger Artists: Fasting and Asceticism in Rabbinic Culture* (New York: Oxford University Press, 2003).

[6] On self-cultivation: Jonathan Wyn Schofer, *The Making of a Sage: A Study in Rabbinic Ethics* (Madison: University of Wisconsin Press, 2005).

[7] See Gwynn Kessler, *Conceiving Israel: The Fetus in Rabbinic Narratives* (Philadelphia: University of Pennsylvania Press, 2009); Jonathan Wyn Schofer, *Confronting Vulnerability: The Body and the Divine in Rabbinic Ethics* (Chicago: University of Chicago Press, 2010); Peri Danit Sinclair, "When Rabbis Conceive Women: Physiology and Gestation in Leviticus Rabbah Chapter 14" (PhD diss., The Jewish Theological Seminary of America, 2014). On temporality: Kaye, "Law and Temporality in Bavli Mo'ed"; Gribetz, "Conceptions of Time and Rhythms of Daily Life in Rabbinic Literature, 200–600 CE."

[8] Balberg, *Purity, Body, and Self in Early Rabbinic Literature*; Wasserman, *Jews, Gentiles, and Other Animals*.

[9] On performative perception: Belser, *Power, Ethics, and Ecology in Jewish Late Antiquity*. On epistemological limitations: Kraemer, *The Mind of the Talmud*; Chaya T. Halberstam, *Law and Truth in Biblical and Rabbinic Literature* (Bloomington, IN: Indiana University Press, 2010). On self-deception: Stein, "Rabbinic Legal Loopholes." On the impact of the self's subjective state upon legal status: Joshua Levinson, "From Narrative Practice to Cultural Poetics: Literary Anthropology and the Rabbinic Sense of Self," in *Homer and the Bible in the Eyes of Ancient Interpreters*, ed. Maren Niehoff (Leiden: Brill, 2002), 345–67; Balberg, *Purity, Body, and Self in Early Rabbinic Literature*; Libson, "Radical Subjectivity."

[10] On the *yetzer*: Rosen-Zvi, *Demonic Desires*. On projection: Christine Elizabeth Hayes, "Displaced Self-Perceptions: The Deployment of Minim and Romans in B. Sanhedrin 90b–91a," in *Religious and Ethnic Communities in Later Roman Palestine*, ed. Hayim Lapin (Potomac: University Press of Maryland, 1998), 249–89. On dreams: Haim Weiss, *Dreams in Rabbinical literature* (Tel Aviv: Modan, 2013); Yehuda Septimus, *On the Boundaries of Talmudic Prayer* (Tübingen: Mohr Siebeck, 2015), 89–142.

these hidden or cryptic dimensions of the self is the public self, the self whose body is clothed, hair is styled, and feet are sandaled, who moves through the marketplace, neighborhood, and study house, walks along the highway and travels on the sea, defining and being defined by those spaces.[11]

Let me illustrate how this abundance of selves might accommodate the animal. The "sensory self" can make room for the deaf ox featured in Chapter 2 and the lusty ox of Chapter 3. The "suffering self" is found in Rav Ivya's ox with a backbite in Chapter 2 and in the overburdened donkey of Chapter 4. The "cultivated self" might include the ox who gores only on the Sabbath but restrains himself the rest of the week, featured in Chapter 2, and the "wild" animals said to be domesticated out of their dangerous natures, discussed in Chapter 5. The "emerging self" is embodied by the gestating animal mentioned in Chapter 5, while the "relational self" finds form in the animal who serves as the wall of a sukkah, mentioned in Chapter 6. "Reflexive selves" might include Rav Pappa's clever ox and Rabbi Pinhas ben Yair's pious donkey, both appearing in Chapter 2. A good place to find the "public selves" of animals would be tractate Shabbat's chapter on animal "clothing," a subject I hope to treat elsewhere.[12] Animals are waiting to join the ranks of the

---

[11] On the public/private distinction and how classical rabbis conceptualized public space: Cynthia M. Baker, *Rebuilding the House of Israel: Architectures of Gender in Jewish Antiquity* (Palo Alto, CA: Stanford University Press, 2002); Charlotte Fonrobert, "Neighborhood as Ritual Space: The Case of the Rabbinic Eruv," *Archiv Für Religionsgeschichte* 10 (2008): 239–58; Charlotte Elisheva Fonrobert, "Gender Politics in the Rabbinic Neighborhood: Tractate Eruvin," in *Introduction to Seder Qodashim: A Feminist Commentary on the Babylonian Talmud V*, ed. Tal Ilan, Monika Brockhaus, and Tanja Hidde (Tübingen: Mohr Siebeck, 2012), 43–61; Gil P. Klein, "Torah in Triclinia: The Rabbinic Banquet and the Significance of Architecture," *Jewish Quarterly Review* 102, no. 3 (2012): 325–70; Daniel Boyarin, *A Traveling Homeland: The Babylonian Talmud as Diaspora* (Philadelphia: University of Pennsylvania Press, 2015); David Charles Kraemer, *Rabbinic Judaism: Space and Place* (New York: Routledge, 2016).

On dress, hair, shoes: Ishay Rosen-Zvi and Dror Yinon, "Male Jewels/Female Jewels: A New Look at the Religious Obligations of Women in Rabbinic Thought," *Reshit* 2 (2010): 55–79; Gail Labovitz, "The Omitted Adornment: Women and Men Mourning the Destruction," in *Introduction to Seder Qodashim: A Feminist Commentary on the Babylonian Talmud V*, ed. Tal Ilan, Monika Brockhaus, and Tanja Hidde (Tübingen: Mohr Siebeck, 2012), 127–45; Naftali S. Cohn, "What to Wear: Women's Adornment and Judean Identity in the Third Century Mishnah," in *Dressing Judeans and Christians in Antiquity*, ed. Alicia J. Batten, Carly Daniel-Hughes, and Kristi Upson-Saia (Burlington, VT: Ashgate Publishing, Ltd., 2014), 21–36; Marjorie Lehman, "Dressing and Undressing the High Priest: A View of Talmudic Mothers," *Nashim* 26 (2014): 52–74.

[12] I presented on this material at the Jewish Law Association Annual Meeting of 2017.

many selves being found in the pages of rabbinic literature. When they do, our sense of those selves will inevitably and unpredictably expand.

ANIMALS AND THE RABBINIC OTHER

The rabbinic Other is the more obvious category with which to be considering animals.[13] Others become such by being compared to animals. Others associate with the wrong animals. Others relate to animals in ways that they shouldn't. It is hard even to imagine the Other without the animal, who is the Other par excellence.[14] The main axis of otherness for rabbinic culture is Jew/non-Jew, or in more native rabbinic terms, *yisrael/ goy*.[15] Sometimes the non-Jewish Other is marked as pagan or gnostic, sometimes Christian or Zoroastrian; often it difficult to tell who exactly the Other is, and of what type he is, whether religious or ethnic.[16] There are also an enormous variety of "internal" Jewish others, as Christine Hayes calls them, among them the heretic, Samaritan, Noahide, convert, and non-rabbi (*am ha-aretz*), all of whom breathe life into the right-believing, right-practicing, ethnically Jewish rabbi. "Others" are not static ontologies but depend on context and are subject to change.

[13] Christine Elizabeth Hayes, "The 'Other' in Rabbinic Literature," in *The Cambridge Companion to the Talmud and Rabbinic Literature*, ed. Charlotte Elisheva Fonrobert and Martin S. Jaffee, Cambridge Companions to Religion (New York: Cambridge University Press, 2007), 243–69. See also Sacha Stern, *Jewish Identity in Early Rabbinic Writings* (New York: Brill, 1994).

[14] The alterity of the animal is a foundational theme in continental animal philosophy; see, for example, Calarco and Atterton, *Animal Philosophy*.

[15] On the emergence of the binary, see Rosen-Zvi and Ophir, "Goy"; Ishay Rosen-Zvi and Adi Ophir, "Paul and the Invention of the Gentiles," *Jewish Quarterly Review* 105, no. 1 (2015): 1–41. On dialogues between Jews and non-Jews, see Jenny R. Labendz, *Socratic Torah: Non-Jews in Rabbinic Intellectual Culture* (New York: Oxford University Press, 2013). On restrictions on trade and other interactions with non-Jews in tractate Avodah Zarah, see Christine Elizabeth Hayes, *Between the Babylonian and Palestinian Talmuds: Accounting for Halakhic Difference in Selected Sugyot from Tractate Avodah Zarah* (New York: Oxford University Press, 1997); Moshe Halbertal, "Coexisting with the Enemy: Jews and Pagans in the Mishnah," in *Tolerance and Intolerance in Early Judaism and Christianity*, ed. Guy G. Stroumsa (New York: Cambridge University Press, 1998), 159–72; Seth Schwartz, "The Rabbi in Aphrodite's Bath: Palestinian Society and Jewish Identity in the High Roman Empire," in *Being Greek Under Rome: Cultural Identity, the Second Sophistic and the Development of Empire*, ed. Simon Goldhill (New York: Cambridge University Press, 2001), 335–61. On purity laws and gentiles, see Christine Elizabeth Hayes, *Gentile Impurities and Jewish Identities: Intermarriage and Conversion from the Bible to the Talmud* (New York: Oxford University Press, 2002).

[16] "In rabbinic halakhah, the gentile can be imagined as an ethnic other *or* as a religious other"; Hayes, "The 'Other' in Rabbinic Literature," 245.

A rabbi can become a heretic, and a non-rabbi can become a rabbi. The Palestinian rabbi is Other when he visits Babylonia, and the Babylonian when he visits Palestine. The convert is most of the time just like a native Jew, but at other times his foreign origins are not forgotten. "Others" occupy gradations of Otherness, with rabbis' wives closer to the rabbinic self than, possibly, King Shapur of Persia.

How do animals contribute to the production of these rabbinic Others and themselves operate as an Other? Consider the case of non-rabbis, the *am ha-aretz*, in Pesahim 49a-b.[17] The passage compares the wife of an *am ha-aretz* to a reptile, and sex with the daughter of an *am ha-aretz* to sex with an animal. The passage permits "tearing an *am ha-aretz* like a fish." Rabbi Akiva is quoted as saying that in his younger days when he used to be an *am ha-aretz* he would have bitten a sage as an ass would. Rabbi Akiva's students compare Akiva's younger self to a dog. Rabbi Meir compares marrying one's daughter off to an *am ha-aretz* to tying her up and putting her before a lion, and likens the sexual advance of the *am ha-aretz* to a lion's trampling and devouring his victim. These animal analogies create an *am ha-aretz* who is, alternately, shameless, voracious, vicious, worthless, something that a rabbi rips up (like the fish), or that rips up a rabbi (like the ass, dog, or lion). Women are particular threats (e.g., the daughter of an *am ha-aretz*), and under threat (e.g., the daughter of a rabbinic Jew). Sexual intercourse with the male *am ha-aretz* is compared not to sex with a lion but to being consumed by one. The *am ha-aretz*, in turn, reinforces the notion that the animal is waiting to pounce, without restraint, nearly demonic.

A Talmud passage on Avodah Zarah 22a-23a "animalizes" the non-Jew rather than the non-rabbi.[18] The mishnah on which the talmudic commentary is based prohibits Jews from paddocking their cattle in the inn of a non-Jew when stopping there overnight on the rather outrageous assumption that non-Jews are "suspect for bestiality" (*hashudin al ha-revi'ah*). The talmudic dialectic contests the assumption, juxtaposing the mishnah with another early rabbinic teaching, a baraita, that permits

[17] See the recent discussion of this passage and references to scholarship in Jonathan A. Pomeranz, "Did the Babylonian Sages Regard the Ammei-ha'Aretz as Subhuman?," *Hebrew Union College Annual* 87 (2017): 115–43. Noteworthy is Jonathan Brumberg-Kraus, "Meat-Eating and Jewish Identity: Ritualization of the Priestly 'Torah of Beast and Fowl' (Lev 11:46) in Rabbinic Judaism and Medieval Kabbalah," *AJS Review* 24, no. 02 (November 1999): 227–62.
[18] A reading of the passage similar in spirit to the one I am offering can be found in Wasserman, *Jews, Gentiles, and Other Animals*.

Jews to purchase an animal from a non-Jew for the purpose of sacrifice. That baraita explicitly rejects the possibility that the non-Jew would have had sex with the animal and thereby disqualified her from sacrifice. In the course of harmonizing these divergent teachings, the later rabbis, the Amoraim, claim that non-Jewish animal owners can be trusted to restrain their deviant sexual impulses when the market value of their animal is at stake. So too can gentile shepherds hold back from sexual partnerships with their flock if they think they might lose their job as a result. The non-Jew emerges from the discussion as coldly calculating, able to restrain their perverse sexual desires when it serves their economic interests. That portrait intensifies when the talmudic dialectic proposes that "[with respect to] them who know each other, they are fearful; [with respect to] us who do not know them, they are not fearful." According to this principle, non-Jews operate on the assumption that their worst habits are well-known to their fellow non-Jews, but that they can deceive Jews into thinking that they are reliable commercial partners. The non-Jew comes across not just as *deviant* but as *devious*. The joke of the passage is that its very existence attests to the fact that Jews (or, at least, rabbis) do, in fact, know the true character of the gentile.

The passage moves from there into an exploration of different kinds of difference – Jewish difference, gender and sexual difference, human difference. Jewish women and rabbinical students are accused of concealing their sexual relationships with the household dog, in a turn of the argument that undermines the initial assumption that gentiles have a monopoly on sexual perversion. The pendulum shifts again as the passage proceeds to some even more outrageous claims about gentiles in what is best understood as an ancient version of a "your momma" joke: gentile men are said to prefer sex with Jewish animals to sex with their own wives. The culmination of the passage is a mythic narrative of humanity's rise, fall, and resurrection whose parallels with Christian theology are striking.[19] The Talmud retells the story of the garden of Eden, but in this version the serpent ejaculates into Eve his "foul poison" (*zohema*) in a primordial act of bestiality that becomes the source of all human perversion.[20] Redemption arrives not with Christ, of course, but with Sinai,

---

[19] Parallels on Shabbat 145b-146a and Yevamot 103b. See discussion in Daniel Boyarin, *Carnal Israel: Reading Sex in Talmudic Culture* (Berkeley: University of California Press, 1993), 82–3. He observes that the rabbinic myth diverges from the Christian notion of original sin in that the rabbinic myth is not about *licit* sexuality.

[20] Sokoloff's definition of *zohema* is filth, foul smell, stink, dirt, sensuality, lust; see Sokoloff, *A Dictionary of Jewish Babylonian Aramaic of the Talmudic and Geonic Periods*, 401.

when Jews alone are said to be freed of the serpent's poison. Non-Jews continue on, according to the myth, in their category-collapsing perversions. Evidence for the myth is found in an anecdote about a non-Jew who purchases a goose in the marketplace and then rapes, strangles, roasts, and eats her. A second anecdote ups the ante. An "Arab" is said to do all the same things, except in his case he has sex with and eats only the animal's thigh. Through these animal stories, the portrait of the non-Jew progresses from deviant, to devious, to utterly monstrous.

<h2 style="text-align:center">DISRUPTIVE ANIMALS</h2>

This book's aim has not been to prove that animals have selves in the Talmud, or that they are cast as Other, though both those things are true. It is to point out the ways that the animals of the Talmud complicate and transcend the self/Other, human/animal binary, as Balaam's donkey does, the animal who opened Chapter 1. Each of the talmudic texts I have examined trade in the human/animal binary while illustrating its inadequacies. Chapter 2's clever ox, able to ignite a fire in order to harvest the ashes so as to heal his wound, overturns the passage's initial presumption that animals are incapable of advanced cognition of this sort. The passage develops a vocabulary for anthropomorphism – "his ox is similar to him" – that advocates cross-species comparison and argues against absolute species difference. In Chapter 3, when the talmudic editors consider a range of opinions regarding whether animals possess moral consciousness, they cast doubt on the completeness of any moral consciousness. Chapters 4, 5, and 6 feature talmudic editors casting doubt on a variety of anthropocentric habits: indifference to animal suffering; projection of danger onto animals; objectification of animals. These talmudic passages alert their readers to anthropodenial, consider the motivations for it, and expose its failures. These talmudic texts suggest not only that animal selves might exist – they clearly do, sometimes – but also that they have the power to disrupt schemes of subjectivity and to throw into question the basic binaries that structure the rabbinic nomos. Animals persist in the rabbinic imagination as bodies to be sacrificed, eaten, traded, inherited, worked, milked, etc., but they also exceed those uses and make themselves known as presences in their own right.

The disruptive potential of the animal can be observed also in today's Jewish culture when one considers new Jewish rituals for pets. Jewish pet funeral scripts include some of the same elements that Jewish human funerals do – the recitation of the prayers *el male rahamim* ("God full of compassion") and *kaddish*; the eulogy (*hesped*); lighting a "yahrzeit" memorial candle; sitting shiva (the initial seven-day mourning period) – but the scripts are also tailored to animals in their inclusion of psalms and talmudic passages that feature the human/animal relationship.[21] Jewish rituals have emerged also to mark the adoption of a companion animal. A Jewish blessing of the animals is recited either on Friday night, mimicking the traditional blessing of children, or on a selected day of the year, adapting the blessing of the animals in churches on St. Francis of Assisi day.[22] These Jewish pet rituals can border on, if not go well past, the absurd. Joan Rivers celebrated a "Bark Mitzvah" for her dog Spike on daytime television, with Spike dressed up in prayer shawl (tallit) and head covering (kippah).[23] There are "chewish" dog toys, and a book called *How to Raise a Jewish Dog*, written by the fictional "rabbis of the Boca Raton Theological Seminary."[24] Some rabbis object to Jewish pet

---

[21] For an ethnographic and personal narrative of the stages and rituals of Jewish mourning, see Samuel C. Heilman, *When a Jew Dies: The Ethnography of a Bereaved Son* (Berkeley: University of California Press, 2001). For some examples of animal funeral scripts, see Reconstructionist Rabbinical College, "Honoring Our Animal Companions," *Ritualwell*, accessed March 7, 2016, http://ritualwell.org/categories/15; Rabbi Janet Offel, "When a Beloved Pet Dies," accessed March 7, 2016, http://kalsman.huc.edu/articles/Offel_WhenABelovedPetDies.pdf; "Jewish Resources for Mourning a Dog (with Inclusive Mourner's Kaddish)," *After Gadget*, January 11, 2011, https://aftergadget.wordpress.com/grief-resources/jewish-resources-for-mourning-a-dog-with-inclusive-mourners-kaddish/; "Burying a Pet," accessed March 7, 2016, www.clal.org/rl17.html. For discussion of these ritual practices, see Aubrey L. Glazer, "Taking the Circumcised Dog by the Throat: A Critical Review of Contemporary Rituals for Dogs in America," in *A Jew's Best Friend: The Image of the Dog Throughout Jewish History*, ed. Phillip Ackerman-Lieberman and Rakefet Zalashik (Portland, OR: Sussex Academic Press, 2013), 230–50. On the phenomenon of new Jewish rituals more generally, see Vanessa L. Ochs, *Inventing Jewish Ritual* (Philadelphia: Jewish Publication Society, 2010).

[22] See Rebecca Meiser, "Forget the Bark Mitzvah: Cleveland Rabbi Offers Jewish Blessing of the Animals Ceremony," *Tablet Magazine*, October 10, 2013, www.tabletmag.com/scroll/148298/the-rabbi-who-blesses-jewish-pets.: "I figured if it was good enough for St. Francis it was good enough for us," [Rabbi Eddie] Sukol told the 40 participants and yarmulke-clad dogs with a laugh, "so I stole it from them."

[23] For an interview of the woman who performed the bark mitzvah, see Debra Galant, "Where Your Pet Can Be Groomed or Become a Bride – The New York Times," *The New York Times*, January 5, 1997, www.nytimes.com/1997/01/05/nyregion/where-your-pet-can-be-groomed-or-become-a-bride.html. On Tracy Morgan's wildly popular werewolf bar mitzvah on the television show Thirty Rock, see Edward Wyatt, "Werewolf Bar Mitzvah – 30 Rock – TV," *The New York Times*, October 25, 2007, sec. Television, www.nytimes.com/2007/10/25/arts/television/25were.html.

[24] Michael Kaminer, "'Chewish' Dog Toys (What's Next?)," *The Forward*, accessed March 3, 2016, http://forward.com/the-assimilator/151106/chewish-dog-toys-whats-next/;

rituals, arguing that they violate the sanctity of classic Jewish rituals.[25] Journalists covering these phenomena tend to take a skeptical or comical tone, calling the bark mitzvah a "dubious religious trend" and asking with respect to Jewish dog toys, "What next?"

Like all jokes, this one is also serious. Jewish animals are helping to shape today's Judaism, its families, rituals, laws, ethics, economics, and sense of identity. Aside from pets raising a variety of halakhic questions – Must a dog eat kosher food? May a dog enter the synagogue? Is neutering or spaying permitted? Is it permitted to walk a dog on a leash on the Sabbath? – pets afford Jews important opportunities to express and explore their Jewishness.[26] Kitschy Jewish dog books and toys and trinkets put on display the adaptability of the owners' Jewish identity. They also give Judaism its own perch within American commercial culture. The bichromatic blue-and-white Jewish pet accessories, littered with stars of David, create a lifestyle brand for Judaism to rival other popular branding schemes, especially those of Christian America.[27] Jewish pet discourse also allows Jews to boil down their Jewishness to its essence: *How to Raise a Jewish Dog* describes a Jewish dog as Jewish in so far as he "has an exaggerated sense of his own wonderfulness" accompanied by an "exaggerated sense of his own shortcomings," thereby illustrating what the authors (jokingly) take to be the fundamental traits of the Jew. Their contrast between an "ordinary dog" and a "Jewish

---

Ellis Weiner and Barbara Davilman, *How to Raise a Jewish Dog*, ed. Barbara Davilman (New York: Little, Brown and Company, 2007).

[25] An articulation of this view can be found in: Karen Tucker, "Sitting Shiva for Spot?," *The Forward*, April 27, 2012, http://forward.com/articles/155303/sitting-shiva-for-spot/.:

See also Meiser, "Forget the Bark Mitzvah":

Rabbi Mark Dratch, executive vice president of the Rabbinical Council of America, explained. "We believe it's not our right or prerogative to create new ceremonies like this ... even if pets are an important part of the family."

[26] For treatment of some of the halakhic issues related to pets, see Howard Jachter, "Halachic Perspectives on Pets," *Journal of Halacha and Contemporary Society* 23 Spring (1992): 33–40; Fred Rosner, "Good Dogs and Bad Dogs in Jewish Law," *B'Or Ha'Torah* 23 (2014): 163–9. A less sober, more conversational treatment is found in Rabbi Ronald Isaacs, *Do Animals Have Souls? A Pet Lover's Guide to Spirituality* (Brooklyn, NY: Ktav, 2013).

[27] On religious branding and the commercialization of religion, see Leigh Eric Schmidt, *Consumer Rites: The Buying & Selling of American Holidays* (Princeton, NJ: Princeton University Press, 1995); Mara Einstein, *Brands of Faith: Marketing Religion in a Commercial Age* (New York: Routledge, 2008).

dog" makes a strong claim for Jewish exceptionalism. Jewish pet naming practices – I knew a dog in Brooklyn named Shelomo, the Hebrew
version of "Solomon," and one in New Haven named Nesli, Hebrew for
"my miracle" (I imagine most people who heard the dog being called
thought he was named after the food and beverage company) – contribute to the Jewish expression of their human companions and form
part of the contemporary Jewish onomasticon. Finally, in the compet-
itive marketplace of American religion, Jewish pet rituals offer rabbis
a path to reach Jewish audiences who might otherwise dispense with
rabbis, synagogues, and Judaism altogether.[28] Just as the ancient Israelite
once brought their animal to be sacrificed by the priests in the Jerusalem
Temple, so now the contemporary American Jew might bring their pet
to be blessed by a local rabbi.

Animals, and dogs in particular, have long inspired Jews to articulate
the boundaries between themselves and others. In his sixteenth-century
gloss on the law code *Shulkhan Arukh*, Polish rabbi Moses Isserles cites a
position on dog ownership that permits it because Jews now "live amidst
the gentiles and the nations."[29] The implication is that Jews need dogs
to protect themselves from inimical gentiles. Two centuries or so later,
German rabbi Jacob Emden calls dog ownership "the behavior of the
uncircumcised."[30] This sense that dogs are "goyish" is embodied in the
joke with which this chapter began and may in part be the motivation
for new Jewish pet rituals.[31] Jewish pet funerals or blessings combat the
long-standing notion that having an animal companion is not Jew-ish.

---

[28] See, for instance, Meiser, "Forget the Bark Mitzvah":

> When Sukol first started this service twelve years ago, he knew of no other rabbis doing
> anything similar. But since he's started, he's noticed the trend has taken off in cities in
> Florida, Michigan, New York, and California by rabbis who are looking for new ways
> to connect with their congregants.

> On American religion as a marketplace, see Wade Clark Roof, *Spiritual Marketplace:
> Baby Boomers and the Remaking of American Religion* (Princeton, NJ: Princeton
> University Press, 1999).

[29] Moses Isserles, 1520–1572, Poland; *Mappah* on Hoshen Mishpat 409, part 3.
[30] Jacob Emden, 1697–1776; She'elat Yaavetz number 17. See discussion in Jachter,
"Halahic Perspectives on Pets."
[31] The conflation of the dog with the goy conforms to what Zalashik and
Ackerman-Lieberman call a persistent approach to the dog among Jews as the "oth-
er's other – the attempt of subaltern Jews to create their own subaltern"; Phillip
Ackerman-Lieberman and Rakefet Zalashik, "Introduction," in *A Jew's Best Friend?
The Image of the Dog Throughout Jewish History*, ed. Phillip Ackerman-Lieberman and
Rakefet Zalashik (Portland, OR: Sussex Academic Press, 2013), 1–11.

At the same time, some contemporary Jewish animal rituals discard the concern for pristine Jewishness altogether. One rabbi jokes about "stealing" from Christianity to create a Jewish blessing of the animals.[32] For Jews today, and for the ancient rabbis, animals present the possibility that anyone or anything can assume a self, whether it be dog, *goy*, or any other figure considered by Jewish convention to lie outside the bounds of community and personhood. Animals suggest that the circle of moral consideration, social legibility, and recognizable subjectivity is never fully closed.[33]

---

[32] See footnote 23.

[33] This formulation is inspired by the reading of Levinas in Calarco, *Zoographies*, 55–77: "Rather than trying to determine the definitive criterion or criteria of moral considerability, we might, following Birch and the reading of Levinas I have been pursuing, begin from a notion of 'universal consideration' that takes seriously our fallibility in determining where the face begins and ends. Universal consideration would entail being ethically attentive and open to the possibility that anything might take on a face; it would also entail taking up a skeptical and critical relation to the determinations of moral consideration that form the contours of our present-day moral thinking" (p. 73).

Works Cited

Aaltola, Elisa. "Personhood and Animals." *Environmental Ethics* 30, no. 2 (2008): 175–93.

Abbou, Julie, and Fabienne H. Baider, eds. *Gender, Language and the Periphery: Grammatical and Social Gender from the Margins.* Philadelphia: John Benjamins Publishing Company, 2016.

Ackerman, Jennifer. *The Genius of Birds.* New York: Penguin, 2016.

Ackerman-Lieberman, Phillip, and Rakefet Zalashik, eds. *A Jew's Best Friend? The Image of the Dog Throughout Jewish History.* Portland, OR: Sussex Academic Press, 2013.

"Introduction." In *A Jew's Best Friend? The Image of the Dog Throughout Jewish History,* edited by Phillip Ackerman-Lieberman and Rakefet Zalashik, 1–11. Portland, OR: Sussex Academic Press, 2013.

Adams, Carol J. *The Sexual Politics of Meat: A Feminist-Vegetarian Critical Theory.* New York: Bloomsbury USA, 2015.

Adams, Carol J., and Lori Gruen, eds. *Ecofeminism: Feminist Intersections with Other Animals and the Earth.* New York: Bloomsbury Publishing USA, 2014.

Agamben, Giorgio. *The Open: Man and Animal.* Palo Alto, CA: Stanford University Press, 2004.

Akhtar, Sahar. "Animal Pain and Welfare: Can Pain Sometimes Be Worse for Them Than for Us?" In *The Oxford Handbook of Animal Ethics,* edited by Tom L. Beauchamp and Raymond Gillespie Frey, 495–518. New York: Oxford University Press, 2011.

Alaimo, Stacy, and Susan Hekman, eds. *Material Feminisms.* Bloomington, IN: Indiana University Press, 2008.

Alexander, Philip S. "What Happened to the Priesthood after 70?" In *A Wandering Galilean: Essays in Honour of Seán Freyne,* edited by Zuleika Rodgers, Anne Fitzpatrick McKinley, and Margaret Daly-Denton, 5–34. Boston: Brill, 2009.

Allen, Barbara. *Animals in Religion: Devotion, Symbol and Ritual.* London: Reaktion Books, 2016.

Allen, Colin, and Marc Bekoff. *Species of Mind: The Philosophy and Biology of Cognitive Ethology*. Cambridge, MA: MIT Press, 1997.

Amit, David, and Yonatan Adler. "The Observance of Ritual Purity after 70 C.E.: A Reevaluation of the Evidence in Light of Recent Archaeological Discoveries." In *Follow the Wise: Studies in Jewish History and Culture in Honor of Lee I. Levine*, edited by Zeev Weiss, 121–43. Winona Lake, IN: Eisenbrauns, 2010.

Aptowitzer, Victor. "The Rewarding and Punishing of Animals and Inanimate Objects: On the Aggadic View of the World." *Hebrew Union College Annual* 3 (1926): 117–55.

Armbruster, Karla. "What Do We Want from Talking Animals? Reflections on Literary Representations of Animal Voices and Minds." In *Speaking for Animals: Animal Autobiographical Writing*, edited by Margo DeMello, 17–33. New York: Routledge, 2013.

Armstrong, Philip. *Sheep*. Chicago: University of Chicago Press, 2016.

Armstrong, Susan Jean, and Richard G. Botzler, eds. *The Animal Ethics Reader*. New York: Routledge, 2008.

Athias-Robles, Hillel. "'If the Eye Had Permission to See No Creature Could Stand Before the Mezikin': Demons and Vision in the Babylonian Talmud." MA thesis, Columbia University, 2015.

Atterton, Peter. "Levinas and Our Moral Responsibility toward Other Animals." *Inquiry* 54, no. 6 (2011): 633–49.

Avalos, Hector, Sarah J. Melcher, and Jeremy Schipper, eds. *This Abled Body: Rethinking Disabilities in Biblical Studies*. Atlanta, GA: Society of Biblical Literature, 2007.

Baars, Bernard J. *The Cognitive Revolution in Psychology*. New York: Guilford Press, 1986.

Baird, Ileana. "Introduction: Peregrine Things: Rethinking the Global in Eighteenth-Century Studies." In *Eighteenth-Century Thing Theory in a Global Context: From Consumerism to Celebrity Culture*, edited by Ileana Baird and Christina Ionescu, 1–16. Burlington, VT: Ashgate, 2013.

Bakels, Jet. "Animals as Persons in Sumatra." In *The Politics of Species: Reshaping Our Relationships with Other Animals*, edited by Raymond Corbey and Annette Lanjouw, 156–63. New York: Cambridge University Press, 2013.

Baker, Cynthia M. *Rebuilding the House of Israel: Architectures of Gender in Jewish Antiquity*. Palo Alto, CA: Stanford University Press, 2002.

Bakhos, Carol, and M. Rahim Shayegan, eds. *The Talmud in Its Iranian Context*. Tübingen: Mohr Siebeck, 2010.

Balberg, Mira. *Blood for Thought: The Reinvention of Sacrifice in Early Rabbinic Literature*. Berkeley: University of California Press, 2017.

——. *Purity, Body, and Self in Early Rabbinic Literature*. Berkeley: University of California Press, 2014.

Balcombe, Jonathan. *Second Nature: The Inner Lives of Animals*. New York: Macmillan, 2010.

Balsdon, John Percy Vyvian Dacre. *Life and Leisure in Ancient Rome*. New York: McGraw-Hill, 1969.

Barak-Erez, Daphne. *Outlawed Pigs: Law, Religion, and Culture in Israel.* Madison: University of Wisconsin Press, 2007.

Beard, Mary. "A Don's Life." *A Pig's Epitaph*, March 15, 2015. http://timesonline .typepad.com/dons_life/2015/03/the-pigs-epitaph.html.

Becker, Adam H. "The Comparative Study of 'scholasticism' in Late Antique Mesopotamia: Rabbis and East Syrians." *AJS Review* 34, no. 01 (2010): 91–113.

Beirnes, Piers. "The Law Is an Ass: Reading EP Evans' the Medieval Prosecution and Capital Punishment of Animals." *Society & Animals* 2, no. 1 (1994): 27–46.

Bekoff, Marc. *The Emotional Lives of Animals: A Leading Scientist Explores Animal Joy, Sorrow, and Empathy – and Why They Matter.* Novato, CA: New World Library, 2008.

Wild Justice: The Moral Lives of Animals. Chicago: University of Chicago Press, 2009.

Bekoff, Marc, Colin Allen, and Gordon M. Burghardt, eds. *The Cognitive Animal: Empirical and Theoretical Perspectives on Animal Cognition.* Cambridge, MA: MIT Press, 2002.

Bekoff, Marc, and Dale Jamieson, eds. *Readings in Animal Cognition.* Cambridge, MA: MIT Press, 1996.

Belser, Julia Watts. *Power, Ethics, and Ecology in Jewish Late Antiquity: Rabbinic Responses to Drought and Disaster.* New York: Cambridge University Press, 2015.

"Reading Talmudic Bodies: Disability, Narrative, and the Gaze in Rabbinic Judaism." In *Disability in Judaism, Christianity, and Islam: Sacred Texts, Historical Traditions, and Social Analysis*, edited by Darla Schumm and Michael Stoltzfus, 5–27. New York: Palgrave Macmillan, 2011.

Benjamin, Andrew. *Of Jews and Animals.* Edinburgh: Edinburgh University Press, 2010.

Berg, Jessica. "Elephants and Embryos: A Proposed Framework for Legal Personhood." *Hastings Law Journal* 59 (2007): 369–406.

Berkowitz, Beth A., and Marion Katz. "The Cowering Calf and the Thirsty Dog: Narrating and Legislating Kindness to Animals in Jewish and Islamic Texts." In *Islamic and Jewish Legal Reasoning: Encountering Our Legal Other*, edited by Anver M. Emon, 61–111. London: Oneworld, 2016.

Berman, Paul Schiff. "Rats, Pigs, and Statues on Trial: The Creation of Cultural Narratives in the Prosecution of Animals and Inanimate Objects." *New York University Law Review* 69 (1994): 288–326.

Berthelot, Katell. "Philo and Kindness towards Animals (De Virtutibus 125–147)." *The Studia Philonica Annual*, no. 14 (2002): 48–65.

Bieder, Robert E. *Bear.* Chicago: University of Chicago Press, 2005.

Bland, Kalman P. "Construction of Animals in Medieval Jewish Philosophy." In *New Directions in Jewish Philosophy*, edited by Aaron W. Hughes and Elliot R. Wolfson, 175–204. Bloomington, IN: Indiana University Press, 2010.

Boddice, Rob, ed. *Anthropocentrism: Human, Animals, Environments.* Boston: Brill, 2011.

Boggs, Colleen Glenney. *Animalia Americana: Animal Representations and Biopolitical Subjectivity.* New York: Columbia University Press, 2013.

Bokser, Baruch M. "Rabbinic Responses to Catastrophe: From Continuity to Discontinuity." *Proceedings of the American Academy for Jewish Research* 50 (1983): 37–61.

The Origins of the Seder: The Passover Rite and Early Rabbinic Judaism. Berkeley: University of California Press, 1984.

Bondeson, Jan. *The Feejee Mermaid and Other Essays in Natural and Unnatural History*. Ithaca, NY: Cornell University Press, 1999.

Bough, Jill. *Donkey*. Chicago: University of Chicago Press, 2011.

Boustan, Ra'anan S. *From Martyr to Mystic: Rabbinic Martyrology and the Making of Merkavah Mysticism*. Tübingen: Mohr Siebeck, 2005.

Boyarin, Daniel. *A Traveling Homeland: The Babylonian Talmud as Diaspora*. Philadelphia: University of Pennsylvania Press, 2015.

Carnal Israel: Reading Sex in Talmudic Culture. Berkeley: University of California Press, 1993.

Dying for God: Martyrdom and the Making of Christianity and Judaism. Palo Alto, CA: Stanford University Press, 1999.

"Hellenism in Jewish Babylonia." In *The Cambridge Companion to the Talmud and Rabbinic Literature*, edited by Charlotte Elisheva Fonrobert and Martin S. Jaffee, 336–63. Cambridge Companions to Religion. New York: Cambridge University Press, 2007.

Socrates and the Fat Rabbis. Chicago: University of Chicago Press, 2009.

Boyce, Mary. *A Persian Stronghold of Zoroastrianism*. Oxford: Clarendon Press, 1977.

Brafman, Yonatan Yisrael. "Critical Philosophy of Halakha (Jewish Law): The Justification of Halakhic Norms and Authority." PhD diss., Columbia University, 2014.

Brakke, David, Michael L. Satlow, and Steven Weitzman, eds. "Introduction." In *Religion and the Self in Antiquity*, 1–11. Bloomington, IN: Indiana University Press, 2005.

Brettler, Marc Zvi, and Adele Berlin, eds. *The Jewish Study Bible: Featuring the Jewish Publication Society Tanakh Translation*. New York: Oxford University Press, 2004.

Brody, Robert. "Irano-Talmudica: The New Parallelomania?" *Jewish Quarterly Review* 106, no. 2 (2016): 209–32.

Brown, Bill. "The Secret Life of Things (Virginia Woolf and the Matter of Modernism)." *Modernism/modernity* 6, no. 2 (1999): 1–28.

ed. *Things*. Chicago: University of Chicago Press, 2004.

Brown, Francis. *The Brown, Driver, Briggs Hebrew and English Lexicon: With an Appendix Containing the Biblical Aramaic: Coded with the Numbering System from Strong's Exhaustive Concordance of the Bible*. Peabody, MA: Hendrickson, 1996.

Brożek, Bartosz. "The Troublesome 'Person.'" In *Legal Personhood: Animals, Artificial Intelligence and the Unborn*, edited by Tomasz Pietrzykowski and Visa A. J. Kurki, 3–13. New York: Springer, 2017.

Brumberg-Kraus, Jonathan. "Meat-Eating and Jewish Identity: Ritualization of the Priestly 'Torah of Beast and Fowl' (Lev 11:46) in Rabbinic Judaism and Medieval Kabbalah." *AJS Review* 24, no. 02 (November 1999): 227–62.

Burnside, Jonathan Patrick. *God, Justice, and Society: Aspects of Law and Legality in the Bible.* New York: Oxford University Press, 2011.

"Burying a Pet." Accessed March 7, 2016. www.clal.org/rl17.html.

Cahan, Joshua. "Tza'ar Ba'alei Ḥayim in the Marketplace of Values." *Conservative Judaism* 65, no. 4 (2014): 30–48.

Calarco, Matthew. *Thinking Through Animals: Identity, Difference, Indistinction.* Palo Alto, CA: Stanford University Press, 2015.

———. *Zoographies: The Question of the Animal from Heidegger to Derrida.* New York: Columbia University Press, 2008.

Calarco, Matthew, and Peter Atterton, eds. *Animal Philosophy: Essential Readings in Continental Thought.* New York: Continuum, 2004.

Campbell, Gordon Lindsay, ed. *The Oxford Handbook of Animals in Classical Thought and Life.* New York: Oxford University Press, 2014.

Carere, Claudio, and Dario Maestripieri, eds. *Animal Personalities: Behavior, Physiology, and Evolution.* Chicago: University of Chicago Press, 2013.

Carey, Benedict. "Male Fruit Flies, Spurned by Females, Turn to Alcohol." *The New York Times,* March 15, 2012. www.nytimes.com/2012/03/16/health/male-fruit-flies-spurned-by-females-turn-to-alcohol.html.

Castricano, Jodey, ed. *Animal Subjects: An Ethical Reader in a Posthuman World.* Waterloo, ON: Wilfrid Laurier University Press, 2008.

Cheney, Dorothy L., and Robert M. Seyfarth. *Baboon Metaphysics: The Evolution of a Social Mind.* Chicago: University of Chicago Press, 2007.

Chengzhong, Pu. *Ethical Treatment of Animals in Early Chinese Buddhism: Beliefs and Practices.* Newcastle upon Tyne: Cambridge Scholars Publishing, 2014.

Chen, Mel Y. *Animacies: Biopolitics, Racial Mattering, and Queer Affect.* Durham, NC: Duke University Press, 2012.

Chris, Cynthia. "Boys Gone Wild: The Animal and the Abject." In *Animals and the Human Imagination: A Companion to Animal Studies,* edited by Aaron S. Gross and Anne Vallely, 152–73. New York: Columbia University Press, 2012.

Clark, Gillian. "The Fathers and the Animals: The Rule of Reason?" In *Animals on the Agenda,* edited by Andrew Linzey and Dorothy Yamamoto, 67–79. Urbana: University of Illinois Press, 1998.

Clough, David L. *On Animals: Volume I: Systematic Theology.* London: A&C Black, 2012.

Coetzee, J. M. *The Lives of Animals.* Princeton Classics. Princeton, NJ: Princeton University Press, 2016.

Cohen, Esther. "Law, Folklore and Animal Lore." *Past & Present* 110 (1986): 6–37.

Cohen, Noah J. *Tsa'ar Ba'ale Hayim–The Prevention of Cruelty to Animals: Its Bases, Development and Legislation in Hebrew Literature.* Washington, DC: Catholic University of America Press, 1959.

Cohen, Shaye J. D. *The Significance of Yavneh and Other Essays in Jewish Hellenism.* Tübingen: Mohr Siebeck, 2010.

———, ed. *The Synoptic Problem in Rabbinic Literature.* Providence, RI: Brown Judaic Studies, 2000.

Cohn, Naftali S. *The Memory of the Temple and the Making of the Rabbis.* Philadelphia: University of Pennsylvania Press, 2013.

———. "What to Wear: Women's Adornment and Judean Identity in the Third Century Mishnah." In *Dressing Judeans and Christians in Antiquity*, edited by Alicia J. Batten, Carly Daniel-Hughes, and Kristi Upson-Saia, 21–36. Burlington, VT: Ashgate Publishing, 2014.

Coole, Diana, and Samantha Frost, eds. *New Materialisms: Ontology, Agency, and Politics.* Durham, NC: Duke University Press, 2010.

Cooper, Alan. "The Plain Sense of Exodus 23: 5." *Hebrew Union College Annual* 59 (1988): 1–22.

Crane, Jonathan K., ed. *Beastly Morality: Animals as Ethical Agents.* New York: Columbia University Press, 2015.

Creegan, Nicola Hoggard. *Animal Suffering and the Problem of Evil.* New York: Oxford University Press, 2013.

Cupp Jr., Richard L. "Dubious Grail: Seeking Tort Law Expansion and Limited Personhood as Stepping Stones toward Abolishing Animals' Property Status." *Southern Methodist University Law Review* 60 (2007): 3–54.

Dalal, Neil, and Chloe Taylor, eds. *Asian Perspectives on Animal Ethics: Rethinking the Nonhuman.* New York: Routledge, 2014.

Danziger, Kurt. "Historical Psychology of Persons: Categories and Practice." In *The Psychology of Personhood: Philosophical, Historical, Social-Developmental, and Narrative Perspectives*, edited by Jack Martin and Mark H. Bickhard, 59–80. New York: Cambridge University Press, 2012.

Darwin, Charles, and Francis Darwin. *Charles Darwin's Works: The Descent of Man and Selection in Relation to Sex.* New York: D. Appleton, 1896.

Davis, Lennard J., ed. *The Disability Studies Reader.* New York: Routledge, 2013.

Dawkins, Marian Stamp. *Through Our Eyes Only? The Search for Animal Consciousness.* New York: Oxford University Press, 1998.

Dayan, Colin. *The Law Is a White Dog: How Legal Rituals Make and Unmake Persons.* Princeton, NJ: Princeton University Press, 2011.

———. *With Dogs at the Edge of Life.* New York: Columbia University Press, 2015.

Deane-Drummond, Celia, and David L. Clough, eds. *Creaturely Theology: On God, Humans and Other Animals.* London: SCM Press, 2009.

Deane-Drummond, Celia, David L. Clough, and Rebecca Artinian-Kaiser, eds. *Animals as Religious Subjects: Transdisciplinary Perspectives.* London: Bloomsbury T&T Clark, 2013.

Deckha, Maneesha. "Critical Animal Studies and the Property Debate in Animal Law." In *Animal Subjects 2.0*, edited by Jodey Castricano and Lauren Corman. Waterloo, ON: Wilfrid Laurier University Press, 2016.

Deleuze, Gilles. *Francis Bacon: The Logic of Sensation.* Minneapolis: University of Minnesota Press, 2003.

Delise, Karen. *The Pit Bull Placebo: The Media, Myths and Politics of Canine Aggression.* Sofia, Bulgaria: Anubis Publishing, 2007.

Derrida, Jacques. "The Animal That Therefore I Am (More to Follow)." Translated by David Wills. *Critical Inquiry* 28, no. 2 (January 1, 2002): 369–418.

DeVries, Scott M. *Creature Discomfort: Fauna-Criticism, Ethics and the Representation of Animals in Spanish American Fiction and Poetry.* Leiden: Brill, 2016.

Diamond, Cora. "Eating Meat and Eating People." *Philosophy* 53, no. 206 (October 1978): 465–79.

"Eating Meat and Eating People." In *Animal Rights: Current Debates and New Directions,* edited by Martha Craven Nussbaum and Cass R. Sunstein, 93–107. New York: Oxford University Press, 2004 [Reprint of Cora, "Eating Meat and Eating People," 1978.].

Diamond, Eliezer. *Holy Men and Hunger Artists: Fasting and Asceticism in Rabbinic Culture.* New York: Oxford University Press, 2003.

Dickey, Bronwen. *Pit Bull: The Battle Over an American Icon.* New York: Knopf Doubleday, 2017.

Dinzelbacher, Peter. "Animal Trials: A Multidisciplinary Approach." *Journal of Interdisciplinary History* 32, no. 3 (2002): 405–21.

Donalson, Malcolm Drew. *The Domestic Cat in Roman Civilization.* Lewiston, NY: Edwin Mellen Press, 1999.

Doniger, Wendy. *Implied Spider: Politics and Theology in Myth.* New York: Columbia University Press, 2010.

Donovan, Josephine, and Carol J. Adams, eds. *The Feminist Care Tradition in Animal Ethics: A Reader.* New York: Columbia University Press, 2007.

Dunkle, Roger. *Gladiators: Violence and Spectacle in Ancient Rome.* New York: Routledge, 2013.

Echoing. "What Is It Like to Be a Bat?" In Thomas Nagel, *Mortal Questions,* 165–80. New York: Canto, 1979.

Edminster, Avigdor. "Interspecies Families, Freelance Dogs, and Personhood: Saved Lives and Being One at an Assistance Dog Agency." In *Making Animal Meaning,* edited by Linda Kalof and Georgina M. Montgomery, 127–44. East Lansing: Michigan State University Press, 2011.

Edrey, Meir. "The Dog Burials at Achaemenid Ashkelon Revisited." *Tel Aviv* 35, no. 2 (2008): 267–82.

Einstein, Mara. *Brands of Faith: Marketing Religion in a Commercial Age.* New York: Routledge, 2008.

Elazar, Kochva. "Venomous Snakes of Israel: Ecology and Snakebite." *Public Health Reviews* 26, no. 3 (1998): 209–32.

Ellis, Albert, Mike Abrams, and Lidia Abrams. *Personality Theories: Critical Perspectives.* Los Angeles: Sage, 2009.

Elvin, Jesse. "Responsibility, 'Bad Luck', and Delinquent Animals: Law as a Means of Explaining Tragedy." *The Journal of Criminal Law* 73, no. 6 (2009): 530–58.

Engels, Donald W. *Classical Cats: The Rise and Fall of the Sacred Cat.* New York: Routledge, 1999.

Epplett, Chris. "Roman Beast Hunts." In *A Companion to Sport and Spectacle in Greek and Roman Antiquity,* edited by Paul Christesen and Donald G. Kyle, 505–19. Hoboken, NJ: Wiley Blackwell, 2016.

Epstein, Marc Michael. *Dreams of Subversion in Medieval Jewish Art and Literature.* University Park: Pennsylvania State University Press, 1997.

"The Elephant and the Law: The Medieval Jewish Minority Adapts a Christian Motif." *The Art Bulletin* 76, no. 3 (September 1, 1994): 465–78.

The Medieval Haggadah: Art, Narrative, and Religious Imagination. New Haven, CT: Yale University Press, 2011.

Evans, Edward Payson. *The Criminal Prosecution and Capital Punishment of Animals.* New York: Dutton, 1906.

Ewald, William. "Comparative Jurisprudence (I): What Was It Like to Try a Rat?" *University of Pennsylvania Law Review* 143, no. 6 (1995): 1889–2149.

Favre, David. "A New Property Status for Animals: Equitable Self-Ownership." In *Animal Rights: Current Debates and New Directions*, edited by Cass R. Sunstein and Martha Craven Nussbaum, 234–50. New York: Oxford University Press, 2004.

Favre, David S. "Judicial Recognition of the Interests of Animals: A New Tort." *Michigan State Law Review* 2005 (2005): 333–67.

Feliks, Yehuda. *Ha-Hai ba-Mishnah.* Jerusalem: Institute for Mishna Research, 1982.

Fine, Steven. "Did the Synagogue Replace the Temple?" *Bible Review* 12 (1996): 18–27.

Finkelstein, Jacob J. "The Goring Ox: Some Historical Perspectives on Deodands, Forfeitures, Wrongful Death and the Western Notion of Sovereignty." *Temple Law Quarterly* 46, no. 2 (1972): 169–290.

The Ox That Gored. Vol. 71. Philadelphia: American Philosophical Society, 1981.

Flesher, Paul Virgil McCracken. *Oxen, Women or Citizens? Slaves in the System of the Mishnah.* Atlanta, GA: Scholars Press, 1988.

Foer, Jonathan Safran. *Eating Animals.* New York: Little, Brown and Company, 2009.

Foltz, Richard. *Animals in Islamic Traditions and Muslim Cultures.* London: Oneworld, 2014.

"This She-Camel of God Is a Sign to You": Dimensions of Animals in Islamic Tradition and Muslim Culture." In *A Communion of Subjects: Animals in Religion, Science, and Ethics*, edited by Paul Waldau and Kimberley Patton, 146–59. New York: Columbia University Press, 2006.

"Zoroastrian Attitudes toward Animals." *Society & Animals* 18, no. 4 (2010): 367–78.

Fonrobert, Charlotte Elisheva. "Neighborhood as Ritual Space: The Case of the Rabbinic Eruv." *Archiv Für Religionsgeschichte* 10 (2008): 239–58.

"Gender Politics in the Rabbinic Neighborhood: Tractate Eruvin." In *Introduction to Seder Qodashim: A Feminist Commentary on the Babylonian Talmud V*, edited by Tal Ilan, Monika Brockhaus, and Tanja Hidde, 43–61. Tübingen: Mohr Siebeck, 2012.

Fonrobert, Charlotte Elisheva, and Martin S. Jaffee, eds. *The Cambridge Companion to the Talmud and Rabbinic Literature.* Cambridge Companions to Religion. New York: Cambridge University Press, 2007.

Fox, Michael Allen, and Lesley McLean. "Animals in Moral Space." In *Animal Subjects: An Ethical Reader in a Posthuman World*, edited by Jodey Castricano, 145–75. Waterloo, ON: Wilfrid Laurier University Press, 2008.

Fraade, Steven D. "Navigating the Anomalous: Non-Jews at the Intersection of Early Rabbinic Law and Narrative." In *Legal Fictions*, 345–64. Supplements to the Journal for the Study of Judaism. Leiden: Brill, 2011.

"The Temple as a Marker of Jewish Identity before and after 70 CE: The Role of the Holy Vessels in Rabbinic Memory and Imagination." In *Jewish Identities in Antiquity: Studies in Memory of Menahem Stern*, edited by Lee I. Levine and Daniel R. Schwartz, 237–65. Tübingen: Mohr Siebeck, 2009.

Francione, Gary L. *Animals, Property, & The Law*. Philadelphia: Temple University Press, 1995.

"Equal Consideration and the Interest of Nonhuman Animals in Continued Existence: A Response to Professor Sunstein." *University of Chicago Legal Forum*, no. 1 (2006): 231–52.

Francione, Gary L., and Robert Garner. *The Animal Rights Debate: Abolition or Regulation?* New York: Columbia University Press, 2010.

French, Roger Kenneth. *Ancient Natural History: Histories of Nature*. New York: Routledge, 1994.

Frey, Raymond Gillespie. *Interests and Rights: The Case against Animals*. New York: Oxford University Press, 1980.

"Utilitarianism and Animals." In *The Oxford Handbook of Animal Ethics*, edited by Tom L. Beauchamp and Raymond Gillespie Frey, 172–97. New York: Oxford University Press, 2011.

Friedland, Paul. *Seeing Justice Done: The Age of Spectacular Capital Punishment in France*. Oxford: Oxford University Press, 2012.

Friedman, Shamma. "Towards a Characterization of Babylonian Baraitot: 'Ben Tema' and 'Ben Dortai.'" In *Neti'ot Le-David: Jubilee Volume for David Weiss Halivni*, edited by Yaakov Elman, Ephraim Bezalel Halivni, and Zvi Aryeh Steinfeld, 195–274. Jerusalem: Orhot, 2004.

Frisch, Amos. "The Story of Balaam's She-Ass (Numbers 22: 21–35): A New Literary Insight." *Hebrew Studies* 56, no. 1 (2015): 103–13.

Fudge, Erica. "A Left-Handed Blow: Writing the History of Animals." In *Representing Animals*, edited by Nigel Rothfels, 3–18. Bloomington, IN: Indiana University Press, 2002.

Furstenberg, Yair. "Am ha-Aretz in Tannaitic Literature and its Social Contexts." *Zion* 78, no. 3 (2013): 287–319.

Gafni, Isaiah. *Land, Center and Diaspora: Jewish Constructs in Late Antiquity*. Sheffield, UK: Sheffield Academic Press, 1997.

Galant, Debra. "Where Your Pet Can Be Groomed or Become a Bride – The New York Times." *The New York Times*, January 5, 1997. www.nytimes.com/1997/01/05/nyregion/where-your-pet-can-be-groomed-or-become-a-bride.html.

Garland, Robert. *The Eye of the Beholder: Deformity and Disability in the Graeco-Roman World*. London: Bloomsbury Academic, 2010.

Genzlinger, Neil. "The Lives of Animals, Disabled and Otherwise." *The New York Times*, April 8, 2014. www.nytimes.com/2014/04/09/arts/television/the-lives-of-animals-disabled-and-otherwise.html.

Gilhus, Ingvild Sælid. *Animals, Gods and Humans: Changing Attitudes to Animals in Greek, Roman and Early Christian Ideas*. New York: Routledge, 2006.

Giliker, Paula. *Vicarious Liability in Tort: A Comparative Perspective*. New York: Cambridge University Press, 2010.

Gillespie, Kathryn, and Rosemary-Claire Collard, eds. *Critical Animal Geographies: Politics, Intersections and Hierarchies in a Multispecies World*. New York: Routledge, 2015.

Girgen, Jen. "The Historical and Contemporary Prosecution and Punishment of Animals." *Animal Law* 9 (2003): 97–133.

Glazer, Aubrey L. "Taking the Circumcised Dog by the Throat: A Critical Review of Contemporary Rituals for Dogs in America." In *A Jew's Best Friend: The Image of the Dog Throughout Jewish History*, edited by Phillip Ackerman-Lieberman and Rakefet Zalashik, 230–50. Portland, OR: Sussex Academic Press, 2013.

Goldhill, Simon. *The Temple of Jerusalem*. Cambridge: Harvard University Press, 2005.

Gomez, Juan Carlos. "Are Apes Persons? The Case for Primate Intersubjectivity." In *The Animal Ethics Reader*, edited by Richard George Botzler and Susan Jean Armstrong, 138–43. New York: Routledge, 2003.

Grant, Robert McQueen. *Early Christians and Animals*. New York: Routledge, 1999.

Greenberg, Moshe. "Some Postulates of Biblical Criminal Law." In *Studies in the Bible and Jewish Thought*, 25–42. Philadelphia: Jewish Publication Society, 1995.

Green, Deborah A. *The Aroma of Righteousness: Scent and Seduction in Rabbinic Life and Literature*. University Park: Pennsylvania State University Press, 2011.

Gribetz, Sarit Kattan. "Conceptions of Time and Rhythms of Daily Life in Rabbinic Literature, 200–600 CE." PhD diss., Princeton University, 2013.

Griffin, Donald Redfield. *Animal Minds: Beyond Cognition to Consciousness*. Chicago: University of Chicago Press, 2013.

　　The Question of Animal Awareness: Evolutionary Continuity of Mental Experience. New York: Rockefeller University Press, 1981.

Grimm, David. *Citizen Canine: Our Evolving Relationship with Cats and Dogs*. New York: PublicAffairs, 2014.

Groot, Maaike. *Animals in Ritual and Economy in a Roman Frontier Community: Excavations in Tiel-Passewaaij*. Amsterdam: Amsterdam University Press, 2008.

　　Livestock for Sale: Animal Husbandry in a Roman Frontier Zone. Amsterdam: Amsterdam University Press, 2016.

Gross, Aaron S. *The Question of the Animal and Religion: Theoretical Stakes, Practical Implications*. New York: Columbia University Press, 2015.

Gross, Aaron S., and Anne Vallely, eds. *Animals and the Human Imagination: A Companion to Animal Studies*. New York: Columbia University Press, 2012.

Gulak, Asher. "Shepherds and Breeders of Domestic Cattle after the Destruction of the Second Temple." *Tarbiz* 12 (1940–1941): 181–9.

Gross, Simcha M. "Irano-Talmudica and Beyond: Next Steps in the Contextualization of the Babylonian Talmud." *Jewish Quarterly Review* 106 no. 2 (June 22, 2016): 248–55.

Haber, Ruth. "Rabbis on the Road: Exposition En Route in Classical Rabbinic Texts." PhD diss., University of California, 2014.

"Hachi Garsinan: The Friedberg Project for Talmud Bavli Variants." Accessed July 17, 2017. https://bavli.genizah.org/Global/homepage?lan=eng&isPartia l=False&isDoubleLogin=False&TractateID=0&DafID=0.

Hachlili, Rachel. *Jewish Funerary Customs, Practices and Rites in the Second Temple Period*. Leiden: Brill, 2005.

Halberstam, Chaya T. *Law and Truth in Biblical and Rabbinic Literature*. Bloomington: Indiana University Press, 2010.

Halbertal, Moshe. "Coexisting with the Enemy: Jews and Pagans in the Mishnah." In *Tolerance and Intolerance in Early Judaism and Christianity*, edited by Guy G. Stroumsa, 159–72. New York: Cambridge University Press, 1998.

Halivni, David Weiss. *The Formation of the Babylonian Talmud*. Translated by Jeffrey L. Rubenstein. New York: Oxford University Press, 2013.

Halpern, Baruch. "The Canine Conundrum of Ashkelon: A Classical Connection." In *The Archaeology of Jordan and Beyond: Essays in Honor of James A. Sauer*, edited by Michael D. Coogan, Lawrence E. Stager, and Joseph A. Greene, 133–44. Winona Lake, IN: Eisenbrauns, 2000.

Haran, Menahem. "Seething a Kid in Its Mother's Milk." *Journal of Jewish Studies* 30, no. 1 (1979): 23–35.

Haraway, Donna Jeanne. *The Haraway Reader*. New York: Routledge, 2004.

When Species Meet. Minneapolis: University of Minnesota Press, 2008.

Harden, Alastair. *Animals in the Classical World: Ethical Perspectives from Greek and Roman Texts*. New York: Palgrave Macmillan, 2013.

Harris, Marvin. "The Abominable Pig." In *The Sacred Cow and the Abominable Pig: Riddles of Food and Culture*, 67–87. New York: Simon & Schuster, 1987.

Harrod, Howard L. *The Animals Came Dancing: Native American Sacred Ecology and Animal Kinship*. Tucson: University of Arizona Press, 2000.

Hartsock, Chad. *Sight and Blindness in Luke-Acts: The Use of Physical Features in Characterization*. Leiden: Brill, 2008.

Hauptman, Judith. *Rereading the Mishnah: A New Approach to Ancient Jewish Texts*. Tübingen: Mohr Siebeck, 2005.

Hayes, Christine Elizabeth. *Between the Babylonian and Palestinian Talmuds: Accounting for Halakhic Difference in Selected Sugyot from Tractate Avodah Zarah*. New York: Oxford University Press, 1997.

"Displaced Self-Perceptions: The Deployment of Minim and Romans in B. Sanhedrin 90b–91a." In *Religious and Ethnic Communities in Later Roman Palestine*, edited by Hayim Lapin, 249–89. Potomac: University Press of Maryland, 1998.

Gentile Impurities and Jewish Identities: Intermarriage and Conversion from the Bible to the Talmud. New York: Oxford University Press, 2002.

"The 'Other' in Rabbinic Literature." In *The Cambridge Companion to the Talmud and Rabbinic Literature*, edited by Charlotte Elisheva Fonrobert and Martin S. Jaffee, 243–69. Cambridge Companions to Religion. New York: Cambridge University Press, 2007.

Hegedus, Chris, and D. A. Pennebaker. *Unlocking the Cage*. Documentary. HBO Documentary Films, 2016.

Heilman, Samuel C. *When a Jew Dies: The Ethnography of a Bereaved Son*. Berkeley: University of California Press, 2001.

Herbrechter, Stefan. *Posthumanism: A Critical Analysis*. New York: Bloomsbury Academic, 2013.

Herman, Geoffrey, ed. *Jews, Christians, and Zoroastrians : Religious Dynamics in a Sasanian Context.* Piscataway, NJ: Gorgias Press, 2014.

Her Many Horses, Emil, and George P. Horse Capture, eds. *A Song for the Horse Nation: Horses in Native American Cultures.* Golden, CO: Fulcrum, 2006.

Hezser, Catherine. "Travel and Mobility." In *The Oxford Handbook of Jewish Daily Life in Roman Palestine,* edited by Catherine Hezser, 210–26. New York: Oxford University Press, 2010.

Hinson, Joy. *Goat.* Chicago: University of Chicago Press, 2015.

Hobgood-Oster, Laura. *Holy Dogs and Asses: Animals in the Christian Tradition.* Urbana: University of Illinois Press, 2008.

Hoffner, Harry. "Incest, Sodomy, and Bestiality in the Ancient Near East." In *Orient and Occident: Essays Presented to Cyrus H. Gordon on the Occasion of His Sixty-Fifth Birthday,* edited by Harry Hoffner, 81–90. Neukirchen-Vluyn, Germany: Neukirchener Verlag, 1973.

Horovitz, H. Saul, and Israel Abraham Rabin, eds. *Mechilta d'Rabbi Ismael.* Jerusalem: Wahrmann Books, 1970.

Horowitz, Alexandra. *Inside of a Dog: What Dogs See, Smell, and Know.* New York: Scribner, 2010.

Howard, Cameron B. R. "Animal Speech as Revelation in Genesis 3 and Numbers 22." In *Exploring Ecological Hermeneutics,* edited by Norman C. Habel and Peter L. Trudinger, 21–29. Atlanta, GA: Society of Biblical Literature, 2008.

Hribal, Jason. *Fear of the Animal Planet: The Hidden History of Animal Resistance.* Oakland, CA: AK Press, 2010.

Humphrey, Nicholas. *The Mind Made Flesh: Essays from the Frontiers of Psychology and Evolution.* New York: Oxford University Press, 2002.

Hunter, Susan, and Richard A. Brisbin. *Pet Politics: The Political and Legal Lives of Cats, Dogs, and Horses in Canada and the United States.* West Lafayette, IN: Purdue University Press, 2016.

Iacub, Marcela. "Paternalism or Legal Protection of Animals? Bestiality and the French Judicial System." In *French Thinking about Animals,* edited by Louisa Mackenzie and Stephanie Posthumus, 121–34. The Animal Turn series. East Lansing: Michigan State University Press, 2015.

Ilan, Tal. *Massekhet Hullin: Text, Translation, and Commentary.* Tübingen: Mohr Siebeck, 2017.

"Inside the Animal Mind – BBC Two." *BBC.* Accessed July 10, 2017. www.bbc.co.uk/programmes/b03thwhf.

Irshai, Oded. "The Role of the Priesthood in the Jewish Community in Late Antiquity: A Christian Model?" In *Jüdische Gemeinden Und Ihr Christlicher Kontext in Kulturräumlich Vergleichender Betrachtung: Von Der Spätantike Bis Zum 18. Jahrhundert,* edited by Christoph Cluse, Alfred Haverkamp, and Israel J. Yuval, 75–85. Hannover, Germany: Hahnsche Buchhandlung, 2003.

Isaacs, Rabbi Ronald. *Do Animals Have Souls? A Pet Lover's Guide to Spirituality.* Brooklyn, NY: Ktav, 2013.

Isaacs, Ronald H. *Animals in Jewish Thought and Tradition.* Northvale, NJ: Jason Aronson, 2000.

Jachter, Howard. "Halachic Perspectives on Pets." *Journal of Halacha and Contemporary Society* 23, Spring (1992): 33–40.

Jackson, Bernard S. "Reflections on Biblical Criminal Law." In *Essays in Jewish and Comparative Legal History*, 25–63. Leiden: Brill, 1975.

Jackson, Deirdre. *Lion*. Chicago: University of Chicago Press, 2010.

Jacobowitz, Tamar. "Leviticus Rabbah and the Spiritualization of the Laws of Impurity." PhD diss., University of Pennsylvania, 2010.

Jacobs, Louis. "The Story of R. Phinehas Ben Yair and His Donkey in B. Hullin 7a-B." In *A Tribute to Geza Vermes: Essays on Jewish and Christian Literature and History*, edited by Philip R. Davies and Richard T. White, 193–205. New York: Bloomsbury, 1990.

Jaffee, Martin S. *Torah in the Mouth: Writing and Oral Tradition in Palestinian Judaism, 200 BCE–400 CE*. New York: Oxford University Press, 2001.

Jamieson, Philip. "Animal Liability in Early Law." *Cambrian Law Review* 19 (1988): 45–68.

Jassen, Alex. "Tracing the Threads of Jewish Law: The Sabbath Carrying Prohibition from Jeremiah to the Rabbis." *Annali Di Storia Dell'esegesi* 28, no. 1 (January 2011): 253–78.

Jastrow, Marcus. "Dictionary of the Targumim, the Talmud Babli and Yerushalmi, and the Midrashic Literature." Accessed July 13, 2017. www.tyndalearchive.com/TABS/Jastrow/.

Jennison, George. *Animals for Show and Pleasure in Ancient Rome*. Manchester, UK: Manchester University Press, 1937.

"Jewish Resources for Mourning a Dog (with Inclusive Mourner's Kaddish)." *After Gadget*, January 11, 2011. https://aftergadget.wordpress.com/grief-resources/jewish-resources-for-mourning-a-dog-with-inclusive-mourners-kaddish/.

Jones, David. *Buddha Nature and Animality*. Fremont, CA: Jain, 2007.

Joosten, Jan. *People and Land in the Holiness Code: An Exegetical Study of the Ideational Framework of the Law in Leviticus 17–26*. Leiden: Brill, 1996.

Joselit, Jenna Weissman. "Jews and Animals, A Very Modern Story." *The Forward*, March 3, 2010. http://forward.com/culture/126414/jews-and-animals-a-very-modern-story/.

Kalechofsky, Roberta. "Hierarchy, Kinship, and Responsibility: The Jewish Relationship to The Animal World." In *A Communion of Subjects: Animals in Religion, Science, and Ethics*, edited by Paul Waldau and Kimberley Patton, 91–99. New York: Columbia University Press, 2006.

Kalmin, Richard Lee. *Jewish Babylonia between Persia and Roman Palestine*. New York: Oxford University Press, 2006.

——— *Migrating Tales: The Talmud's Narratives and Their Historical Context*. Berkeley: University of California Press, 2014.

——— "The Bavli, the Roman East, and Mesopotamian Christianity." *Jewish Quarterly Review*, 106, no. 2 (June 22, 2016): 242–7.

——— "Josephus and Rabbinic Literature." In *A Companion to Josephus*, edited by Zuleika Rodgers and Honora Howell Chapman, 293–304. Malden, MA: Wiley Blackwell, 2016.

Kalof, Linda, and Amy Fitzgerald, eds. *The Animals Reader: The Essential Classic and Contemporary Writings*. New York: Berg, 2007.

Kaminer, Michael. " 'Chewish' Dog Toys (What's Next?)." *The Forward*. Accessed March 3, 2016. http://forward.com/the-assimilator/151106/chewish-dog-toys-whats-next/.

Kasher, Hannah. "Animals as Moral Patients in Maimonides' Teachings." *American Catholic Philosophical Quarterly* 76, no. 1 (2002): 165–80.

Katz, Steven T., ed. *The Cambridge History of Judaism: The Late Roman-Rabbinic Period.* Vol. 4. New York: Cambridge University Press, 2006.

Kaye, Lynn. "Law and Temporality in Bavli Mo'ed." PhD diss., New York University, 2012.

Kemmerer, Lisa. *Animals and World Religions.* New York: Oxford University Press, 2012.

Kessler, Gwynn. *Conceiving Israel: The Fetus in Rabbinic Narratives.* Philadelphia: University of Pennsylvania Press, 2009.

Killebrew, Ann E. "Village and Countryside." In *The Oxford Handbook of Jewish Daily Life in Roman Palestine,* edited by Catherine Hezser, 189–209. New York: Oxford University Press, 2010.

Kim, Claire Jean. *Dangerous Crossings: Race, Species, and Nature in a Multicultural Age.* New York: Cambridge University Press, 2015.

King, Barbara J. "Anti-Stress Serenity Injection: The Chimpanzee Waterfall Video." *NPR.org.* Accessed January 14, 2016. www.npr.org/sect ions/13.7/2012/03/28/149531687/anti-stress-serenity-injection-the-chimpanzee-waterfall-video.

How Animals Grieve. Chicago: University of Chicago Press, 2013.

Kirova, Milena. "Eyes Wide Open: A Case of Symbolic Reversal in the Biblical Narrative." *Scandinavian Journal of the Old Testament* 24, no. 1 (2010): 85–98.

Kitchell, Jr., Kenneth F. *Animals in the Ancient World from A to Z.* New York: Routledge, 2014.

Klawans, Jonathan. *Purity, Sacrifice, and the Temple: Symbolism and Super-sessionism in the Study of Ancient Judaism.* New York: Oxford University Press, 2006.

Klein, Gil P. "Torah in Triclinia: The Rabbinic Banquet and the Significance of Architecture." *Jewish Quarterly Review* 102, no. 3 (2012): 325–70.

Kluger, Jeffrey. "What Are Animals Thinking? (A Lot, as It Turns Out)." *Time.* Accessed July 10, 2017. http://time.com/3173937/what-are-animals-thinking-hint-more-that-you-suspect/.

Knust, Jennifer Wright, and Zsuzsanna Várhelyi, eds. *Ancient Mediterranean Sacrifice.* New York: Oxford University Press, 2011.

Koosed, Jennifer L., ed. *The Bible and Posthumanism.* Atlanta, GA: Society of Biblical Literature, 2014.

Kooten, Geurt Hendrik van, and J. van Ruiten, eds. *The Prestige of the Pagan Prophet Balaam in Judaism, Early Christianity and Islam.* Themes in Biblical Narrative Conference. Leiden: Brill, 2008.

Korsgaard, Christine M. "Interacting with Animals: A Kantian Account." In *The Oxford Handbook of Animal Ethics,* edited by Tom L. Beauchamp and Raymond Gillespie Frey, 91–118. New York: Oxford University Press, 2011.

Kraemer, David Charles. *Jewish Eating and Identity through the Ages.* New York: Routledge, 2007.

Rabbinic Judaism: Space and Place. New York: Routledge, 2016.

Reading the Rabbis: The Talmud as Literature. New York: Oxford University Press, 1996.

Responses to Suffering in Classical Rabbinic Literature. New York: Oxford University Press, 1994.

The Mind of the Talmud: An Intellectual History of the Bavli. New York: Oxford University Press, 1990.

Krech, Shepard. *Spirits of the Air: Birds & American Indians in the South.* Athens: University of Georgia Press, 2009.

Kulp, Joshua, and Jason Rogoff. *Reconstructing the Talmud: An Introduction to the Academic Study of Rabbinic Literature.* New York: Hadar Press, 2017.

Kuzniar, Alice. "'I Married My Dog': On Queer Canine Literature." In *Queering the Non/Human,* edited by Myra J. Hird and Noreen Giffney, 205–26. Burlington, VT: Ashgate, 2012.

Kyle, Donald G. *Spectacles of Death in Ancient Rome.* New York: Routledge, 2012.

Labendz, Jenny R. *Socratic Torah: Non-Jews in Rabbinic Intellectual Culture.* New York: Oxford University Press, 2013.

"The Book of Ben Sira in Rabbinic Literature." *AJS Review* 30, no. 02 (2006): 347–92.

Labovitz, Gail. "The Omitted Adornment: Women and Men Mourning the Destruction." In *Introduction to Seder Qodashim: A Feminist Commentary on the Babylonian Talmud V,* edited by Tal Ilan, Monika Brockhaus, and Tanja Hidde, 127–45. Tübingen: Mohr Siebeck, 2012.

Lapin, Hayim. *Rabbis as Romans: The Rabbinic Movement in Palestine, 100–400 CE.* New York: Oxford University Press, 2012.

Lawrence, Louise J. *Sense and Stigma in the Gospels: Depictions of Sensory-Disabled Characters.* New York: Oxford University Press, 2013.

Leeson, Peter T. "Vermin Trials." *Journal of Law and Economics* 56, no. 3 (2013): 811–36.

Lehman, Marjorie. "Dressing and Undressing the High Priest: A View of Talmudic Mothers." *Nashim* 26 (2014): 52–74.

Levine, Baruch A. *Leviticus = Va-Yiqra: The Traditional Hebrew Text with the New JPS Translation.* Philadelphia: Jewish Publication Society, 1989.

Numbers 21–36: A New Translation with Introduction and Commentary. Vol. 4A. The Anchor Bible. New York: Doubleday, 2000.

Levinson, Bernard M. *Deuteronomy and the Hermeneutics of Legal Innovation.* New York: Oxford University Press, 1997.

Levinson, Joshua. "From Narrative Practice to Cultural Poetics: Literary Anthropology and the Rabbinic Sense of Self." In *Homer and the Bible in the Eyes of Ancient Interpreters,* edited by Maren Niehoff, 345–67. Leiden: Brill, 2002.

Levy, Shimon. "Angel, She-Ass, Prophet: The Play and Its Set Design." In *Jews and Theater in an Intercultural Context,* edited by Edna Nahshon, 3–21. Leiden: Brill, 2012.

Lewy, Israel. *Introduction and Commentary to the Talmud Yerushalmi: Bava Qamma Chapters 1–6.* Jerusalem: Kedem, 1969.

Libson, Ayelet. "Radical Subjectivity: Law and Self-Knowledge in the Babylonian Talmud." PhD diss., New York University, 2014.

Lieberman, Saul, ed. *Tosefta according to Codex Vienna.* The Order of Nezikin. New York: The Jewish Theological Seminary of America, 2001.

Tosefta Ki-Fshuṭah: A Comprehensive Commentary on the Tosefta. Parts VI–VII: Order Nashim. New York: The Jewish Theological Seminary of America, 1995.

Tosefta Ki-Fshuṭah: A Comprehensive Commentary on the Tosefta. Parts IX–X: Order Nezikin. New York: The Jewish Theological Seminary of America, 2001.

Tosefta Ki-Fshuṭah: A Comprehensive Commentary on the Tosefta. Part II: Order Zera'im. New York: The Jewish Theological Seminary of America, 2001.

Tosefta Moed. New York: The Jewish Theological Seminary of America, 2002.

Linzer, Dov. "Tza'ar Ba'alei Chaim (Animal Suffering): A Case Study in Halakha and Values." In *Mishpetei Shalom: A Jubilee Volume in Honor of Rabbi Saul Berman,* edited by Yamin Levy, 383–402. Riverdale, NY; Jersey City, NJ: Ktav, 2010.

Linzey, Andrew. *Animal Gospel.* Louisville, KY: Westminster John Knox Press, 2000.

Why Animal Suffering Matters: Philosophy, Theology, and Practical Ethics. New York: Oxford University Press, 2009.

Linzey, Andrew, and Dorothy Yamamoto, eds. *Animals on the Agenda: Questions about Animals for Theology and Ethics.* Urbana: University of Illinois Press, 1998.

Luck, Chad. *The Body of Property: Antebellum American Fiction and the Phenomenology of Possession.* New York: Fordham University Press, 2014.

Lundblad, Michael. "From Animal to Animality Studies." *Proceedings of the MLA* 124, no. 2 (2009): 496–502.

Lurz, Robert W., ed. *The Philosophy of Animal Minds.* New York: Cambridge University Press, 2009.

Macdonald, Helen. *H Is for Hawk.* New York: Grove/Atlantic, 2015.

Mackenzie, Louisa, and Stephanie Posthumus, eds. *French Thinking about Animals.* The Animal Turn series. East Lansing: Michigan State University Press, 2015.

MacKinnon, Michael. "Pack Animals, Pets, Pests, and Other Non-Human Beings." In *The Cambridge Companion to Ancient Rome,* edited by Paul Erdkamp, 110–28. New York: Cambridge University Press, 2013.

Macuch, Maria. "On the Treatment of Animals in Zoroastrian Law." *Iranica Selecta: Studies in Honour of Professor Wojciech Skalmowski on the Occasion of His Seventieth Birthday.* Silk Road Studies VIII (2003): 167–90.

Magnússon, Sigurður G., and István M. Szíjártó. *What Is Microhistory? Theory and Practice.* New York: Routledge, 2013.

Martin, Jack, and Mark H. Bickhard, eds. *The Psychology of Personhood: Philosophical, Historical, Social-Developmental, and Narrative Perspectives.* New York: Cambridge University Press, 2012.

Marvin, Garry. *Wolf.* Chicago: University of Chicago Press, 2012.

Marx, Dalia. "The Missing Temple: The Status of the Temple in Jewish Culture Following Its Destruction." *European Judaism* 46, no. 2 (September 1, 2013): 61–78.

Masri, Al-Hafiz Basheer Ahmad. *Animal Welfare in Islam.* Markfield, UK: The Islamic Foundation, 2016.

Masson, Jeffrey Moussaieff. *When Elephants Weep: The Emotional Lives of Animals.* New York: Random House, 2009.

Mazzoni, Cristina. *She-Wolf: The Story of a Roman Icon.* New York: Cambridge University Press, 2010.

McCance, Dawne. *Critical Animal Studies: An Introduction.* Albany: State University of New York Press, 2013.

McFarland, Sarah E., and Ryan Hediger, eds. *Animals and Agency: An Interdisciplinary Exploration.* Leiden: Brill, 2009.

McHugh, Susan. *Dog.* Chicago: University of Chicago Press, 2004.

McKay, Adam. *The Big Short,* 2015. Film.

McKay, Heather A. "Through the Eyes of Horses: Representation of the Horse Family in the Hebrew Bible." In *Sense and Sensitivity: Essays on Reading the Bible in Memory of Robert Carroll,* edited by Alastair G. Hunter and Philip R. Davies, 127–41. London: Sheffield Academic Press, 2002.

Meir, Ofra. "The She-Ass of R. Pinhas ben Yair." *Folklore Research Center Studies* 7 (1983): 117–37.

Meiser, Rebecca. "Forget the Bark Mitzvah: Cleveland Rabbi Offers Jewish Blessing of the Animals Ceremony." *Tablet Magazine,* October 10, 2013. www.tabletmag.com/scroll/148298/the-rabbi-who-blesses-jewish-pets.

Menzel, Randolf, and Julia Fischer, eds. *Animal Thinking: Contemporary Issues in Comparative Cognition.* Cambridge, MA: MIT Press, 2011.

Midgley, Mary. *Utopias, Dolphins, and Computers: Problems of Philosophical Plumbing.* New York: Routledge, 1996.

Mikhail, Alan. "Dogs in Ancient Islamic Culture." *OUPblog,* July 13, 2017. https://blog.oup.com/2017/07/dogs-ancient-islamic-culture/.

———. *The Animal in Ottoman Egypt.* New York: Oxford University Press, 2013.

Milgrom, Jacob. *Leviticus 1–16: A New Translation with Introduction and Commentary.* Vol. 3. The Anchor Bible. New York: Doubleday, 1991.

———. *Leviticus 17–22: A New Translation with Introduction and Commentary.* Vol. 3A. The Anchor Bible. New York: Doubleday, 2000.

———. *Numbers = [Ba-Midbar]: The Traditional Hebrew Text with the New JPS Translation.* JPS Torah Commentary. Philadelphia: Jewish Publication Society, 1990.

Miller, Patricia Cox. *The Poetry of Thought in Late Antiquity: Essays in Imagination and Religion.* Burlington, VT: Ashgate, 2001.

Miller, Stuart S. *At the Intersection of Texts and Material Finds: Stepped Pools, Stone Vessels, and Ritual Purity Among the Jews of Roman Galilee.* Göttingen, Germany: Vandenhoeck & Ruprecht, 2015.

Mizelle, Brett. *Pig.* Chicago: University of Chicago Press, 2011.

Moazami, Mahnaz. "A Purging Presence: The Dog in Zoroastrian Tradition." *Anthropology of the Middle East* 11, no. 1 (Spring 2016): 20–9.

———. "Evil Animals in the Zoroastrian Religion." *History of Religions* 44, no. 4 (2005): 300–17.

Molloy, Claire. "Dangerous Dogs and the Construction of Risk." In *Theorizing Animals: Re-Thinking Humanimal Relations*, edited by Nik Taylor and Tania Signal, 107–28. Leiden: Brill, 2011.

Montgomery, Sy. *The Soul of an Octopus*. New York: Simon & Schuster, 2015.

Moore, Stephen D., ed. *Divinanimality: Animal Theory, Creaturely Theology*. New York: Fordham University Press, 2014.

Morell, Virginia. "Animal Minds – National Geographic Magazine." Accessed July 10, 2017. http://ngm.nationalgeographic.com/2008/03/animal-minds/virginia-morell-text.

Morris, Desmond. *Leopard*. Chicago: University of Chicago Press, 2014.

Moscovitz, Leib. *Talmudic Reasoning: From Casuistics to Conceptualization*. Tübingen: Mohr Siebeck, 2002.

"'The Actions of a Minor Are a Nullity'? Some Observations on the Legal Capacity of Minors in Rabbinic Law." Edited by Berachyahu Lifshitz. *Jewish Law Annual* 17, Part I (2008): 63–120.

"'The Holy One Blessed Be He ... Does Not Permit the Righteous to Stumble': Reflections on the Development of a Remarkable BT Theologoumenon." In *Creation and Composition: The Contribution of the Bavli Redactors (Stammaim) to the Aggada*, edited by Jeffrey L. Rubenstein, 125–80. Tübingen: Mohr Siebeck, 2005.

Moss, Candida R., and Jeremy Schipper, eds. *Disability Studies and Biblical Literature*. New York: Palgrave Macmillan, 2011.

Moyer, Clinton J. "Who Is the Prophet, and Who the Ass? Role-Reversing Interludes and the Unity of the Balaam Narrative (Numbers 22–24)." *Journal for the Study of the Old Testament* 37, no. 2 (2012): 167–83.

Muers, Rachel. "Setting Free the Mother Bird: On Reading a Strange Text." *Modern Theology* 22, no. 4 (2006): 555–76.

Nadler, Steven M. *Rembrandt's Jews*. Chicago: University of Chicago Press, 2003.

Naiden, F. S., and Christopher A. Faraone, eds. *Greek and Roman Animal Sacrifice: Ancient Victims, Modern Observers*. New York: Cambridge University Press, 2012.

Narveson, Jan. "A Defense of Meat Eating." In *Animal Rights and Human Obligations*, edited by Peter Singer and Tom Regan, 192–5. Englewood Cliffs, NJ: Prentice Hall, 1989.

Nayar, Pramod K. *Posthumanism*. Cambridge, UK: Polity, 2014.

Neis, Rachel. *The Sense of Sight in Rabbinic Culture*. New York: Cambridge University Press, 2013.

Neusner, Jacob. *Praxis and Parable: The Divergent Discourses of Rabbinic Judaism: How Halakhic and Aggadic Documents Treat the Bestiary Common to Them Both*. Lanham, MD: University Press of America, 2006.

Newmyer, Stephen Thomas. *Animals in Greek and Roman Thought: A Sourcebook*. New York: Routledge, 2011.

Animals, Rights, and Reason in Plutarch and Modern Ethics. New York: Routledge, 2006.

Nicholson, Peter. *Pure History Specials. Beasts of the Roman Games*. London: Digital Rights Group, 2009. Film.

Nikolsky, Ronit. "Interpret Him as Much as You Want: Balaam in the Babylonian Talmud." In *The Prestige of the Pagan Prophet Balaam in Judaism, Early Christianity and Islam*, edited by Geurt Hendrik van Kooten and J. van Ruiten, 213–30. Themes in Biblical Narrative Conference. Leiden: Brill, 2008.

Nir, Sarah Maslin. "Dog Praised as Hero for Saving Deer (Whether He Meant To or Not)." *The New York Times*, July 18, 2017, sec. N.Y. / Region. www.nytimes.com/2017/07/18/nyregion/dog-rescues-a-drowning-deer-and-becomes-a-social-media-hero.html.

Nocella, Anthony J., Amber E. George, and J. L. Schatz, eds. *The Intersectionality of Critical Animal, Disability, and Environmental Studies: Toward Eco-Ability, Justice, and Liberation*. Lanham, MD: Lexington Books, 2017.

Nocella, Anthony J., John Sorenson, Kim Socha, and Atsuko Matsuoka, eds. *Defining Critical Animal Studies: An Intersectional Social Justice Approach for Liberation*. New York: Peter Lang, 2013.

Noort, Ed. "Balaam the Villain: The History of Reception of the Balaam Narrative in the Pentateuch and the Former Prophets." In *The Prestige of the Pagan Prophet Balaam in Judaism, Early Christianity and Islam*, edited by Geurt Hendrik van Kooten and J. van Ruiten, 3–24. Themes in Biblical Narrative Conference. Leiden: Brill, 2008.

North, Peter. *Civil Liability for Animals*. New York: Oxford University Press, 2012.

"NOVA | Inside Animal Minds." Accessed July 10, 2017. www.pbs.org/wgbh/nova/nature/inside-animal-minds.html.

Nudds, Matthew, and Susan Hurley, eds. *Rational Animals?* New York: Oxford University Press, 2006.

Nussbaum, Martha Craven. *Frontiers of Justice: Disability, Nationality, Species Membership*. London: Belknap, 2007.

"The Moral Status of Animals." In *Animal Rights: Current Debates and New Directions*, edited by Martha Craven Nussbaum and Cass R. Sunstein, 30–6. New York: Oxford University Press, 2004.

Nussbaum, Martha Craven, and Cass R. Sunstein, eds. *Animal Rights: Current Debates and New Directions*. New York: Oxford University Press, 2004.

Nzou, Goodwell. "In Zimbabwe, We Don't Cry for Lions." *The New York Times*, August 4, 2015. www.nytimes.com/2015/08/05/opinion/in-zimbabwe-we-dont-cry-for-lions.html.

Ochs, Vanessa L. *Inventing Jewish Ritual*. Philadelphia: Jewish Publication Society, 2010.

O'Connor, Terry. *Animals as Neighbors: The Past and Present of Commensal Species*. East Lansing: Michigan State University Press, 2013.

O'Donohue, William, Kyle E. Ferguson, and Amy E. Naugle. "The Structure of the Cognitive Revolution: An Examination from the Philosophy of Science." *The Behavior Analyst* 26, no. 1 (2003): 85–110.

Offel, Rabbi Janet. "When a Beloved Pet Dies." Accessed March 7, 2016. http://kalsman.huc.edu/articles/Offel_WhenABelovedPetDies.pdf.

Oliver, Kelly. "Little Hans's Little Sister." *Philosophia* 1, no. 1 (2011): 9–28.

Olyan, Saul M. *Disability in the Hebrew Bible: Interpreting Mental and Physical Differences*. New York: Cambridge University Press, 2008.

Omidsalar, Mahmud. "Cat I: In Mythology and Folklore." *Encyclopaedia Iranica*. Winona Lake, IN: Eisenbrauns, 1990. www.iranicaonline.org/articles/cat-in-mythology-and-folklore-khot.

"Online Treasury of Talmudic Manuscripts." Accessed March 9, 2016. http://jnul.huji.ac.il/dl/talmud/intro_eng.htm.

Origen. *Contra Celsum*. Translated by Henry Chadwick. New York: Cambridge University Press, 1980.

Origen. *Contre Celse*. Translated by Marcel Borret. 5 vols. Paris: Éditions du Cerf, 1967.

Osborne, Catherine. *Dumb Beasts and Dead Philosophers*. New York: Oxford University Press, 2007.

Palmer, Clare. *Animal Ethics in Context: A Relational Approach*. New York: Columbia University Press, 2010.

Payne, Richard E. *A State of Mixture: Christians, Zoroastrians, and Iranian Political Culture in Late Antiquity*. Berkeley: University of California Press, 2015.

Pepperberg, Irene Maxine. *The Alex Studies: Cognitive and Communicative Abilities of Grey Parrots*. Cambridge, MA: Harvard University Press, 1999.

Perlo, Katherine Wills. *Kinship and Killing: The Animal in World Religions*. New York: Columbia University Press, 2009.

Perlove, Shelley, and Larry Silver. *Rembrandt's Faith: Church and Temple in the Dutch Golden Age*. University Park: Penn State Press, 2009.

Perpich, Diane. *The Ethics of Emmanuel Levinas*. Palo Alto, CA: Stanford University Press, 2008.

Petropoulou, M.-Z., ed. *Animal Sacrifice in Ancient Greek Religion, Judaism, and Christianity, 100 BC–AD 200*. New York: Oxford University Press, 2008.

Philo. *Philonis Alexandrini de Animalibus: The Armenian Text*. Translated by Abraham Terian. Chico, CA: Scholars Press, 1981.

Pietrzykowski, Tomasz, and Visa A. J. Kurki, eds. *Legal Personhood: Animals, Artificial Intelligence and the Unborn*. New York: Springer, 2017.

Pinches, Charles, and Jay B. McDaniel, eds. *Good News for Animals? Christian Approaches to Animal Well-Being*. Maryknoll: Orbis Books, 1993.

Pitkowsky, Michael Matthew. "Mipnei Darkhei Shalom ('Because of the Paths of Peace') and Related Terms: A Case Study of How Early Concepts and Terminology Developed from Tannaitic to Talmudic Literature." PhD diss., The Jewish Theological Seminary of America, 2011.

Plutarch. *Plutarch's Moralia*. Translated by William C. Helmbold and Harold Cherniss. Vol. 12. 15 vols. Loeb Classical Library. Cambridge, MA: Harvard University Press, 2001.

Podberscek, Anthony L., and Andrea M. Beetz, eds. *Bestiality and Zoophilia: Sexual Relations with Animals*. Oxford, UK: Berg, 2005.

Pomedli, Michael M. *Living with Animals: Ojibwe Spirit Powers*. Toronto: University of Toronto Press, 2014.

Pomeranz, Jonathan A. "Did the Babylonian Sages Regard the Ammei-ha'Aretz as Subhuman?" *Hebrew Union College Annual* 87 (2017): 115–43.

"The Rabbinic and Roman Laws of Personal Injury." *AJS Review* 39, no. 2 (2015): 303–31.

Porphyry. *On Abstinence from Killing Animals*. Translated by Gillian E. Clark. Ithaca, NY: Cornell University Press, 2000.

Porphyry: On Abstinence from Killing Animals. Translated by Gillian E. Clark. London: A&C Black, 2014.

Porter, Anne M., and Glenn M. Schwartz, eds. *Sacred Killing: The Archaeology of Sacrifice in the Ancient Near East*. Winona Lake, IN: Eisenbrauns, 2012.

Potts, Annie. *Chicken*. Chicago: University of Chicago Press, 2012.

"Printing the Talmud Web Site." Accessed March 9, 2016. http://jewishhistory .com/PRINTINGTHETALMUD/home.html.

Probyn, Elspeth. *Carnal Appetites: FoodSexIdentities*. New York: Routledge, 2003.

"Rabbinics Resources Online." Accessed March 9, 2016. www.rabbinics.org/.

Radford, Mike. "'Unnecessary Suffering': The Cornerstone of Animal Protection Legislation Considered." *Criminal Law Review* (1999): 702–13.

Raphael, Rebecca. *Biblical Corpora: Representations of Disability in Hebrew Biblical Literature*. New York: Bloomsbury T&T Clark, 2009.

Reconstructionist Rabbinical College. "Honoring Our Animal Companions." *Ritualwell*. Accessed March 7, 2016. http://ritualwell.org/categories/15.

Regan, Tom. *Defending Animal Rights*. Urbana: University of Illinois Press, 2001.

The Case for Animal Rights. Berkeley: University of California Press, 2004.

Renders, Hans, and Binne de Haan, eds. *Theoretical Discussions of Biography: Approaches from History, Microhistory and Life Writing*. Leiden: Brill, 2014.

Rogers, Katharine M. *Cat*. Chicago: University of Chicago Press, 2006.

Rohman, Carrie. *Stalking the Subject: Modernism and the Animal*. New York: Columbia University Press, 2012.

Roof, Wade Clark. *Spiritual Marketplace: Baby Boomers and the Remaking of American Religion*. Princeton, NJ: Princeton University Press, 1999.

Rosenberg, Daniel. "Short(hand) Stories: Unexplicated Story Cues in the Babylonian Talmud." PhD diss., New York University, 2014.

Rosenberg, Meisha. "Golden Retrievers Are White, Pit Bulls Are Black, and Chihuahuas Are Hispanic: Representations of Breeds of Dog and Issues of Race in Popular Culture." In *Making Animal Meaning*, edited by Linda Kalof and Georgina M. Montgomery, 113–26. East Lansing: Michigan State University Press, 2011.

Rosenblum, Jordan. *Food and Identity in Early Rabbinic Judaism*. New York: Cambridge University Press, 2010.

The Jewish Dietary Laws in the Ancient World. New York: Cambridge University Press, 2016.

Rosen-Zvi, Ishay. *Demonic Desires: Yetzer Hara and the Problem of Evil in Late Antiquity*. Philadelphia: University of Pennsylvania Press, 2011.

Rosen-Zvi, Ishay, and Adi Ophir. "Goy: Toward a Genealogy." *Dine Israel* 28 (2012): 69–122.

"Paul and the Invention of the Gentiles." *Jewish Quarterly Review* 105, no. 1 (2015): 1–41.

Rosen-Zvi, Ishay, and Dror Yinon. "Male Jewels/Female Jewels: A New Look at the Religious Obligations of Women in Rabbinic Thought." *Reshit* 2 (2010): 55–79.

Rosner, Fred. "Good Dogs and Bad Dogs in Jewish Law." *B'Or Ha'Torah* 23 (2014): 163–9.

Ruane, Nicole J. *Sacrifice and Gender in Biblical Law.* New York: Cambridge University Press, 2013.

Rubenstein, Jeffrey L. *Rabbinic Stories.* Mahwah, NJ: Paulist Press, 2002.

Talmudic Stories : Narrative Art, Composition, and Culture. Baltimore: Johns Hopkins University Press, 1999.

The Culture of the Babylonian Talmud. Baltimore: Johns Hopkins University Press, 2005.

Rudy, Kathy. *Loving Animals: Toward a New Animal Advocacy.* Minneapolis: University of Minnesota Press, 2011.

Ryan, Derek. *Animal Theory: A Critical Introduction.* Edinburgh: Edinburgh University Press, 2015.

Rydström, Jens. *Sinners and Citizens: Bestiality and Homosexuality in Sweden, 1880–1950.* Chicago: University of Chicago Press, 2003.

Safrai, Shemuel, ed. *The Literature of the Sages, First Part: Oral Tora, Halakha, Mishna, Tosefta, Talmud, External Tractates.* Vol. 3. Compendia Rerum Iudaicarum Ad Novum Testamentum. Philadelphia: Fortress Press, 1987.

Safrai, Zeev. "Agriculture and Farming." In *The Oxford Handbook of Jewish Daily Life in Roman Palestine*, edited by Catherine Hezser, 246–63. New York: Oxford University Press, 2010.

Satlow, Michael L. "Beyond Influence: Toward a New Historiographic Paradigm." In *Jewish Literatures and Cultures: Context and Intertext*, edited by Anita Norich and Yaron Eliav, 37–54. Providence, RI: Brown Judaic Studies, 2008.

Schaefer, Donovan O. "Do Animals Have Religion? Interdisciplinary Perspectives on Religion and Embodiment." *Anthrozoös* 25, no. 1 (August 1, 2012): 173–89.

Religious Affects: Animality, Evolution, and Power. Durham, NC: Duke University Press, 2015.

Schaffner, Joan. *An Introduction to Animals and the Law.* New York: Palgrave Macmillan, 2011.

Schick, Shana Strauch. "Intention in the Babylonian Talmud: An Intellectual History." PhD diss., Yeshiva University, 2011.

Schmidt, Leigh Eric. *Consumer Rites: The Buying & Selling of American Holidays.* Princeton, NJ: Princeton University Press, 1995.

Schochet, Elijah Judah. *Animal Life in Jewish Tradition: Attitudes and Relationships.* Brooklyn, NY: Ktav, 1984.

Schofer, Jonathan Wyn. *Confronting Vulnerability: The Body and the Divine in Rabbinic Ethics.* Chicago: University of Chicago Press, 2010.

The Making of a Sage: A Study in Rabbinic Ethics. Madison: University of Wisconsin Press, 2005.

Schremer, Adiel. "Stammaitic Historiography." In *Creation and Composition: The Contribution of the Bavli Redactors (Stammaim) to the Aggada*, edited by Jeffrey L. Rubenstein, 219–36. Tübingen: Mohr Siebeck, 2005.

Schwartz, Baruch J. *The Holiness Legislation: Studies in the Priestly Code (Torat ha-Qedushah: 'iyunim ba-Huqah ha-Kohanit sheba-Torah).*Jerusalem: Magnes Press, 1999.

Schwartz, Daniel R. "Rabbinic Law between Biblical Logic and Biblical Text: The Pitfalls of Exodus 21:33–34." *Harvard Theological Review* 107, no. 3 (July 2014): 314–39.

Schwartz, Joshua. "Cats in Ancient Jewish Society (The Place of Domesticated Animals in Everyday Life and the Material Culture of 2nd-Temple Judaism and Ancient Palestine)." *Journal of Jewish Studies* 52, no. 2 (2001): 211–34.

"Good Dog-Bad Dog: Jews and Their Dogs in Ancient Jewish Society." In *A Jew's Best Friend: The Image of the Dog Throughout Jewish History*, edited by Phillip Ackerman-Lieberman and Rakefet Zalashik, 52–89. Portland, OR: Sussex Academic Press, 2013.

Schwartz, Seth. "The Political Geography of Rabbinic Texts." In *The Cambridge Companion to the Talmud and Rabbinic Literature*, edited by Charlotte E. Fonrobert and Martin S. Jaffee, 75–96. Cambridge Companions to Religion. New York: Cambridge University Press, 2007.

"The Rabbi in Aphrodite's Bath: Palestinian Society and Jewish Identity in the High Roman Empire." In *Being Greek Under Rome: Cultural Identity, the Second Sophistic and the Development of Empire*, edited by Simon Goldhill, 335–61. New York: Cambridge University Press, 2001.

Secunda, Shai. "Talmud and the Absurd: The Elephant in the Sukkah." *The Talmud Blog*, October 10, 2011. https://thetalmudblog.wordpress.com/2011/10/10/talmud-and-the-absurd-the-case-of-the-elephant-sukkah/.

"'This, but Also That': Historical, Methodological, and Theoretical Reflections on Irano-Talmudica." *Jewish Quarterly Review* 106, no. 2 (June 22, 2016): 233–41.

Secunda, Shai, and Uri Gabbay, eds. *Encounters by the Rivers of Babylon: Scholarly Conversations between Jews, Iranians, and Babylonians in Antiquity.* Tübingen: Mohr Siebeck, 2014.

Segal, Eliezer. "Justice, Mercy and a Bird's Nest." *Journal of Jewish Studies* 42, no. 2 (1991): 176–95.

Seps, Christopher D. "Animal Law Evolution: Treating Pets as Persons in Tort and Custody Disputes." *University of Illinois Law Review* 4 (2010): 1339–73.

Septimus, Yehuda. *On the Boundaries of Talmudic Prayer.* Tübingen: Mohr Siebeck, 2015.

Septimus, Zvi. "The Poetic Superstructure of the Babylonian Talmud and the Reader It Fashions." PhD diss., University of California, Berkeley, 2011.

Sherwood, Yvonne. "Cutting up 'Life': Sacrifice as a Device for Clarifying – and Tormenting – Fundamental Distinctions Between Human, Animal and

Divine." In *The Bible and Posthumanism*, edited by Jennifer L. Koosed, 247–97. Atlanta, GA: Society of Biblical Literature, 2014.

Shoshan, Arieh. *Ba'ale hayim be-sifrut Yisrael: ben Yehudi li-vehemto*. Rehovot, Israel: Shoshanim, 1971.

Shyovitz, David I. "Christians and Jews in the Twelfth-Century Werewolf Renaissance." *Journal of the History of Ideas* 75, no. 4 (2014): 521–43.

——. "'How Can the Guilty Eat the Innocent?' Carnivorousness and Animal Eschatology in Medieval Jewish Thought," in manuscript.

Siebert, Charles. "Should a Chimp Be Able to Sue Its Owner?" *The New York Times*, April 23, 2014. www.nytimes.com/2014/04/27/magazine/the-rights-of-man-and-beast.html.

Siegal, Michal Bar-Asher. *Early Christian Monastic Literature and the Babylonian Talmud*. New York: Cambridge University Press, 2013.

Sinclair, Peri Danit. "When Rabbis Conceive Women: Physiology and Gestation in Leviticus Rabbah Chapter 14." PhD diss., The Jewish Theological Seminary of America, 2014.

Singer, Peter. *Animal Liberation: The Definitive Classic of the Animal Movement*. New York: Ecco, 2009.

——. "Animal Protection and the Problem of Religion." In *A Communion of Subjects: Animals in Religion, Science, and Ethics*, edited by Paul Waldau and Kimberley Patton, 616–28. New York: Columbia University Press, 2006.

Singh, Arvind Kumar. *Animals in Early Buddhism*. Delhi: Eastern Book Linkers, 2006.

Slifkin, Natan. *Man and Beast: Our Relationships with Animals in Jewish Law and Thought*. Brooklyn, NY: Zoo Torah; Yashar Books, 2006.

Sluijter, Eric Jan. *Rembrandt and the Female Nude*. Amsterdam: Amsterdam University Press, 2006.

Smith, Julie Ann, and Robert W. Mitchell, eds. *Experiencing Animal Minds: An Anthology of Animal-Human Encounters*. New York: Columbia University Press, 2012.

Smith, Steven D. *Man and Animal in Severan Rome: The Literary Imagination of Claudius Aelianus*. New York: Cambridge University Press, 2014.

Snead, Stella, Wendy Doniger, and George Michell. *Animals in Four Worlds: Sculptures from India*. Chicago: University of Chicago Press, 1989.

Sokoloff, Michael. *A Dictionary of Jewish Babylonian Aramaic of the Talmudic and Geonic Periods*. Baltimore: Johns Hopkins University Press, 2002.

Sorabji, Richard. *Animal Minds and Human Morals: The Origins of the Western Debate*. Ithaca: Cornell University Press, 1993.

Sorenson, John. *Critical Animal Studies: Thinking the Unthinkable*. Toronto: Canadian Scholars' Press, 2014.

Spittler, Janet E. *Animals in the Apocryphal Acts of the Apostles: The Wild Kingdom of Early Christian Literature*. Tübingen: Mohr Siebeck, 2008.

Stager, Lawrence E. "Why Were Hundreds of Dogs Buried at Ashkelon?" *Biblical Archaeology Review* 17, no. 3 (1991): 26–42.

Steinbock, Bonnie. *Life before Birth: The Moral and Legal Status of Embryos and Fetuses*. New York: Oxford University Press, 1992.

Stein, Dina. *Textual Mirrors: Reflexivity, Midrash, and the Rabbinic Self.* Philadelphia: University of Pennsylvania Press, 2012.

Stein, Elana. "Rabbinic Legal Loopholes: Formalism, Equity and Subjectivity." PhD diss., Columbia University, 2014.

Stern, Sacha. *Jewish Identity in Early Rabbinic Writings.* New York: Brill, 1994.

Stone, Christopher D. *Should Trees Have Standing? Law, Morality, and the Environment.* New York: Oxford University Press, 2010.

Strack, Hermann L., and Gunter Stemberger. *Introduction to the Talmud and Midrash.* Translated by Markus Bockmuehl. Reprint edition. Minneapolis, MN: Fortress Press, 1992.

Stutesman, Drake. *Snake.* Chicago: University of Chicago Press, 2005.

Sue, Derald Wing. *Microaggressions in Everyday Life: Race, Gender, and Sexual Orientation.* Hoboken, NJ: John Wiley & Sons, 2010.

Suen, Alison. "From Animal Father to Animal Mother: A Freudian Account of Animal Maternal Ethics." *Philosophia* 3, no. 2 (2013): 121–37.

Sunstein, Cass R. "Slaughterhouse Jive: Introduction to Animal Rights: Your Child or the Dog? By Gary L. Francione." *New Republic,* January 29, 2001, 40–5.

Swartz, Michael D. "Ritual about Myth about Ritual: Towards an Understanding of the Avodah in the Rabbinic Period." *The Journal of Jewish Thought and Philosophy* 6, no. 1 (1997): 135–55.

Sztybel, David. "Animals as Persons." In *Animal Subjects: An Ethical Reader in a Posthuman World,* edited by Jodey Castricano, 241–57. Waterloo, ON: Wilfrid Laurier University Press, 2008.

Tabory, Joseph. "זקה חוליש: לע סחיה ביו טעמ הומתוה לבי דיניה." In *(Studies in Halakhah and Jewish Thought)* לאונמע סחנמ הרב דוככל סישגומ : לארשי תבשחמבו הכלהב סירקח תורובגל תיעיגהב ומקר, edited by Moshe Beer, 121–41. Ramat Gan, Israel: Bar-Ilan University, 1994.

Taylor, Nik. " 'Never an It': Intersubjectivity and the Creation of Animal Personhood in Animal Shelters." *Quantitative Sociology Review* 3, no. 1 (April 2007): 59–73.

Taylor, Nik, and Richard Twine, eds. *The Rise of Critical Animal Studies: From the Margins to the Centre.* Abingdon, UK: Routledge, 2014.

"TheGemara.com – A Historical and Contextual Approach." *TheGemara.com.* Accessed July 11, 2017. http://thegemara.com/.

"The Saul Lieberman Institute | Home Page." Accessed March 9, 2016. http://eng .liebermaninstitute.org/.

"The Society for the Interpretation of Talmud." Accessed July 17, 2017. www .talmudha-igud.org.il/content.asp?lang=en&pageid=1.

"The Talmud Blog." *The Talmud Blog.* Accessed March 9, 2016. https://thetalmud blog.wordpress.com/.

Tigay, Jeffrey H. *Deuteronomy = [Devarim] : The Traditional Hebrew Text with the New JPS Translation.* Philadelphia: Jewish Publication Society, 1996.

Tlili, Sarra. *Animals in the Qur'an.* New York: Cambridge University Press, 2012.

Toner, Jerry P. *The Day Commodus Killed a Rhino: Understanding the Roman Games.* Baltimore: Johns Hopkins University Press, 2014.

Tooley, Michael. "Are Nonhuman Animals Persons?" In *The Oxford Handbook of Animal Ethics*, edited by Tom L. Beauchamp and Raymond Gillespie Frey, 332–70. New York: Oxford University Press, 2011.

Toperoff, Shlomo Pesach. *The Animal Kingdom in Jewish Thought*. Northvale, NJ: Jason Aronson, 1995.

Toynbee, J. M. C. *Animals in Roman Life and Art*. Barnsley, UK: Pen & Sword Books, 2012.

Tucker, Abigail. *The Lion in the Living Room: How House Cats Tamed Us and Took Over the World*. New York: Simon & Schuster, 2016.

Tucker, Karen. "Sitting Shiva for Spot?" *The Forward*, April 27, 2012. http://forward.com/articles/155303/sitting-shiva-for-spot/.

Tulloch, John, and Deborah Lupton. *Risk and Everyday Life*. Thousand Oaks, CA: Sage, 2003.

Ullucci, Daniel C. *The Christian Rejection of Animal Sacrifice*. New York: Oxford University Press, 2012.

Valer, Shulamit. *Sorrow and Distress in the Talmud*. Translated by Sharon Blass. Boston: Academic Studies Press, 2011.

Vidas, Moulie. *Tradition and the Formation of the Talmud*. Princeton, NJ: Princeton University Press, 2014.

Višak, Tatjana. *Killing Happy Animals: Explorations in Utilitarian Ethics*. Basingstoke, Hampshire: Palgrave Macmillan, 2013.

Waal, Frans B. M. de. *Chimpanzee Politics: Power and Sex among Apes*. Baltimore: Johns Hopkins University Press, 1998.

   The Ape and the Sushi Master: Cultural Reflections of a Primatologist. New York: Basic Books, 2001.

Waal, Frans B. M. de, and Pier Francesco Ferrari, eds. *The Primate Mind: Built to Connect with Other Minds*. Cambridge, MA: Harvard University Press, 2012.

Waal, Frans B. M. de, and Peter L. Tyack, eds. *Animal Social Complexity: Intelligence, Culture, and Individualized Societies*. Cambridge, MA: Harvard University Press, 2003.

Waldau, Paul. *Animal Studies: An Introduction*. New York: Oxford University Press, 2013.

   The Specter of Speciesism: Buddhist and Christian Views of Animals. New York: Oxford University Press, 2002.

Waldau, Paul, and Kimberley Patton, eds. *A Communion of Subjects: Animals in Religion, Science, and Ethics*. New York: Columbia University Press, 2006.

Wallace-Hadrill, David Sutherland. *The Greek Patristic View of Nature*. New York: Barnes & Noble, 1968.

Wapnish, Paula, and Brian Hesse. "Pampered Pooches or Plain Pariahs? The Ashkelon Dog Burials." *The Biblical Archaeologist* 56, no. 2 (1993): 55–80.

Warren, Mary Anne. *Moral Status: Obligations to Persons and Other Living Things*. Oxford: Clarendon Press, 1997.

Wasserman, Edward A., and Thomas R. Zentall, eds. *Comparative Cognition: Experimental Explorations of Animal Intelligence*. New York: Oxford University Press, 2006.

Wasserman, Mira Beth. *Jews, Gentiles, and Other Animals: The Talmud After the Humanities.* Philadelphia: University of Pennsylvania Press, 2017.

Watson, Alan, trans. *The Digest of Justinian.* Vol. 1. Philadelphia: University of Pennsylvania Press, 2009.

Way, Kenneth C. *Donkeys in the Biblical World: Ceremony and Symbol.* Winona Lake, IN: Eisenbrauns, 2011.

Wegner, Judith Romney. *Chattel or Person? The Status of Women in the Mishnah.* New York: Oxford University Press, 1988.

Weil, Kari. *Thinking Animals: Why Animal Studies Now?* New York: Columbia University Press, 2012.

Weiner, Ellis and Barbara Davilman. *How to Raise a Jewish Dog.* Edited by Barbara Davilman. New York: Little, Brown and Company, 2007.

Weiss, Haim. *Dreams in Rabbinical literature.* Tel Aviv: Modan, 2013.

Weiss, Roslyn. "Maimonides on 'Shilluaḥ Ha-Qen.'" *Jewish Quarterly Review* 79, no. 4 (1989): 345–66.

Weitzenfeld, Adam, and Melanie Joy. "An Overview of Anthropocentrism, Humanism and Speciesism in Critical Animal Theory." In *Defining Critical Animal Studies: An Intersectional Social Justice Approach for Liberation,* edited by Anthony J. Nocella, John Sorenson, Kim Socha, and Atsuko Matsuoka, 3–27. New York: Peter Lang, 2013.

"When Animal 'Legal Personhood' Gets Personal." *Advocate Magazine, Lewis & Clark Law School,* Summer 2014. https://law.lclark.edu/live/news/26010-when-animal-legal-personhood-gets-personal.

Wimpfheimer, Barry S. *Narrating the Law: A Poetics of Talmudic Legal Stories.* Philadelphia: University of Pennsylvania Press, 2011.

Wise, Steven M. "Legal Personhood and the Nonhuman Rights Project." *Animal Law* 17 (2010): 1–11.

——— *Rattling the Cage: Toward Legal Rights for Animals.* Cambridge, MA: Perseus Books, 2000.

——— "The Capacity of Non-Human Animals for Legal Personhood and Legal Rights." In *The Politics of Species: Reshaping Our Relationships with Other Animals,* edited by Raymond Corbey and Annette Lanjouw, 241–5. New York: Cambridge University Press, 2013.

——— "The Legal Thinghood of Nonhuman Animals." *Boston College Environmental Affairs Law Review* 23, no. 2 (1996): 471–546.

Wolfe, Cary. "Human, All Too Human: 'Animal Studies' and the Humanities." *Proceedings of the MLA* 124, no. 2 (2009): 564–75.

——— *What Is Posthumanism?* Minneapolis: University of Minnesota Press, 2010.

Wolfe, Cary, and Jonathan Elmer. "Subject to Sacrifice: Ideology, Psychoanalysis, and the Discourse of Species in Jonathan Demme's Silence of the Lambs." *Boundary* 2 (1995): 141–70.

Wyatt, Edward. "Werewolf Bar Mitzvah – 30 Rock – TV." *The New York Times,* October 25, 2007, sec. Television. www.nytimes.com/2007/10/25/arts/television/25were.html.

Wylie, Dan. *Elephant.* Chicago: University of Chicago Press, 2009.

Wynne, Clive D. L. *Do Animals Think?* Princeton, NJ: Princeton University Press, 2004.

Zamir, Tzachi. "Literary Works and Animal Ethics." In *The Oxford Handbook of Animal Ethics*, edited by Tom L. Beauchamp and Raymond Gillespie Frey, 932–56. New York: Oxford University Press, 2011.

Zellentin, Holger M. *Rabbinic Parodies of Jewish and Christian Literature*. Tübingen: Mohr Siebeck, 2011.

Zuckermandel, Moses Samuel, ed. *Tosephta; based on the Erfurt and Vienna codices (Tosefta al-pi Kitve-yad 'Erfurt Vinah)*. Jerusalem: Wahrman, 1970.

Index

Abaye, 78
admonition to keep young animals with
    their mothers, 91
Agriprocessors kosher meat plant, 22
am ha-aretz, 185
Amoraim, 33
animal-centric anthropomorphism, 5
animal consciousness
    distinction as an ontological category, 77
animal control legislation
    explanations of, 124
    role of children in driving moral
        panic, 143
animal danger
    as act of God or divine
        punishment, 128–31
    discourse, 122–23
    epistemology of, 122
    Freudian explanations of, 124
    irrationality of legislation, 123
    Mishnaic perspectives, 132
    social explanations of, 124
    tam and muad animals, 126–28
animal funerals, 180
animal intelligence
    Aristotle, 41
    Augustine, 43
    Christian views, 43
    Cynic, Platonist, and Pythagorean
        views, 41
    implications for sacrifice, 43
    legal implications, 40
    limits of, Mishnaic perspectives, 50–52

natural historical perspectives, 44
    Origen, 43
    Philo, 42
    Plutarch, 42
    Porphyry, 42
    reason, 40
    shame, 60
    Stoic views, 41
animal moral capacity, 80
animal moral culpability
    animals and non-Jews. *See* animals and
        non-Jews
    Babylonian Talmud, 75–80
    capacity to derive pleasure from
        sin, 79–80
    capacity to sin, 77
    inanimate or animate objects, 76
    Mishnah, 73–74
    Mishnah Sanhedrin 7 on bestiality, 71
    ontology of animals, 76
    similarities between animals and
        Gentiles, 81
animal profiling
    Mishnah Bava Qamma, 124
animal sacrifice, 42
animal studies
    Derrida, 9
    difference theorists, 10
    early philosophical arguments against
        specieism, 10
    identity theorists, 10
    indistinction of animals and humans, 11
    Peter Singer, 9

animal studies and subjectivity, 63
  instability of subjectivity, 84–85
animal suffering
  complexity of human reactions to, 91
  conflict between "ascendancy" and
    "kindness", 118
  cooking a kid in its mother's milk, 92
  as an impetus for animal planning and
    action, 58
  inherent contradiction in rabbinic
    perspectives on, 119
  lack of concern for in the Mishnah, 106
  limited nature of Biblical concern for, 92
  modern scholarly arguments for its role
    in Jewish law, 117
  obligation to help the animal, 108
  paradoxical nature, 92–93
  parental bonds, 92
  perspectives from the Babylonian
    Talmud, 111–16
  prevention of as a form of virtue
    training, 92
  Rava, 108–10
  reception of Rava in contemporary
    Jewish scholarship, 116–18
  schizophrenic nature of human concern
    for, 93
  sending of the nest, 90–92
  Stammaitic testing of earlier rabbinic
    traditions for, 113
  Sumatran hunters and apologetic
    slaughter, 93
  tannaitic interest in, 107–8
animal sukkahs, 164
  perspectives from the Babylonian
    Talmud, 169–73
animal tort cases
  owner's share of damages, 125
animal trials, 46
  contemporary advocacy for animals, 67
  early modern European versions
    of, 64
  in film, 64
  historical and contemporary, 64–67
  Mishnah, 71–73
  modern advocacy for, 66
  scholarly explanations for, 65
animalistic
  use as critique of human behaviors, 14
animality
  definition, 13
  elasticity of, 14

erecting boundaries with humanity, 14
  formation of rabbinic hierarchy, 62
  nonhuman subjectivity, 13
  novelty of the Babylonian Talmud's
    perspective on, 19
animals
  and the *am ha-aretz*, 185
  as bad property, 154, 167
  capabilities of, 12
  damages caused by in Mishnah, 126–28
  death and control, 176
  and differential human responses
    to, 90
  as instrument for rabbinic
    self-critique, 151
  as legal edge cases, 38
  as marginalized group, 63
  in modern Jewish ritual practice,
    187–89
  and non-Jews, 185–87
  as nouns, 153
  owner's liability for, 51
  and the rabbinic other, 184–85
  rabbinic terminology for, 47
  recipients of God's mercy, 82
  ritual concerns as a result of the animal's
    death, 168
  as ritual objects, 162–66
  role in divine economy, 81
  use in sealing off graves, 165
  use of for divorce writs, 165
  and viral videos, 89
animals as property
  biblical law, 154
  in early modern and modern
    Anglo-American legal tradition, 155
  in Institutes of Gaius, 155
  Roman law, 155
animals in texts
  mediated nature of, 8
anthropocentric anthropomorphism
  Fran de Waal's definition, 5
anthropocentrism, 8
anthropodenial
  critique of continuity between humans
    and animals, 14
anthropomorphism, 5
  anthropocentric, definitions of, 5
  desire to understand animal
    subjectivity, 6
apes
  animal intelligence, 46

Aquinas, 23
Aramaic, 33
Augustine, 23

ba'ale hayim, 47
Baby raccoon in Brooklyn, 89–90
Babylonian Talmud, 33
  animals and Temple substitution, 17–19
  cultural context, 16–17
  cultural world, 16
  intelligence of animals, 38
  manuscripts, 35
  Stam, 15–16
  Syriac and Zoroastrian contexts, 16
  traditions of interpretation, 34
  Western Jewish traditions and
    Hellenism, 17
Babylonian Talmud Avodah Zarah
  22a–23a, 185
Babylonian Talmud Bava Metzia
  32a–b, 109–16
Babylonian Talmud Bava Metzia 85a, 97–98
Babylonian Talmud Bava Qamma
  34b–35a, 55–59
Babylonian Talmud Bava Qamma
  80a, 139–44
Babylonian Talmud Pesahim 49a-b, 185
Babylonian Talmud Sanhedrin 55a,
  74–86, 87
Babylonian Talmud Sukkah 22b–23b,
  162–63
Babylonian Talmud Sukkah 23a, 162–63
Balaam, 1–4, 6–8
Balaam's donkey, 1–3, 6
  biblical story, 4
  dialogue between Balaam and the
    donkey, 6
  ironies inherent in the story, 4
  Maimonides' reading of incident, 8
  Numbers 22, 2, 4
  Rembrandt's depiction, 1
  speech of, 6–8
  subjectivity of, 7
  Symbolism of in early modern
    Holland, 2
  viewer's gaze in Rembrandt's painting, 2
Balak, 2
ban on raising dogs, 137
bark mitzvahs, 180
behemah, 47, 79, 108, 127, 128, 138,
  170, 176
bestiality, 67, 187

ambiguity of animal and Gentile sin, 75
ancient Near Eastern law, 68
the animal's guilt, 70
animals and Gentiles, dimensions of
  sin, 75
animals and non-Jews in the Babylonian
  Talmud, 75
bestiality and Gentiles, 68
in the Bible, the animal's guilt, 68
Biblical law, 68–70
in Biblical law, ambiguity of
  language, 70
criminalization of, 67
culpability of animals, 79
death penalty for, scribal creation of, 69
differential punishment for men and
  women, 70
execution of offenders, 69
and Gentiles, 186
Gentiles, mercy toward animals, 82
Hittite law, 68
moral consciousness of gentile, 78
obstacle, 81
punishment for animal in
  Mishnah, 70–71
reasons for animal's execution in
  Mishnah, 71
unwittingly committed, 85–86
bestiality and Eve
  as Talmudic retelling of the Fall, 186
The Big Short, 31
Bint Jua
  gorilla who saved a boy, 12
bloodhounds, 120
Brooklyn hipsters, 90

camel-back sukkahs, 161
canine profiling, 123
cats, 122
  Rav's decree against, 141
  role in the Roman world, 149
  Sassanian and Zoroastrian treatment
    of, 148
cats in mosaics
  Roman Empire, 149
cats in worship
  Isis and Bubastis, 149
Circe, 42
clever animals
  donkey of Pinhas ben Yair, 62
  prophetess rat, 62
  snake of House Akhore, 62

clever ox
  anthropomorphism, 57
  Babylonian Talmud, 55–61
  concrete examples of, 58–59
  making use of ashes, 55, 58
  other cases, 59
  other clever animals, 62
  Palestinian Talmud, 53–55
  Rav Pappa's ox with a toothache, 59
  shor piqe'ah, 58
  violating the Sabbath and productive
    dimensions of, 54–55
cognitive ethology, 38–40, 94
  historical development, 39
cooking a kid in its mother's milk, 91
critical animal studies
  the ancient world, 24–25
  "difference theorists," 10–12
  Jewish Studies, 23
  philosophy, 10
  religious studies, 23–24
  scientific perspectives, 12–13

dangerous animals
  as acts of God, 130
  bloodhounds, 120
  damages owed by owner of, 129
  dangerous species of, 47
  discourse of, 131–32
  dogs, 121
  domestication of, 129
  trials of, Mishnah Sanhedrin, 129
  as walking weapons, 130
dangerous dog laws, 121
dangerous species
  fundamental biological link in rabbinic
    discourse, 131
Darwin, 39
de Waal, 94
  moral behaviors of primates, 12
Deuteronomy 22:26–27, 91
Deuteronomy 22:4, 101
difference theories of animal studies
  encounter with the animal as Other, 10
Digest of Justinian, 43
disability and animals
  Mishnah, 45
distinctions between humans and animals
  grammatical, 62
dogs, 26
domesticated animals, 168
  dangers of, 138

dominionist ideology
  in the Bible, 23
  critiques of, 96
donkey struggling beneath his burden
  animal suffering, 93
dream interpretation, 182

elephants as sukkah walls, 171–72
empathy with animals
  stereotypes about, 150
Epicureans, 41
ethology
  contributions to understanding of
    animals, 94
exegetical rule
  no two verses teach the same thing, 107
exhausted ox
  Deuteronomy–essentialness of animal to
    situation, 103
Exodus 21:29, 126
Exodus 21:29–30, 73
Exodus 23:5, 100

factory farms, 26
feminist animal ethics
  affective dimensions of, 95–96
Francis of Assisi, 97
  blessing of the animals, 188

Ge'onim, 34
goring ox, 38, 45
  areas in which owners are more liable
    than their animals, 50
  complex cognition, 44
  in the Mishnah, 44–45
  severity of biblical punishment, 126

honoring father and mother, 92
human-animal hybrids, 46
human characteristics of animals, 12
hunting, 137

Immanuel Kant, 92
impossible animals, 37
indistinction
  as an approach to animals, 11
  commodification and capitalism, 11
  Gilles Deleuze, 11

Jane Goodall, 94
  chimpanzee religion, 12
Jerusalem Temple, 15, 17

Jewish dog toys, 189
"chewish," 188
Jewish kitsch, 189
Jewish pet funerals, 188
liturgical elements of, 188
Jewish pet rituals, 187–89
halachic aspects of, 189
Jews and dogs
in contemporary American life, 189–90
Jacob Emden on dogs, 190
Moshe Isserles on dogs, 190
Jews and pets, 189–91
Joan Rivers, 188
Jonathan Safran Foer, 23
Josephus, 17
Judah the Patriarch, 32
and the family of weasels, 97–98

Kaufmann manuscript, 35
King Shapur, 185
Kosrow II
treatment of cats, 148

labor on the Sabbath
destructive forms of labor, 52
Mishnah Shabbat 13:3, 52
late antique turn away from the animal, 41
later rabbinic movement, 33
Leiden manuscript, 35
Leviticus 20:15–16, 68
lions
contemporary reactions to hunting of, 122
livestock
linguistic complexities concerning, 153

Maimonides, 92
micro-aggression, 20–21
microhistory, 20
as technique for reading rabbinic
literature, 20
micro reading
and its relationship to master narratives, 20
Mishnah, 33
approaches to animal intelligence, 44
history of early rabbinic movement, 32
manuscripts, 35
Orders of, 32
understanding of animals, 38
views on animal intelligence, 48
Mishnah Bava Metzia 2:10, 103
exegetical explanations for, 107
Mishnah Bava Metzia 2:9, 47

Mishnah Bava Qamma 1:4, 124–26
Mishnah Bava Qamma 3:10, 49
Mishnah Bava Qamma 4:2, 44
Mishnah Bava Qamma 4:5, 73
Mishnah Bava Qamma 4:6, 45
Mishnah Bava Qamma 5:6, 45
Mishnah Bava Qamma 7:7, 132
Mishnah Bekhorot 5 and 6, 46
Mishnah Eruvin 1:7, 164
Mishnah Niddah 5:4–5, 82
Mishnah Sanhedrin 1:4, 46, 72, 129
Mishnah Sanhedrin 7:4, 70–71
Mishnah Shabbat 5 and 6, 46
Mishnah Shevuot 3:8, 37
Mishnah Sukkah 2:3, 161
Mishnah Sukkah 2:6, 47
Mishnah Yadayim 1:5, 46
muad
based on location, 128
shor muad, 128
walking and eating, 128
Munich manuscript, 35

Neoplatonism, 42
non-Jew as animal, 185–86
non-Jews as deviants, 186
Numbers 22:28–31, 6

Origen
Against Celsus, 43
ownership and knowledge of animals, 38
ox
liability for acts of damage from, 49

Palestinian Talmud, 15, 33
manuscripts, 35
Palestinian Talmud Bava Qamma
3:10, 52–55
parody
rabbinic literature, 148
Talmudic, the fall of man, 186
patriarchate, 98
personhood of animals, 157–59
definitional problems, 158–59
ethnographic perspectives, 157–58
modern legal debates, 155–57
religious studies perspectives, 160
Peter Singer
animal liberation, 94
critiques from theology and religious
studies, 96–99
ethological critiques of, 95

Peter Singer (*Cont.*)
  feminist critiques of, 97
  foundational influence on critical animal
    studies, 9–10
  speciesism of his arguments, 10
Pharisees, 32
Philo, 17
pitbulls, 121
  not recognized as an actual breed, 123
priesthood after 70 CE, 18
prohibition on slaughtering a parent and
    its young on the same day, 91
Pythagorean views of animals, 41

rabbinic categorization of animals
    in Mishnah, 137–38
rabbinic deference, 140
rabbinic honor, 140–41
rabbinic masculinity, 151
the rabbinic other
    various forms of, 184–85
rabbinic prohibitions of domestic animals
    rabbinic prohibitions of small
      cattle, 132–33
    rabbinic small cattle ban, 133–38
    the small cattle ban and rabbinic
      flaws, 143–45
rabbinic self
    different forms of, 181
    historiography of, 181–83
    the role of animals in forming, 183–84
rabbis and cats, 138–43
    conflicting legal traditions about, 150
    distinctions between black and white
      cats, 147–48
    historical and cultural context, 148–50
    rabbinic traditions about, 145–46
raising chickens
    threat posed to Jerusalem sacrifices and
      pure foods, 136
raising pigs
    distinctiveness of Jewish avoidance of, 137
Rashi, 34, 40, 163
Rav Sheshet, 75–77
Rava, 79–80, 109
    Stammatic misreading of, 111
Rembrandt, 1–3, 4, 8
    Peter Lastman's version of Balaam's
      donkey, 2
Remonstrants and
    Counter-Remonstrants, 2
replacement of the Temple

continuing symbolic power of the
    Temple, 18
rabbinic strategies for, 18
resting donkey
    a-z-v, 101
    Exodus, 99–101
    Exodus 23–as tempting target of
      interest, 102
    Exodus 23-etymology of verb to
      leave, 100–1
resting donkey and exhausted ox
    biblical perspectives, 99–103
    Deuteronomy 22, 102
    independent obligation to the
      animal, 108
    Mishnaic perspectives, 103–8
    reloading versus unloading as
      obligations, 106
    socially constructive elements of
      Mishnah's treatment of, 104
resting donkey and the exhausted ox
    Rava's reframing of biblical
      verses, 108–10

Sabbath labor
    destructive acts, 56
    productive acts, 53
Schoolhouse Rock, 153
sending of the nest, 91
    interpretation of by Maimonides and
      Nahmanides, 92
    means of reinforcing family values, 92
Septuagint, 17
serpents, 186
shame
    distinctions between Jews and
      Gentiles, 78
    Gentiles, 80
    role in separating animals from
      humans, 60
shepherds and herders
    rabbinic prejudice against, 134
Shulkhan Arukh, 190
sin
    consequences for luring someone to
      sin, 75
small cattle ban
    Babylonia, 143, 144
    Babylonia, Rav Huna's violation of, 144–45
    practical implications, 133
    zooarcheological evidence for violation
      of, 134

small cattle in the house, 135
  Yehudah ben Bava, 135
Stam, 15
Stammaim
  historical context, 34
  literary project, 34
Stoics, 48
subjective self
  animal as means to destabilize self, 63
sugya, 33
Syriac literature, 16

talking animals, 5
talking dogs
  Lucian's dialogues, 5
tam and *muad*, 126, 128
Tannaim, 32
Ten Commandments
  role of animals within, 154
thingness of animals
  complexities and legal debates, 173–78
  complexities of owning living
    things, 167–69
  cultural and legal contexts, 178–79
  definitional problems, 153–54
  legal contexts, 154–55
  Zoroastrian views of, 178–79

Tony the Tiger, 5
Torah's terminology for animals
  rabbinic views on, 48
Tosafists, 34
Tosefta Bava Metzia 2:12, 107
Tosefta Hullin 1:1, 46
transmigration of souls, 43
travel sukkahs, 161–62
tza'ar ba'ale hayim, 110, 115

utilitarian ethics
  limits of such ethics, 95

vegetarianism, 25–26, 95–96, 99
  contexts for, 26
virtue training, 92

wild animals, 128–32
from the words of both of them it can be
    learned
  Rava, 109

yetzer, 116, 182

zooarcheology in the ancient world, 25
Zoroastrian literature, 16
Zoroastrian religious views of animals, 179